TEMP

Also by Louis Hyman

Shopping for Change,
with Joseph Tohill

American Capitalism: A Reader,
with Edward E. Baptist

Borrow

Debtor Nation

LOUIS HYMAN

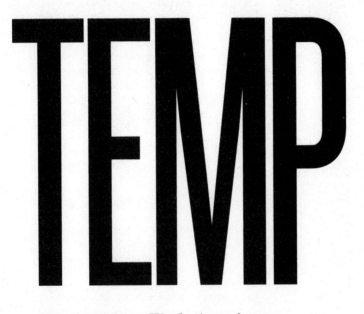

How American Work, American
Business, and the American Dream
Became Temporary

VIKING

VIKING

An imprint of Penguin Random House LLC
375 Hudson Street
New York, New York 10014
penguin.com

ISBN: 9780735224070 (hardcover)
ISBN: 9780735224094 (ebook)

Printed in the United States of America
1 2 3 4 5 6 7 8 9 10

Set in Parkinson Electra Pro
Designed by Francesca Belanger

While the author has made every effort to provide accurate telephone
numbers, internet addresses, and other contact information at the
time of publication, neither the publisher nor the author assumes any
responsibility for errors or for changes that occur after publication.
Further, the publisher does not have any control over and does
not assume any responsibility for author or third-party
websites or their content.

For Kate

Somebody must do the work and it might as well be you.

—ELMER WINTER

CONTENTS

How We All Became Temps

During the worst recession since the Great Depression, Elmer Winter gave a speech condemning the complacency of American businessmen. Winter was the president of Manpower Inc., a temporary labor agency, but also one of America's largest employers. He delivered his speech as a call to arms—a plea for nothing less than to save the country itself.

Winter fixed on "deadly fears of the future" as a theme—developments Americans believed would undermine their economic safety. Some of these fears came from abroad, like Chinese twenty-five-cents-an-hour labor or Russia's ever subtle global diplomacy. Most of Winter's fears, however, were about America itself, about the disconnect between our hopes and our realities. "Foremost in the thinking of every man and woman who works is the basic question," Winter said, "'How secure is my job?'" The hope of the man on the street today in America, he told the shareholders, is "a good job—good health and security—for himself and for his family."[1]

Ever the realist, Winter told the businessmen that this dream of economic security, in the form of a steady, well-paid job, would no longer be possible. He told them that the "old days are gone . . . and plans must be the order of the day." Winter's vision was to bring down costs, especially labor costs, by providing a flexible workforce without job guarantees, buttressed by new automation technology. American business would need to work smarter and harder to overcome the hue and cry that "we can't compete with foreign products where our labor rates are three or four times higher than theirs." Manpower, and other temporary agencies like them, would provide that labor.

Winter's speech—you might be surprised to learn—was delivered not in 2008, but in 1958. He gave it in the first brief downturn of the postwar economy. The end of American job security was not in the past, but still in the future.

His prognostications came true, partially because he—and others like him—believed them so zealously and worked so hard to bring them about. The rise of our flexible economy—how we all, to some degree, have had to come to terms with the withering of the postwar job—is not just the story of Elmer Winter. His company, Manpower Inc.—the first major temporary agency, which in 2017 still employed more than 3 million people or 50 percent more than Wal-Mart—would play an important role in transforming the world of work from one of security to insecurity, but it would not be alone.[2] This transformation was not a conspiracy, but was carried out in public to much acclaim. Presidents, CEOs, and stock markets the world over celebrated the dismantling of the postwar prosperity.

Most people kept their jobs, but you don't need to replace everybody to make the rest insecure. Temps define the limits of what is possible in labor, casting a long shadow over the rest of the workforce. Beginning in the midst of the postwar boom in the 1950s, American jobs were slowly remade from top to bottom: consultants supplanted executives at the top, temps replaced office workers in the middle, and day laborers pushed out union workers at the bottom. On every step of the ladder, work would become more insecure as it became more flexible.

This new economic arrangement produced opportunities and wealth for those at the top, but for most people, flexibility produced economic uncertainty. For some of the new temps, like consultants, the work is glamorous and lucrative. For others, like office workers, it is a dead end. For those day laborers waiting outside Home Depot, it is work with little pay and much danger. Despite pay gaps, education gaps, and citizenship gaps, temps have come to define our workplaces today in ways that *Mad Men*-era secretarial temps—white gloved and beautiful—never could have imagined.

Temp is the history of this transformation, of how the postwar world, which to our eyes worked so well, came undone neither by economic accident nor by technological inevitability, but by human choice.

Many of us who came of age in the 1970s, '80s, and '90s expected those postwar days to return. We believed that whatever the recession that Winter—or Carter, or Reagan, or Clinton—had been addressing, it was only temporary. The good years, the permanent onward progress of prosperity, would surely return. For most Americans, they have not. Where did all the good jobs go?

The answer goes deeper than Uber and further back than downsizing, and contests the most essential assumptions we have about how our economy and our businesses work.

The Rise and Fall of the Postwar Economy

A postwar world of work and business that brought two generations of unprecedented prosperity came to an end in the 1970s, and in its stead a new era of wage stagnation and income inequality began—though it was hard at first to see that this change was permanent. For a while, the wage problem was hidden, first by more women entering the workforce (raising household income) and then by rising house prices (raising household equity). But in the collapse of 2008, we all suddenly became aware that while the economy had grown for forty years, the 10 percent at the top received 87 percent of all that growth (compared with 29 percent from 1933 to 1973).[3] The much-maligned 1 percent alone received 56 percent of all the growth from 1975 to 2006. In the aftermath of the Great Recession of 2008, we discovered that our society not only was unequal, but also had been becoming steadily more so for a long time. Instead of progress, we had been in decline (at least if you were not in the 1 percent). In 2018, despite a booming stock market, we are still wrestling with the aftershocks of that recession, but the real roots of today's insecurity go much deeper than credit default swaps and underwater mortgages.

Temporary labor and flexible corporations first emerged when that hard-won dream—job security—appeared to be the inevitable and happy result of a mature capitalism. The foundations of job security were, as the leading postwar economist, John Kenneth Galbraith, believed, in the risk aversion of the postwar corporation. In his best-selling 1967 exegesis of the American corporation, *The New Industrial State*, Galbraith explained that the modern corporation was defined by risk minimization, not profit maximization. The investments required for manufacturing in the postwar economy required sums of capital (and an investment of time) unseen before. The first Model T may have been produced with an investment of a few tens of thousands of dollars, but a Mustang factory of the 1960s cost millions. World War I-era planes could be brought from blueprint to battle in only a few months, but by the '60s, just the design of jet planes took years. To actually build a jet factory took that much longer. Executives planned for long time horizons, eschewing short-term opportunities for long-term gain.

This dull steadiness produced unrivaled economic progress, both in terms of GDP and technology. In the 1950s, U.S. real GDP growth rates hit as high as 8.7 percent a year—as fast as China's today. None of the top one hundred corporations failed to earn a profit in the postwar period. Long-term investment in corporate science made this growth possible. Products were not just incremental novelties, but truly disruptive technologies. In these labs, the Bells, the Polaroids, the Lockheeds, and the Xeroxes launched the digital revolution. This was when American scientists invented plastics, transistors, computers, jets, fiber optics, computer networks, cell phones, and nearly every other technological marvel that still defines our world today (and that most of us think were invented very recently). Corporations invested in manufacturing, in research and development, and most important, in employees. Well-paid workers, meanwhile, could buy American products without borrowing too much. With steady profits and a long-term vision, corporations could focus on real progress.

Firms needed to know that the workers would, in turn, show up. The strategies of corporations required stability not just for their investments, but for their employees, and by extension for all of American life. Paper pushers of the middle class could count on their jobs as their families grew. Working stiffs knew the plant would be open the next year and that their industrial union would get them a raise, but not a revolution. An unwavering workforce was needed if investments in heavy manufacturing were to pay out. The jobs might have been repetitive, but so were the paychecks. Capitalism worked for nearly everyone. For the first time, inequality fell and growth accelerated. Policy makers, corporate planners, and labor leaders fashioned a world after World War II that promoted security not only for the elite—and their investments—but for nearly everybody.

This investment certainty was in part possible because of the unusual politics of Cold War Keynesianism, which appeared to have transformed capitalism's periodic crises into unending expansion. Lucrative defense contracts with fixed rates of profit swelled to make up a third of the GDP. Government services accounted for another fifth. Although nuclear brinkmanship was terrifying, the economy, at least in the U.S. and the West, was oddly calm. The Bretton Woods order, centered on the U.S. dollar, produced a twenty-five-year run of prosperity. Consumer purchasing power rose every year since World War II. But the true certainty came from the technological progress made possible by these political arrangements, not just the odd alignment of global politics. It was a broad commitment to steady progress, not disruptive wealth creation, that turned all that cutting-edge science into new industries.

Galbraith may have been right about the postwar corporation, but he was wrong about the future of capitalism. Around 1970, we decided to go in a completely different direction.

Elmer Winter was not the only one advocating for another vision of the American workforce, and this vision—supported by economists, but more important, by business leaders and their paid consultants—began to focus on leanness instead of stability. The postwar institutions—big unions, big corporations, powerful regulators—that insulated us from volatility and made possible the steady economic growth and broad equality of the postwar era were swept aside in the name of resurgent faith in the "market." This transformation was not a conspiracy of a few, but a consensus of the many. At the top, the risk-taking entrepreneur supplanted the risk-averse, but loyal, company man as the capitalist ideal. Risk became sought after because it was increasingly seen as the way to maximize profits. Without risk, the new portfolio theorists chided, there could be no return. The right way to view a corporation, economists and consultants told business leaders, was to see a firm not as something that produced valuable goods and services but as a way to make money. Managers began to hop from firm to firm, focusing less on climbing the ladder (i.e., investing for the long term) than on garnering the biggest bonuses. Even for founders, getting acquired, rather than building a firm, became the new goal. No one at the top was committed to the long haul, so why would they be committed to job security for anyone else? These market fundamentalists believed their own hype and turned their backs on the ideas and institutions that had made the postwar boom a reality.

The key features of the postwar corporation—stable workforce, retained earnings, and minimized risk—became liabilities rather than assets. The American corporation was taken in a more financial direction, abandoning thirty years of manufacturing success. In the place of long-term investment and stable workforces, the new ideal for American firms was short-term returns and flexible labor. The elements of the reorientation that promoted and made possible this temporary transformation—consultants, temps, day laborers—emerged from different places and for different reasons, but as their ideas, practices, and institutions interwove, they remade the corporation—and America.

In Dallas, just around the same time that Elmer Winter was starting Manpower, a young electrician named James Ling discovered that if he wanted his one-man shop to grow, the easiest way was to sell some stock and buy out the competition. Ling was not alone. A strictly financial view of the firm—most tangible in the newly ascendant conglomerates from Texas, like Ling-Temco-Vought and Litton Industries—contested the long-term outlook of big industry, encouraging the use of debt leverage, not innovation, to buy their way to the top. In the 1960s, these conglomerates began to buy out everybody, from Hollywood studios to jet plants to basketball manufacturers. When the conglomerate bubble burst in 1969, Ling and Litton were erased from popular memory, but their privileging of finance over production lived on through the investment banks, like Lehman Brothers and Goldman Sachs, that had issued their stocks and bonds. Capital became temporary, and corporations began to focus on short-term profit. In the conglomerate collapse, alternative theories of corporate organization became popular—especially those sold by consultants.

In Boston and New York, management consultants acquired a new currency as theorists of business organization in a time of rapid technological change. Rather than just deliver the new computer technology or perform old efficiency studies, as consultancies like Arthur D. Little had since the turn of the twentieth century, the new consultants offered entirely new growth strategies for the corporation. McKinsey's Marvin Bower and

Boston Consulting Group's Bruce Henderson emerged, along with their firms, as the most sought-after voices to understand change. Offering an interpretation of the failure of the conglomerate—bloated bureaucracies that fell to market forces—they justified the restructuring of the American corporation and, of course, carried it out on the ground as well, not only remaking General Electric and Citibank, but privatizing Fannie Mae. Stability, as rethought by these consultants, became a problem to be solved rather than an aspiration. Their myopic solutions actually undid the real solutions developed during the 1930s that had contained capitalism's tendency toward short-term profit and income inequality. Helping these pure consultancies along were the public accountancies, like Coopers & Lybrand and Price Waterhouse, which used their access as accountants to offer even more lucrative consulting services. The corporation, under the consultants' helm, was no longer an enduring venture; it became a momentary assemblage whose value was not in tomorrow's progress but in today's stock price.

In California and Texas, electronics, the fastest growing industry in the U.S., finally became by the late 1970s the largest industry in America, and its metronome—Moore's Law—became the new time signature of capitalism. In 1965, Gordon Moore, cofounder of Fairchild Semiconductor, predicted that every eighteen months technologists could double the number of components on an integrated circuit. This exponential growth meant that investments in electronics factories had horizons measured in months, not years or decades. Short-term investment and flexible production found their natural home, and Silicon Valley became a model of success for the rest of the country. While Marshall McLuhan saw media as the key driver of the cultural speedup, electronics were actually speeding up the economy. This speedup came from incremental advances in technology (slightly better-made transistors and integrated circuits) rather than any breakthroughs. While new industries produced bonanza profits, this incrementalist industry did not. With a time scale so short, capital needed a way to keep its labor cheap and flexible, so it did not produce the good, stable jobs of prior leading industries. Silicon Valley pioneered transistors, but it also pioneered the use, through subcontractors, of undocumented labor at an industrial scale.

In both electronics and construction—again both California and Texas boom industries—firms discovered that if American labor cost too much, or was too inflexible, the easiest thing to do was to use workers who had no legal rights—the undocumented. With the end of the bracero, or agricultural guest worker, program in 1964, the 20 million Mexicans who had, since World War II, annually migrated to work in U.S. fields found themselves without jobs. Some—as historians have well documented—continued to work in the fields illegally, but just as many—as historians have largely ignored—began to work on construction sites, on factory floors, and in chemical shops. Although Americans may not have wanted to work in the fields, they did want to work industrial jobs. Migrant labor, unprotected by the state, created an alternative to the American worker. This cheap labor made key parts of the 1980s boom possible, whether in Houston's strip malls or Silicon Valley's electronics factories.

The postwar prophecies of office automation finally came in the 1980s, but instead of giving us leisure, they gave us the pink slip. Dovetailing with the consultant-promoted vision of the flexible workforce, temporary labor shifted from an emergency replacement to an essential part of employment strategy. Electronics pioneered outsourcing, first domestically and then overseas, in the 1970s; by the late 1980s, firms everywhere followed the leader. Blue-collar workers saw their manufacturing jobs going overseas. White-collar workers soon faced the same consolidation, as one manager's spreadsheet could replace a room of analysts and a word processor could replace the entire secretarial pool. While temps had already replaced workers inside the firm, by the 1990s, the bulk of white-collar back-office operations could be outsourced as well. Call centers, accounting, and many other formerly internal functions were subcontracted to the lowest bidder, gutting the broad middle class. Middle managers were, in a term invented during the recession of 1991, downsized. Wherever possible, functions that had been part of the postwar corporation—and jobs that had been part of that stability—were moved into the market.

With the quick growth of the internet in work placement in the late 1990s, first through Craigslist and today through Upwork, this process only accelerated. Short-term work acquired a new name: gig labor. Craigslist made it easy to find workers to do nearly anything for any price. Most temps were still hired by corporations, but in the corners of the marketplace, the gig economy began to grow. Although Craigslist was free, it was also hard to use. Over the 2000s, start-ups began to carve off pieces of it to create new digital labor platforms: Elance, oDesk, TaskRabbit, Uber, and all the rest. After the Great Recession, Americans in need of work turned to the gig economy to get them through, and once again Silicon Valley had a boom. Firms that had formerly outsourced through temp agencies and consultancies could now do so with a website as the middleman.

Today's tech boom may create market value, but it has not created that many jobs, especially compared to the big postwar industries. Google might have fifty thousand employees, but even old-economy Sears still has two hundred thousand. The iPhone has probably been as socially disruptive as the car, but Apple doesn't employ like General Motors. App companies are game changing for some college graduates, but only 30 percent of Americans have a bachelor's degree. This gig economy may appear to be driven by new technology, or even just Uber, but behind it is a deep history of the making and unmaking of what most of us consider to be our dream— economic security—and that story is more about management ideas and business values than about any app.

The Second Industrious Revolution

When we learn about the industrial revolution in school, we hear about coal, steam engines, maybe the power loom. But another revolution in capitalism occurred before that, in what historians now call the industrious revolution, which reorganized people, not machines. Before the industrious revolution of the eighteenth century, people worked where they lived, whether a farm or a shop. Earlier manufacturing, like textiles produced through cottage industry, relied on networks of farmers who spun fibers and wove cloth. They worked on their own; they were not employees. In the industrious revolution, manufacturers gathered workers under one roof, where the work could be divided and supervised. For the first time, home and work were separated on a massive scale. Workers no longer controlled how they worked, receiving a wage instead of the profits of their efforts. The industrial revolution of the nineteenth century consolidated these new relationships with new technologies, but those technologies were only possible because people's relationship to work had already changed. Social disruption caused technological innovation, not, usually, the other way around.

Today's new technologies dazzle us and lead some experts to call this the second machine age. Yet as in the eighteenth century, today's reorganization of people matters as much as, if not more than, the new machines. It's been happening for forty years, and in the last few years computers and other technologies have begun to accelerate it, just as steam engines accelerated the industrious revolution. The technology, even so-called artificial intelligence (AI), is not particularly impressive from a historical perspective. AI will be able to perform repetitive tasks, but it will never be true intelligence; its very name is a misnomer. Human strength and human skill will be encoded into machines, as they have for hundreds of years. All sorts of exciting technologies will reinforce this industrious revolution, but it is not the technology that deserves our attention. Technological innovation only solves for social disruption.

Rather than a second machine age, we should instead think of our current moment as the second industrious revolution. The technologies analogous to the steam engine (like artificial intelligence, virtual reality, and the like) haven't fully arrived, but those technologies are being developed in ways that address principally the business problems of an already insecure world, not workers' well-being. The choices we make today will determine whether those steam engines of tomorrow make us all wealthier, or just a few.

Just as modern wage work and bureaucratic corporations emerged from industrial capitalism, so are new forms of labor and capital emerging from this early period of our digital economy. Most Americans (84 percent) still rely on traditional employment as their main source of income, but that is not where the economy is growing. In the last ten years, 94 percent of net new jobs have appeared outside of traditional employment.[4] Already approximately one third of the workforce participates in this alternative world of work, either as a primary or supplementary source of income. The digital labor platforms, like Uber, Upwork, Lyft, and the like, make up less than 1 percent of the workforce, but that is poised for growth as well.[5] In the economic expansion of this second industrious revolution, the employee receiving a regular wage or salary is giving way to independent contractors, consultants, temps, and freelancers. At the same time, the corporation as we know it is disappearing.[6] No longer are the resources of a corporation needed when a "flash team" can be assembled from an online platform, execute a task, and then just as easily disappear.[7] What is truly novel today is not technological change, but organizational breakthrough—the possibility that workers might be able to be as productive on their own as within a firm, with access to the same global distribution and production regimes. An independent person can function as a multinational, sourcing and selling globally through digital platforms.[8] We all can fund, design, launch, and sell products anywhere in the world. Every assumption about labor and capital that underpinned the postwar economy and corporate capitalism has been drawn into question.

What is truly shocking is how wage labor and the corporation might begin to retreat. Wages and corporations will never disappear, and we will certainly need to rethink our labor laws, but digital platforms and independent work are ascendant like never before in capitalism. Capitalism without corporations would truly be a historical break. A large swath of our population might no longer need to have a boss. In our new awakening, we have the chance to return to old dreams.

Yet the recent past does not justify such optimism. Today's economy is not as bleak as the industrial revolution, but there are echoes, and it feels like it is getting worse.[9] Inequality is higher than it has been since the 1920s.[10] Rural America feels disconnected from the urban growth. Drugs and despair are cutting life spans short.[11] Something has gone dangerously wrong in our democracy. While unemployment is down, that metric, which reflects only those who have looked for work in the past two weeks, conceals the new reality: it is harder than ever to find a job, much less a full-time job that pays the bills and provides benefits. We are told at every turn to be entrepreneurial, to make our own work. For some people—a special few—this option works, but for most people, a secure job is still the goal. We are blamed for our own failure to find that job that we have all believed was our right as Americans. We don't know what to do, since the old paths seem to be closed. Even a college education no longer seems like the road to middle-class security.

Job insecurity is both what is new and what has become expected. Even where old-fashioned permanent jobs remain, workers must contend with a new truth: they can be replaced with a phone call. Americans cannot typically rely on just one job anymore, certainly not over a lifetime, and—for the working poor—frequently not even at one time. Though day laborers, office temps, and management consultants—as well as contract assemblers, Craigslist freelancers, adjunct professors, Uber drivers, Blackwater mercenaries, and every other kind of worker filing an IRS Form 1099—span the income ranks, what they do have in common is what we all have in common in this post-1970s economy: they are temporary.[12]

Just as our business and policy leaders made choices to bring about this insecurity, we are at a moment when we can once again choose to remake our economy. To do so, however, we must confront some uncomfortable truths about how American capitalism has been remade from top to bottom. For some, the rise of the gig economy is liberation from the stifled world of corporate America. It is a return to the autonomy and independence of an economy before wage labor. No desk. No boss. Every consultant is her own master. Yet for the vast majority of workers the freedom from a paycheck is just the freedom to be afraid. It is the severing of obligations between firms and employees. It is the collapse of the protections that we, in our laws and our customs, fought hard to enshrine.

After a long history of insecurity in the labor market, not until the mid-twentieth century, in the heyday of postwar capitalism, did we find a way to create economic security in America's wage-work economy—a steady paycheck, health insurance, and quality housing. The New Deal ended this century-long war over who would benefit from rising industrial productivity. New Deal policy embedded security into a particular kind of industrial-era, full-time, employer-employee relationship that was itself born of a historical moment when automobiles and aerospace defined the leading sectors of the economy. Policy makers, in ways that are now forgotten, supported business to invest in these radical new technologies, while at the same time making sure that workers got their fair share of the wealth.

At the same time, we should not romanticize the postwar period and its associated protections. For those excluded from those jobs—women, Latinos, African Americans, undocumented migrants—the rest of the economy was not so glorious, and their work helped make that economy possible. In many ways, as *Temp* shows, the experiences of the people who were left out of the good postwar jobs became the rehearsal for most people's jobs today. As the century progressed, these groups would work, but their labor would not be as protected, as valued, as white men's labor. The New Deal protections remained on the books, but were not renewed along with the economy, making them ever more peripheral; in the end, even white men were not protected from this new reality, contributing to the Trump victory in 2016. Again and again, we must ask the same question: Who counts? At the same time, we must not forget that even for those white men who had the good paychecks, working on an assembly line or in a mine was dehumanizing, backbreaking, and most important, soul-breaking work. Whatever the wages and benefits, humans should not do the work of robots.

If we should not romanticize the postwar salaryman, neither should we, at the same time, romanticize the freelancer. This capitalism of independent workers and flexible firms will not naturally be better. Industrial capitalism did not naturally provide the well-paid, stable factory work for which we are nostalgic. For a century, there was a bloody struggle between labor and capital over how capitalism's growth was divvied up. For workers, industrialization meant decades of fear, growing inequality, and shortened life expectancies.[13] By the end of the nineteenth century, industrial capitalism had produced a world of grinding poverty, substandard tenements, and political unrest. To deny, dismiss, or simply overlook this wrenching reality that went hand in hand with industrialization, by making only the case that new jobs and economic growth were the result, ignores the reality of that brutal world.

Most of us aren't consultants, temps, or day laborers, but that world of flexibility defines our work lives. These workers, whether they are at the top, like McKinsey consultants, or at the bottom, like undocumented workers, offer employers alternatives to providing secure employment. We can't turn back the clock, but neither is insecurity inevitable. Only by understanding how these ideas and institutions came to be so powerful can we meaningfully act to once again make capitalism work for us, not work us over. Laws matter in how capitalism plays out, but organized power—of both labor and capital—matters more. Reading this history will, I hope, point us toward a better understanding of our lives to come.

Temp is the history of how American work and American business—and perhaps even the American dream itself—became temporary. This history traces the rise of the stable work and stable investment that happened after World War II, in that period that historians called the postwar—from 1945 to 1970—and how it came undone. Although the first part has an easy name, "postwar," the second part, the fall, does not. Various terms have been proferred: neoliberalism, age of turbulence, postindustrialism, the service economy, late capitalism, the regressive era, post-Fordism, post-Jim Crow, new Jim Crow, age of Reagan, and many others. Notice how none of the -isms have stuck. We are still living in this post-postwar moment that has yet to be completed, and when you live in a moment it is hard to name. But perhaps not for long.

This book, then, should not be seen as either for or against temping (or consulting, or freelancing). Though it focuses on a few firms and leaders, it is not even really about Manpower or McKinsey, Elmer Winter or Marvin Bower, but about how work and society in every business has changed because of choices made. Today, if our emergent flexible economy was all bad or all good, there would be no need to even make a choice. The ambiguity and complexity demand that we understand all sides of these issues, and formulate policies to separate the good from the bad, in order to make the best of the situation. Just as the industrial economy offered inequality and growth, so, too, will the digital economy. We need to understand that this flexible workforce can be, depending on the choices that we make, either the liberation from wage work that Americans have so long yearned for or damnation to insecure lives in an unequal society. The decision is ours.

CHAPTER ONE

Making Company Men

Before the 1930s, Americans assumed that individuals, especially if they were men, were responsible for their own work
lives. Workplace rights owed more to union bargaining—a manly showdown, not a legal negotiation—than federal regulation.[1] Suckers were born
every minute, and it was every man's own responsibility to make his way in
the world. Markets were king. Popular faith in markets reached a crescendo
during the heady days of the 1920s, when it appeared that the economy
would continue to grow without bound. Contemporaries called it a New
Era, when the recessions of the past would never happen again. A new kind
of corporation, pioneered by General Motors, showed how a modern firm
could be run and deliver truly innovative products. Industrial peace had
been achieved, it seemed, through rising wages, not through Russian-style
revolution. Exciting new products based on the proliferation of urban electricity could be found everywhere those cables traced out their power. The
stock market went up, up, up. All these new gizmos and rising stock prices
nonetheless hid a weakness in the economy.

When the Great Depression came, the industrial economy unspooled,
but just as important, so, too, did the stories that explained how the economy worked. Men—good men—lost their jobs. Fortunes disappeared, but so
did companies. Supply and demand may have worked in theory, but in reality they just worked you over. In this crisis, with everything up for grabs, industrialists, unionists, and policy makers put American capitalism on a new
footing of stability. If the 1920s made the corporation more productive,
then the 1930s—through the machinations of labor leaders, clever policy
makers, and bureaucratic entrepreneurs—brought that productivity to the
rest of America. The political and business choices of the 1930s created a
new industrial security—for labor and for capital—that enabled the postwar
good life.

In the process of this reinvention of the industrial corporation came new kinds of work: legal industrial unionists, management consultants, certified public accountants, and temporary foreign farmhands. As the corporation remade industrial capitalism, it pulled in its wake a whole host of new ways of working.

The Invention of the Modern Corporation

Historians of the corporation traditionally look to the railroad as the birthplace of its bureaucracy, but the growth of the corporate bureaucracy didn't really take off until the twentieth century, when manufacturing—with the cars and chemicals it created—became much more complex.[2] Like railroads, the new manufacturing corporations required precise coordination over time and space—or engines exploded. These new entities required a level of complexity that one person, or even a small group of people, could not oversee by themselves. For the first time, layers of management were needed in order to effectively run an enterprise. As American capitalism transitioned from simply moving wood and grain to creating steel and cars, the necessity for coordination grew in all big companies that used the railroads. After the Civil War, huge industrial concerns used holding companies to buy out their rivals, as well as their suppliers. Steel magnate Andrew Carnegie bought into Henry Frick's business, not because Frick made steel, but because he supplied the coal to run Carnegie's plants. To the public, the purpose of these trusts appeared to be monopolistic control (and sometimes it was), but that was not the only goal. For the industrialists, it was just as often about guaranteeing necessary supplies. Markets could not be trusted.

Coordinating activities across national and international distances required a lot of confidence—a level of faith that market transactions often could not provide. Eliminating markets was the dream of the nineteenth century—and not just in terms of suppliers. From 1895 to 1904, eighteen hundred industrial firms consolidated, with three quarters of them merging five or more companies.[3] Accelerating in the 1890s, trusts began to dominate every area of the U.S. economy. These grand consolidations included the epochal U.S. Steel, but also lesser-known oligopolists like American Chicle, American School Furniture, American Seeding Machine, American Snuff, and American Stogie—all of which controlled more than 70 percent of their respective markets (except U.S. Steel, which only controlled about two thirds of the U.S. steel market).[4] Every industry had its trust, amalgamating smaller entities from the old manufacturing regimes. Out of this burst came the grand industrial names of the twentieth century: DuPont, Eastman Kodak, International Harvester, National Biscuit, Amalgamated Copper, and International Paper. Industrial "markets" were monopolies in disguise, with vast, centrally controlled networks of supply.

The formation of U.S. Steel, through which J. P. Morgan combined Carnegie Steel with a few other major firms, was significant not only in its size (as the first billion-dollar firm), but in its meaning for the twentieth-century corporation. Morgan realized that by the turn of the twentieth century, the holding company had encountered its limit. Holding companies were flexible affairs, but in the absence of the market's discipline, they offered none of their own. For ever more complex manufacturing, access to supplies, like iron or coal, was not enough. The industrial corporation of the twentieth century offered more control than a holding company, but without sacrificing its scale. This careful balance was worked out, for the first time, at General Motors, as it was transformed from a holding company into the archetype of the modern corporation.

Unlike all the would-be auto magnates, such as Henry Ford, William Durant, who would later found General Motors, was no mechanic. He had no interest in futzing with engines. Durant believed in selling, not making. He believed in growth, not management.[5] Durant had started his working life as an insurance salesman in Flint, Michigan, which was, at that time, a boomtown filled with possibilities. He made his first million by selling horse carts, starting in 1885. And when he started selling them, he subcontracted their assembly. Like Nike many decades later with shoes, Durant never made his own carts.

By the late 1890s, Durant was a millionaire many times over. Little interested in actual manufacturing, Durant moved his headquarters to New York to be near other important businessmen and to make the financial connections to expand his interests. By 1908, he had begun to notice that the automobile industry was finally emerging from mechanics' garages, threatening to upset his cart business. As Henry Ford rolled out his Model

T, Durant set about creating his own automobile empire, but on a completely different basis. Where Ford relied on his mechanical genius, Durant relied on his genius for selling. Ford refused outside investment, especially from Wall Street bankers, while Durant relied on borrowed money and stock swaps to buy out the competition.[6] In a few short years, he bought the distressed assets of Buick, Oldsmobile, and other auto manufacturers, assembling them into a holding company that he called General Motors.

Durant's interests continued to grow, but he brought no discipline to his enterprises. He bought out as many suppliers and assemblers as he could, seeking to expand General Motors as quickly as possible. In the process, he so wildly overextended himself that his creditors, a group of Boston bankers, briefly took control of GM. Through an elaborate stock-swap maneuver, however, Durant regained control in 1915. Between 1915 and 1920, the company grew eightfold, but Durant had not learned from his mistakes. This second time around, he reorganized GM in 1917 into an operating corporation rather than a holding company. All the various companies previously held by GM, and allowed to be relatively autonomous, were remade into corporate divisions but were still run mostly like separate firms. But while Durant added companies, he did not add oversight. He was more concerned with sales growth than with profit growth. Making this expansion possible were the chemical fortunes of DuPont, who wanted a piece of the automobile action. During the upheavals of 1915, as Durant resumed control, Pierre du Pont, the head of the DuPont Company, committed more than half of his private fortune to investing in GM. DuPont, the company, invested more in GM than had any other company in U.S. history in another firm.[7] Pierre wanted to make sure his investment panned out.

The freewheeling nature of GM suited Durant's ego, but it definitely rubbed the du Ponts the wrong way. As long as the expansion continued, the du Ponts held their tongues. Lucky for GM—and the only reason you know its name today—one of those companies that Durant acquired during his binge made roller bearings. The Hyatt Roller Bearing Company was headed by an MIT-trained engineer, Alfred Sloan, who would redefine the corporation.

Brooklyn-raised Alfred Sloan had joined the Hyatt Roller Bearing Company fresh out of his electrical engineering program. The company made an antifriction bearing that found uses in "cranes, paper-mill equipment, mine cars, and other machinery."[8] Like many firms, however, it made a good product, but not much profit. In 1898, only twenty-three years old, backed by his father and his father's friend, Sloan invested five thousand dollars and, after success in raising revenues, became its general manager. His real breakthrough came with the rise of the automobile, which needed many, many bearings. Sloan positioned himself as "a kind of consulting sales-engineer" to these early car companies, and they included his roller bearings in their designs. He had turned Hyatt from a technologically sophisticated but stagnant firm into a prosperous one. Through his sales, Sloan made contacts and grew familiar with the entire automobile industry. He was no salesman, but he did not need to be. He sold bearings to large manufacturers; with only a few customers, he could produce in volume. As an engineer, however, he had a very different vision of the corporation than Durant, the consummate salesman.[9]

When Durant acquired Hyatt in 1916 as part of his expansion, he paid $13.5 million for the firm, 60 percent of which Sloan and his family owned. Now forty years old, Sloan wanted to be part of something bigger than roller bearings.[10] He took half of his payment in GM stock, became the head of a division at GM, and seized the opportunity that presented itself to him.[11] At GM, Sloan brought his systematic thought and organizational talents to bear on a much larger challenge. As head of the division of GM that manufactured parts and accessories, he had to coordinate and compare the performance of many different kinds of manufacturing. He set up unified accounting. He standardized organizational hierarchies. Lines of authority and responsibility became clear with a well-structured organization chart. It became the best-managed division of GM. Unlike the other division heads, Sloan could provide clear and reliable information that no other division at GM could.

Durant cared little about Sloan's bookkeeping, of course, because he imagined that GM would eventually become the car monopoly. Before Sloan's intervention, Durant did not even have accountants review GM's books, and according to Sloan, "did not have a sound concept of accounting as such."[12] Sloan nonetheless slowly began to organize the finances of GM behind the scenes.

Unfortunately for Durant, the postwar recession of 1920–21 undid his dreams. By the end of April 1920, GM had $167 million in unused inventories. By October, inventories hit $210 million and the demand for automobiles had disappeared. Ford cut his prices 20 to 30 percent. Durant tried to maintain his prices, but volume fell to about one quarter of what it had been only months earlier.

As you might expect, during all of this, GM's stock collapsed. Durant, always committed to his personal responsibility for success or failure, attempted to buy all the stock on credit. In the end, he could not, as one man fighting the market, stop the price drop. By November 1920, as his attempt was found out and the company spiraled toward bankruptcy, he was ousted.

Into this gap, the du Ponts, who had assumed control of the company, looked to the sober leadership of the engineer Alfred Sloan, who had impressed the du Ponts with his attention to financial details. Sloan, in turn, offered a reorganization plan for GM with a structured hierarchy of responsibilities, echoing what he had done in his division, and in doing so defined the twentieth-century corporation.

Sloan's corporation, which would be called the multidivisional, or M-form, corporation, would attempt to synthesize market pricing with bureaucratic coordination.[13] Unlike Durant, who thought market domination led to profits, or Ford, who believed in vertical integration, Sloan had a more nuanced conception of how corporations succeed. Imagine you run a corporation and that corporation has ample but limited capital. How to invest that capital? Should it be in a mine? Should it be in a factory? How to choose? It seems obvious, but Sloan decided to go with whatever was more profitable. If a product, like roller bearings, could be had cheaper in the market, Sloan would shut down the roller-bearing division and take that capital to invest in a more profitable division. Of course, shutting down a GM division would not happen instantaneously; an effort would be made to improve it. But if that did not work, the market could be relied on. In this way of expanding and pruning, profits could be increased.

To make that possible, Sloan standardized accounting practices across the divisions so that apples could be compared to apples (if apples were revenues, oranges were costs, and so on). He centralized functions that were replicated across Durant's empire (like real estate, taxes, and accounting) into the headquarters, where a core staff could oversee everything. This re-organization into a bureaucracy increased control and reduced duplication, yet the layers of hierarchy allowed units to operate semi-independent busi-nesses. Sloan's financial policy imitated that of the du Ponts—direct finan-cial control.[14] Whereas before, each unit had controlled its own cash, all money would now be centrally allocated. All incoming money went to the finance department. Divisions would submit monthly reports on expenses, revenues, and anticipated needs. Money would then be dispersed or not dis-persed depending on whether the financial executives thought it would be prudent.

At any point, Sloan, and by extension the du Ponts, could understand any part of the business—and trust managers to run their own divisions. In-ternally, other shifts were made to make central control more practical. The heads of the Olds, Oakland, Cadillac, and Chevrolet divisions were all fired. These managers dated from the time when these were independent companies. Their style could not fit with the larger aims of Sloan and the du Ponts. The du Ponts loved it.[15]

Sloan's vision for a car company looked nothing like Durant's, or even Henry Ford's. Ford spent the 1920s trying to perfect his monumental River Rouge plant, which could take in raw iron ore (from Ford's own mines) and output Model Ts. Ford made cars cheaply. Sloan made cars profitably.

By 1923, Sloan had re-created the entire line of GM cars to offer a spread across price points, to make sure he could sell a car to nearly any-body. Cadillac was the most expensive, then Buick, then Oakland, then Oldsmobile, then Chevrolet. Because of a price gap between Olds and Chevy, GM created Pontiac. Instead of selling to one kind of customer (like Ford), GM pioneered market segmentation in a rational way that no con-sumer goods company before it had done. At the same time, though nineteenth-century industrialists faced sporadic and uncertain supplies of basic goods in the market—remember Carnegie's problem with coal—by 1920, these markets were well developed. Production would not shut down for want of coal, or steel, or rubber. So Sloan decided to forgo owning the less profitable mines and concentrate his investments on the more profitable car-assembly business.

As GM rose, the holding company fell. General Motors' centralized bureaucracy and multidivisional structure would be the blueprint for the industrial corporation of postwar America. Rebuilding America's corporations to this blueprint required a new class of professionals—accountants and consultants.

The Emergence of Accounting and Consulting

In the 1920s, finance had simply become too exciting to resist. All the speculation (and fraud) made some rich (and others poor), but it didn't create the orderly world that Sloan envisioned. After the Great Depression, Americans longed for order, especially at work. To make that happen required keeping the corporations honest and modernizing their organizations. To do this, a new cadre of professionals emerged: accountants and consultants. These two professions seem very different—accountants checking the books, and consultants telling firms how to run themselves. Indeed, at their origins, and in their paths over the subsequent decades, their two very different roles tangled—and not always for the good. The line between them in the 1920s was far blurrier, and more consequential, than one might imagine, and is so today.

Public accountancy, as a profession, preceded consulting by only a few decades, but in the 1920s, the age of the M-form corporation, it assumed a centrality to the most basic operation of capitalism: investment. The separation of management and ownership required a certain transparency in how the business was actually being run. Clear facts about the books were necessary if the stockholders were to know what they were investing in. Public accountants, with their codes of ethics and annual audits, smoothed over some of the conflicting interests of shareholders and top management. Glenn Petty was a young accountant at Lybrand, Ross Bros. and Montgomery, only a few years out of Wharton, when the Great Depression struck. He'd watched from his Philadelphia office as the bank across the street folded and his coworkers rushed out with the rest of the crowd to get their deposits. But while banks collapsed, accountancies did not. In fact, work increased. In the aftermath of the crash, scrutiny of corporations increased. In 1932, the New York Stock Exchange required independent audits of all corporate statements, which was reinforced in 1934 by a new federal agency to oversee the financial system—the Securities and Exchange Commission (SEC).

In its oversight capacity, the SEC demanded—for the first time—that publicly traded corporations have their accounts audited, and that these audits be made public. Never before had corporations been forced to open their books to the world. In the previous two decades, corporations had grown more complex. All this oversight came with a price—more accountants. Corporate auditing by independent accountants was seen, both on Wall Street and in Congress, as a safeguard against any more tomfoolery. Public accounting became the go-to bulwark against capitalist crisis. Petty, like other public accountants, had clients who had "new sets of rules to comply with" and "many reports." Someone, for the first time, was "looking over our shoulder on the reports" on corporations. The information needed to be correct or there would be legal consequences. More forms meant more work. Accounting was just one of the new ancillary professional services to expand.[16]

If accounting helped executives understand what was happening in these multidivisional corporations, then consultants helped those executives decide what to do with that information. Management consulting grew out of the same origin as Sloan's modern corporation—scientific management paired with managerial accounting. But over the decades, it would become something much more important: a vehicle for rapidly collecting and then selling ideas about how businesses ought to be organized.

In 1926, James "Mac" McKinsey had started a company in Chicago that, building on the teachings of industrial engineer Frederick Winslow Taylor, helped businesses to better manage their operations, but through careful analysis of the accounts, not the production line. McKinsey, like Sloan, believed in the synergy of research, accounting, and management. University of Chicago trained, he became a certified public accountant in 1919. In 1922, he published one of the first books on how to use accounting to manage firms, *Budgetary Control,* followed by *Managerial Accounting* in 1924. Unlike his contemporary engineers, who understood a business through the machines on the production line, McKinsey started with the accounts, with the abstraction of numbers.[17] The thinking here, reasonably enough, was that if you knew a lot about a firm's balance sheets, you could probably help them make more money. McKinsey offered this analysis to clients, starting his own eponymous firm in 1926. It would eventually become the most influential consultancy in the world. But then, McKinsey & Company, like many advisory firms, blurred the lines between accountant and "management engineer."[18]

That same year, a young Marvin Bower, the future leader of McKinsey & Company, thought he would become a lawyer, only to have those hopes dashed. He grew up in a middle-class family in Cleveland, Ohio, and had made his way to Brown University in 1921, where he studied philosophy and the new field of economics.[19] He followed Brown with Harvard Law, going to Cambridge in 1925. He graduated, but his grades in law school would not get him a job at his choice Cleveland law firm—Jones, Day.[20] To join that firm, a graduate needed to be in the top 5 percent of his class or on the *Harvard Law Review*.[21] Bower, now twenty-five, made the unusual choice in 1928 to cross the Charles River and enroll at Harvard Business School for an MBA. The dean of Harvard Law tried to offer him a job at International Paper, telling him, "My God, Bower, you are about to graduate from the greatest educational institution in the world and you are going to *that* place!"[22] After two years, Bower graduated, but in those two years American business had gone from dizzying growth to vertiginous collapse.

When he *did* join Jones, Day, Bower found himself handling the wreckage of the Great Depression. His firm, which had been involved in the bond issues of leading Cleveland manufacturing companies, now tried to maximize the return for those bondholders by helping the companies get back on track. With his unusual combination of degrees, Bower found himself meeting with the CEOs of leading firms like Midland Steel and Studebaker. Their troubles were not legal troubles but business troubles. "No one asked why these companies had failed," he later said.[23] In this moment, Bower started to feel his true calling: consulting with CEOs to wring value out of firms in crisis. As a lawyer, he oversaw the reorganization of eleven firms over the next three years—despite being the tender age of twenty-seven—and learned firsthand how to bring change to corporations.

When firms began to default on their bond payments, Jones, Day would help them restructure their debts. Bower designed these new capital structures, which he thought was fun.[24] Actually implementing them involved writing long legal documents, which was boring. Even as he enjoyed thinking about business, he realized that his approach was amateurish, at least in comparison to the professional expertise of his firm's legal partners. He thought there should be a comparable professional firm for business problems.

By 1933, Bower decided that he liked consulting more than law, but the kinds of advisory services he offered didn't fit well with existing professional firms, and more than anything Bower thought of himself as a professional, not as a technician. Accountants audited and prepared the books. Management engineers optimized factory production, but they were few and far between, and when they did exist, they parroted Taylor and found ways to cut costs. Bower did something harder than just cost cutting. He looked for ways for companies to grow.

He started to look around, and one of his old professors at Harvard Business School suggested that he contact James McKinsey, who ran a hybrid accounting/management engineering company in Chicago. McKinsey, like Bower, was well educated, and his firm worked on the kinds of problems that interested Bower. Still, Bower wasn't sure about leaving his high-prestige job for this small, unknown firm far away from his native Cleveland. But as Jones, Day threatened to cut all salaries by 25 percent (it was still the middle of the Great Depression), he decided to trek to Chicago to meet with McKinsey. Bower told him about his work at Jones, Day. He told him that the business problems interested him much more than the law problems and that he longed to be part of a consulting firm that was run as professionally as his law firm. McKinsey told him, "Why don't you join us and enjoy your work completely?"[25] "My colleagues in Cleveland thought I was out of my mind when I left a leading law firm to join an unknown firm in an unknown field," Bower said, "but I was confident that I was taking advantage of a great opportunity."[26]

The firm advised industrial companies on how to best use their labor, their machines, and their capital, combining the skills of public accounting, corporate law, and management science. During the 1930s, as businesses collapsed, services to cut costs and improve efficiency were in demand.

McKinsey spoke widely and publicly on business issues, helping to found the American Management Association. The firm grew rapidly and opened a branch office in 1932 in New York City.

From the beginning, McKinsey had tried to standardize the analytic approach of the firm. With his General Survey Outline—perhaps the first business framework, as we would call it today—all management engineers were supposed to be able to understand any firm's operations. Following a checklist, an associate or partner would start with the industry, then the company, then "all major functions: marketing, manufacturing, facilities, control, finance, personnel, etc."[27]

Bower appreciated the reliance on numbers, but disagreed with Mac that the same person should audit the accounts and then decide, as a management engineer, what to do with them. Students do not grade themselves, and neither should consultants. The people who counseled a business on how it should be run, Bower thought, should not at the same time be in charge of determining whether those choices were profitable. The conflict of interest was suspect and made such an arrangement unprofessional.[28] Some accountants (who were intimates of the businesses they audited) nonetheless provided that assistance, though often in hushed tones. At Ernst & Ernst, for instance, these "special services" smacked a bit of going against the impartiality of public accounting. Mac McKinsey thought that the "favorable economics" made it irresistible, and that Bower's troubles with the system were unfounded.[29] As an associate, and then a junior partner, Bower politely agreed to disagree with Mac.

At McKinsey & Company, Bower did enjoy all his work. Within a year, he was overseeing the New York office.[30] Like Mac, Bower believed in the power of facts to change firms. McKinsey's facts came from the accounts, but Bower's facts came from everywhere. He believed in interviewing workers from the bottom to the top to find out how a business actually worked.

A turning point for McKinsey came in 1935, when they landed the biggest engagement yet—Marshall Field. Consultants had a reputation, Bower feared, for being called in as "business doctors" only when a business was dying. It was hard to convince clients to bring McKinsey in, because it signaled ill health. But Bower knew that if they could succeed with a big name like Marshall Field, McKinsey & Company would be on the path to success.[31]

Marshall Field, the venerable Chicago catalogue operation and department store, hired McKinsey to examine its operations, which spanned wholesale, retail, and manufacturing. Mac oversaw the Chicago engagement, but Bower traveled to examine its textile factories in the South and its buying operations in New York. The investigations revealed what had been suspected—Marshall Field's wholesale and manufacturing operations were bad investments. The McKinsey report "call[ed] for the liquidation of the wholesale business, sales of the mills, and the Mart," which was then the largest office building in the world. It was a stunning intervention, but the Marshall Field leadership was convinced. In September, Mac was offered the chief executive position at Marshall Field to carry out the transformation while still running his own business. He accepted, and looked for a way to keep his own firm going. He decided to merge James O. McKinsey & Company with another accounting firm, Scovell, Wellington & Company, in 1935.[32]

This "shotgun marriage," as Bower later referred to it, did not succeed. The cultures of the two firms could not have been more different. First names were used at McKinsey, Mr. So-and-So at Scovell. Senior partners got copies of every letter at Scovell, while McKinsey partners believed in confidentiality (especially with clients). Moreover, Bower's long-standing suspicion of accounting came to the fore. Frustration with the situation forced Bower to consider in a systematic way how he thought a consulting firm ought to be organized.[33]

The next two years were volatile. The merged firm landed some big names—U.S. Steel, H. J. Heinz, United Parcel Service, Lukens Steel—all of which struggled with new federal laws and the Great Depresssion.[34] Despite attracting important new clients, the merged firm also lost their most important one. In May 1937, U.S. Steel withdrew from its engagement after only a year, eliminating 55 percent of the firm's revenues. That business tragedy was soon followed by a human tragedy.[35]

In November 1937, McKinsey suddenly died from pneumonia. In the aftermath of McKinsey's death, Bower stepped in and led the firm, building on Mac's legacy, but with his own vision. The reason that McKinsey & Company is the global consulting phenomenon it is today is Marvin Bower—Harvard Business School graduate, former lawyer, and young management engineer.

With a few other senior investors, over the next two years, he bought out the New York and Boston operations of the firm and set about remaking it as he thought it should be: professional and fact driven, but independent from accounting.[36] The Chicago office went to another partner, A. T. "Tom" Kearney, who still believed in the older way of doing things.[37] McKinsey, Kearney & Company became, within a few years, the more familiar A. T. Kearney & Company. The New York office and the name McKinsey & Company went to Bower.

First, Bower jettisoned the accounting department. He stopped doing anything that could compromise the appearance of objectivity or present a conflict of interest. He believed in professional ethics before all else. He stopped, for instance, executive recruiting, since it seemed to tarnish the firm's impartiality. In his view, consultants did not hire and fire individuals; they defined job requirements. Recruiting smacked of subjectivity. He ran McKinsey, in short, like a law firm, and in 1939, he stopped calling his colleagues management engineers and gave them a new, more professional, title: management consultants.

How the New Deal Created the Good Job

If General Motors defined the new organization of capital, it also, despite itself, defined the organization of labor as well. It would be at General Motors that the promise of industrial democracy—workers sharing in industrial productivity—would be realized, but not without a fight. The fight would be on the factory floor, but it would also be in the courts. This new labor model—good pay, job security—would be possible only because of the success of the M-form corporation. But it would be new laws and, more important, new labor organizations that turned industrial growth into democratic prosperity. For the first time, the wealth of the industrial revolution was extended to the rest of America. Just as Sloan had organized the industrial corporation in the 1920s, another man, John L. Lewis, would organize industrial labor in the 1930s.

It had started in Washington, D.C., just around the same time that Marvin Bower had joined McKinsey. During his first hundred days in office, President Franklin Delano Roosevelt offered legislation intended to remake the U.S. economy, from farm to factory. FDR announced his policy ideas that came to form the core of the bill on May 3, 1933, during his second Fireside Chat, a weekly radio broadcast in which FDR addressed the nation. He called for a partnership in planning between government and business that would give the government the power to directly interfere in business practices like union negotiations and wage setting.

Two weeks after the chat, FDR delivered his legislation to Congress. The National Industrial Recovery Act (NIRA) intended "to promote the organization of industry for the purpose of cooperative action among trade groups"—that is, to allow them to meet to set wages, a meeting that would ordinarily have been in violation of antitrust laws. These codes, organized through the National Recovery Administration (NRA), set standards for every industry and were, in large part, to be written by industry leaders. Roosevelt's ambition was to create codes of fair competition with standard wages and business practices. Colluding through these codes, manufacturers, in concert with government regulators, could agree on fair wages and working conditions. Child labor, for instance, could be banned, for the first time, from Southern textile mills. Such controls would, in turn, stabilize a downward spiral of wages. The only hiccup in this plan was that it was both unconstitutional and at odds with traditional economic thought. Child labor, for example, had been repeatedly ruled by the Supreme Court as beyond the federal government's ability to regulate. One of his advisers questioned his programs: "You realize then that you're taking an enormous step away from the philosophy of laissez-faire?" FDR replied in kind: "If that philosophy hadn't proved to be bankrupt, Herbert Hoover would be sitting here right now. I never felt surer of anything in my life than I do of the soundness of this passage."[38]

Nestled deep in the NIRA as well was the small provision that would have big consequences: section 7(a). This section granted workers the right to collectively bargain for wages and hours. This provision was shockingly radical. The federal government had long restrained the rights of workers to organize. The Sherman Antitrust Act, intended to curtail monopolies, had mostly been used against unions. Codifying the right to form a union was a bold divergence from previous federal policy.

If you are thinking that these two parts of the bill seem contradictory, you are correct. One part granted business the right to create standard wage and hour codes, and the other gave labor the right to organize unions to contest those codes. From the very start, New Deal policy was inconsistent—sometimes in the very same bill, like in the NIRA. For Roosevelt and his advisers, the key issue after the Great Depression was rejuvenating industrial capitalism and, in doing, so figuring out how to break free from policy assumptions rooted in an agricultural economy. Keynesian economics was not yet invented. There was no road map. All these policy makers knew was that the assumptions of an agricultural world, from which laissez-faire derived its logic, no longer applied. Better to experiment than to let the Great Depression run its course. Radical as it was, the NIRA had a sunset clause built into it—it was, after all, an experiment. It would need to be renewed in two years, in 1935.

No one recognized the opportunity of the NIRA more than John Lewis, the leader of the United Mine Workers (UMW). Fifty-three, powerfully built, and missing an eye, John Lewis had been the head of the UMW since 1920, leading it through a long decline during the 1920s. Membership dropped from four hundred thousand in 1920 to one hundred thousand in 1933. Lewis saw section 7(a) as the chance to rebuild the union. He organized a summertime campaign in 1933 throughout Kentucky, West Virginia, Pennsylvania, and Illinois, announcing from loudspeakers on trucks: "The president wants you to unionize. It is unpatriotic to refuse to unionize. Here is your union."[39]

Along with other labor leaders in the garment, steel, and automobile industries, Lewis began a national campaign to organize workers who had been considered, a generation earlier, unorganizable: unskilled industrial workers. Unlike the old American Federation of Labor (AFL) craft unions, like the carpenters' union or bricklayers' union, these industrial unions were organized by industry. Whatever you did at a mine or factory, you were part of the union, whether you were a highly skilled artisan or an unskilled janitor. Everyone, of course, has some skills, but what this term meant then, and now, is someone who has either a common skill or a skill that nearly anyone can learn quickly.[40] If a skill can be easily learned, a worker can be easily replaced, making strikes nearly impossible. For the AFL, since its inception in 1888, the lesson of American labor was to stick to organizing skilled workers. Every time labor leaders tried to organize the unskilled, it ended in failure.[41] The focus on skilled workers had kept the AFL alive, just barely, through the 1920s, but in a rapidly industrializing economy, that focus had also limited the labor movement's scope. Because of the new support from the federal government, however, strikes were not as necessary for organizing. Lewis believed that the unskilled could finally be organized.

In an unprecedented way, the federal government set up a new organization, the National Labor Board, to decide if a union truly represented the employees. If it did, then the corporation had to negotiate with the union. This election would be supervised by the government. As one NLB member said to a mill owner, "This is America and that's the way we do things here."

Corporations were not democracies. Sloan's hierarchy allowed for no bottom-up voice, just top-down control. That was the point. The worker obeyed the owner. Chains of command enforced by the possibility of unemployment enforced relations of power. Industry was not "America." You may have been free outside of work, but for eight, or ten, or twelve hours a day, you obeyed.

Owners grew incensed at not being able to simply fire union organizers and install their own "company" unions. They merely refused to recognize the rulings of the NLB, which, in the end, had no real enforcement powers. By the spring of 1934, companies freely flouted the NLB. A crisis mounted. On the one hand, FDR wanted to placate business to facilitate the NRA, but at the same time, section 7(a) was an important part of the NIRA. Roosevelt confronted a Supreme Court that still did not think the NRA, or by extension the NIRA, was constitutional. In May 1935, the Supreme Court declared the NRA and the NIRA unconstitutional.[42]

FDR took this decision as an opportunity rather than a setback. The NRA, with little public and political support, was all but dead anyhow. Regrouping, Roosevelt announced that certain aspects of the NIRA would be distributed among different agencies. Child labor, wages, hours, and union oversight would all be divvied up, forcing their constitutionality to be decided separately.

Section 7(a) was remade into the National Labor Relations Act (also known as the Wagner Act) of 1935. Out of the Wagner Act came the re-christened National Labor Relations Board, which had the clear right to supervise union elections and to enforce those elections in courts. Codifying the rest of the NIRA took a few years.

While these new laws kept the federal government from stopping unionization, industrial workers continued to organize themselves. The law helped the organizing, but it was the workers themselves who made the Committee for Industrial Organization grow, not the government. Like Roosevelt, Lewis took the opposition (in his case, the AFL) as an opportunity. Through a series of organizing campaigns and strikes that were sometimes militant, Lewis's unskilled union's membership—which in 1935 was known as the CIO, encompassing the group of AFL unions trying to organize unskilled workers. These CIO unions grew to 4 million members, even in the midst of the Great Depression, defying all expectations. The most audacious of the strikes was without a doubt the Flint sit-down strike of 1936, which transformed the United Auto Workers (UAW) into one of the most powerful unions in America.

Walter Reuther, who would become the leading voice of autoworkers, and then of the CIO, was born in West Virginia in 1907. He had spent his early years working at Ford in the tool and die department. After he was fired for attempting to organize in 1932, he went, in a youthful enthusiasm for communism, to the USSR to see how they organized their auto plants. When he got back, the CIO was in full swing, and so he joined with the UAW to help organize autoworkers at GM.

Unionists weren't sure about the new NLRB. What they did know was that after years of depression, their backs were against the wall. Unemployed workers were everywhere, and management seemed to have the upper hand in every negotiation. Sporadic strikes kept breaking out in the industrial heartland, like the rubber workers' strike in Akron, Ohio. Reuther and the UAW did not want to organize one plant; they wanted to organize an industry. Trying to take down the world's largest corporation in the middle of the Great Depression might seem quixotic, but the UAW understood that what made GM strong also, paradoxically, made GM vulnerable.

By 1936, General Motors was not one factory. It was a string of factories across the country that each concentrated on one part of the car. One factory might make chassis, another might make headlights. Moreover, behind those factories were other companies that supplied steel and lightbulbs and every other part of the car. Without the flow of those supply chains, the assembly of a car—where it was "made" in Detroit—could not occur. Methodically, the UAW planned a strike through the entire supply chain.

GM management caught wind of the planning and decided to move a set of body dies out of the Flint Fisher Body Plant No. 1 in the middle of the night on December 30, 1936, so they could keep production going. A body die is the machine that bends the sheet metal into a car body. These dies are incredibly expensive, heavy, unique, and essential. Without car bodies, no cars are possible. GM simply could not store large numbers of car bodies in anticipation of a disruption in supply. If they ran out, car assembly would stop, and behind that, all along the supply chain, back to the bulb manufacturers and the steel processors, work would stop.

The Flint workers anticipated this and had rigged a red warning light if GM attempted to run away with the dies. With the flick of a switch, three thousand men swarmed the Fisher Body plant. The strike was on. Workers occupied the factory, and the first major sit-down strike (or sit-in) in U.S. history had begun. The demands were mostly simple: shorter hours, union recognition, and a minimum wage "commensurate with an American standard of living."

When the UAW shut down that one factory—which employed only a few hundred workers—all of GM stopped. Production collapsed from fifty thousand cars a month to nearly zero. The largest corporation in America had been brought to its knees. Police could not forcibly storm the plant because they could not risk the irreplaceable machines being damaged. GM could not wait six months for the workers to give up, nor could they wait six months to make new dies. Forty-four days later, the UAW was recognized as the sole bargaining agent for General Motors, and all the autoworkers in America got raises. The eight-hour workday would remain, and the union would not have input on production schedules, but it was a victory nonetheless, in the middle of what had seemed like certain defeat. Workers did not need to control every GM plant, just the one that made what could not be reproduced anywhere else.[43] With that audacious strike in Flint, GM recognized the United Auto Workers, and Walter Reuther became a national figure. Between the new industrial unions and the new laws, American labor enjoyed success like never before in its history.

Yet this new labor movement had abandoned the radical critique of its earlier years, even as it embraced innovative methods. Gathering on July 5, 1936, in Homestead, Pennsylvania—the site in 1892 of one of the best-known and most controversial strikes of the industrial era—a group of unionists read a declaration of independence of their own making: "Through this union we shall win higher wages, shorter hours, and a better standard of living. We shall win leisure for ourselves and opportunity for our children. We shall abolish industrial despotism. We shall make real the dreams of the pioneers who pictured America as a land where all might live in comfort and happiness." These new unionists did not want to overthrow capitalism or even form a political party; they just wanted "comfort and happiness."

Out of this moment, and in particular a contract between the CIO and U.S. Steel in 1936, the radicalism of earlier industrial workers was exchanged for the security of a comfortable life. Reporters came to U.S. Steel headquarters expecting to hear of a massive strike, and instead they heard that a new contract had been signed. In this contract, U.S. Steel recognized the CIO's Steelworkers Organizing Committee, as well as the forty-hour workweek, time and a half, paid vacation, seniority, and grievance procedures. Workers even got paid holidays on the Fourth of July, Labor Day, and Christmas. It was an amazing coup that reversed decades of industrial strife. In the following month, forty-one other steel companies followed suit, in the first instance of what came to be called pattern bargaining. These contracts were only for a year, and were a delaying action, as the steel executives certainly believed that the Wagner Act would, like the NIRA, be declared unconstitutional.

In 1937, the Supreme Court supported the legality of the Wagner Act, demanding that Jones & Laughlin, one of the "Little Steel" companies—that is, any steel company that was not U.S. Steel—hold and recognize NLRB-overseen elections.[44] The NLRB ruled that Jones & Laughlin had to stop financial support for company-funded unions and hold fair elections. The elections were held, and the CIO union won (seventeen thousand for the union, seven thousand against). Other steel companies did not go so easily. At Bethlehem, Republic, Inland, and Youngstown, steelmakers refused to go along with U.S. Steel's easy capitulation, especially now that it seemed the NLRB was constitutional. On May 28, 1937, a strike of seventy-eight thousand steelworkers spanned seven states in the Steel Belt from Homestead to Chicago. The Little Steel Strike of 1937 showed that business would not accommodate unionization even in the face of federal directives. Little Steel companies came prepared. They each bought tens of thousands of dollars' worth of tear gas, gas grenades, pistols, and rifles to supply the local police and corporate guards to stop a strike. A congressional investigation found that the companies together had purchased $178,000 worth of such armaments. Bethlehem Steel had directly paid the policemen's salaries. In Chicago, on Memorial Day, came the climax of the strike, when a thousand strikers took American flags and began to walk toward the steel mill. When told to disperse by police, they refused. The police fired on the crowd in what was reported as the Memorial Day Massacre, killing seven and wounding ninety. Most of the injured were shot in the back. The strike fell apart soon after. Yet the legal machinery, which now mattered most of all, continued. Four years later, in 1941, the NLRB ruled that the Little Steel companies had to capitulate. Workers were remunerated with back pay. Those who had been fired were reinstated. The injured were compensated.

In the wake of the strike, instead of collapsing, the CIO was energized. By 1938, these unions were so successful that the AFL pushed the Committee for Industrial Organization to surrender those members who could join the craft unions. Of course, if the CIO unions did that, they would lose their solidarity—and their funding. Fundamentally, industrial firms could not be organized by craft methods. Lewis refused to give the AFL any money. In 1938, the CIO unions—more radical, more unskilled—broke from the AFL, creating a new backronym from CIO: Congress of Industrial Organizations. That year, industrial standards and industrial unions became a legitimate part of the economy.

Basic standards for industrial work were now part of the law. In 1938, Congress passed the Fair Labor Standards Act (FLSA), which redelivered aspects of the NIRA. Child labor was outlawed at the national level. Any industrial worker, regardless of unionization, could expect injury compensation, time and a half for overtime, and even breaks. Industrial workers could expect a minimum wage, regardless of market conditions. Through labor law, employer excesses were limited. If a factory ran through the night, the bosses would have to pay their workers more. The laws acknowledged the new relationship between industrial workers and industrial corporations. To think the laws created worker prosperity is to confuse cause and effect. The workers made their own New Deal.[45]

The laws ratified the new power of the industrial unions, but only for the kinds of workers in those industrial unions. Fair labor standards applied only to industrial jobs: while the labor laws of the 1930s celebrated and defended factory and office work, they specifically excluded agricultural and domestic work. Not coincidentally, these jobs were done by workforces that were darker and more feminine than the protected industrial jobs. These different protections were rooted in assumptions about whose work needed to be secure—and who had power in society. As the government saw it, men, especially white men, needed to earn money to support a wife and family—the so-called family wage. Workers in the home (women) and workers in the field (first African Americans and then Mexicans) were less deserving of these protections. Though 1938 may have been a turning point for white men, it was not for black men and black women, who still labored under the rule of Jim Crow. White men's work counted. Everybody else's did not.

Migrant Labor in the Industrial Age

Although we think of the Great Depression as beginning with the stock crash of 1929, for rural America it began earlier. The Roaring Twenties never came to the farm. The rural U.S.—where half the country continued to live—had been in a funk since 1920. During World War I, farmers borrowed to buy the new mechanized tractors and supply a hungry Europe. As European farmers returned to the fields, there was a worldwide oversupply. Wheat, corn, and other agricultural products entered a price free fall. While we think of the Great Depression as the fall in stock prices, or even house prices, we could just as easily mark its onset with the fall of wheat prices a decade earlier.

Wheat is a commodity. Usually we just toss that word around as if it were a synonym for a product or good. However, "commodity" has a very special meaning: it is a good (or service) that is identical to any other of its type and can be made by anyone. So while any Model T is identical to any other Model T, it is not a commodity because it can be made only by Ford. Most commodities are agricultural, but this is not because all plants are the same.

Wheat varies from farm to farm, even field to field, much less from Iowa to Bavaria! Plants are similar but never the same. Making plants into commodities takes a willingness to overlook those differences. In the late nineteenth century, standards began to be established for wheat, and other farm products, that picked a few aspects among the inevitable variety—like kernel hardness or color—and decided that these would determine the kind of wheat. Sorted into grades, the wheat from Hank in Iowa and Hans in Bavaria could be directly compared to one another. These standards made a global equivalence in wheat possible and made wheat into a commodity, because anybody meeting the standards could now sell wheat interchangeably.

This commodification of wheat is why prices could fall so quickly after World War I. Wheat in Europe was equivalent to wheat in the U.S., and this equivalence meant that there was a truly global supply of wheat, and a global price. Wheat was interchangeable with wheat. Through prices, farms in Europe and farms in America competed. Seeking cheaper ways to produce more, American farmers mechanized. This digression on wheat mattered because whenever anything could be graded, it could be commodified—even work.

Long before robots replaced factory workers, tractors replaced farmworkers. The mechanization of agriculture in the 1920s utterly transformed American work. Agricultural workers went from 31 percent of the workforce in 1910 to 18 percent of the workforce in 1940.[46] And the number kept declining. By 1960, only 6 percent of Americans worked in agriculture. What had been the most common human occupation for six thousand years disappeared over the course of a few decades.

Rural Americans, desperate for jobs, began to flood the cities. Car companies were growing at a breakneck pace, but it was the new factories turning out vacuums, fridges, and radios—all powered by the new electrical grid—that needed the ex-farmers. While car factories were relatively streamlined by the 1920s, the variation in these new appliances meant that manufacturers needed lots of handy people. New industries always require more people than a mature industry. In a mature industry, the managers have ironed out the kinks, engineers have replaced inefficient routines with best practices, machines have been invented to cut down on bottlenecks. In new industries, with all the profit and possibility of the new, men could find work. Urban America, with its electrical grid and its electrical products, employed millions of Americans who otherwise would have been jobless. Equally important, these industries absorbed the idle millions of dollars that would otherwise not have been invested. While rural America endured year after year of depression, urban America had the best decade in U.S. history.

Most farmers were long deeply entwined with the market economy. Farmers might not have had annoying bosses, but they did have annoying bankers. Mortgages, taken out in times of rising prosperity in the 1910s, came due amid the falling prices of the 1920s, crushing their American dreams as quickly as any house foreclosure today. The utter collapse of the mortgage markets in the early 1930s, coupled with the Dust Bowl, was the final nail in the coffin. Farmers deserted the land, traveling to nearby cities or, less often, across the country.

Someone still needed to bring in the crops. Especially when the country went to war in 1941.

As mobilization began, American officials realized that if the men were at war and the women were in the factories, somebody would still need to grow the food. Immigration had been effectively banned since the early 1920s, and now, twenty years later, more people were needed. Rather than open the borders, President Roosevelt negotiated with the Mexican president Manuel Camacho to allow the first official American guest workers—the Bracero Program. Starting with a few thousand beet harvesters in 1942, the number of braceros expanded during the war and continued afterward until, by the 1950s, hundreds of thousands of Mexican migrant workers harvested America's food—without becoming citizens. The Bracero Program was for the benefit of the growers, who could not find workers at what the Immigration and Naturalization Service (INS) called "prevailing wages."[47]

Braceros had few options once they arrived. Ramón Avitia, a bracero, later recounted that "growers didn't always respect the contract or pay us what it said. But it was hard to advocate for ourselves and our rights. We were far from home, didn't speak the language, and often had no one to go to for help."[48] Despite his hardships, when Avitia returned to Mexico with the money he earned, he "built [his] house and bought a few cows."[49]

The trip north could bring rewards but it was also exhausting, dehumanizing work. On some farms, workers were referred to only by number, like in a prison. When the men could no longer travel, they told their younger male relatives—"sons, younger brothers, nephews, and eventually grandchildren"—how to make the trip. In this way, the Bracero Program became a lure for the next generation of migrants.[50] Felipe Casteñeda, of Santa Angelica, Durango, said, "For me, it was an opportunity, sort of. My family has a house. My kids got shoes. I went lots of times. Although life got better, the opportunity came at a cost."

During the war, braceros supplied a small but, for some kinds of farming, important source of labor. The wartime braceros, 219,500 farm laborers, were only 3 percent of the farm labor workforce, but in California—which employed 63 percent of the total bracero workforce overall, and 90 percent in the off-season—they mattered much more.[51] As the coastal California shipyards and airplane factories drew in laborers from across the state, someone needed to fill the labor shortage.[52] The women of the canneries moved into other, better-paid factories. Only citizens could work in defense-industry jobs, so employers with nondefense jobs (which paid less) had to look elsewhere. Canneries began to hire large numbers of ethnic Mexicans, a massive shift from the whites-only policies of the 1930s. Canneries, by the end of the war, employed mostly Mexican women.[53]

Texas, in contrast, had a longer history of exploiting Mexicans working across the border, and the Mexican government insisted that no braceros be employed in Texas (though they were, and in the early days hired at the border). In California, however, the Bracero Program supplied a new source of labor to harvest the crops just when aerospace was drawing the native population to Los Angeles. This contract labor population came from far away, often from remote parts of Mexico. Once the work was done, they could be sent home. The obligations of the employer to braceros lasted only for the duration of the work, and not a minute more. Moreover, since agricultural work was excluded from the FLSA, the kinds of protections that industrial workers enjoyed did not apply to braceros, even as legal workers. Workers could not form unions or protest in any way.

For groups like the antiunion Associated Farmers, which had campaigned through the 1930s to keep unions out of the fields, the braceros were a welcome change. In the canning factories and dried-fruit plants of San Jose (now the center of Silicon Valley), workers, mostly Italian immigrants and their children, could (and did) form unions based on the Wagner Act.[54] Before the union, crowds of Italian women would show up in the morning outside the factory gates, begging for work—the shape-up.[55] Those who didn't cause trouble and did whatever the supervisor told them got work. Those who didn't stayed outside. Canners averaged $8 a week in 1933 (roughly $151 in 2017).[56] Ten- and twelve-hours days were routine, though eighteen-hour days were possible. With unionization in 1937, these women had job security and more reasonable wages, as well as protection from the arbitrary whims of supervisors. The growers felt the omnipresent threat of organizing, even though the field workers had no legal protections.

The Bracero Program legally imported workers, but it also sanctified existing illegal immigrants. This process of "drying out the wetbacks," as the INS referred to it at the time, enabled farmers to use undocumented Mexicans already on their farms.[57] In the late 1940s, this sanction covered more farmworkers than the Bracero Program. In the summer of 1947, the INS legalized 55,000 undocumented farmworkers in Texas alone, compared to the officially admitted 31,331 braceros in the whole country.[58] Former braceros who could not get another contract easily became undocumented migrants.[59] Historians estimate that a half million undocumented workers went north every year in the late 1940s and early '50s. With the Bracero Program as cover, it was easy to mix other Spanish-speaking workers in with a legal farm crew.

The head of the U.S. Border Patrol, Willard Kelly, later told Congress in 1952 that "it would almost seem that the reason for the failure of the United States to properly protect its borders is to make way for the illegal entry of cheap alien labor."[60] From the start, as a complaint to a senator from the members of a south Texas farm association reveals, growers cared little whether farmworkers were here legally or illegally. The growers cared only that the INS leave their workers alone and deport those who were "bad citizens."[61] Since none of them were actually citizens (good or bad), the growers simply wanted the INS to deport troublemakers. From its first years, then, growers looked to the INS as a source of discipline for workers who had no rights.

As American citizens left the farms for the cities, first machines and then Mexicans took their place. These workers had few protections. Despite what the U.S. negotiated with Mexico, actual wages and labor conditions bore little resemblance to the agreements. The older laissez-faire model still existed, but only in the fields, where documented and undocumented Mexican laborers alike could not organize. Citizenship had become a bright line between those who had rights and those who did not. At first that line would matter only in the fields, but as the postwar era progressed, that legacy, particularly in California and Texas, would come to matter for industry as well.

The Good Industrial Job

For industrial workers, however, labor protections meant that there was at least the possibility of industrial capitalism finally giving workers a fair share. The path to the good industrial job, even after unions were legalized, was not inevitable, but hard won through struggle. In the end, it was state power allied with worker organization that produced that life of comfort and happiness. In return, capital and government expected stability in their workforce. During the war, the UAW and every other union pledged not to strike. Wages were stabilized and, through price controls, inflation was kept in check.

For those left out of this comfort and happiness, the war challenged the white man's industrial order. Factories on the home front converted from producing cars to tanks (thanks to federally backed loans). In Detroit, 30 percent of the industrial workforce left for war.[62] As millions of men (of all races) went abroad to fight, the labor gap was filled with people—women, African Americans, and rural folks—who had not been in factories, much less unions, before. Women had always worked in factories—only half of those Rosie the Riveters had not worked in industry before. What was truly new was not women working, or women working in factories, but women in men's roles in those factories. In heavy manufacturing, as elsewhere, gender had determined the kind of work that men and women did. Women, dressed in men's clothes while working on an assembly line, contested the naturalness of men's work itself. Meanwhile, the UAW swelled to more than 1.2 million members.[63] A union woman said, "Some of us don't have a stove to cook on, our husbands have died overseas. We have orphaned children to support and we are entitled to a decent wage and a decent living."

While the U.S. government launched a propaganda campaign to get white women into the factories, black men and women had to fight to get access to those same jobs. As America prepared for war, FDR learned that there was a planned march on Washington led by black union leader A. Philip Randolph. The march was to protest discrimination against hiring African Americans into the war plants. To quell potential African American protest, FDR issued Executive Order 8802 to create the Committee on Fair Employment Practices (CFEP) to oversee defense plants. Through this executive order (not legislation), workers could not be discriminated against on the basis of "race, creed, color, or national origin." The executive order had little real power. Was the U.S. going to cancel tank contracts over racial discrimination? Yet over the objections of Southern congressmen, FDR increased the budget of the Fair Employment Practices Committee (FEPC) over the course of the war. What the FEPC lacked in enforcement power, it made up in moral suasion. During the war, a million black Americans became industrial workers, moving from 2 percent of war workers in 1942 to 8 percent in 1944.[64] The wartime arrangements across gender and race lines were fragile, and everyone knew that with victory would come a battle over what they would mean in peacetime.

Demand for workers should have driven up wages, but in the name of patriotism, workers did their part (even as corporations saw windfall profits). As soon as the war ended, however, the gloves came off.

When President Truman announced victory over Japan on August 17, 1945, American workers celebrated by launching the largest strike wave in U.S. history over the next twelve days. The causes of these strikes were complex—rooted in fears of recession and frustrations over race mixing, as well as simply feeling underpaid during the war.

Starting with small walk-offs by autoworkers in Detroit and longshoremen in New York, the strike wave quickly spread. Thousands of strikers across all industrial industries challenged the meaning of victory. Would industrial workers be victorious if there was another depression? Workers and executives both feared that in this reconversion would come another recession, like after World War I, or even a return to the Great Depression. If the postwar economy was dependent on government demand, there would be a return to depression. Government demand alone could not sustain the peacetime economy, and decreasing demand after the war was apparent.

In the reconversion, workers would lose jobs, wages, and hours. Simply losing overtime, going from forty-eight hours to forty hours, for example, meant a 30 percent pay cut. Moreover, because of wartime no-strike clauses, unionists felt that while big corporations made profits, they had not gotten their fair share. Ten million draftees (mostly white men) were coming home as well, and they needed jobs. The no-strike pledge had been honored, at least by the union leadership, and now the workers wanted their due.

Reuther believed that with the end of the war, industrial workers would need to continue to fight for a greater share of industrial productivity.[65] With all the simmering wildcats during the war, it was essential, he thought, to have a big top-down strike.[66] He kicked off one of the biggest postwar strikes with a radical demand on GM management: 30 percent wage increases with no increase in prices for consumers. Following the CIO line, Reuther wanted to increase the comfort of workers, but not at the cost of other consumers' pocketbooks. To that end, he wanted access to GM's accounts.

Philip Murray, the head of the CIO, insisted that Reuther drop these demands to see the books and to control prices. Murray, unlike Reuther, had never supported communism. Murray didn't want the CIO to be branded too radical, and he wanted the support of Truman. Truman had, in the fall of 1945, used federal troops to end a strike at oil refineries, denouncing a "few selfish men" who favored their pockets over the national reconversion. In 1946, he pushed for a bill giving himself the power to draft strikers into the army if they left their jobs. The bill failed, but Truman's position was clear. In early 1946, then, Murray moved to make sure that planned support strikes among auto-, steel-, and electrical workers did not happen. For the UAW to be seen as a reliable partner, Reuther needed to make sure that contracts were upheld and that unionized labor could be counted on. Sympathy strikes in other industries would threaten the industrial peace.

Reuther's strike ended with a modest raise, but not access to the books or control over who paid for that raise—corporate profits or consumer pocketbooks. The strike was a success in terms of wages, and it enabled Reuther to become UAW president in 1946.[67] Yet in Reuther's capitulation to Murray and GM, we can see the limits of American unionism. Workers would get a good wage, but not control over the workplace. The strike ended the hopes of the left that unions would have greater control in public affairs. After this point, the UAW looked toward securing benefits for its membership in what has been deemed a private welfare state, rather than broadly reforming class relations or corporate control. Only two years later, UAW unionists got guaranteed raises tied to cost-of-living increases and productivity increases. In return, union leaders gave up the quest for workplace control.

All these strikes and pay increases have been partially credited with returning control of Congress to the Republicans in the 1946 elections. The Democrat Truman, with approval ratings in the low thirties, also did not help. Americans were terrified, and felt that Truman had ended the war but the victory seemed Pyrrhic. The USSR was now as strong militarily as America was and a real threat, which it had not been in the 1930s. Democrats were blamed for the loss of Eastern Europe as the Soviets annexed the Eastern bloc after the war, promising free elections but never allowing them. Strike waves were everywhere. The economy seemed precarious. The new push for anticommunism, and suspicion of communist-tinged unions, led to the Taft-Hartley Act in 1947.

The passage of Taft-Hartley put the last legal piece in place for the postwar industrial workplace: constraining the rising power of industrial unions. It banned secondary strikes and boycotts, as well as the closed shop (which mandated that only union members could be hired). Foremen, and by extension any level of management, could not be unionized.[68] Taft-Hartley also enabled states to pass right-to-work laws, which allowed them to ban the union shop (which required workers to join the union). Most striking, Taft-Hartley required an affidavit that union members were not communists in order to utilize the legal machinery of the NLRB. Communists who signed affidavits were charged with perjury. For industrial unions, this compromise provided recognition by the state, even by Republicans, as part of the governing order. Instead of an ongoing battle with capital, unions could negotiate. Lawyers could be used instead of strikers. This alternative was appealing, and the AFL and the CIO, in the end, chose to entrench their legal power, uncertain of further battles. In time, this reliance on the power of the state, rather than the power of the workers, would prove to be organized labor's downfall, but at the time, it was a choice for stability and peace.

Most crucial for our story was that the most radical union, and the third largest in the CIO, the United Electrical workers (UE), found itself gutted by Taft-Hartley and then McCarthyism. The CIO expelled the UE and formed a more moderate union, the International United Electrical workers (IUE). Over the next few decades, they fought over the electrical workers of America, and in the process dwindled in size to only tens of thousands of workers.[69] As the electronics industry became America's leading sector, there would be no strong union to organize those workers.

Taft-Hartley made law what Murray had done in practice: set limits to the radicalism of industrial workers. Negotiations would be held between one union and one company, not between all unionists and society (the result of banning secondary strikes). At the same time, the act reaffirmed the New Deal labor laws, setting the stage for the growth of those good manufacturing jobs.

After Taft-Hartley, Walter Reuther accepted the new reality. The young radical had become more pragmatic and now saw unions as creating a new "middle class" of labor. And he was right. In terms of income, union workers were no longer the exploited proletarians of the nineteenth century, but right at the center of American consumer capitalism. In return for giving up the ability to have massive, sudden increases in income, unionists received steady increases. In return for radical strikes, they got government arbitration.

The 1950 GM-UAW agreement, the so-called Treaty of Detroit, defined this new world of work. Everything we consider today to be the good job was in this agreement for the first time: cost-of-living adjustments, health insurance, and pension funds. In return, workers would not strike. Disputes would be resolved by arbitration. The contract brought an end to the disruptive strikes. Its length, five years, allowed GM to invest, with a knowledge of labor costs, for many years at a time. This capitalist five-year plan caught on. Other auto manufacturers replicated the arrangement, and this pattern of bargaining spread through the automotive industry, and then through others (with slight variations). A GM spokesperson explained it simply: "Rewards gained from stability will outweigh" the increased labor costs. GM's position, of course, was at odds with several decades of fighting such an accommodation, but in the face of political and worker power, they began to focus on the advantages.

The foundation of the postwar economy was heavy manufacturing, which required incredible capital investments. The machines, at first glance, would appear to weaken labor. Individual worker skill no longer mattered—Turn that wrench! Push that button!—since the machine contained the expertise. But expensive machines required the workers to show up, and if any of them did not or, God forbid, went on strike, the investment in machines would not be realized. No matter how skillful the machine, it still required a human operator—no matter how deskilled. While most work had historically been individual—Can that carpenter fit that joint?—the industrial work on the assembly line relied on every single person showing up and doing their job. The value of workers was not in their individual skills, but in the group. Industrial unions faced a strategic landscape entirely different from earlier skilled-labor craft organizations like the American Federation of Labor. Only group disruption of the operation of the machines could bring prosperity—and it did.

This de-skilling of work made everyone replaceable, but this shift, which seemed like it would boost management's power, actually contained an Achilles heel. These investments needed to be defended. Whatever the labor cost, it cost less than the machines going idle. Shutting down an assembly line or a supply chain could disrupt an entire industry. Machines, not labor, were now the biggest expense and the efficient use of those machines the primary goal. The interests of capital and labor aligned in this particular moment, because although machines were ascendant, labor was still necessary to run them. Unions may have cost more than nonunionized workers, but to the heavy manufacturers they offered the most tantalizing quality: stability.

Fortune magazine said that the Treaty of Detroit was the first contract that accepted "the existing distribution of income between wages and profits as 'normal' if not 'fair.'" Workers could live in middle-class suburbs. They could drive the same cars as office workers. They could shop at the same department stores. Labor unions had delivered the good life to workers and stability to corporations. For a generation that had lived through depression and war, that kind of clockwork predictability sounded pretty appealing. Most important to understand is that it was exactly that instability that had motivated a generation of working people, with political allies, to struggle for and achieve this good life. Industrial capitalism did not naturally produce good jobs. More than ever before, the Treaty of Detroit mattered because of where Americans were working.

The wartime investments changed the composition of American capitalism. Big business became not just big profit centers, but big employers. Before the war, big firms (those with more than ten thousand employees) hired 13 percent of the workforce. By the end of the war, they accounted for 31 percent of the workforce. During the war, a half million small businesses went under, but big business took up the slack workforce as the economy doubled in size (in constant 1939 dollars) from $80 billion GDP to $153 billion. Workers at small and medium-size firms (fewer than five hundred workers) fell from 52 percent of the workforce to 38 percent. Most Americans, in other words, started working for big corporations.

As industry concentrated, so, too, did unionization rise, from 12.7 percent before the war to 22.2 percent after the war, from about 7 million union members in 1940 to 13 million by 1944. The CIO doubled in size. The most monopolized, most heavily capitalized industries also had the most unionists. In manufacturing, two thirds of workers were in unions, as were two thirds of those in transportation. In the biggest sectors—like automobiles—virtually all workers were in unions.

Job stability, then, was not just for white-collar workers but for factory men as well. It had come not from the goodwill of employers, but from workers using law and strategy to demand better lives. Unions organized

industrial America like never before, but the legal transformations of the
New Deal affected everyone. Whether through the union or through the
court, new expectations about pay and security found their way into American culture. Americans, regardless of class, believed that steady work at a
reasonable wage was their right as citizens. Instead of breaking capitalism,
surprisingly, these market interventions accelerated economic growth. Job
security would come from that growth and from the way in which their
new rights allowed workers to demand a share of it—at least if they lived in
cities.

The Perils of Permanent Stability

Before he became the world's first business guru, at thirty-four, the young-
ish Peter Drucker was just another professor of politics and recent émigré
from Austria. When he was invited to General Motors in the fall of 1943 to
discuss a possible book project, he had already published two well-received
books on the industrial economy—particularly *The Future of Industrial
Man* (1942), which had sought to explain how the shift from agriculture to
industry required not only a change in our economy, but in our imagination
of democracy. Drucker's broad-reaching books led him to the offices of
GM, where Alfred Sloan and the senior management asked him to examine General Motors in depth. Drucker later wrote that the book that resulted from his study, *Concept of the Corporation*, was "the first study of a
big corporation from within, of its constitutional principles, of its structure,
its basic relationships, its strategies and policies."[70]

Sloan was sixty-seven and had overseen GM for decades. It was the largest corporation in America; it employed hundreds of thousands of workers
and supplied millions with their cars. Sloan, by force of will, had steered the
firm from its uncertain early days through the equally uncertain days of the
Depression.

Drucker's account was celebratory but critical. Instead of confirming
that GM was the future, the book shockingly revealed its flaws. Drucker
had questioned the "labor and employee relations, the use and role of
central-office staffs, and dealer relations" in GM, but he actually went much
further than such superficial criticisms.[71] To Drucker, the industrial

corporation was a necessary evil. It allowed production at scale, but at the cost of worker independence. Although the worker received a steady paycheck and the executives rose up the ranks, neither of these gains provided "the same satisfaction as was given by advancement in the small business society. Even a responsible executive in a big corporation is often not 'independent' but dependent," which Drucker believed foreswore any harmony between industrial corporations and American democracy, whatever the pay.[72] Job security had come at the cost of independence—for worker and for executive.

Still, while the corporation inhibited a more abstract independence, the stable income was concrete. Job certainty, after the Great Depression, mattered more than anything. Drucker thought that big businesses like GM offered a key advantage for society over the small business: long-term interest. He saw that "bigness can contribute to social stability because a big business can subordinate temporary gains to long-term policies." Workers could be kept "even in bad times. . . . A small business could rarely afford to sacrifice the immediate saving in cost."[73] To the degree that the corporation absorbed the volatility of the market and efficiently produced goods, it had a social value.

But still the corporation had fatal flaws.[74] Bureaucratic ossification could counter the higher productivity of the assembly line. As much as possible, Drucker believed that the top-heavy centralized management would need to be kept in check by a competitive market. Decentralized corporations, which combined flexibility and scale, were the ideal, but such a condition ran counter to the desire for executive control and seemed destined to fail. In short, Drucker challenged the value of the very GM leaders who had allowed him into their confidence. The book understandably became "unmentionable in GM for many years."[75]

Those years would become, much later, the heart of Sloan's own autobiography, *My Years with General Motors*, which was the book, it seems, that GM leaders had intended Drucker to write. *My Years* set out ways to think about the professional manager; Drucker's more capacious book hinted at the fractures already evident in the foundation of the postwar corporation. The corporation's success was antithetical, in a basic way, to American values of indepedence. For Drucker, *Concept of the Corporation* was a stepping-stone to a fantastic career as the first management guru, which began with the publication of *The Practice of Management* in 1954.

From top to bottom, the policies of the New Deal produced an economy that created security, but security rooted in a particular vision of Americans—native-born white male workers, for whom the corporation provided a foundational stability at the cost of autonomy. Other kinds of people figured into this stability either as dependents (like married women) or as outsiders (like Mexicans). "Less than ten years ago," Drucker wrote in the introduction to *Concept of the Corporation*, "it still seemed to be a vital issue of American politics whether to have Big Business or not. Today the very question is meaningless if not frivolous." World War II "made clear that it [was] the large corporation which determines the economic and technological conditions under which our economy operates." They "set the [labor] standards for the nation, their wage scale determines the national wage scale, their working conditions and working-hours are the norm."[76] The industrial economy had bested the agricultural economy at last, and the necessity of industrial production had proved essential not only to the American economy, but to American survival over the Axis powers.

Drucker believed that, unlike the nineteenth-century trusts, this postwar corporation would be permanent. Shareholders might come and go, but the corporations themselves would endure, providing a bedrock of stability in American life. "The maintenance of the 'going concern,'" Drucker wrote, was more important than the "individual rights of shareholders, creditors, workers, and, in the last analysis, even of consumers."[77] Nothing mattered more.

Yet the stability of labor and capital would begin to fall apart almost as soon as it had been won.

CHAPTER TWO

Temporary Women

E lmer Winter was not a modest man. Rarely when one reads the About the Author page of a book is more gleaned than a hometown or perhaps a college degree. Winter, in his many, many books, took his time to list his copious achievements, including his art collection, which showcased his genius, he thought, for more than business. Winter envisioned himself as a transformer of the world, yet at the same time he had a profound anxiety about what he was doing. After all, his temp agency, the ironically named Manpower Inc., was predicated on women working.[1]

As he professed in his 1961 A *Woman's Guide to Earning a Good Living*, Winter was old-fashioned.[2] He believed that "every married woman's first duty is to her family," which, for a company who mostly hired women, was rather odd. Women's paid labor, unlike housework, was a choice. Divorcées and widows, as well as older women, all worked for money. But for Winter, the situation was murkier when it came to wives. "If there is already a breadwinner in the family," he wrote, "what economic reason does a wife have for taking a job?"[3]

A wife's time, almost by definition, was superfluous. She might "go to school, take a job, or play canasta with the girls" and there would be no difference in the family's well-being.[4] Unlike the necessity of her husband's work, a wife's work provided the extras that a neighbor across the street might have and that both wanted: the redone rec room, the second car, or even the deep freeze in the garage.[5] Her work was a luxury, her income supplemental. Winter envisioned a job that would be flexible, giving her enough time to care for home, children, and husband.[6] Her labor wasn't supposed to matter—and that moral distinction about who deserved stable work made the invention of temporary labor possible in a time when permanent work was celebrated.

Even as temp labor caught on, it quickly encountered limits. Corporations readily embraced the emergency replacement for a sick secretary, or even a few extra hands when needed, but in general they shunned an attempt to replace permanent workers with temps. By the 1960s, Manpower would already be able to deploy entire shifts of replacement workers, complete with supervisors; all Elmer Winter needed to do was convince managers that no one had a right to job security. The decision to use or not use temps was not only about costs, but about beliefs—beliefs about the proper organization of the labor force.[7] Although other temp agencies emerged during this period—Kelly Girl, Olsten, and hundreds of local agencies— Manpower led the charge, setting up a radical new way of working, all in the name of the traditional family. But temporary labor would help, in the long run, to destabilize the security of the family wage on which the archetypal temporary worker—a married white woman—was supposed to rely.[8]

The Emergence of Temporary Labor

Like most business innovations, the temp agency emerged from a crisis: in this case, a middle-aged attorney who found himself unable to find a secretary to type a long and exacting brief for the Supreme Court.[9] Elmer Winter, who had somehow managed to start a career in law in the middle of the Great Depression and then serve in the Office of Price Administration during the war, was by 1948 again in private practice, and he could not type. After calling all the employment agencies that provided permanent secretaries, he found that none could provide short-term help.

Desperate, he and his partner, Aaron Scheinfeld, called a former secretary who had left to have a baby.[10] She came in to type, and the brief was filed. The emergency was overcome, but the two men realized that their need for temporary labor could not be unique. They hatched a plan that, though modest at first, would ultimately remake how America worked.[11]

Winter and Scheinfeld placed a help-wanted ad (much like Uber ads today) in a Milwaukee newspaper that stated: "Work when you want as long as you want."[12] The ad produced hundreds of applicants, all women looking to find work on their terms. While the help-wanted pages promised steady work, these women, constrained by marital and family obligations, did not want steady work. They wanted work for "one day, one week, or longer," as another advertisement offered, on a time scale that fit their lives.

The firm they conceived would not be an employment agency, but something new: a temporary labor agency.[13] Unless an employer was resourceful like Winter, if he needed a worker in a pinch he would have to scrounge. Placing a newspaper ad, interviewing prospective workers, and training them for their positions took weeks. Personnel departments simply could not wave a magic wand and produce "five experienced key punch operators ready to start work tomorrow" or find "100 file clerks in two different cities."[14] Employment agencies might offer to find temporary employees—defined in California, for instance, as anything less than ninety days—but they took just as long to locate a temp as a perm. For a one-day job, they couldn't help. Manpower's labor model—in which the temp worked for Manpower and not for the company—was a truly novel way to work. "Three Manpower girls, one blonde, one redhead, one brunette," could be found with a morning's phone call "for [a] month long promotional tour of shopping centers in connection with Helena Rubenstein 'color lift' campaign."[15] Manpower would be that magic wand.

Manpower opened its first office in Milwaukee, on Thirty-third Street between Wells and Kilbourn.[16] Scheinfeld and Winter were not only business partners, but brothers-in-law; their wives, Sylvia Scheinfeld and Nannette Winter, were sisters.[17] Scheinfeld was thirteen years older than Winter when they started Manpower, and his seniority got him 60 percent of the stock, but Winter had the power.

Shoring Up Permanent Employment

The magic of Manpower was that it could supply a worker for nearly any task with just a phone call. Through the 1950s, the primary role of their temps was as emergency support. "You are a rescue worker," Winter explained to potential temps, there to relieve the pressure.[18] Temps, of course, could do one-off jobs—emergency or not—that part-timers could not. Some were kooky. Manpower supplied temps for a "search for $2,000 worth of diamonds which were lost while the owner attended a picnic in a Kentucky tomato patch" and offered "secretaries to take dictation at poolside from

Hollywood directors who wanted to work while swimming." Naturally, temps were also available to "unload a carload of butter which lay . . . outside a Cleveland food processing plant on a sizzling day."[19] By 1961, if you were, as one mortician was, desperate to demonstrate the virtues of your new product, which "lifted a body from a slab," you didn't need to hire a full-time employee; you could simply call Manpower Inc. and request a "girl" to move your dead body—using your new apparatus.

Manpower was not alone in its magic. Its main rival, Kelly Girl, was also founded after World War II.[20] When the first *beep-beeps* were heard from Sputnik, *BusinessWeek* reported, "the Harvard Observatory asked Kelly Girl for two mathematicians with master's degrees." A few hours later, they were calculating Sputnik's orbit.[21] Kelly Girl would play second fiddle to Manpower, but as temporary staffing grew, they offered similar kinds of services.[22] The business of temporary labor, though trailblazed by Manpower, was not unique to Manpower.

From today's perspective, some of these positions were at best creepy and at worst rank exploitation. UCLA needed "human guinea pigs" to test the effects of smog on the human eye. Manpower supplied them. A French strawberry farmer needed pickers in Lyon. Manpower helped not by finding agricultural workers, but by contacting the local mental health hospital for inpatients, which the supervising "doctors" approved. A Tokyo office needed a "size 10 secretary" to double as secretary and model. Manpower found her. Most jobs, however, were less sensational, at least in the day-to-day requirements, and if they were exploitative, it was subtler than smog in the eyes.[23]

In emergencies, workers did not need to be replaced entirely; temps could just substitute for them, shoring up the gaps in the model of permanent employment. A permanent worker could use her sick days without worry that the paper would pile up. A temp could substitute for her. Instead of simply being replaced by someone the next day—as might have happened when Americans were desperate for work—she could come back in a few days and without a backlog. Vacation days, those newfangled novelties, could be taken. Consider "a Milwaukee secretary" who had "given up several weekends to help her employer prepare for a million-dollar deal" and was then rewarded with a "three-week vacation with all the expenses paid."

Her employer showed his appreciation not only by giving her three weeks off and paying for her trip (!), but also by employing a temp in her absence. When she returned, she was delighted to discover that her replacement had kept up the calendar and the filing, and that "her own desk was as immaculate as she had left it." The temp even left memos updating her on what had happened.[24] Temps helped ensure the security of the permanent workforce by enabling sick days, vacations, and all the perks of the postwar office.

Temps, even in the 1960s, were cheaper than permanent workers. Because of the generous benefits of the postwar period, temps could make financial sense even if the wage cost per hour seemed higher. Manpower hired a management consultancy to answer the million-dollar question: "Can companies effect savings through the use of a temporary help service as compared to hiring permanent staff?"[25] The answer was a definitive yes. This idea of instant staff that could be "turned on when needed" might appeal to the manager of the 1960s who faced rising wages.[26] Comparing area wage surveys with Manpower rates for typists, stenographers, and secretaries showed that temps were cheaper, overall, in the sixteen cities examined. A typist from Manpower might cost $1.88 an hour, whereas a permanent employee would cost $1.68—until you included the fringe costs and hiring costs. If you just needed a typist for a week, hiring her would cost a firm $106.37, but a Manpower temp would cost only $29.66. In fact, it would not be advantageous to hire permanent employees unless you expected to keep them at least ten weeks.[27] Two and a half months is a long time to break even.

New staff had costs, Manpower argued, that were both visible and hidden. Finding a new employee obviously cost money, but according to a study cited by Winter, those search costs made up only 3 percent of her first-year price (outside of wages). Training, which only some firms tracked, still made up 19 percent. The real, usually hidden, expense of new employees was their initial lack of productivity, which accounted for 28 percent of all new employee costs in inefficient use of wages. Even worse, new people who didn't know their jobs made errors, which also cost money. Winter estimated that errors were nearly half the expense of a new employee. Temps avoided all this waste. Temps had no recruitment costs. Temps were used to starting work at a new place. If a temp made an error, she could be replaced with someone else that afternoon.[28] If she worked fewer than four hours, Manpower wouldn't even charge the client. The transaction costs for new permanent employees were much higher than for temporary workers, even in 1962.[29] A Manpower survey found that "a typist who receives $70 of straight pay a week with fringes, with all the hiring costs, etc., actually costs the company $92 a week. When you use our type of service the cost is not $92 a week. It is less than that."[30]

What made temp work possible was how similar everyday tasks were from office to office. When Winter described what a temporary was, he inevitably wrote "a secretary is a secretary."[31] "Writing letters and answering the phone for a [movie] star," he said, "is not essentially different from performing the same services for a food broker or a contractor who suddenly found himself without the services of his regular Girl Friday." The temporary worker could perform a nearly endless variety of jobs, but what made temp labor possible was interchangeability. A microfilmer could archive records at banks or delis. A mailer could stuff envelopes in the city or the suburbs. Filing was stultifyingly similar.[32] Winter claimed that one of the exciting aspects of temp work was meeting new people and being in new places, but temps who did nothing but microfilm experienced little of that larger world. The commodification of these jobs ran counter to Winter's claims of variety. The workplaces might change, but the work would remain the same. The hours might shift, but the filing cabinets didn't.

Manpower could supply nearly any skill because they could test for nearly any skill. Employers knew what they were getting without having to interview anyone. And if you were a temp, you didn't need a credential. You just took a test at Manpower. Think you are a bookkeeper? Take a "written test about keeping" and a math test on "number accuracy and arithmetic." Think you can use a "ten-key adding machine"? Take a special written test and then enter some numbers on the in-house adder. Would-be legal secretaries were asked to "transcribe dictation on the proper legal forms." Supposed medical stenographers "would be tested with [medical] records." And so on. Applicants on the cusp might be given additional materials in typing or dictation to train themselves at home.[33]

Interchangeable work is a fantasy, like the belief that two apples, even from the same farm, are actually the same. Work is always different. What matters is how completely the tasks are the same. Work, like apples, then, can only incompletely be transformed into an interchangeable commodity.[34] Most offices have idiosyncrasies that make them unique—different forms, even if the typewriters are the same. Last week a temp "may have worked for a cosmetic manufacturer who wanted his letters typed in block format with six copies on pink tissue," and next week letters might need to be in small caps on carbon copy.[35] Dictation might require knowing special terms. Names, of course, could always be a challenge. Yet temps would never receive the kind of training that a permanent employee would receive. New typists at a New York City bank received two weeks of training, including slide films on the "Role of the Commercial Banking System."[36] Permanent workers were expected to have a sense of the big picture, while temps filled a very specific role. Manpower offered a few manuals on different specialized vocabularies—legal, banking, insurance—to help acclimate temps, but nothing like a normal onboarding process for a job.[37]

Despite the aid for a sick day or a boring task, a secretary might be made nervous if she could be replaced with a phone call. Manpower was understandably careful to create policies that minimized the social friction between temps and perms. Part of that comfort came from Manpower's insistence that their temps were choosing to work flexible hours; temps didn't want permanent, full-time jobs.

Manpower took pains to reassure full-time workers that their jobs were being secured, not threatened. The best way for firms to use temps was to plan to use temps—and explain how they were supporting the job security of the permanent staff. Permanent, full-time jobs were the norm, and Winter did not want to change that—at first. He encouraged firms to create "clear-cut policies governing temporary or part-time help."[38] These rules would make explicit the difference between these workers: the "regular work force will have greater job security," or a draftee would have "no re-employment rights." He encouraged employers to distinguish "probationary" and "temporary" workers. While both kinds might be on the job for only a short time, doing the same work, the understanding of their roles was completely different. Regulars needed to understand why a temp was coming in, and that it was a special situation because someone was ill or on vacation. The "temporaries are in no way competing with the regular workers" was Winter's reassuring refrain.[39] In turn, Winter suggested that temps be "friendly" but "industrious"; that is, detached from the permanents. When a temp arrived, it was important to make her feel welcome, though not to make her feel like "part of the family." The work "family" may not have been as real as the home family, but it was often invoked to connote the same kinds of feelings: loyalty, mutuality, patience. None of these ethics applied to temps.

The temp was a guest. Winter suggested that she be told where to find the lunchroom, the supplies, and, of course, the restroom. It was best to "get across her duties," especially "the telephone technique preferred by the man she's working with" and how letters were to be typed.[40] Winter encouraged firms to use a multipurpose room to house temps so that the mixture of perms and temps could be kept to a minimum, and so as not to remind perms that temps were on-site, with the implicit threat of replacement.[41] The isolation, Winter argued in turn, would enable greater productivity for the temps. Intrigue would not be possible for temps, but neither would compassion. Temps preparing the payroll might not gossip, but neither would they "wonder whether Joe put in for all of his overtime or whether the boss intended to give Mary sick-pay credit for the day she was called home when her son broke his arm." The social life of work would be erased. Workers would be disconnected from each other, and from the firm. If temps looked for acceptance or a social connection in the workplace, they were not going to find it.

For the regular staff, temps made vacations easier. Temps helped out when their work friends were sick. Temps made the good life possible.

A Step Forward for Women

In 1966, Dr. Joyce Brothers, the "eminent psychologist, newspaper and magazine columnist, and radio-TV personality," wrote a promotional pamphlet for Manpower: *So You're Thinking of Returning to Office Work.*[42] In choosing Brothers to write the pamphlet, Manpower selected one of the most trusted experts in America, and as a woman, she had a special authority when speaking to her audience of potential temps. Brothers framed the decision to work as a step forward for women: "Society no longer controls your decisions. The choice today is up to you."[43]

Working was a choice, but for the intended audience of women, it was a choice that was limited by the other kinds of obligations that only women had. Most of Brothers's pamphlet focused on the demands on women outside of work or women's social identities, with chapters like "Solving the Problems of Husband and Home," "But What About the Children," "Solving the Problem of 'You,'" "If You Are Widowed or Divorced," or "How Old Is 'Too Old.'"[44] Women's work in the office could not even be considered without first thinking about women's life—and work—at home.

Justifying women's work without undermining male authority was Winter's true genius. His perspective on women seems, in some ways, surprisingly progressive for the era—supporting women working—yet still very much committed to women's subordination. At every step, the pamphlet carefully balanced ideas of the proper woman (as consumer, as wife, as sex object) with work opportunities—never too far in either direction, and always attentive to placing women in their proper role.

Temporary workers, Winter insisted, were nothing like regular (male) workers—they were married women who worked by choice, not necessity, and temps all had families to whom to return. This narrative of choice reassured the anxious that temps were not destabilizing homes. A temp was not a career girl. Family would always come first. The work might not threaten the patriarchy, but Brothers knew that husbands would still object, invoking the need for the wife to watch the children, make dinner, or take care of the house. Brothers dismissed this "male ego" and encouraged women to refocus the conversation on the concrete. If she worked late, she'd prepare a "casserole—your favorite" ahead of time.[45] Women could emphasize the "positive" effects ("Darling, I think I've figured out a way for us to get that new station wagon") rather than pointing out the husband's inability to provide ("If you can't get us the thing we need, I guess I'll have to").[46] More than men, Winter believed, women were deeply invested in social status, whether in the shops or on the job. "Women are more money-conscious than men," he felt, which was why, in his mind, so many women turned to work for luxury goods.

Luxury offered a way out of insulting the male ego. Since a working wife made the success of the breadwinner suspect, this disjuncture could be resolved by claiming that luxuries had become necessities—as Winter did. "If there is already a breadwinner in the family," he wrote, "what economic reason does a wife have for taking a job?" The postwar family had the husband's income already budgeted—home mortgage, car payment, installment loan—and these forms of credit crowded out savings. The wife's income could be used for saving.

Or it could be used for more consumption. When "a neighbor buys a second car or builds a recreation room, pressure is on to follow this pattern, and the wife's returning to work often provides the answer." Joining the temporary workforce would put not only "a spring in her step" and "a twinkle in her eye," but a luxurious color TV in her house. By being able to afford beauty treatments and gifts for the children, she could provide her family with what they wanted, even if the husband provided what they needed.

The real suburban melancholy, Winter wrote, came from too much luxury. "Even the latest deep-freeze model or washer-drier is not precisely stimulating." Work was the best cure for "housewifeitis." Wives needed an "escape for a while from the four walls of their home," and temp work could be the answer to suburban ennui.[47] "Just being a housewife sort of got me into a rut," said a Mississippi temp. After working, she felt like "a new woman and just rarin' to go."[48] But women's most important role, Winter insisted, remained that of consumer and wife.[49]

Although Winter and Brothers tapped into widespread assumptions about the natural differences between men and women, they did so carefully, so as to support the day-to-day practices at Manpower. All these ideas justified a kind of work that provided no career path, no true stability, and less money than a regular job. Women's work, in the end, could not be as consequential as men's work—otherwise the rest of the world no longer made sense.

Selling White-Gloved Women

If wifeness presented a problem for paying women, womanness presented an opportunity for selling them. In the fall of 1961, Elmer Winter had a problem. His business was mostly sending women to work in offices, yet his company's name began with the word "man."[50]

In 1962, Manpower inaugurated its White Glove Service—with what would be its iconic white-gloved girl—to highlight "a high quality of service that encompasses neatness, efficiency, competence, and capability."[51] Winter believed that "our girls received the idea extremely well and consider the white gloves as a badge of honor, which, in effect, requires them to do their job in accordance with our high standards," but without receiving incentive pay.[52] Manpower branded itself through that icon of feminine sexuality—the white glove. Manpower chose white gloves as a symbol because "they seemed to represent everything that is feminine, neat, and proper. They symbolize quality and efficiency."[53] The gloves sold the temp as a woman.

Manpower training manuals of the 1960s covered not only how to type, but also how to dress. Before a Manpower employee became a White Glove Girl she was expected to study a series of training manuals like "Adapting Quickly to New Office Routine and Advanced Telephone Technique," "How to Be an Effective Vacation Replacement," and—my favorite—"The White Glove Girl's Book of Beauty, Wardrobe, and Personal Grooming."[54]

These were educated and experienced women, and yet Manpower took pains to instruct them on how to dress and comport themselves, making sure that they aligned themselves with dominant beauty standards. Winter noted that "almost all (95.1 percent) had once been full-time office workers," and their average full-time experience of nine years was considerable. In fact, these temps were more educated than most women. About one third had gone to college, and a third had gone to "business school," by which Winter meant secretarial school.[55] Manpower proudly announced that "all of our female employees have been given a pair of white gloves which they wear to all assignments," and according to the women, "both customer and employee reaction has been extremely favorable."[56]

Their sexuality was as valuable as their skillfulness. Secretarial work remained the primary business of Manpower into the 1960s, and being a good secretary was not just about words per minute. "A temporary isn't called in to beautify an office," Winter wrote, "but if she does, she's all the more appreciated."[57] Winter explained that "to *his* customers, you represent *him*." The same way a beautiful wife raised the value of a husband, so, too, did a beautiful secretary raise the value of an executive. The transference from one role to the other was undeniable. In fact, many employers would not hire above a certain age: thirty-five, thirty, twenty-six, or even twenty-one.[58] For women who did not fit the standard mold of beauty, especially in terms of race or age, finding clerical work could be difficult.

The "80,000 women who work for Manpower" were transformed through this rebranding into middle-class women of leisure—beautiful and efficient, of course, but at the same time still making a choice to work and having the flexibility to return to their normal lives without a job. The white gloves, spotless and pure, made clear that these women were still women. Work was something dainty and feminine. Dr. Joyce Brothers told women that while "your clothes and hair . . . might be all right for shopping and family activities," they might not work for the office.[59] With white gloves, the role of beautiful woman trumped that of ink-stained office worker. That work remained optional was as alluring as the women themselves.

Resisting hiring older workers was not just about beauty discrimination. Employers assumed that older women, who might only be in their thirties, would be unmanageable in comparison with—the thinking went—docile younger women. Interviews by the National Manpower Council with potential employers found that older female workers were perceived as "inflexible, set in their ways, and find it difficult to get along with their superiors and fellow workers."[60] Winter defended older women. Older workers displayed all the traits desired by employers: autonomy, conviviality, punctuality, dependability. They might not know all the new technologies, but studies found them to be just as efficient, if not more so, than younger workers.[61] Systematically hiring older women undercut the ways that the pay structure was naturalized by ideas of age and gender. Older people *should* be paid more for their experience, but in reality they were not. Moreover, if an older woman needed to work, it put the entire system of the family wage and male earning power under suspicion. Older temps existed, but there were not nearly as many as young temps.

While gender circumscribed what kinds of jobs women could get, racial discrimination did as well, creating a barrier even more obstinate than age. Only 7 percent of African American women working in 1950 found positions as clerical or sales workers, whether as temps or perms. Before the growth of the more racially inclusive government bureaucracy of the 1960s, African Americans found themselves shut out of office work at white corporations. Discussions of race rarely appeared in Manpower's promotional materials, and black women were absent from its White Glove Girl advertisements. A postwar national survey found, however, in its analysis of gender and work, that one of the main explanatory variables in white women's labor force participation was the "size of the Negro population." "Wherever the Negro population is large," they discovered by comparing cities, "the percent of [white] women in the labor force is above average."[62] White women could go to offices when black women could go to their homes "as domestic servants." Home appliances didn't enable white women to work; black women did.[63]

By 1965, the gender underpinnings of temp labor were being contested (though not always successfully). Manpower's rationalizations worked only as long as women's work remained optional, and as the '60s became the '70s, that ideal matched up less and less with reality, as white, middle-class women more often began to work full time by necessity. Emergency replacements, moreover, had limited growth potential. The big money would be in workforce planning.

The Realities of Women's Work

Nuclear family ideals, of course, clashed with the reality of many women's lives. Women worked for many different reasons—some for extra income, to be sure, but just as many because they had to. In the 1960s, 21 percent of the female workforce was widowed or divorced and another 24 percent was single; neither group could count on a husband's wage.[64]

The reality of family life was less rosy than Dr. Joyce Brothers suggested. A little less than half of White Gloves Girls found that their "work had 'improved my family life and home life generally.'"[65] Working as a temp, like working in general, was fraught with anxieties for men and women as they defied convention. Winter framed temporary work as a bridge to an "enlightened new world for women," where their efforts garnered respect and they were seen as more than household drudges. He suggested it would lead to "more help from your husband as he recognizes your new status as a fellow wage-earner."[66] If only men's attitudes toward women's household work derived from such a strong sense of class solidarity among wage earners. Even for those women whose husbands supported their work, it was support that did not ring of enlightenment. One temp remarked, "My husband is enthusiastic. He says I'm a better housekeeper, mother, and wife."[67]

In surveys of Manpower temps, many husbands objected to their wives working, but recognized the value of the extra paycheck. "At times my husband objects because of his strong attitude on his wife working," an Oshkosh, Wisconsin, temp wrote, "but readily agrees that without Manpower our money problems would be worse."[68] Although Winter insisted that the income was discretionary, it was still income, whether to make up for an unemployed husband, to pay children's medical bills, or simply to avoid a husband's meddling in her spending.

Survey responses revealed a range of situations: husbands who were indifferent or supportive; women who found satisfaction and self-esteem through work and sometimes through spending. Many women talked about how they balanced their work lives with their home lives. Temp work allowed them to be home when children left for school or to take care of aged parents. In an ideal world, all jobs would allow us to meet our social obligations and still have rewarding work. In the postwar era, and for most working people today, that is not the reality. We work because we must.

In the early 1960s, most White Glove Girls, 80 percent, reported that their work was a choice to earn extra money. Only 7 percent of White Glove Girls claimed they worked "to earn a living."[69] Yet the motivations for work appeared to be more mixed than the 80 percent figure suggests. While for some the pay was extra, the differences in husband's incomes among the White Glove Girls also suggest that the work was not as discretionary as the women might have liked to say it was. Three times as many White Glove Girls had husbands who earned less than $100 a week as women whose husbands earned more than $200.[70] A similar ratio existed between women whose husbands worked in factories (31 percent) and women whose husbands worked as professionals or executives (11 percent). For women who needed to get paid, the lower wages of temps relative to permanent workers was not a benefit.

These working women also faced higher costs in going to work than men did. Earning money cost money. Childcare and home care, seen as their responsibility, was not cheap. When opportunity knocked—or called on the phone, as was the case with temps—the woman had to decide quickly whether, as Winter said, "she can afford to put off some important home task or whether she should entrust the children to a substitute baby-sitter whom she does not know very well."[71] A typist averaged $74 a week in the late 1960s. Of that $74, a woman with children would pay out $15—or about one fifth, before taxes. Between lunches, transportation, and childcare, simply going to work meant spending about a third of the money earned.[72] Men incurred the same transportation and food costs, but the cost of childcare was a particular burden for mothers, since they were, with few exceptions, responsible for children. The husband's wage was dependent on the wife's unpaid care work. Whether going to work provided a "break away from the domestic routine," it certainly cost more for a woman than it did for a man.[73]

Women often wanted full-time work, despite the fact that Winter spoke of the attractiveness of temp work. He said that temps "like the idea of working when they want for as long as they want." He opined that "if you think about it, we would all like to work on this basis." "Unfortunately for most of us," that is, men who had a steady job, "economics don't permit us to work on that basis. But there are tens of thousands of people, particularly housewives, who like the idea of working only part time or on a temporary basis."[74] Yet even Manpower's own survey data contradicted his claims. The surveys, as reported by Winter, did not reveal whether these temps wanted more hours ("to succeed") or whether they actually preferred half time, as he seemed to imply.[75] On average, White Glove Girls worked about eighty hours a month—or two weeks full time. Other measurements, like twenty-one weeks per year, corroborated that White Glove Girls worked about half time, but it is less clear how much that was by choice.

Most telling, Manpower went to great lengths to keep its temps from finding a permanent job, belying the argument that all temps just wanted part-time work.[76] The screening cost of potential temps was real, but not as high as the cost to the worker of being unable to transition to a permanent job. Manpower, for instance, "had a bit of trouble losing its help to clients," forcing them to create contracts forbidding temps from making arrangements for "permanent employment" for six months after the temporary job ended.[77] Temps who went to work for the client firm had to pay a financial settlement with the agency—or at least their employer did. Of course, Manpower preferred that its temps, if they wanted steadier work, "switch to a permanent job . . . they have found for themselves in a company where they have never worked for Manpower."[78]

While Elmer Winter celebrated women's choices, the reality was more muddled. Like everyone else with a job, temps chose to work, but they did so given a particular context: of suburban ennui and modern luxury to be sure, but often just to pay the bills. For women hemmed in by tight money and gender expectations, temp work was the only choice they had.

CHAPTER THREE

Consulting Men

F or the consultant, ideas are, and were, the coins of the realm. Marvin Bower believed that consulting was the "most natural bridge between theory and practice of management."[1] He saw consultants as bees pollenating the flowering corporations of the world, enabling the best ideas to circulate widely. Consultants could take academic abstraction and turn it into corporate concrete, building a better tomorrow. Over the decades, every firm would release reports, journals, and books to establish themselves as the preeminent thought leaders in a particular area.

McKinsey began this tradition when it started a newsletter in 1939, then called *Top Management Notes*, which it sent to client executives, followed, in 1940, with *Supplementing Successful Management*, which went out to 2,600 clients and prospective clients.[2] On the copy I have, the business card of a McKinsey partner named John Neukom is stapled to the front.

When Neukom put his card on the book, he and the other partners who did likewise were endorsing that vision personally, aligning their worldview with that of Bower and McKinsey. Managerial ideas went hand in hand with the day-to-day experiences of consultants. Like all consulting publications, *Supplementing Successful Management* was used to sell services, but Marvin Bower thought the true value of the book was in the way that it established the philosophy and strategy of McKinsey.[3]

John Neukom, who would later head the San Francisco office, had joined McKinsey in 1934, about a year after Marvin Bower. At that time, McKinsey had a handful of partners, with fifteen to twenty-five associates in two offices in New York and Chicago.[4] On Sunday afternoons, consultants would leave their homes to catch a train to their industrial clients in nearby cities. "The great American Pullman car," as Neukom put it, took consultants overnight from Chicago to their destinations, promising on-time arrivals to one hundred cities by the next morning. No consultant in

Chicago could expect to leave in the morning and have a full day of work upon arrival, unless he was going to nearby Milwaukee. Travel in this time before airplanes made consulting either very local or very grueling. Neukom had the grueling. In 1936, he spent 112 nights in Pullman cars, traveling 31,000 miles.[5]

Over the years, he devoted those hours to thinking about consulting, and as the firm expanded its associate training in the postwar period, Neukom wrote a great deal of the material that explained to new consultants exactly how an engagement should be run, and more important, what it would mean, both for McKinsey and for their clients. As they took their own overnight Pullmans, and later planes, the same structure of how to conduct an engagement would remain in place. The purpose, too, would remain unchanged: to supplement management.

To supplement successful management was to support successful executives, McKinsey argued—like a temp coming in during an emergency. The executive had to run an entire company and could not devote his time to a particular problem, no matter how important. Like Elmer Winter's many publications, the ambition of *Supplementing Successful Management* was to show that consultants did not fix "sick" companies, but augmented successful ones. Consultants were not there to replace executives, but to back them in times of need. Solving a problem, whether it was rethinking an org chart or repricing potato chips, was their only task. These groups had little specific knowledge of the particular company or product, but their expertise, it was believed, was in a general ability to ask the right questions and come up with the right answers, filtering the meaningful out of the noise of the known. McKinsey consultants could make that problem, whether "increasing sales or reducing manufacturing and operating costs," their "full-time responsibility."[6] Like temps, consultants could solve the "special problems [that] generally occur infrequently."[7]

As with Manpower's temps, with McKinsey there would always be one-off problems, even emergencies—an unprofitable unit, an unwieldy org chart—that required some consultants. After the emergency passed, McKinsey hoped they could have an ongoing relationship with the firm's executives. Although they stressed that consultants "supplement management[,] we do not supplant any of its functions," the reality was more complicated. If the proper role of management is strategic planning, then asking someone else to solve that problem is tantamount to abdicating that responsibility. Management would execute the strategy, but the ideas would come from the consultants. They had to be trusted.

Long-term relationships with CEOs were the foundation of McKinsey's business plan. The "capacity to keep confidences," Bower believed, is what kept clients coming back again and again.[8] These recurrent studies were the bread and butter of management consulting. Bower's relationship with David Ogilvy, the head of the leading postwar advertising firm Ogilvy & Mather, meant that McKinsey continually studied them for years. This study benefited Ogilvy, who said in his autobiography that "no other agency had accumulated such a corpus of knowledge, and as a result they had no consistent discipline." Ogilvy may have spent "millions of dollars," but he certainly felt it was worth it. Other ad agencies, he thought, "were forced to fly blind."[9] McKinsey, of course, got the millions.

Making a Consultant

Mac McKinsey, like other management engineers, believed that the best way to gain credibility was to hire "mature executives," as Bower put it.[10] Engineering, despite Bower's renaming, remained through the 1950s the touchstone of consulting. National organizations like the Association of Consulting Management Engineers (ACME) kept the word in their names, giving them an aura of science and objectivity. Yet even these management engineers realized that their work was, in fact, not like engineering at all. If the problem had a solution in a textbook, then the consultant would be out of a job. An ACME guidebook to hiring, published in 1961, explained the key trait of the management engineer—intelligence. Raw intelligence was essential. ACME estimated the IQ cutoff required for consulting, 120 points, eliminated 90 percent of the population.[11] But this intelligence would need to be balanced by a certain kind of mind that took in chaos and put out order. A consultant would need to "plan and organize much of his own work" in often "complex and hazy" situations.[12] The trick was that because these situations were often unlike anything that had been seen before—in theory—there was no textbook. Consultants had to write the textbook as they went, rethinking how businesses worked.

Unlike most professional fields, you could not get a degree in consulting.[13] Hiring postwar consultants was trickier than hiring lawyers or engineers, who had clear credentials.[14] Every consultancy screened their applicants carefully, but there the hiring similarities ended. There was generally a mix of unstructured and preplanned interviews, as well as the requisite evaluation by a trained psychologist.[15] The process was highly idiosyncratic.[16]

Experience, for most firms, mattered more than education. When an ACME survey was done in 1959, consulting firms preferred to hire men in their thirties, with five years' experience and a master's degree—though in some cases a doctorate in psychology was acceptable.[17] The consultant had to be "book smart," with superior intelligence, but also "person smart," with the ability to "persuade and influence people toward a sound course of action by reason rather than authority." These men had a "proven ability to make decisions and solve problems."[18]

Bower decided to do things differently at McKinsey.

He believed that the firm should be run in all ways like a law firm, including hiring new consultants directly out of school so that they could be trained to think like a consultant. He believed in the value of the blank slate. Older hires would be fixed in their ways and unable to see problems from the McKinsey perspective. These junior consultants, called "associates" like at a law firm, would nonetheless be advising much older executives on corporate policy. It was a radical move. McKinsey pioneered hiring directly out of business schools, and it hired from the best, Harvard Business School, like Bower himself.

For Bower, educational credentials like his were the best expression of meritocracy. Unlike when he was coming up in the postwar period, the MBA was becoming more commonplace, and he thought Harvard's pedagogy, which was focused on the case study, made for perfect consultant training. Unlike CPAs who knew accounting or industrial engineers who knew machines, the MBA had spent years thinking about a wide variety of businesses and problems rather than the regimented application of rules.

This kind of consultant looked for the novel rather than the tested, employing abstract reason in the development of solutions rather than experience.

Taking a young business school graduate and molding him into a McKinsey man was possible in a way that was more difficult with an older, more experienced man. "Failure is higher for associates," Bower said, "with substantial business experience than for those with less."[19] The experienced hires found it hard to adjust to their lack of status when they began at McKinsey. Even experienced hires began as associates (though they might be promoted faster). The "pride and self-assurance gained through past success," Bower cautioned, "make it impossible for him to summon the humility and motivation that are required for the essential learning."[20] Recruiting younger consultants with little previous experience made a more homogenous culture—and a homogenous problem-solving approach—possible.

Senior executives may have bristled at the youngsters, but the Harvard brand made up for what a McKinsey administrator at the time called the fuzzy-cheeked associates. From 1950 to 1959, consultants with MBAs grew from 20 percent of the firm to 80 percent.[21] The typical McKinsey consultant had an MBA, JD, or PhD, and a third of the MBAs were from Harvard.[22] The larger pool of consultants, even inexperienced business school graduates, allowed the firm to double in size, which then allowed McKinsey to act more broadly in the economy. Bower did, however, make sure that no matter how young they were, the associates dressed like old men—black socks, dark suits, and conservative hats.[23]

Education, however, was just the starting point for success in consulting. Like Manpower, McKinsey prided itself on screening—and they screened for more than just smarts. McKinsey could supply the skill in diagnosis that came from a combination of technical knowledge and analytic skill, but the consultant's most important attribute was the ability to ferret out the key facts that would be needed to make a business decision—what Neukom called judgment.

Judgment was not the same as intelligence. The basic training materials of McKinsey distinguished between intelligence, which was more rational, and judgment, which was more intuitive.[24] Clients came to McKinsey because they had problems. Obvious problems with textbook solutions could be solved by a corporation's staff; consultants tackled complex situations to find the basic problem.[25] A consultant could easily find an answer to any standard problem. The hard part for a consultant was figuring out what the real, underlying problem was.

When facts could be used, that was best, but, as John Neukom wrote in the McKinsey training materials, "business problems are not solved by facts alone," since the facts were often incomplete. Facts about what problem? The hard part was not finding facts, but asking the right questions. A consultant's judgment, therefore, mattered as much as his intelligence or research skills. His intuition about how the world worked and what ought to be done helped him ask better questions.[26]

As much as consulting was mental, it was also athletic. The consulting life was hard and the consultant needed stamina. The work was challenging to the mental health of associates, who required, Bower said, "self-confidence . . . and emotional stability."[27] Spending ten to fourteen hours a day in a room with colleagues you had probably never met before was a recipe for disaster unless the associates had exceptional social skills or similar social backgrounds. By recruiting from the same elite schools, McKinsey helped reinforce a shared social background. Bower said that in the 1940s he would only hire an associate he "would be glad to go on a tiger hunt with."[28]

Self-presentation mattered as much as ideas. Even though Bower believed in intellectual iconoclasm, he also believed in social conformity. McKinsey men did not look better or worse than their clients. They were to be equals. Conformity in style meant that the clients would listen to the new ideas. Style underpinned substance. When top management wore hats, so did consultants (except in California, where no one wore hats). When a McKinsey team worked at Shell, they wore the same ties as the management. Bower thought it was no coincidence that when they did a study at DuPont, the client thought they were "smart" and that "they even look like DuPonters."[29] Social conformity mattered for the team, then, but also for the clients.

As the job description piled up—intellectual, technical, emotional, social—it becomes understandable why McKinsey, and most elite consulting firms, had such high turnover rates. To succeed at McKinsey you had to be Marvin Bower—or close to it. For Bower, of course, this was effortless.

He saw consulting as "self-expression and personal fulfillment," so that "work then is no longer a burden."[30] For the rest, tests might reveal intellectual capacities, but it was far more difficult to screen for the wide range of character attributes required for the job. To impress his vision on the firm, Bower always attended when starting associates took part in the introductory training program, which was intended to provide specific training in problem solving. The two-week program brought consultants from all the offices together as part of the one-firm philosophy.[31] Bower attended every single session until the 1990s—decades after he had formally retired from the firm. In a very real sense, Bower's vision of the firm was the way every associate was taught to see consulting.

Few men would stay at McKinsey—or any other consultancy—for their careers. Annual recruiting at business schools like HBS offset the huge turnover. Unless associates worked their way up to partner, they were let go. This up-or-out policy meant that only the most committed, most suitable, most McKinsey consultants stayed.[32] Consultants could never expect to last a long time. But the McKinsey training—intellectual, cultural, ethical—meant they would approach business in this way for the rest of their careers. Their consulting experiences would guide their managerial decisions forever.

The Engagement

Already by the 1940s, Alfred Sloan's multidivisional bureaucracy, which had been pathbreaking in the 1920s, seemed to be encountering limits. Consultants were there to help. The value of consultants was simple: they got things done. In a modern firm, there was corporate inertia that needed to be overcome. Firms could, in theory, search for someone to solve a particular problem, but it would be exhausting. Like Manpower, McKinsey could supply the talent that was needed and, when the project was done, leave.

John Ellsworth was the president of a company in the 1960s that was like most companies—moderately sized and little known. His Ensign-Bickford Company, a munitions manufacturer headquartered in Simsbury, Connecticut, wasn't in the same league as the General Electrics of the world, but the same pressures to become more flexible were already apparent, even in Simsbury. Ellsworth's experiences with consultants dated back to when they were simply management engineers. In the 1920s, he hired such an engineer to resdesign his incentive structure, which allowed the company to ride the boom of the 1920s and survive the '30s. In the '40s, he had brought in management consultants to provide an outside perspective on how Ensign-Bickford ought to be organized, ensuring proper lines of authority, executive compensation, and succession planning, to turn it into a well-run multidivisional corporation. In short, consultants helped him structure his firm in the most up-to-date way. Ellsworth believed that "the job of management is to render the corporation proof against the shock of surprise." To do this, he emphasized the value of consultants even to midsize firms. "For the smaller company," Ellsworth said, "cannot as a rule afford the luxury of having persons permanently employed on our staffs who are experts in management and organization."[33] Once in the door, consultants could offer a range of services. The tricky part was selling that first engagement.

"Arrangements for our services are simple," *Supplementing Successful Management* informed potential clients. An executive simply needed to have a chat with a partner. After discussing the problem, a study could be arranged. The fees could be by the day or by the project, as dictated by the project and by the client's preferences. There would be no contract or future obligation. McKinsey sought "no permanent arrangements."[34] Because a contract was unseemly, a letter outlining the engagement, called a letter of proposal (LOP), would serve as a guide to the scope, timing, and cost of an engagement.[35] An initial study would reveal whether McKinsey was equipped to solve the problem. Everything was done as gentlemen, as professionals, not as salesmen.

Bower thought that a hard sell and promotion were unbecoming to the professional. The clients should come to them, not the other way around—and there were practical reasons for this as well. "If the client initiates the study," Bower wrote, "we are in the better position to push for results." That was, however, balanced with his idea of client "exposure." There was, Bower said, a "fine line between making the Firm more widely known and actually soliciting clients," but to grow, McKinsey would need to straddle that line.[36] Ideas helped acquire new clients. McKinsey's growth was not the result of advertising. There were no ad campaigns for white-gloved McKinsey men.

McKinsey was able to gather these clients through the quality of its work and with an active outreach program. Beginning in 1940, Bower hosted clinic dinners, which acted as seminars on business topics, for a couple of dozen executives and a guest speaker. These events proved an effective way to educate prospective clients about McKinsey's abilities to grapple with cutting-edge issues. Other consultancies did the same, and though Bower dismissed their seminars as mere "promotional activity," it is hard to see how McKinsey's seminars differed.[37]

During the 1950s, as McKinsey's reputation grew, the firm became more selective about their clients. Bower wanted McKinsey to be an elite firm with an elite clientele, particularly in industry and finance. After the war, McKinsey had switched to a fixed fee schedule per month or per project. The idea was to avoid nickel-and-dime situations with lesser clients. A client who would not be comfortable knowing in advance that there would be a high monthly fee would not be a client the firm wanted to serve. The quality should, in the end, justify the high cost.[38] Bower condemned the foot-in-the-door approach of low pricing.[39] McKinsey's reputation, not low cost, should sell engagements. Growth should be a by-product of client service, not a goal. Any other approach was déclassé. It was—and this was Bower's greatest possible insult—unprofessional.[40]

Once McKinsey acquired a new client, the next step was the engagement itself. For a first engagement with a client, Bower preferred to do a total analysis of the business, following Mac McKinsey's General Survey Outline, which functioned as a checklist for any business, running through its finances, operations, and markets, as well as its competition. Sometimes what clients thought was the problem was just a symptom of a different, more important problem. The general survey could be done for "the management or for outsiders such as commercial and investment bankers, insurance companies, and security owners' committees," and could be useful whether management wanted to improve operations or wanted to issue stock. Following this survey, McKinsey would do a special study on "organization planning; marketing, distribution and merchandising; manufacturing and operations; management controls (costs, budgets, executive reports); office, plant, and warehouse operating methods and procedures; personnel management and labor relations; financial planning." These special studies came second because McKinsey often found that "the roots of what appears to be an isolated problem extend rather widely."[41]

McKinsey prided itself on its independent analysis. Though clients would frequently try to share a business plan with Bower and get his quick opinion (and perhaps avoid fees), Bower dismissed this approach.[42] Without independent fact-finding, the basis of those plans might be flawed. In a study, McKinsey needed to be given free rein and total access in order to find the underlying causes of problems and the data that might suggest answers. Every study, they claimed, may have shared a kind of analysis, but every answer was tailor-made for the client. They were not selling what Bower dismissively called "systems."[43]

To carry out these engagements, McKinsey sent a team to the client. On site, the team was led by a project manager, called an engagement manager, or EM in McKinseyese, along with a couple of associates. First, the team verified that the problem they had been asked to solve was the right problem. "The principal activity on a study," Bower explained, "is solving problems."[44] Problem solving at McKinsey had a very specific set of meanings. At the beginning of the engagement, the team developed a feasible hypothesis of what the problem was and a possible solution.[45]

Testing their hypothesis against data, the team validated their approach. The bulk of the study consisted of gathering facts to prove or disprove the hypothesis (and possibly rework it). Consultants did this by interviewing staff, examining records, comparing firms, and conducting other kinds of research.

In the team room on site, consultants would debate. A key part of the process was that everybody, if they made sense, would be heard, though in practice, the lack of hierarchy was more iffy. Bower thought of consulting as a "role not a job," in which "the consultant has no subordinates and no authority." In his vision, consultants swayed others by reason alone. On the ground, of course there was hierarchy and deference, but lackeys and yes-men would not be able to do the job. Neither would tyrants. To succeed in consulting meant combining the intellectual resources of the team.[46]

The hierarchy of the firm, Bower believed, was based on merit, not office politics. When two associates told him why an office in Switzerland needed to be closed in the 1950s, he listened, considered their points, and closed the office. It is hard to imagine a junior executive going to Alfred

Sloan and getting the same result. Bower's vision of McKinsey may have been rose tinted, but certainly everyone at the firm believed in the "obligation to dissent."[47] If an idea was questioned in a fact-based manner, the critique was appreciated—no matter who said it. Bower believed that quality came out of this creative disagreement among equals.

While the multidivisional corporation's bureaucracy operated through an organizational chart of cascading responsibilities and authorities, the associate, in contrast, "had no in-box and out-box." He had no "defined activity and authority."[48] The associate "must really make his own work." In this way, a consultant's work process was more ambiguous than a lawyer's, who at least knew in advance how to read a contract. Even a professor knew what it was to teach (at least in theory). Unlike most professionals, who worked within a much more structured environment, consultants lived in a world of work very different from the one they advised.

Bower believed that "an open society in which highly talented people prefer to work" was the best way to organize the workplace, but this ideal was quite different from the corporate hierarchy.[49] In practice, of course, there were hierarchies even at McKinsey. The engagement director (the partner overseeing the study) ultimately had responsibility to the client, but ideas flowed more freely than in most postwar workplaces. No consultant could solve a problem alone. Successful teams distilled the expertise of a firm; they were backed by the research and experience of the entire firm and of the partners.

Part of the value of McKinsey was the experience of partners across different firms. Consultants occupied a tricky position regarding confidential information. Sharing other clients' core secrets, like secret formulas, was obviously verboten, but so was discussing pricing. At some point, however, these secrets became best practices that could be generalized from a particular firm. As much as firms wanted McKinsey to keep their secrets, they also wanted access to consultants' experience of similar firms. Management consultants sold themselves as first-rate problem solvers, but with an institutional memory of the "hundreds, or rather, thousands of companies" they had served, and they, as the London director of McKinsey told the BBC, "try to make that general experience available to our clients."[50] A well-known executive said in *Supplementing Successful Management,* "Your firm helps us trade ideas with other leading companies."[51] For smaller companies, like the Ensign-Bickford Company, the value proposition was even more extreme. A small firm could have access to the same solutions as the most prestigious corporations in the country. There would be no need to maintain a permanent staff of specialists. "Market research and industrial engineering" could be done by McKinsey on "a temporary and, therefore, more economical basis."[52] Consultants spread ideas across boundaries that ordinarily would have been impassible.

This fluidity extended across the firm. Though McKinsey's managing director was nominally in charge, he was not a CEO. In practice he simply coordinated the activities of the partners across the offices. Partners and directors were meant to be leaders, not executives.[53] Gil Clee, who would be Bower's first successor, compared being the managing director of McKinsey to being the "president of a university. You don't order the faculty to do anything—the basic objective is to create a working environment in which the individual has a maximum opportunity for innovation, freedom with the discipline of teamwork, and fairly rigid quality control."[54]

As McKinsey grew, Bower's strong cultural indoctrination held this capitalist anarchy together. For Bower and other leaders, the source of the firm's success was this open culture, this rejection of ranks that defined so many postwar firms. Most important, they all believed that collaborative decision making through facts and persuasion—which came from a lack of hierarchy—was the source of their success. "A thorough and complete exchange of ideas and opinions without artificial limitations" was essential to do the work, as was a lack of "pride of authorship."[55] The report issued at the end of an engagement would have no author except McKinsey & Company. No consultant who thought themselves smarter than their colleagues could succeed. Any egoists who liked seeing their names in print should look to other lines of work.

The Presentation

The best solutions were worthless if the client could not be convinced. After the team was convinced that a particular approach was correct, they would create a presentation. The presentation was not a by-product but an important project milestone. As the hypotheses connected, the consultants developed a story line that explained how to go from the problem to the solution.[56] Logic was (and is) seldom enough, Neukom wrote, to convince most people. Talking to the clients in a language that they understood was necessary if the recommendations were to be adopted.[57] Analysis needed to become narrative, and that narrative needed to appeal not only to reason but also to feelings. Stories, not data, moved people to act. *Supplementing Successful Management* said, "As consultants, we exercise no authority." Their authority came from their ability to convince "client executives on the basis of recognized company benefits, soundness of substantiating facts, and effectiveness of presentations."[58] McKinsey's guidelines on presentations, therefore, were just as long as its guidelines on problem solving.

An effective presentation was a brief presentation. Decades before PowerPoint, the "highly synthesized presentation of problems and solutions at minimum depth" pointed to quick answers rather than long-term challenges.[59] In the early 1950s, the standard for the end of an engagement had been the narrative report. These reports, with their rich details and complex arguments, had "continuing values for studies of a fundamental character which deal with long-range questions," but they were often long and difficult to read.[60] By the 1960s, consultants were encouraged to use more streamlined reports with more of a graphic component. Whole pages of text in the 1950s were reduced to single topic sentences in the 1960s.

Whereas Mac McKinsey had thought that the report was the goal, Bower believed it was just a starting point. To Bower, the objective was to make sure the recommendations were implemented. The most important role of a consultant, he argued, was as a teacher. The "gold-lettered blue or black bound final report" was not nearly as important as how the consultant coached management to "open executive minds to new areas of professional competence."[61] Nonetheless, for many engagements, the report was physical proof of the work, and so looks mattered—just like the associates' hats.[62]

Before the final presentation, the consultants checked their findings with every key stakeholder.[63] Executives needed to be heard, their opinions incorporated, and their feelings soothed. Meetings were never to be surprises. All the decisions were actually made ahead of time. The work was in getting all stakeholders to agree to the presentation before the final presentation was made.

When McKinsey reorganized Citibank, then officially called First National City Bank, in the 1960s, for example, the very first page of the final report laying out the structure of the new bank emphasized that it was the result of the "combined thinking of a great number of Citibank officers and McKinsey consultants." The report did "not provide a total record of all the analyses, findings and conclusions of the organization planning study," but it did include the "agreed-on organizational structures" as they had been presented to the bank's officers. McKinsey didn't surprise Citi. At every step along the way, they had shown data to support their recommendations, though only some of those facts made it into the final report. Everything in that report had already been seen and vetted by Citi. Ideas didn't sell themselves. Stakeholders needed to be brought along with the team's thinking.

Such presentations distilled complicated situations down to the most relevant facts, and then reasoned from those facts to make recommendations. With their behind-the-scenes corralling, those recommendations would be carried out.[64] McKinsey's approach worked. Every year, about three quarters of all billings came from repeat customers. "Year after year," Bower wrote, "client executives generally value our services."[65]

Meritocracy and Insecurity

While clients returned to McKinsey year after year, consultants did not. Consultants themselves were temps, though highly paid, and they had reconciled themselves to a worldview that accepted that insecurity. When these men worked at firms like McKinsey, their days were numbered. While permanent executives might work on a project for years on end, consultants measured their projects in terms of days or weeks, only rarely in months. Assembling in teams that might never have met each other before, they received a problem from the chief executive or one of his lieutenants and then dispersed. The work was temporary, but so, too, was their time with the consultancy.

Promotion or dismissal on "merit" was a core tenet of Bower and

McKinsey's philosophy.[66] For inspiration he looked to leading law firms and universities. He thought the up-or-out policy was best for the firm and probably good for the consultant; after all, "faculty members separated from Harvard usually get good positions in other universities."[67] Compromise killed excellence. For Bower, the answer was simple: if "there is doubt whether a candidate for advancement really qualifies, it is better to pass him over."[68] Electing partners was a long-term decision. "Superior people stimulate one another," and lowering standards would spur the elite to leave.[69] While management engineering firms sought experienced hires, Bower sought the brilliant young. While public accountancies promised long-term careers, Bower promised only short-term excitement. In both ways, Bower made the practice of consulting extoll fresh ideas and new faces.

Despite their short-term work projects and lack of job security, consultants were well respected—and well paid. Marvin Bower described their pay as modest, but it was, perhaps, not as modest as he suggested. Even as early as the 1940s, each partner earned the equivalent of $176,000 today, including a share of the $10 million a year in profits generated at that time.[70] The value of partnership only grew over the decades, and aspirants worked hard to move up.

But McKinsey's up-or-out policy meant that few consultants would. Every evaluation contained the possibility of promotion or firing. It was not enough for the consultant to do his job, to be a workhorse.[71] Along with his productivity, he would be judged on whether "he ha[d] real promise for long-term success with the Firm based on his performance and his character."[72] He had to do it so well that he demonstrated a trajectory of even more success in the future. Failure to show this promise had the same result as not doing his current job well—he would be fired.[73] Even partners were not secure. If one was deemed no longer on that trajectory of excellence, he, too, would be separated. No one was spared from the unforgiving meritocracy.

In the 1960s, consultants at the top firms like Booz Allen and McKinsey & Co. had similar career paths. On average 17 percent of post-MBA consultants made partner, while 83 percent left their firms within six years. Most of the older consultants, those over thirty-five, joined major corporations, while the younger consultants struck out in a more entrepreneurial direction. The average tenure at these new firms was about three years. Few consultants could expect to make a career of consulting. Those who did thought of themselves as the best of the best. Meritocracy, more than pedigree, defined the value system of the consultant.

The insecurity took a toll. Researchers in the 1960s found that consultants—more than their peers with stable jobs in corporations— exhibited the telltale signs of distress: "less conformity," "more emotional instability," "less motivation to exercise power over others," and perhaps most distressing, "a less favorable disposition toward assuming a masculine role."[74] These "compulsively driven" "inner-directed" misfits sound suspiciously like the middle-management professionals whose stability they helped destroy. The instability of the world could not help but produce instability in the soul. Yet it was exactly this world that consultants recommended for all of us.

Leaving McKinsey was not the way it is when most of us leave jobs—it was more like graduating from college. Unlike temps, consultants exited toward a great future. Jobs might pay more for an ex-McKinsey consultant because of the "prestige of the firm"[75]—the so-called McKinsey multiplier. Clients even asked to be told if any consultants would be leaving.[76] In fact, this hiring away was part of the consulting firms' business model.

Losing one's job as a consultant was not failure, it was opportunity. Even those who were fired, or "counseled to leave," would receive generous severance packages. McKinsey treated them not as failed consultants, but as McKinsey alumni. As in college, you might be a consultant for only a few years, but you would be an alum for life. Placement counselors helped them find good jobs outside the firm, where, McKinsey hoped, they would hire McKinsey in the future. The up-or-out policy meant that highly trained, highly indoctrinated consultants were spread through the upper echelons of corporations. The influence of consultants was felt not only when they worked for Boston Consulting Group (BCG) or McKinsey—it was felt after they left. This logic, peculiar to this very niche world, would later be projected onto the economy at large. The instability and high pay of the consulting world fed on itself, as the people who believed in this model of management cut the staffs of corporations, and, when that was done, joined the staffs. It worked for them. Why would it not work for the rest of America?

Robert Waterman—McKinsey partner, management guru, and coauthor of *In Search of Excellence*—would later attribute this lack of career safety as one of the core reasons for McKinsey's success. Consultants at any level, even partners, had to produce constantly or lose their jobs. "The culture valued performance, no favorite sons," and even partners could be pushed out unless they were promoted to director. This meritocracy was made possible by the systems that Bower put in place.[77]

The excellence of McKinsey, in other words, was a result of the way in which employees could not count on job security. Bringing that excellence, and insecurity, to their clients—first in the U.S. and then abroad—would reshape the future of the corporation.

CHAPTER FOUR

Marginal Men

S ecure work for most white men began to disappear in the 1970s, but for Mexican migrants, African Americans, and even some unfortunate white men, it had happened earlier. If temporary labor was justified by concepts of the breadwinner and the wife, then the male temp presented a conundrum. While Elmer Winter wrote book after book, article after article, on how to use women as temporary labor, men rarely appeared in his writings. Men might be useful as temps, but this would undermine the postwar logic of family wages. In reality, though, behind the celebration of white-gloved women at Manpower, as early as 1960, a third of the temp workforce was male. In 1959, the office division accounted for 60 percent of sales, but the industrial division, mostly men, was 30 percent.[1] Gloveless, these men worked as temps in factories and warehouses. Perhaps only some women needed jobs at Manpower, but all the men did.

Insecure work was not just an economic problem, but also a political problem. In the cities roiled by protest, Manpower also worked with government and business to bring youth, especially black youth, into the workforce, if only temporarily. And Mexican migrants, as Congress ended the Bracero Program, found themselves in cities on construction and industrial sites—albeit illegally. Drawing lines between those who counted and needed to be folded into American society and those who could be pushed out of that society, the Great Society of the 1960s wrestled with the political meaning of insecurity.

The growth of these temporary male workforces, while substantial, remained peripheral. Most employers chose to employ men permanently and full time. Yet even if they were special cases, these marginal men rehearsed a new economy to come.

Braceros

In 1954 *The I&N Reporter*, the house organ of the INS, published an article by Willard Kelly, the assistant commissioner of the Border Patrol, on a
pressing question of the day: what he called "The Wetback Issue." He recounted very succinctly the old relationship between Mexican labor and
American bosses in a statement that he heard frequently: "My granddaddy
worked wetbacks," Kelly quoted, "and my grandchildren will."[2] This new
migration was different, because so many migrants had come through the
wartime guest worker program, the Bracero Program. These "wetbacks"—a
term for economic migrants from Mexico who crossed the Rio Grande—
came because they were invited. Kelly knew that this migration was the result of manpower shortages during World War II, but he was, like many
Anglo Americans, wary of the vast numbers who came to work the American fields illegally. This federal policy resulted, he said, in "the greatest
peacetime invasion ever complacently suffered by any country." Unlike
most invaders, they were looking for jobs, not spoils.

In 1952, the same year that the Immigration and Nationality Act went
into effect, officials like INS commissioner Argyle Mackey complained of
"the human tide of 'wetbacks'" as the "most serious enforcement problem
of the Service." Most ended up in agriculture, but a smaller fraction, it
seemed, ended up in industry. For "every agricultural laborer admitted
legally, four aliens were apprehended," and of those 875,000 captures, only
30,000 were in trade and industry. Kelly emphasized that "not all 'wetbacks'
come to work on farms . . . unknown thousands have entered the trades and
industries [and], incidentally, many are members of our labor unions" but
the overwhelming majority were farmworkers.[3] Americans might have
abandoned the farms, but they wanted to work in the cities. While the first
Mexicans may have come to the fields legally through the Bracero Program,
the reports of good work to "the Mexicans left at home . . . [had] turned the
trickle into the flood."[4]

These pressing concerns led the INS to launch, in 1954, the Special
Mobile Force Operation, or what the INS colloquially called Operation
Wetback, which swept California and Texas. The INS deported 1.1 million
migrants in 1954. Relatively few of these deportations occurred in cities.

Work camps on farms were easier to find than apartments of factory workers. Sweeps of Spokane, Chicago, and Kansas City were "continuing to discover illegal aliens who ha[d] eluded initial sweeps" but found only "20,174 illegal Mexican aliens [in] industrial jobs."[5]

The INS declared a year later that the "so-called 'wetback' problem no longer exist[ed]."[6] In 1955, "less than 250,000" migrants were deported. An INS statistician could confidently report that, thanks to the efforts of 1954 and '55, "the southern border has been secured." Over the 1950s, the composition of illegal aliens detained by the INS changed dramatically. In 1954, for instance, 99 percent of deportable aliens were Mexican. By 1962, less than a third of deportees were Mexican. The difference was made up by people from other Western countries and from China. In 1962, the number of deportations relative to the size of the annual legal inflow was puny. Only 18,000 Mexicans were deported.[7]

Mexicans continued to form the overwhelming majority of agricultural laborers admitted to the U.S., but they came legally. From 1953 to 1962, 3.6 million workers came north from Mexico to work American fields. Canadian loggers (67,800) and West Indian field-workers (84,006) constituted the next largest labor pools.[8] Basque sheepherders, a category that INS administrators considered important enough to constitute its own category, numbered 1,274. The annual number of Mexican laborers varied between 178,000 and 447,000 over that period, averaging about 350,000 per year.

Beginning in 1962, as the Bracero Program began to cut back legal slots and a drought hit Mexico, the number of undocumented Mexicans captured and deported by INS began to rise again.[9] American agriculture now depended on migrant labor, legal or illegal, even as public opinion swung against the program. These marginal men would still come, but now illegally. Changing the law would not change the economy.

Manpower Men: Temporary Laborers in a Union Economy

Not all industrial jobs were just for men, of course, though most were. Manpower could supply men or women to these jobs, depending on how gender shaped the local workforce. While Manpower highlighted its auxiliary services for the industrial economy, it did offer to replace the entire permanent workforce if need be. Its list of "services unlimited" for this sector included "Factory Work (Men and Women)." Specifying both men and women meant that while permanent jobs could be eliminated, gendered divisions of industrial work need not be.[10] Factory men wouldn't have to work alongside temp women, and in factory settings that did use women, like canning, women could be provided as well.

The jobs that men did at Manpower took more muscle, but in the 1950s, like the women's jobs, they were also irregular. Men found themselves employed more in physical distribution work than in offices. Their work sometimes involved skilled labor—Manpower's technical division offered temps like "Senior Engineer," "Junior Designer," or "Laboratory Technician"—but these areas in the postwar period were very small.[11]

Consider just one morning in 1959, when Manpower provided all kinds of men. Ten men unloaded a shipment of lumber in Niagara Falls. Fifteen men did an overnight supermarket inventory in Miami. Twenty-seven men loaded "19 inch Admiral TV sets in station wagons for delivery throughout three state area" in Newark.[12] Lumberyards needed to unload wood, but as one Midwest lumberman complained, they were "constantly plagued with the problem of finding employees to work on a short-term basis unloading cars" of wood. Before Manpower, he "maintained a force of extra laborers" to unload the cars, but with temps he saved money because he paid "only for the hours actually worked."[13] For the firm that wanted to relocate, either from the city to the suburbs or from the north to the south, Manpower could "provide packers, laborers and truck drivers to move the warehouse" and anything else.[14] Just as with female temps, these temporary men were characterized as supplementary, emergency replacements. For employers, the more they used these men, the more they realized they could serve other roles as well—especially during labor disputes.

Temp workers at Manpower, Kelly, and other agencies were not unionized. Like the rest of those left out of the good jobs, they were, on average, less skilled and darker. Two thirds of Manpower's industrial jobs were unskilled, and one third of those jobs were held by "Negroes."[15] It certainly did not lead to unionization.

With labor laws intended to protect long-term employment, temporary labor allowed companies to find legal ways to employ short term. Even if a company wanted to hire and fire men on a daily basis—day laborers—the costs could be high, because of unemployment compensation. A "large steel company," Elmer Winter wrote, needed between twenty and a hundred men. Keeping everyone on the payroll was not practical, and so they hired by the day, but the state's unemployment compensation was designed for long-term workers. A man "who worked on Wednesday" could file "on Thursday for unemployment compensation." The firm paid $81,000 a year in unemployment out of its $3 million payroll. Hiring workers through Manpower dropped its unemployment costs to $15,000 a year.[16] The Manpower workers cost only $50,000, which was less than the difference in unemployment compensation. Winter claimed that the AFL-CIO shop of one Midwest manufacturer went along with temporary workers because of "its highly seasonal production pattern." The core workers were all union, but the temporary workers were not. Winter claimed that skilled union help was not particularly interested in working for just a short time. This claim seems strange given that so many union jobs, including the ones mentioned by Winter—welding, fabricating, assembling, and shipping—were elsewhere handled on a flexible basis by a hiring hall. Manpower tiptoed around the power of industrial unions, carefully avoiding the label of scab, but it still made inroads at the edges of men's industrial labor.

Elmer Winter was careful nonetheless in the 1950s and '60s not to tread directly on unions. Temps were an obvious way to replace striking workers, and yet Manpower, in its everyday practices, respected unions. Picket lines were not crossed—at least not blatantly.[17] Winter said nothing publicly against unions. He told a group of stockbrokers in 1962 that "we will not send people in to break a strike—the unions know that."[18]

To a meeting of franchisees in 1967, in private, he said, "unions are still a problem. It might get stronger. The United Automobile Workers are quite difficult these days." For Winter, of course, the greatest threat would be that "they want contracts which eliminate any kind of subcontracting." Winter didn't think that Manpower and unions could find a middle ground. He didn't think "that unions that are looking for their people to make $3.00 to $3.50 an hour are going to [be] very impressed with us when we talk about our wage rates to them."[19] That may have been true, but the employers of union workers often were. Instead of directly confronting unions in the 1960s, Manpower maneuvered around them.

A ready supply of temp replacements could be appealing to companies resisting union organizing. In 1964, for instance, oil workers in Wichita, Kansas's Southwest Grease and Oil Company began to discuss forming a union. Management caught wind, and the owner told the personnel manager that "he did not 'give a damn'" how they kept the union out, but that he'd "close the fucking doors" before he let in a union—or at least that is what one pro-union employee who was fired, Hans Nitch, told the NLRB inquiry. Nitch and thirty-three other employees were let go. The difference in workforce was made up by Manpower. Ordinarily Manpower cost a company about 40 cents for every dollar paid to its own workers. During this period, Manpower received $1.70 for every dollar paid to the company's workers. Clearly the fourfold increase was to make up for the fired would-be unionists. The NLRB gave the company a slap on the wrist and told them to put up a sign saying that unions were legal. The "gripers and complainers," as the owner described them, lost their jobs.

Manpower workers could be used as a threat as well as a replacement. After the boxcar loaders at Rust Sales Company (a Denver commercial bakery) joined the Teamsters, the management began to cut overtime—and to use Manpower workers to make up the difference. Manpower usage, before unionization, varied from 7 to 74 hours per week. After unionization, it settled down between 120 and 197 hours per week.[20] Whatever Winter's public rhetoric, Manpower industrial workers were being used to replace or supplement union workers.

"Who is the real employer" was one of the key questions for temporary labor—and an issue that would haunt temps (and then independent contractors) for decades. Under those 1930s labor laws, the employer-employee relationship had a specific set of rules. If an employee worked for Manpower, that meant one thing, but if they worked for a unionized employer, like a big meatpacker, then that worker would have a different set of rights. While Manpower claimed that the temps worked just for Manpower, the National Labor Relations Board had a different opinion.

In 1966, Armour, the national meatpacking company, contracted with Manpower for drivers for its Tennessee operation. Although Armour had contracts with many unions (in the case of its drivers, the Teamsters), Manpower refused to recognize any union. The Teamsters demanded that the NLRB treat the Manpower drivers as covered under their contract with Armour.[21] The NLRB found that although "only Manpower can hire and fire the drivers, Armour can request certain drivers . . . and can refuse to accept the driver referred to it by Manpower." Armour's dispatchers directed the Manpower drivers. Armour disciplined a driver. Perhaps most telling, "of the seven drivers who have consistently been driving for Armour, only one had made a trip for another company and then only on one occasion." Formally they worked for Manpower (from whom they got paid), but they took direction from Armour. This control led the NLRB to rule that these temps were "jointly employed" by Manpower and Armour and had the rights of collective bargaining under the Wagner Act. This question of "who is the real employer" was essential in enforcing labor law and guaranteeing collective bargaining rights, but was far murkier for temps than it was for truck drivers.

The NLRB's decision in 1966 would not be the last time that lawyers attempted to fit new, flexible labor into old New Deal law. What made that law enforceable was not just the power of the state, but the power of the union, too.

A Great Society of Temporary Labor

In 1965, Elmer Winter addressed a roomful of Milwaukee businessmen at the headquarters of Allis-Chalmers. He recounted how over the previous fifteen years, they made strides in developing Milwaukee—stadiums, library additions, railroad stations, even a zoo! What they had not developed, he told them, was "a section of our town which consists of about twenty-five square blocks in the heart of Milwaukee . . . what is known as the 'Negro Ghetto.'" In this territory, he said, "eighty thousand Negroes" lived, "represent[ing] over ten percent of our population," and received, to his estimates, disproportionate "relief." He had only the aggregate numbers of unemployed, not neighborhood, not even race, but he believed that these "Negroes" made up most of the relief rolls of Milwaukee. He issued a challenge to the group: "What can we, as employers, do about this?"[22]

Young people, black and white, were disenchanted with American society. White hippie kids protested. Black ghetto kids rioted. For Winter, all the youth protests emerged from the employment crisis. "Businessmen can and must play," he said in 1968, a "role . . . in the social revolution that is taking place in this country today."[23] "You can't win young people over as part of the establishment if you can't give them jobs," he later told the *Pittsburgh Press*.[24] Winter was interested in quelling social revolution, but at the same time he was promoting his own vision of workplace revolution. For Winter, the natural answer was to use the methods with which he had been successful: he created Youthpower, a nonprofit version of his Manpower, focused on temp jobs for young people.

Youthpower

Youthpower emerged from a meeting in April 1964 of "Milwaukee civic leaders . . . school officials, police, clergy, and social workers," who "warned businessmen to prepare for possible trouble" because of the "14,000 local high-school boys and girls" looking for work.[25] Jobs would keep them out of trouble. Winter took it upon himself to present an answer, and that answer came out of his own business of providing temporary labor. As *Reader's Digest* related, while "many local professional men, merchants and industrialists were eager to help . . . few had work to offer."[26] Winter, however, was experienced in connecting job seekers with job providers. Manpower provided office space, "typewriters and telephones, printed application forms," and utilities for a group of eighty-seven volunteers to begin the process of creating Youthpower. They mailed ten thousand postcards "reporting that messengers, handymen, yard workers, window washers, car hops and other proficient young people were available and eager."[27] On the radio and on the television, young people learned about the program, and on its first day hundreds applied for work.

Winter did for summer jobs what he had done for permanent work—created a temp labor pool. With a phone call, employers could find through Youthpower a short-term worker who had been vetted and inspected. Like the jobs at Manpower, most jobs at Youthpower were rarely full time. Only about a third of Youthpower jobs were full-time summer jobs. Youthpower was modeled on Manpower, but with a nonprofit twist. Manpower paid for one full-time employee to coordinate Milwaukee's Youthpower program. Such a lean model emerged directly from Manpower's own experiences, where a permanent staff of a few hundred oversaw the deployment of hundreds of thousands of temps every year. Unlike Manpower, Youthpower did not take a percentage of the wages. There was no fee for the service at all. At Manpower's training center, would-be data entry operatives processed the Youthpower applications into an IBM 360 for job matching. Volunteers, themselves teenagers, staffed the office, overseen by an "adult adviser, the only paid member of the staff, who act[ed] as coordinator, record keeper, community relations man, and problem solver."[28]

Youthpower was also meant to be an antidote to the hippie wave that seemed to be sweeping the country. Journalist John Chamberlain observed, on a visit to a Youthpower office, that he "couldn't help contrasting their appearance and attitudes with the sight of the non-studying students I had seen slouching about the university gates at Berkeley, Calif., in bare feet and professional slob dress."[29] Work provided a solution for many of society's apparent problems. "Newspaper editors," *Better Homes and Gardens* opined, "are exposed every day to the consequences of teen-age idleness, restlessness, and rootlessness."[30] Little wonder, then, that newspapers would "bend over backwards to support any community effort to solve the problem."[31]

It is not difficult to imagine that Winter thought of Youthpower as a win-win for Manpower. He was helping redress the recurrent summer crises, especially in the ghettos, and simultaneously producing a fresh crop of temp-ready workers already familiar with the flexible work regime. The teenagers who worked for Youthpower, according to the *Herald Tribune*, "are training themselves for job opportunities in the parent organization, which has been signing them up for after-graduation jobs."[32] Manpower, and the demand for temporary labor business more generally, was growing faster than the supply of workers. If there were too few jobs for youth, there were too many open jobs for women, at least the kind of women that Manpower regularly sent out to "type, take dictation or do bookkeeping."[33] Winter estimated in 1966 that he was fifty thousand women short.[34] Unskilled work, like demonstrating products, taking surveys, and doing factory work, was also in short supply. Taking thousands of young people and giving them temp jobs showed them a way of working that would have been alien to their parents, and produced a new crop of Manpower employees.

The following summer, the other founder of Manpower, Aaron Schein-feld, opened the second Youthpower location on Chicago's mostly African American South Side. Building on this outreach in Chicago, Youthpower, as the years went on, emphasized job placement for the black poor, opening offices in ghetto areas of the West Side, as a way "to help Negro youths."[35] The success of Youthpower excited Scheinfeld because "you realize that most of these young people would have gone unemployed had it not been for Youthpower." In 1968, according to *BusinessWeek*, "Youthpower put greater emphasis on getting Negro radio stations and newspapers to devote more time and space to spreading the Youthpower message."[36] Special "job recruiting stations were set up in ghetto sections of some cities, including St. Louis, Birmingham, and Milwaukee." In the first summer in Chicago, Youthpower found four hundred jobs for twelve hundred applicants—or about a third. On the basis of that success, Scheinfeld opened two more of-fices in Chicago to "develop new employment areas for young people." Winter told *BusinessWeek*, "We are making a greater effort to place mi-nority group members. We're not discriminating in reverse, but we do want a better balance than in the past."[37]

The Problem of the "Instant Negro"

Winter's interest in jobs for black Milwaukee, and all American cities, pre-ceded the urban riots, but the growing unrest made his efforts more press-ing. Before the riots, that same group of Milwaukee executives worked with the Urban League to try to match black job seekers with work through a skills bank. An equal opportunity employer would create a written nondis-crimination policy and retrain its recruiting personnel. "Over the years," Winter said, "Negroes have consistently been given jobs as laborers, jani-tors, maids, etc.," and "the time has come where we have to open up other jobs in our companies." As with women, he imagined that temp labor for black youth would be a bridge to better work—or at least, he said so.

Winter believed in racial equality, but Youthpower also promoted Man-power's model of flexible labor, especially through the fawning praise that the program received in the media. From his perspective, it was the "employers in this country who have a real stake ... in making certain that the training that is going to take place under the various poverty programs will be training people for the jobs of tomorrow."[38] Of course the jobs of tomorrow would turn out to be temp jobs at Manpower rather than well-paid manufacturing jobs at Allis-Chalmers (which would be dissolved by 1985). Rather than the "tired American" who might say "I'm fed up with the riots. . . . Let the Negroes sink or swim as they see it. I'm through," Winter felt that "there are twenty million Negroes in this country who I would prefer to turn into buyers of our goods and services rather than haters and disillusioned people who, without jobs, will swell our relief rolls for generations to come."[39]

Business leaders would need to address the urban crisis. Winter was no particular fan of the Great Society efforts. He said to the group, "You may not believe in the program, but I ask you—can we abdicate by saying, 'We have no interest—these are purely government programs?'" To Winter the answer was clear.[40] The solution to urban poverty would need to come from the private sector, not the government. The only alternative to "government largess, well-meaning as it might be," was to have "private self-help," and it must help young people and minority people in a "real, live alternative—not just 'free enterprise' philosophy."[41] The intervention of employers to provide job prospects for the young was essential for steering them "in the direction of free enterprise, rather than in the direction of socialism."[42]

Creating paths to employment, especially for young black people, was essential to stabilizing America. Winter enjoined the businessmen not to "write off the young people of this community because of the excesses of the two percent who cause us trouble"—that is, black activists.[43]

Winter wanted better schools and training, but he also thought that hiring standards for African Americans should be relaxed. "The days of finding the skilled Negro," he told the crowd, "the instant Negro, seem to have disappeared." Expecting "to hire minority workers [who] are qualified" was no longer "realistic." Firms would need to take on the responsibility for the "training of Negroes who do not have the full skills that we normally require" if they were to "cut down the cost of relief and social benefits." He paraphrased Whitney Young of the Urban League: "We can't expect every

Negro secretary to have the appearance of Lena Horne, or every accountant to be another Ralph Bunche."[44]

Young's words, and Winter's choice of those words, deeply reflected some of the assumptions bouncing around in that room of white executives. Ralph Bunche might have known accounting, but he knew more about political science, in which he had a doctorate from Howard. He had also done a postdoc in anthropology at the London School of Economics. He might even be considered an expert in human rights, having been a key contributor to the UN Universal Declaration of Human Rights after the war. He was, however, not an accountant. Lena Horne, in contrast, was a beautiful woman in addition to being a renowned singer. Yet her beauty and voice would appear to have no bearing on the skill set of a secretary. If secretaries had to be beautiful, and the standards of beauty were white standards, then finding secretarial work for black women would be difficult. If black men needed PhDs and senior positions at the UN to qualify to be an accountant, that would have been even harder.

Winter ignored all this, believing that lowering standards would be the only way to solve black unemployment, and, by extension, urban unrest. If business was "to make a success of our minority hiring programs, we are going to have to hire the person who is not always qualified and make him into a qualified worker."[45] Requirements like a high school diploma would bar black applicants, and Winter encouraged Manpower franchisees to consider whether it was necessary, "so that you can bring in more minority workers."[46]

The story was different for industrial firms, where personnel directors might blame union contracts for forbidding hiring nonunion (black) labor. Winter recounted conversations: "I am willing to put Negroes into an apprenticeship or training program, but the union is balking and won't go along." Winter said, "This is an easy way out." Union locals could be forced to "negotiate out problems" because the "top leadership of the International Unions has made supporting Equal Employment Opportunity" a priority.[47]

Youthpower in Chicago built on deep connections with the black community and addressed the different needs of unemployed black youth. A state senator cut ribbons at the opening of an office. One of the offices was provided not by Manpower, but by the black newspaper the *Chicago Daily Defender*.[48] The first director was a local black elementary-school teacher (who presumably knew all about neighborhood kids). The Youthpower locations in ghetto areas received extra attention and resources. Chicago offices had five paid adult positions, instead of the usual one, so that the young people could receive more personal guidance.[49] These locations were often open year-round instead of just in the summer. The director of the office described their job seekers as "hav[ing] completed their schooling for the present"—in other words, dropouts. At this Youthpower office, the positions were straight factory work "at jobs that [would] give them skills leading to lifetime trades" and a source of self-respect.[50]

The job training was not just occupational, but clearly meant to instill self-pride both as a worker and as an African American. Youthpower sponsored training sessions with a curriculum offering "how to get a job, your Negro-African culture, markets for African products in the U.S., black art in America, and developing a full-time occupation from part-time work."[51] Following Winter's belief that self-respect and labor discipline were entangled, it made sense that learning African history would connect with temporary work.

Youthpower, with its high-level contacts and existing Manpower relationships and methods, found job placement much easier than local nonprofits or even government agencies. In 1968, in Milwaukee alone, Youthpower received 2,011 applications and found jobs for 1,253—or 62 percent.[52] It was at that time in seventeen cities around the country. The standard applications and evaluations, just like at regular Manpower offices, made job candidates more eligible to potential employers who ordinarily would not hire young black people, especially young black people from particular neighborhoods.

For more hard-pressed workers, having job placement assistance at zero cost was essential. A. D. McGee, for instance, had dropped out of school in the seventh grade and worked some construction "back home in Missouri," but wanted to find factory work in Chicago. Youthpower offered a path to that job. Katie Boga dropped out of high school her senior year when she became pregnant. A year later, she needed a paycheck and "hope[d] to work in an office."[53] Without Youthpower, that office job would have been harder to find. These young workers were not the same as college kids looking for book money, but they needed real work, too. Stanley Williams, the local Youthpower director, remarked in 1968 that "three or four years ago when people in [black] Lawndale went job hunting doors were closed to them, but now the doors are opening." Youthpower had relationships with more than 150 companies and had regular job fairs for ghetto residents.

Getting those ghetto workers to the suburban jobs required extra effort on the part of Youthpower, and the offices provided transportation if there wasn't public transit available. Employers "on the fringes of the city," or more accurately, the suburbs, would, according to Williams, "never get into the ghetto" without these job fairs and Youthpower's intervention. Williams's job, then, wasn't just educating teenagers but, as Scheinfeld told the *Chicago Daily Defender*, "educat[ing] businessmen in outlying areas as to the jobs needs of the Lawndale community."

What's in It for Manpower?

Addressing a private group of assembled Manpower office franchisees in 1967, Winter explained how he thought white flight would remake the cities, the suburbs, and the temp industry. The rhetoric in this private lecture to franchisees was, needless to say, blunter than the public voice Winter usually used. Developing a flexible, urban, and especially black workforce was important to Winter, not just for social justice reasons, but to ensure a sustained supply of urban temps in an era of white flight. He told the franchisees that in some cities, the dominant population was, now, black: "In Washington today the population is sixty-three percent Negro, in Newark it is fifty-one percent." He recounted "that in fifteen years there are a number of cities where half of the population of the city will be Negro, including Chicago, Cleveland, Detroit, Oakland, Philadelphia, St. Louis and Trenton." "To have half a city Negro" meant that the "downtowns are going to change" from being areas where white people were comfortable. For instance, "in Philadelphia there are problems of getting [white] girls to come in to the downtown office because they have to take a bus that passes through a Negro area." It caused enough anxiety that "[white] women prefer to be working out in the suburbs." White anxiety made a pressing business case for hiring more black temps for those downtown office buildings.

At the same time, white flight increased temp demand in the suburbs, in those new office plazas. Franchisees were also encouraged to reconsider expanding in cities and instead look to the new suburban industrial parks. Plant closures in the downtowns, as well as office closures, "particularly those adjacent to the Negro area," meant that temporary staffing firms needed to follow their clients—and their preferred, white employees. He felt that the "Negro problem" was at the same level of social importance as the computer revolution, but business came first.[54] Franchisees needed, whenever possible, to create work opportunities for African Americans, but client service came first.

Providing summer employment to ghetto residents had been a win-win way to calm the streets of the American city, to provide moral cover for the expansion of temporary labor, and to train black workers as temps while white workers retreated to the suburbs. Youthpower had provided valuable public relations to Manpower, justifying its expense. In the first five years, Manpower spent about $135,000 (about $965,000 in 2018 dollars) on Youthpower.[55] Articles about Youthpower invariably mentioned Manpower and Elmer Winter, and these articles, which appeared in newspapers and magazines across the country, loved the idea of a private solution to "juvenile delinquency" (if the kids were white) and "ghetto unrest" (if the kids were black). As the summers of the 1960s became the summers of riot and rage, these two separate issues became intertwined, but as those summer riots ended, the pressing need for Youthpower came to an end as well.

Manpower ended its involvement in Youthpower in 1975, citing "declining interest by young persons and a particularly poor job market predicted for this summer."[56] The peak of the program had come in 1968, with five thousand applicants and three thousand jobs. By 1974, there were two thousand applications and fifteen hundred jobs, which doesn't seem like a particularly large drop in demand or success.

More likely than declining interest from job seekers was that Manpower Inc. had a declining interest in Youthpower. The riots, while not forgotten, had not occurred in years. The Great Society was dead. Youthpower's success granted Manpower and Winter political access that led him to provide business educational services to the government during the Johnson administration.

Manpower became a key part of the Great Society's Manpower Development and Training Group as a subcontracted educational organization. The government said to Manpower Inc., as Winter told his franchisees, "When we train people to be welders, Manpower, you train these people to read and write first." Manpower contracted with the government to train the long-term or, as *Fortune* called them, "hard-core unemployed."[57] With revenues of $1.7 million a year, Manpower expected 10 to 15 percent profits. In 1968, Winter had been appointed by President Johnson to serve as the metropolitan Milwaukee chairman of the National Alliance of Businessmen, which set a goal of providing "one hundred thousand jobs for the hard-core unemployed" and "two hundred thousand jobs for youth from low-income families."[58]

When President Johnson left office, he sent Winter a personal telegram to "express [his] very deep personal appreciation" for his work. When Nixon became president, Winter's relationship with the White House continued. Nixon appointed him to his White House Conference on Children and Youth, and he had already been a member of the White House Task Force on Employment and Economy. With the contracts and contacts secure, Manpower's need for Youthpower abated. Perhaps more crucially, Youthpower had served its role of helping to legitimate the proliferation of temporary labor and provide valuable public relations at a moment when the traditional permanent job was still able to be defended.

Uniquely, the same program reached out to both middle-class white and poor black teenagers. Youthpower tailored its methods differently to the suburbs and the ghettos, but rolled both under the same name, with many of the same methods. Through Youthpower, Manpower deployed itself as a resource to help urban youth get their first jobs and understand what it meant to be a worker—and learn just how precarious that work could be. More resources were devoted to ghetto youth because of Winter's views, but the underlying method, like that of Manpower, was the same, promoting a unified vision of labor for men and women, black and white, ghetto and suburb.

Youthpower, Manpower claimed, had provided more than 75,000 positions, but those positions had largely been temporary.[59] Youthpower gave those 75,000 teenagers a preview of the economy to come. When Youthpower coordinator Ronald Franzmeier encouraged job seekers to "look beyond the conventional summer job" and "accept childcare or yard work as substitutes for a full time job" in 1970, because of the bleak job market, it is hard not to think of this as but a portent.[60] Though Winter wanted to provide a job for every young person, the meaning of jobs, in part due to his own efforts at Manpower, was about to change. Youthpower, for black and white alike, became a rehearsal of a new flexible economy in the offing. In the years to come, jobs would be provided, but they would be of the sort that Manpower provided: uncertain, low paid, and precarious, not the kinds of jobs that Allis-Chalmers and other manufacturers had offered the white working class. Regardless of race, in the future, jobs would be temporary.

From Legal to Illegal Migration

In 1964, the controversial Bracero guest worker program officially ended and the very next year, 1965, Congress passed a sweeping revision to U.S. immigration law. Since the 1920s—and reaffirmed in 1952's Immigration and Nationality Act—immigration from the Old World had been capped, initially as a way to reduce the numbers of seemingly unassimilable (and endless) Eastern and southern Europeans. Part of the post–World War I era return to normalcy was to reduce the numbers of all those people—Italians, Poles, Jews, Slovaks, etc.—whose English wasn't quite up to snuff. While these restrictions shut the gates across the Atlantic, however, there were no such restrictions on immigration from the western hemisphere. Mexicans, as well as Hondurans, Cubans, Canadians, and the rest of the New World, could come as they pleased.

By 1965, the sons of those unassimilable immigrants from the 1920s were now congressmen who believed that assimilation was not only possible, it was inevitable, at least for those from Europe. In this new immigration regime, however, immigrants from the New World would be restricted. These restrictions were rolled into a new framework of immigration that prioritized reuniting families on the one hand and admitting high-skill labor on the other. The policy, enacted under the Immigration and Nationality Act Amendments of 1965, intended to continue the American policy of keeping the country looking like the people who already lived there, but with a new openness to global talent.

The challenge, of course, was that the kind of labor that American agribusiness had been importing for two generations was not high skilled, at least in the sense of college degrees and earning potential. The immigration laws did not help Mexicans. The legal number of agricultural workers from Mexico fell from 181,738 in 1964 (already less than half the workforce of the 1950s) to only 18,544 in 1966.[61] When the Bracero Program ended in 1965, there was a sharp increase in the number of undocumented aliens, especially from Mexico.[62] By 1966, 65 percent of deportable aliens were "Mexican nationals seeking work in the United States."[63]

Habits of migration and expectations of remittances could not be easily interrupted. While it was hard to count who came to the U.S., it was far easier to count who was deported. In just one year after the end of the Bracero Program, Mexican deportees rose from 55,349 to 89,751—a rise of 62 percent.[64] The next year, 1967, the number increased by another 19,000.[65] These increases in capture happened without any increases in INS personnel, indicating that there was a real rise in the numbers of migrants.[66]

Congress did not intend for these kinds of laborers to become a part of the citizenry after 1965 any more than they had during the Bracero Program, yet such workers remained necessary. A stopgap measure, the H-2 temporary worker program, was kludged onto the INS immigration programs only a year after the end of the Bracero Program. The H-2 program could not provide sufficient labor to tend to all those American fields. In the gap between H-2 and the INS came a new population of undocumented Mexican workers who, unlike their predeessors, came to work in cities, not the country.

The General

Leonard Chapman had spent his life serving his country. Immediately after graduating from the University of Florida, he had joined the Marines. He rose through the ranks until he found himself, in the last years of the

Vietnam War, as the commandant of the U.S. Marine Corps. After his
retirement, President Nixon appointed him commissioner of the Immigration and Naturalization Service—a seemingly dissimilar job. "Before becoming commissioner," he once told an audience, he "had no idea of the
number or the magnitude of the problems our country faces concerning
immigration and aliens." Chapman found it hard not to see the commonal-
ities between his wartime experience and the "flood of illegal aliens pouring
into this country."[67]

A few years after Chapman's appointment, he addressed a group of
newly minted Americans at their naturalization ceremony.[68] The day
was unimportant—May 11—but the year itself was deeply symbolic: 1976,
the bicentennial, a year in which everyone was thinking through what
it meant to be an American. The previous year, the U.S. received four
hundred thousand legal immigrants. Unacknowledged in his speech, of
course, were the other migrants, those who had come in 1975 and were not
citizens.

In the previous week's address to the American Legion National Commanders Banquet in Indianapolis, Chapman was less circumspect. "As a
military man for thirty-seven years, and Marine commandant for four years,
it has been my responsibility to help ensure that our position against armed
aggression was such that we could turn it back." But in his new role, he told
the attendees that there was, today, "another type of invasion of our country."[69] This invasion was far different from the Soviet invasion that he had
trained for. This one had "gone largely unnoticed. For the perpetrators are
not wearing uniforms, and are not carrying weapons. They are not storming
our beaches under the cover of artillery." This "invasion is a silent one, occurring mainly at night across our unprotected borders." These invaders
were "coming not as an occupation force, but simply to find jobs and to par-
take of the wealth in this great land of ours." Chapman turned the meaning
of "occupation force" on its head. This army was not looking to occupy, but
to work.

This invasion had been turned back before. Operation Wetback had
been pronounced a success. This time, however, the migration was different. As we've seen, it had accelerated in the decade after the end of the Bracero Program—and unlike in 1954, the INS was unable to slow the

migration. In 1965, the INS caught almost 100,000 undocumented aliens. By 1975, that number had risen to about 800,000—nearly all from Mexico.[70]

For two generations, Mexicans had come north to work the fields in far-flung parts of America, just as they had worked the regions along the border since before those lands were part of the United States. The story of this farm labor, both during the Bracero period and afterward, is familiar, as it is a morality tale: Americans don't want these jobs—at least at the prevailing wages. The less studied but perhaps more important side of this story is not what happened in the fields, but what began to happen on the construction sites. Some Mexicans worked in the fields, but many moved to the cities, where they worked in factories and construction.

Every year after 1965, more apprehended undocumented aliens were found working in industry and service than in agriculture.[71] Mexicans came to work in agriculture, but when those legal jobs dried up, they found alternatives. Like temps and consultants, these temporary men would model an alternative for employers. As growth slid into stagnation, however, these migrant men, outside of the postwar labor law, offered a choice for hard-pressed employers.

When INS agents captured and deported these early day laborers, they asked them whether their employers knew that they were undocumented. It turned out that not only did the employers know they were illegal, but the fact that they were illegal was one of the reasons they were hired. Although farm and domestic labor existed, and continue to exist, outside of the labor laws that, since the Fair Labor Standards Act of 1938, guide what employers can and cannot do, construction labor was decidedly regulated. The evasion of those New Deal-era laws was the point.

Chapman challenged the common refrain that the jobs undocumented aliens take are only the low-paying ones no American will have. "Nothing could be further from the truth."[72] Two thirds of the illegal workers apprehended by the INS worked in "industry, service and construction jobs that pay good salaries." In 1975, the year before his American Legion speech, the INS had, for instance, captured 4,700 workers in Chicago, 90 percent of whom were earning over $2.50 ($11.89 in 2018 dollars) an hour. In Seattle, a small factory with only 60 workers had 10 such workers earning $3.21 to $4.25 an hour. The effect was greatest in border states like California and Texas.

Speaking in Houston that year, Chapman estimated that there were between a half million and a million undocumented migrants in Texas alone. Of the migrants apprehended in the previous six months in Houston, "sixty per cent earned over $2.50 per hour," but pay could range much higher, to those who laid utility cables for $6.50 an hour or stevedores who earned "over $6 per hour."[73] These were jobs that Americans, especially Hispanic and black Americans, could no longer have. They were not remote, they were not in fields, they were not badly paid, and they were jobs that Americans wanted. At the time, the INS could not be sure that two thirds of the undocumented actually worked in industry (maybe it was just easier to find people in the cities), but we know now, from those who later applied for amnesty in 1986, that the proportion reflected reality, not policing. Cities were easier to live in than remote farms, especially places like Houston, which had always had a large Spanish-speaking community. Finding a job was easy in Houston's growing economy. Employers, moreover, wanted to hire them, and no law required an employer to check the immigration status of an employee.

Employers preferred illegal laborers for unskilled and semiskilled work for the same reason that office managers preferred temps: benefits and control. The wages might have been good, but the benefits were not—and as Elmer Winter had shown, it was in the benefits that American workers truly became costly. Illegal laborers could be hired or fired at will and forced to do more dangerous work beyond the reach of government inspectors. The undocumented could be compelled to work in conditions that unions, or even the new Occupational Safety and Health Administration (OSHA), which had been founded in 1971, would never permit.

Odd cases defied the general trends in who the INS apprehended. As Chapman told a national assembly of the Sons of Italy in 1976, the undocumented migrants came "from virtually every nation in the world . . . hold[ing] jobs in every income level, from lowly paid busboy through professional positions enjoying earnings of $20,000 a year and even higher." Nonetheless, the main source of migrant labor at this time was Mexico and Latin America, who mostly took jobs not as engineers but as "painters, construction workers, plumbers, welders, [and] clerks." Chapman was sympathetic—he really was—to the desire to come to the U.S. Migrants endured unimaginable hardships in getting here and finding work, but it did not change either the laws broken or the consequences for American workers. At the same time, his relationship to the migrants' condition was fundamentally distant. His speeches are peppered with pronunciations of Spanish names ("Goo-tear-is"), which phonetically reminded him how alien the migrants truly were, even as he attempted to be sensitive to pronunciation.[74]

These migrants were fundamentally different, he would tell audiences like Sons of Italy or the American Legion, from the ones who came legally. Illegal migrants, he told the Legionnaires, "live[d] their lives below the surface of our society," getting by through "deceit and fraud."[75] Separate from mainstream society, they could not assimilate. To Chapman and others who worried about the undocumented migrants, this kind of uncontrolled immigration threatened to create a "mosaic of hundreds of nationalities," rather than a "melting pot."[76] Mexicans could perhaps assimilate, but never if they were undocumented. Of course, these same fears of unassimilable foreigners was exactly why Congress closed the borders in 1921, only opening them again in 1965, after all those Jews and Italians, with their strange foods and exotic languages, had long since been assimilated. But to the men sitting there that night, eating bland convention food—inevitably chicken—Chapman made sense. A "mosaic" could not be a "strong and unified country." For Chapman the issue was certainly cultural, but more important, it was economic. "We cannot," he said, "let America become the haven for all the world's unemployed."

By 1976, Chapman explained, the INS estimated that there were 6 to 8 million undocumented aliens in the U.S., with at least 1 million "holding good jobs that pay well . . . probably another two or three million are holding lesser paying jobs." Studies found that undocumented workers weren't well paid, but most made more than the minimum wage. These were jobs that lesser-skilled Americans—"students, teenagers, minorities, and young Vietnam veterans"—wanted. Of the "forty per cent of black teenagers unable to find a job of any kind," probably some wanted those jobs. With 7 million unemployed, 3 million illegal laborers in jobs that Americans wanted was not a small number. The INS estimated that of a million illegal workers, there were "214,000 in light industry, 150,000 in heavy industry, 335,000 in agriculture and 301,000 in service occupations."[77]

Americans in the grip of stagflation were furious. Polls conducted by the

INS found that 87 percent of Americans thought "the taking of jobs by illegal aliens [was] a serious problem." The number was the same for "persons of Latin American ethnic origin." American citizens, entitled to benefits and protections, believed these migrants made it harder to find work—and they were right. The INS commissioner pointed to studies conducted in cities like San Diego, where INS sweeps had picked up thousands of illegal workers. Contemporary economists estimated undocumented aliens at between 2.2 and 4.1 percent of the entire San Diego labor force.[78] The economists found that within six months those positions that had been held by migrants "were filled by legal permanent residents and other Hispanics." In Chapman's mind, the question wasn't one of "discrimination against foreign appearing applicants," but one of guaranteeing safety and benefits for workers, legal or illegal.

The silver-bullet solution, Chapman and many others thought, was to make employing illegal laborers a crime. More INS agents would cost too much money. Inspecting every worksite in the country would be impossible. Only by bringing fear to employers would the problem be fixed. Otherwise, they took no risk. Employers, of course, resisted such sanctions, and Chapman would never see his solution implemented, because when Jimmy Carter, a Democrat, was elected, Chapman was replaced. Carter may have wanted a solution, but offered only compromise: amnesty for those who had been here for a while, but no new migrants. Carter wanted a more moderate approach to immigration, and looked for someone completely different than the former head of the U.S. Marines.

Constructing Texas

Houston's legal workers got their pride from their work, but also from their unions, which had a contentious relationship with the undocumented. The conventional story of the American South is that it was never unionized, that right-to-work laws kept wages low and the AFL-CIO out. That story is half true. While the industrial unions of the CIO never gained a foothold, the AFL unions, especially in construction, were everywhere in the South, even Houston. These unions were conservative, segregated, and part of the Southern democratic machine. Southern construction unions were strong enough for Nixon to try to break them. When Nixon created the Equal Employment Opportunity Commission, it was, in part, designed to break the southern AFL unions.

Right-to-work laws or not, the South, especially in cities like Houston, was in a construction boom. Skyscrapers were popping up all over the city. Strip malls spread along the highways and frontage roads. Most building trades, like the carpenters' union and the cement masons' union, excluded "blacks and Spanish surnamed Americans." Although most construction unions were white, the Laborers' Union was black—and strong. Despite the seeming interchangeability of unskilled labor, there was a value to having workers show up and do a job on time. When deadlines mattered, having union laborers on site mattered. And contractual deadlines in turn gave those laborers bargaining power.

Consider the 1966 showdown between the Laborers' locals and the Houston builders (represented by the Construction Employers Association of Texas and the Associated General Contractors).[79] The Laborers wanted an exclusive hiring hall. This would have meant a monopoly on all unskilled labor in what was the third or fourth strongest construction market in the country. Weak unions can't make these kinds of outrageous demands. In 1961, the only way that employers had avoided an exclusive hiring hall was through the intervention of the courts; in 1966, the Supreme Court ruled that it was a legitimate issue for bargaining, even in right-to-work states, forcing employers to the bargaining table. Public projects—both in the sense of being paid for by the city and in the sense of being on television—whose financing depended on meeting milestones, like a new airport, a new performing arts center, or a civic center, were all picketed and delayed. The mayor of Houston appeared on television, apparently in support of the strikers, and the employers found themselves blamed for the situation. The employers, in turn, applied pressure by asking lenders, like banks, department stores, and credit clothiers to demand debt repayment so that the workers would have to return to work. After a grinding strike, in which employers missed deadlines on commercial, public, and institutional building work, as well as industrial construction, they came to a compromise.

The strikers didn't get an exclusive hiring hall (something that rarely happened in the U.S.), but they did get, like many other unionists, the promise of a more stable, prosperous life. In Houston at the end of World War II, union laborers made 80 cents an hour ($10.90 in 2018 dollars). Other union workers made more, but none of them received pensions, health care, or vacation days. Back in 1956, the more skilled trades, like electrical workers, got health care and pensions, and even the laborers got a bump to $1.75 ($16.19 in 2018 dollars). By 1963 (during the last contract negotiation), workers in most unions received health care, pensions, apprentice training, and even vacation money. Laborers made $2.41 ($19.65 in 2018 dollars). Then the laborers won the 1966 strike and wages went up even further. Employers now paid into a "health and welfare fund."[80] Union members got double pay on weekends and holidays—and time and half for anything over forty hours. They got paid holidays. They even got special clothes for when it rained heavily (as it does in subtropical Houston nearly every afternoon in the summer). In return, the employers got stability from the laborers, like they got from the electrical workers. They knew what they had to pay, and they knew that the workers would be available and would not strike. The contract enabled Houston builders to bid accurately and efficiently so that they could focus on developing Houston into the most dynamic city in the country—which they did.

Union strength peaked in Houston in the late 1960s. In 1967, for instance, 80 percent of all commercial building were union projects. By 1975, that number had already dropped to 68 percent—just at the moment when migrant Mexicans joined the workforce.

The Bureaucrat

If Chapman feared a silent army of Mexicans to the south, his successor, Leonel Castillo, appointed by President Carter in 1977, felt less anxiety about Mexicans since he was Mexican American himself. Born and raised in Galveston, Texas, on the outskirts of Houston, Castillo grew up speaking Spanish. His father was a union dockworker who had young Leonel help keep the records of union dues at the labor hall because he was literate in both Spanish and English, unlike many of the dockworkers.[81]

After graduating from college and getting a master's degree in social work, he came to Houston in 1967 to become a community organizer, eventually leading protests against the segregated school system in 1969. But the protests, he felt, were ineffective. He wanted a position that would give him more influence. Rather than run for a visible policy making position, he decided to run for the position that controlled the money—comptroller. He thought that it was a winnable office, since the incumbent hadn't had opposition in twenty years.[82] He ran in 1971 and won. Every paycheck and every bill that the city of Houston paid came across his desk. He employed more Hispanics than his predecessor, but his main impact was efficiency, not politics. Instead of purging Anglos from the bureaucracy, as many white Houstonians feared, Castillo set about modernizing the office, installing the first computers (and putting in some nice new curtains). By the mid-1970s, Castillo was one of the most politically powerful Chicanos, not only in Texas, but in the Democratic Party.

The first time Chapman and Castillo met was when Chapman, as the head of INS, came to Houston to make an appearance on a local TV talk show. The show booked Castillo to be his interlocutor. These two men were primed to be antagonists, but afterward they got coffee and, as Castillo later said, "hit it off." Chapman later told him that he "was one of the few Chicanos he'd ever met who didn't yell at him." Castillo, in turn, suggested that Chapman have an advisory committee of Chicanos to help him understand the issues he was confronting. Chapman agreed, because he genuinely could not fathom why Mexican American citizens were wary of his policies. "He'd always dealt with patriotic *mexicanos* in the Marine Corps who were good fighters," Castillo later said, "and he couldn't understand why they weren't being patriotic when it came to defending their border."[83] Militarizing the Border Patrol to defend the border seemed obvious to him. "His life had been geared to military intervention," Castillo remembered, "so when you STOP something, you stop it with an army, or with a package of military activity, with Vietnam-era technology, with more Border Patrol, and sensors, and infrared scopes, and helicopters."

Castillo became the head of the INS in 1977, and saw illegal immigration quite differently than Chapman—as a bureaucratic failure, not a military failure. While Chapman "had managed to get everybody up to a fever pitch about the silent invasion" and "the brown hordes," Castillo tried to humanize the migrants, inside and outside the INS, emphasizing the need to support legal migration rather than just stop illegal migration.[84] Instead of "illegal aliens," Castillo called these migrants, for the first time ever on national TV, "undocumented immigrants."[85]

Castillo still had to secure the borders, but he felt "like a real shit" in doing it. "You're deporting," he said, "young men and women, primarily men, and you knew their sole reason for coming is working."[86] He sat at the border with patrolmen through the dark nights, looking through infrared scopes, and was there as they picked up the migrants.

The undocumented took pride in how hard they worked compared to Americans. In Houston, Castillo visited the apprehended lockup, which he did whenever he visited a city. A young man told him about his life in Houston, working construction, where "many of the workers were undocumented, but the *patrón* really liked the undocumenteds because when it came to work[ing] overtime or under hard conditions the undocumenteds stayed until they were chased off the job." This young man "was real proud of that. 'Americans' would go home at the first *chispas* [raindrops]" while the undocumented would stay.[87] The young man was proud of how the *patrón* believed the undocumented to be "more honorable" because they "worked harder and therefore they were better" than the Americans.[88]

Castillo felt pressure for border enforcement from Mexican Americans, some of whom had crossed the border legally, and some of whom, of course, had had the border cross their ancestors following the Texas revolt and the Mexican-American War. More conservative groups like the League of United Latin American Citizens (LULAC) emphasized the importance of assimilation and legal migration. Even more radical Chicanos, like Cesar Chavez, the famous leader of the United Farm Workers (UFW), demanded that the INS enforce the immigration laws since undocumented workers made organizing legal farmworkers much more challenging.[89] Members of the UFW, according to Castillo, asked to be "deputized" as part of the Border Patrol to "chase the Mexicans and others out of the fields, the worksites." The United Farm Workers were "not any longer the best symbol of Chicanoism. They're a good solid union." Like any union, their strength rested on their ability to exclude new workers and keep employers paying them. In the cities, the competition remained acute.

Indocumentados as construction workers crowded out Americans, including Chicanos.

Castillo's speeches, nonetheless, shifted in emphasis from Chapman's, emphasizing the agricultural labor that "American citizens scorn," rather than the jobs Americans wanted. Castillo didn't pretend that good jobs were not being lost, but it was not his main point. "In Houston, for instance, there are unemployed construction workers," he told a crowd in Washington, D.C., "yet the INS frequently apprehends undocumented aliens working on construction."[90] Castillo agreed that undocumented aliens were displacing legal workers, but did not think it was the main issue like Chapman did. Schools, taxes, medical care, smugglers, and a host of issues mattered as much to him as jobs did. Castillo emphasized service to legal immigrants (like his grandparents) over border enforcement.

Castillo, unlike Chapman, could show up at field offices, dressed normally, and experience being ignored like the other Chicanos without an appointment. Castillo wanted it to be easier for Mexicans, and others, to legally come to the U.S., shifting the focus of the INS away from stopping undocumented aliens to helping legal migrants. Instead of stopping an invasion, Castillo, less dramatically, wanted to automate INS data processing and streamline the bureaucracy.

As with the Houston comptroller's office, Castillo wanted to modernize the INS with office automation. While migrants came illegally across the border, many millions were prevented from coming legally not by a wall of concrete, but by a mountain of paperwork. Immigration applicants waited years to hear back about their cases. Castillo wanted to resolve the 236,000 pending applications quickly. Administrative problems were more easily solved, in some ways, than the policy issues. His predecessor had focused on the battleground; Castillo focused on the office as he had done in Houston, installing the first computers, which could keep track of border entry as well as applications. In New York, for instance, INS "installed a semi-automatic filing system . . . which reduce[d their] space needs by sixty percent and has freed four persons from the file room for other work."[91] Task force teams went from office to office, installing computers and word-processing equipment to increase productivity. Centralized databases of visas were created so that remote offices could dial in and get the data they needed. The backlog was brought under control with these specialized teams, but to keep it manageable, Castillo planned to "automate all handling of files by the end of fiscal year 1980."[92]

Neither Chapman's guns nor Castillo's computers could stop the migration of undocumented Mexicans north. American industry in Texas and California needed workers who would work cheaply, but more important, outside of the law.

Terms of Employment

The rising lack of jobs, both in the U.S. and in Mexico, was the real problem, not the undocumented migrants. Economists, then and now, debated the impact of undocumented migrants on the economy. *Indocumentados* might take jobs, but they also spent money and paid sales tax. Americans could take advantage of their cheaper labor to do other, more lucrative activities, and, of course, as the undocumented spent money they created demand for American goods and services. In the end, a few million jobs this way or that way, in a country of hundreds of millions, where a million people might change jobs in a month, was not really going to push the needle on unemployment too strongly. These macroeconomic variables—except for the low wages of the unskilled, who had nothing to sell but their strong backs—really didn't signify much.

What the undocumented did for employers, as office temps did, was to change the terms of employment for everyone, whether they were legal or illegal. These marginal men were an alternative. The temporary workforce created a space outside of labor law and outside of unions, where the boss was king. The undocumented, like the temps, enabled employers to imagine a workplace without obligations, without regulations, and without oversight.

By the 1970s, the American economy had become dependent on the flexible, cheap labor of Mexicans for its service and industrial work. Within only a few years, the postwar world seemed to suddenly implode, and assumptions about who counted and who deserved stability were up for grabs.

CHAPTER FIVE

Temporary Business

Management consulting had been invented in the 1930s, but it came into its own after World War II, as the preeminent consulting firms like McKinsey & Company skippered postwar corporations across the shoals of a globalizing economy. Manpower Inc. expanded in parallel to McKinsey, both domestically and abroad. That a group of high-skill temps, who pushed corporations to replace their permanent workers with contingent ones, expanded at the same time as the supply of office temps is no coincidence. Manpower and McKinsey both grew from small businesses to international catalysts over the same few decades. Both firms spread nationally in the 1950s and then abroad in the '60s. While McKinsey famously remained one firm, Manpower pushed a new organizational strategy—franchising—to grow. McKinsey's growth, at least in billings, was just as quick, but while Bower focused on quality, Winter focused on quantity. In their growth, American, and then international, corporations began to rely on temps and consultants.

During the war, McKinsey had grown in billings, which increased from $323,000 in 1941 to $979,000 by 1944, but not in staff, as only a handful of associates were hired. The growth came from just a few companies, including the Food Machinery Corporation. FMC was headquartered across the country, in far-off San Jose.[1] To serve FMC and other new clients on the West Coast (which was very hard to get to by train), McKinsey had opened a branch office in San Francisco in 1944. San Francisco was the first, but not the last. McKinsey opened an office in Los Angeles in 1949 and in Washington in 1951, to be at the center of the new government-driven industrial economy.[2] The company even closed the Boston office in 1953. Billings and client growth there had been flat, which Bower attributed to the "negative management attitude toward consultants" in New England. Moreover, none of the partners wanted to move to provincial Boston.[3] The next office would open the same year in Cleveland, which had its own bevy of industrials as well as easy access to Canada, but in the age of airplane travel, consultants could be anywhere. Offices in Dallas, Houston, and Atlanta came in the 1970s.[4] Traveling from New York to San Francisco, as Bower did during the 1940s, would no longer be necessary. These few offices still allowed McKinsey to operate on a national stage.

Manpower may have begun as a family business but, like McKinsey, it rapidly became a national, and then an international enterprise. From 1955 to 1959, Manpower tripled its revenue from $5 to $15 million, unusually fast growth for a family business.[5] With a permanent internal staff of only 375 people, in 1958 Manpower sent out 80,000 temporary workers to the offices of nearly every major American corporation, and its files contained information on 200,000. What made this possible was both the appeal of temps and the canny manner in which Manpower expanded.

Unlike all of the postwar industrial corporations, Manpower's service business required almost no investment. It had no inventories. It had no factories. Its greatest cost remained the labor of its temps, which took up about three quarters of the revenue.[6] As *Fortune* noted, Winter and Scheinfeld needed just enough capital "to buy some office furniture, pay for some advertising, and meet the payroll before the customers pay up." Without the need for heavy investment, any profits allowed them to expand. Expansion, Winter and Scheinfeld realized, was everything. Their business model had meager barriers to entry: price, convenience, quality, and most important, reliability. To establish its reputation for reliability at a national level required expansion; national firms should be able to count on Manpower in every major market. Franchising would make this global presence possible with the minimum of investment.[7]

While we associate the franchise model with McDonald's and the growth of fast food (also in the 1950s), Manpower was actually a pioneer. With its first franchise in 1954, Manpower set about replicating a customer experience for office temps across the country. Franchisees paid for their office. Manpower provided the training for the office managers and staff to make sure they knew what they were doing. In return, Manpower got 5.2 percent of the gross sales. *Fortune* estimated that Manpower spent 1.7 to 2 percent of their franchisees' gross sales on training and support, leaving the firm with 3.2 to 3.5 percent profits, which was "an excellent return with no investment."[8] Company-owned branches returned higher profits (4 to 6 percent) but also required more oversight and investment. As long as standards could be met through the franchisees, Manpower could rapidly take over the industry. It did for work what McDonald's did for the hamburger.

The lure of the franchise was the riskiness of small business. Americans wanted to be in business for themselves, but with a franchise they were not in business by themselves. Winter and Scheinfeld understood the dynamic. They had lost nine thousand dollars in the first year of Manpower from "the usual number of mistakes," and having someone to advise them on advertising and sales promotion, much less know-how, would have been useful.[9] They now offered that expertise to their franchisees.

Prospective franchisees would come to an intensive training course at the Milwaukee office.[10] The initial fee depended on how big the city was, between $20,000 and $75,000, depending on the size of their market.[11] The initial contract was for five years, but could be canceled if the franchisee violated the terms. The franchisees used the Manpower name, as well as the "same advertising materials, sales programs, manuals and forms." By 1956, Manpower had more franchised offices—fifty—than corporate-owned offices—thirty-five. Each year in the 1950s, on average, the company added another nineteen offices.[12] Manpower tried "to keep [its] organizational structure as flexible as possible and to modify it as often as necessary to meet the demands of this growth." A Manpower investigation in 1969 found that these franchisees had done very well: 75 percent of the franchisees earned more than $20,000 ($139,000 in 2018 dollars), 25 percent earned more than $50,000 ($348,000 in 2018 dollars), and 10 percent earned more than $100,000 ($696,000 in 2018 dollars). Three quarters of the franchisees had been with Manpower for ten years or more.[13]

By 1960, Manpower had 200 offices across the country with 130,000 temps and an annual revenue of $35.2 million (around $3 billion in 2018 dollars). More important, 66,000 firms used Manpower services in a year.[14] Winter believed the market for temp help remained virgin territory. A survey commissioned by Manpower in 1960 found that 47 percent of American businesses had never used temporary help.[15] But even the 53 percent who had used temp help was a stunning conquest, considering that this kind of business had been invented in 1948. Supplying business services rather than business products was a clear winner. As Manpower noted in its *Annual Report* in 1962, "Business services are the fastest growing component of our national income, averaging an increase of 10.7 percent annually since 1951." Business services were "five times the size of commercial air transport" but somehow were not considered as "real" as production or transportation.[16]

Franchising enabled Manpower's corporate office growth. The majority of its new locations in the U.S. came through franchising, and this rapid scaling-up brought increased profitability. As Manpower's revenue grew, its earnings per dollar of revenue grew even faster, from 2 percent in 1955 to 4 percent in 1959.[17] With the domestic growth funded by the franchise owners, Manpower's capital was freed up to expand abroad.

Incorporating for Growth

Incorporating enabled both McKinsey and Manpower access to the capital they needed to continue to grow. While Manpower looked to capital markets to fund its growth by selling stocks and issuing bonds, McKinsey used incorporation to act more like a postwar industrial firm by retaining earnings and reinvesting profits.

Manpower's initial public offering (IPO) of its stock in 1959 was as midwestern as the company itself, through the offices of Smith, Barney in Chicago (though it was a New York-based investment bank).[18] After the IPO, Scheinfeld and Winter stilled controlled 71 percent of the stock, selling off only 24 percent to the public market.[19] By the time of its IPO, Manpower served ninety-seven of the top one hundred corporations in the United States.

If the low capital requirements allowed Manpower to expand, it also made it challenging to be evaluated by Wall Street analysts, who, used to pricing industrial corporations, could easily undervalue the firm. A large component of the value of industrial firms was the value of their assets—like factories. Manpower had none of these, and a large fraction of its offices were franchises.

In 1962, Winter tried to clarify to these analysts how to think about Manpower—and its stock price. Winter explained how to compare his no-assets company with a manufacturing enterprise: Service firms did not operate at the scale of Manpower. Manpower had the revenues of a manufacturing company. Manpower was a corporation in Delaware with dozens of subsidiaries across the world. Manpower was publicly traded on the NYSE. Service firms were usually partnerships in one city. How, then, should Manpower be valued on the market? To Winter, "the answer is that the greatest asset that a service industry has, namely its personnel, does not appear on a balance sheet."[20] Winter tried to explain to security analysts that Manpower had a margin on its main cost—workers. Every temp's wages had a standard markup. In 1962, for every dollar billed to a client, the worker's wages and benefits made up seventy-five cents. To keep Manpower managers from cutting those margins, they received bonuses based on profitability, not sales, so there was less incentive to cut prices and grow volume.[21] The IPO happened, and Wall Street found new ways to think about what to value in a firm beyond production.

Manpower was everywhere, but so was McKinsey.[22] McKinsey also incorporated around that time, in 1956, as its scale began to outstrip the legal boundaries of a partnership.[23] On the most basic level, McKinsey "partners" would no longer be actual partners—that is, they would not be liable for the debts of the firm and would be (along with associates and everybody else) personally shielded from lawsuits.[24] McKinsey would incorporate, but, unlike Manpower, it did not sell any of its stock publicly.

Like temp agencies, consulting did not require heavy capital investment, but opening offices abroad still cost some money. While partnerships needed to distribute their earnings, corporations could retain their earnings and reinvest them. McKinsey used its incorporation to fund expansion abroad by enabling greater retained earnings, not, like Manpower, by selling stock. This simple shift allowed McKinsey, which was wildly profitable, to fund their overseas growth in the 1960s.[25] For McKinsey, incorporation also allowed the firm to more easily share its profits across generations.

Unlike at Manpower, equity ownership at McKinsey provided motivation for a broad range of its personnel. Few temps would have expected to own Manpower, but every consultant who wanted a career at McKinsey wanted a share of the profits. As partners retired, they could sell their stock to the next generation and potentially make a tidy profit on the capital gains.[26] In 1956, the U.S. had changed its laws so that a corporation could establish a "tax-sheltered profit-sharing retirement plan."[27] If McKinsey became a corporation, it could contribute up to 15 percent of an employee's income to a fund that would accumulate tax free until retirement. For high-salaried consultants, 15 percent of salary and bonus could really add up. In the following decades, McKinsey's standard would match 12 percent.[28] Even if an associate left, they could count on that retirement fund in their later years. The flexible savings prefigured the 401(k) that we have today. There were no defined benefit plans for consultants.

McKinsey, though incorporated, still operated culturally as a partnership. McKinsey partners (now actually stockholders) owned the firm. Bower idealized the partnership, which for him meant independence from outside shareholder demands, which allowed McKinsey to say no to clients and maintain professional independence. They would not have to sacrifice professional standards for shareholder returns. While other consultancies and accountancies would later dance with going public, McKinsey never did, largely because of Bower's example. At sixty, when he was still the managing director, he sold his shares back to the firm—at book value. "Young people have got to get some shares," Bower said. "They have to gain a sense of ownership."[29] Bower believed in investing for the long-term rejuvenation of McKinsey, even as he focused on the short-term needs of its clients.

The instant wealth of an IPO meant little to Bower compared to his deeply held belief in his firm. During the later "go-go" years of the middle 1960s, Bower would receive IPO offers for McKinsey stock on a regular basis. He told the partners, but he always declined. To sell the stock publicly would eliminate McKinsey's independence, and that independence was everything to him.[30] The pressure for growth, to make that next sale, would hobble other, more important, considerations.

Incorporating these two firms allowed their stock issues and retained earnings to bring the American model of temporary labor and management consulting to Europe and Asia.

Consultants Abroad

Before Gil Clee came to McKinsey, where in 1967 he would become the first successor to Marvin Bower, he had worked as a Latin American loan officer for the World Bank.[31] Before that, he had been a partner in a New York financial consultancy.[32] He was a cosmopolitan, international man, "a conceptual thinker," as Bower described him, which is probably the highest praise Bower could bestow. In the 1950s, Bower and Clee watched their American clients rebuild Europe and then begin to move abroad.

While we tend to think of globalization as a feature of the 1970s, when Americans began buying their cars from Europe and their radios from Japan, American firms had begun moving overseas in large numbers much earlier. The globalization that emerged after World War II was not like the pre–World War I global trade. After World War II, countries didn't simply exchange goods—firms moved their production overseas. They became multinational. While global trade had defined the nineteenth century, global production would define the world after the 1970s, as the president of ACME observed, "multinational companies [moved] factors of production—capital, technology, management techniques—as well as merchandise."[33] Beginning in the late 1950s, consultancies and temp agencies had followed their clients overseas. Bower thought this was "the most important benefit of incorporation," since the enabled growth allowed McKinsey to support American corporations in the reconstruction of Europe and Japan.[34]

At first, in the 1950s, according to Bower, McKinsey partners had no intention of serving international clients, simply of supporting U.S. firms, like when IBM opened a Paris office and needed market-entry support, or ITT asked McKinsey to have a look at their multinational organizational structure.[35] Through these early studies, partners learned what clients needed as they moved overseas. Other firms, like Booz Allen (which was in fifteen countries by the late 1950s), had already trailed their clients, and if McKinsey was to remain competitive domestically, it would need to venture abroad, too.[36]

Their first entrée into a larger world came in 1956, when the head of Royal Dutch Shell, John Loudon, asked McKinsey to examine its organizational structure in its Venezuelan operations. Bower himself oversaw the study, which lasted a year. Though he spent weeks in Venezuela, the engagement manager and associate lived there for the year. During the study, Bower also spent time in London and The Hague, where Royal Dutch Shell had their headquarters. Pleased with the results, Loudon asked McKinsey and Bower to conduct a full organizational analysis of Royal Dutch Shell in 1957.[37]

Bower, two engagement managers (American Lee Walton and British Hugh Parker), and two associates remade Shell, and by extension the organization of multinational corporations, in a way that would endure for three decades. Few examples illustrate the power of consultants as does this McKinsey reorganization of Shell into one of the first matrix corporations.[38] The matrix corporation was the first attempt at reorganizing corporations to acknowledge and take advantage of multinational production.[39] McKinsey's international move, then, helped other corporations operate multinationally.

The first big corporations, like General Motors, were organized by product (Chevrolet, Oldsmobile, Cadillac, etc.). But corporations can be organized along many different lines: by function (marketing, manufacturing), by geography (state, region, country), or by business sector (agriculture, retail). A conventional approach to multinational operations would have been to have marketing divided by region, or region divided by function (like marketing and manufacturing). The matrix form instead allowed for all three axes to intersect in shared governance of an activity, so that, for example, manufacturing in France for retail would be at the intersection of a matrix. Obviously, responsibility can be much more confused than in a traditional hierarchy, but the matrix system allows the quick flow of know-how around a firm, so that, for instance, a multinational's factories in Germany and Wisconsin can be overseen by both manufacturing experts and regional experts. With McKinsey's help, Shell adopted the form in 1959 and it held, with minor changes, until the 1990s, when, once again, McKinsey reviewed its organization.[40]

Building on this success at Shell, McKinsey opened its London office in 1959, with Gil Clee as the partner in charge and Hugh Parker as office manager. Though the motivation was, as the opening announcement read, to support its existing clients in "the emergence of a more highly integrated world economy," McKinsey was also open to new European clients.[41] As they moved overseas, however, the partners insisted that they would not work their way up the ladder from piddling firms to the big players. The consultants would work only on "studies of top-management problems for major corporations." The young European Common Market, which began in 1958, would create many new opportunities in those firms.[42] If McKinsey could not sustain this kind of business, they would, Bower later wrote, "withdraw."[43]

McKinsey did not need to withdraw. The London office, instead, brought the multidivisional corporation to Europe. Over the next few years, they picked up major clients, beginning with Imperial Chemical Industries in 1962, including Cadbury Schweppes, Rolls-Royce, Shell-Mex and BP, and Unilever. U.S. clients needed support, but McKinsey unexpectedly found that most of their billings came from European firms looking for American-style overhaul. When Paul Chambers, the chairman of Imperial Chemical Industries, approached McKinsey, it was to do a study for ICI "like the one you made for Shell."[44]

As McKinsey, Manpower, and other U.S. multinationals grew in Europe, European journalists like Jean-Jacques Servan-Schreiber sounded what a McKinsey partner later called an alarm about American management.[45] In books like his *Le Défi Américain* (*The American Challenge*), Europe was seen as backward. Unless Europeans adopted American managerial styles, Europe would fall behind. The demand for American professional services, like Manpower and McKinsey, increased as Europeans encountered the new management and workforce techniques. "Clients were really knocking down the doors," the partner said, "at a faster rate than McKinsey could serve them." American management methods were welcomed, even if there was a broader anxiety in Europe about American firms taking over their companies. "McKinsey was seen as the way," Bower later said, "to get that American management know-how." The firm became known as reorganization specialists. They even became a verb. A firm that was reorganized was "McKinseyized."[46] McKinsey had no offices in countries like Spain, where there were no multidivisional corporations until the 1980s. In contrast, in Britain, seventy-two of the one hundred largest businesses used the M-form structure by 1970, and nearly half of those had transformed their organization under the guidance of McKinsey itself.[47] As European firms looked to the bigger Common Market, they learned from

McKinsey how they could operate over vast spaces (as in the U.S.).[48] Later, in 1966, a leading UK management journal, *Director*, would describe the arrival of McKinsey in London as "a management revolution in British business."[49]

By the mid-1960s, McKinsey had offices across the continent: Amsterdam, Dusseldorf, and Paris were opened in 1964, and Zurich in 1966.[50] Cultural differences proved challenging, especially when they were at odds with the temporary relationships of consulting. Swiss clients did not like the rotating staff, concerned as they were about stability and secrecy. German companies were more egalitarian than American firms. Bower regarded cultural differences as a serious obstacle, agreeing with anthropologists that "the typical person has acquired his pattern of behavior, including his attitudes and values, by the time he is 25 or 30."[51] Explaining to clients how American consulting worked, and why it worked better, made expansion in Europe harder.

Later, in the 1970s, Peter Drucker would look to these years and remark that "company after company, often with the help of U.S. consultants, has reorganized itself on the decentralized American model—Britain's Imperial Chemical Industries, Germany's Siemens, Japan's Hitachi, the Bank of England and the British Coal Board, Royal Dutch Shell, and France's Renault." Major corporations in every country followed the American M-form model and looked to American consultants to help them shape their organizations. The M-form corporation became part of the global capitalist order.[52]

Unlike today, when a McKinsey associate can work Monday through Thursday in Brazil and live in Manhattan (though with a great deal of red-eye on that Friday in the New York office), associates and partners were expected to relocate overseas, with or without their families. Some resisted.[53] Bower saw this as a failure of character, since he and Clee comfortably did whatever the clients, or the firm, needed. In the U.S., the New York office exported partners to every other office, but it was harder to get consultants to relocate abroad. Many of the new associates and partners were recruited from abroad. Guaranteeing the "same top-management approach" overseen by "American directors" would require vigilance. Though Bower celebrated the idea of one firm, globalizing while maintaining the same standards and culture would prove challenging. The same kind of training that was needed to standardize Manpower's temps and franchise managers would be needed at McKinsey as well.

McKinsey's Tokyo office opened in 1970, though it had been discussed since 1964.[54] If the cultural gaps with Europe were hiccups, in Japan they were asphyxiations. McKinsey relocated the Zurich manager to Tokyo and used Japanese junior staff (who were trained in San Francisco), like Kenichi "Ken" Ohmae, to provide the bridge between cultures.[55] Staffing the Tokyo office proved difficult, though, because of what Bower called "special cultural problems such as 'lifetime' employment by the major companies."[56] His ideal, the up-or-out law firm, turned out to be culturally specific, and undoing professional security in these other countries was more challenging than he had expected.

American management in the 1960s would reshape the world, and McKinsey would become the filter through which these ideas circulated. Hugh Parker, during a BBC interview in 1969, explained it simply: "Germans at one time have led the world in chemistry and the Swiss, if you like, in precision instruments. America, I think, does lead in management, and we can bring that skill to this country."[57] But always, behind these technocratic impulses toward a "universal management" rested other realities: cultures were different, people were different, and, most important, workplaces were different.

Servicing Multinationals

"As the world continues to shrink," Winter told a meeting of investment clubs in 1961, "we are carrying our Manpower program to the four quarters of our globe."[58] The domestic franchises allowed Manpower to focus its efforts overseas, opening 135 corporate-controlled offices in the decade after 1956.[59] As early as 1962, 10 percent of Manpower's revenues came from overseas.[60] Manpower abroad had begun in Paris. The success of the Paris office turned on Michael Grunelius, who came to Manpower after running the Parisian Diners' Club operation. American corporations needed the same temporary support abroad as they had in Milwaukee. Focusing on business-machine operators and security guards, Grunelius rapidly grew the Paris office. Building on that base, Manpower rapidly showed French firms how to use temps as well.

As *Fortune* noted in 1968, "One of the paradoxical consequences of the private welfare state that unions and management have created to safeguard the permanent worker has been to make his temporary colleague look increasingly attractive."[61] When this was written, the temp industry employed at least a million workers. Manpower was twice the size of its nearest rival, now Kelly Services instead of Kelly Girl, but it had become a model for the temp agencies that had sprung up in every city in the United States and abroad. Despite the student occupation of its Paris office during the events of May 1968, Elmer Winter could envision the massive expansion of its European operations in the coming decade. "French businessmen are willing to enter joint ventures and welcome us," Winter said upon his return from a vacation to Nice that year. What the French desired, he remarked, was American management skills and know-how.[62] Manpower was not only serving American multinationals in France—98 percent of its clients were French. It was disseminating American management styles and ideas of work.

As *Fortune* reported on Manpower's growth, it took a derisive, almost colonial, tone when describing the "native businesses" in Tokyo and Bangkok that had "excess personnel because of the abiding paternalism which dictate[d] that once hired no one can be fired except for grievous cause."[63] This, the magazine believed, created an opportunity for Manpower. Domestically, *Fortune* may have pointed to the excesses of the welfare state, but the same critique could extend abroad. Winter observed that "in many countries . . . new social legislation is making it more difficult for companies to terminate an employment relationship. The cost of termination pay is mounting."[64] This attempt to legislate job security only incentivized affected firms to turn to Manpower.

Demand for Manpower continued to grow. By 1968, France alone accounted for 9 percent of Manpower sales, and Paris was its largest office.[65] Manpower opened its first operation in Asia, in Tokyo, that year.[66] By the end of the 1960s, 20 percent of Manpower's sales were overseas.[67]

In many ways, Manpower continued to operate like a family business rather than a multinational during this period.[68] The leadership of the firm was hard to disentangle from the founding personalities of Scheinfeld and Winter. Even though it had been a public firm since 1959, the top two positions into the 1970s were still held by Winter and the son of Aaron Scheinfeld, James Scheinfeld. In the late 1960s, the Scheinfeld and Winter families still held 54 percent of the outstanding stock, making Manpower closer to a privately held family firm than a publicly traded corporation.[69] Unlike most postwar industrials, like General Motors, which were accountable to their boards, Winter and Scheinfeld truly commanded the operation, like industrial magnates of the previous century. Winter believed in Manpower's bold future. In 1968, he told a crowd of franchisees that Manpower would be a billion-dollar company by 1981. "You might ask, 'Have I been taking LSD as part of the "happening"'? I'm standing on firm ground."[70]

Poised for Crisis, Poised for Growth

Marvin Bower's last day as the managing director at McKinsey was October 13, 1967. Though the transition had been in the works for years, it happened, finally, at a lunch at the Princeton Club in New York, when Bower told the crowd that when he sat down, Gil Clee would assume his role. Bower had been the managing director of the firm since 1950, and in a very fundamental sense, it was more his than it was Mac McKinsey's. Bower would remain with the firm into his eighties, but he would never again steer the ship.

In all things, Bower led by example. When he retired, he sold his own shares back to the firm at book value, rather than their actual market value, and made no gigantic fortune from nurturing McKinsey for thirty years. Bower wanted the firm to last "in perpetuity," and that mattered more to him than to "get rich."[71]

Marvin Bower brought, as Hugh Parker later said, "the sort of *Cleveland Plain Dealer* thing" to the world of management consulting.[72] He was a straight shooter in a world filled with would-be hucksters. For years he refused to fly first class, even though he was, by the 1950s, invited to presidential inaugurations.[73] He thought of consulting as a profession, not as a

business. His ethical concerns, authentic and to the bone, were omnipresent. Yet at the same time, his ethics were a businessman's ethics. He believed in honesty, but he also believed in profit.

It is, perhaps, easy to be cynical about Bower's beliefs in integrity and in
character, but in the final analysis, he practiced what he preached. He gave
up his fortune, and in return, he lived the professional independence that
mattered most to him. He and McKinsey were not beholden to any shareholders.

Gil Clee, unfortunately, remained with the firm only a short while.
Maybe second only to Bower, Clee had defined McKinsey in his leadership
of its expansion overseas. The following year, Clee tragically contracted
lung cancer and passed away.[74] After his death, the managing director role
came and went from man to man within a few years. The continuity of postwar leadership had ended. Bower's singular focus on professionalism began
to blur.

Clee's successor, Lee Walton, became managing director in 1968. The
big challenge, as he outlined in a firmwide memorandum, "The Firm 1968:
The Challenge of Self-Renewal," would be to engage with the new finance-
frenzied, technology-driven economy.[75] McKinsey would need to rethink
its relationship with investment banking, venture management, and management information systems to remain viable. The firm seriously considered going public, participating in joint ventures with other firms, and other
kinds of heresy.[76]

Bower's retirement and Clee's passing marked the end of postwar consulting but, in a larger sense, coincided with the end of the postwar economy. Within a few years, the corporate world that Bower had so carefully
stewarded would begin to come apart.

CHAPTER SIX

Office Automation and Technology Consulting

A rthur Gager, the staff director for the National Office Managers Association, framed automation in the 1950s as the choice between flexibility and inflexibility. "Machines should be used instead of people whenever possible," he explained. "Machine power has but one disadvantage—inflexibility," and thus workers' only advantage was flexibility. Machines don't get tired. Machines don't want overtime. "Employees," in contrast, "must be kept happy with Christmas parties, pleasant surroundings, cheerful co-workers, music, morning coffee, personal telephone privileges, and weekly pay periods; machines don't present morale problems."[1] Effective office machines were few and far between, but running those machines required people who would not want, or at least not be able to demand, any Christmas parties either. Temps fit the bill perfectly—but so would computers.

Which to choose? Luckily, these choices were not mutually exclusive. In fact, temps and automation complemented one another. The rise of computers and the rise of temps went hand in hand. Starting as a special project, corporations discovered through the experience of data entry in the 1960s that temporary labor could be a permanent part of their workforce. Behind every computer was a woman inputting data.

Overseeing this migration and implementation would be consultants who focused on cutting costs through technology—but these consultants would, oddly enough, come from accountancies. Cutting costs was only a short step from auditing the books, and accountancies like Coopers & Lybrand found themselves offering consulting services alongside their accounting services. Temps typed and consultants planned, and in the process, office jobs began to be deleted.

Planned Staffing for Profit

Beginning in the late 1950s, Elmer Winter struggled with the natural limits of emergency replacement and began to consider other ways in which temps could be deployed in the workforce. The growth opportunity for temporary labor firms, he figured, was not in the yearly crunch or in the odd emergency, but, as he wrote, in the "regularly occurring tasks that can be performed more cheaply by temporaries."[2] From there, he imagined entire functions being subcontracted to Manpower. By the early 1970s, Winter envisioned Manpower as what we would today call a platform—the basis on which everything else operated. But convincing corporations to abandon how they operated was easier said than done—even if it was cheaper. The best way to convince a firm to use temps was to give them a taste of how useful, and cheap, they could be.

Once a firm started using temps, the opportunities to use them elsewhere became more apparent. First Wisconsin National Bank, headquartered in Milwaukee, "made its first use of leased personnel (for statistical typing)" in 1959. By 1965, Manpower temps were stenographers and typists, but also hostesses and elevator operators during special events. They worked the booth during account promotions (offering free "genuine leather billfolds" for signing up). They even checked the backgrounds of loan applicants, despite that task's highly confidential nature. In just this one company, we can see the quick spread from emergency replacement (stenographer) to flexible workforce (booth promotions) to replacement of core function (credit checking). This bank was in Elmer Winter's hometown, and it is difficult to imagine that location played no part in First Wisconsin's adoption of Winter's vision of workforce management.[3]

More common in 1965, according to *Bankers Monthly*, was the older form of the business: emergency replacement. Although only one instance of workforce planning like that used by First Wisconsin was offered, many examples of emergency replacement were preferred: a five-week stenographer in Chicago, six securities clerks in Houston, interest calculators in Boston.[4] Manpower was not alone. Kelly Girl, by 1961, sold a service that they called "stabilized staffing," which like Manpower helped by "keeping a company's own staff to absolute minimum."[5] Yet, like Manpower's model, it did not catch on.

As early as the 1958 recession, Manpower had introduced their "controlled overhead plan," which had attempted to show firms how to use temps to meet peak demand in their labor force. The most obvious example was the Christmas shopping rush, but such seasonal work also plagued florists at Easter and accountancies at tax time. Greater staffs were needed not just to bring in the harvest, but in all kinds of service-sector work. Cycles did not have to be yearly. They could be monthly or even weekly. As we've seen, firms that staffed up for that periodic work carried too many extra employees the rest of the time; Winter imagined those jobs filled by temps. Taking into account the excess staff during the valleys, Manpower would reckon the cost of those employees against the cost of temporary help during the peaks. Manpower, of course, helped in the cost analysis, and "many managers, when they [took] a close look at the situation [have] been truly amazed by the cost savings."[6] "Billing, filing or preparation of monthly reports" could be done by temps, Winter said, "leaving the regular employees free to give full attention to their normal duties." But what if those jobs *were* the normal duties? These savings would violate all the moral foundations of postwar work. If temps could handle all the routine work, then there was an opportunity to break complex jobs into simpler repetitive tasks—and replace those perms with temps. Everywhere Winter looked, there were opportunities for growth, wherever work was repetitive but variable—yet firms stubbornly refused to replace their staffs.

"Businessmen today are caught in a serious profit squeeze," Elmer Winter told a roomful of Houstonian personnel managers in 1964, "and in order to return a true profit to the company, there must be more precise and dynamic management."[7] The old days of hiring to meet peak demand were over, he insisted. As he had been saying for years, job security was a threat to American security. Speaking to a trade group in 1960, he remarked, "I would support that if you would ask the man on the street today in America what is of greatest interest to him, he would answer: 'A good job, good health, and security for himself and for his family.'" But Winter believed that the "old days are gone . . . and plans must be the order of the day."[8] These plans would bring American labor costs more in line with global forces. The alternative was to lose out to communism. He offered data. He presented examples. Still, few firms took him up on his offer, despite his rhetoric and his data.

Such an ambitious reimagination of work could not really take hold until the business world had a pressing need for alternative labor in the climate of stagnating profits that came in the late 1960s. Winter renewed the push in the mid-1960s under the name Planned Staffing for Profit.[9] The plan considered temporary workers to be a long-term solution to personnel challenges, intended for "advanced planning . . . where management uses the service as a repetitive management tool to be applied in given sets of circumstances." Planned staffing would be as transformational to business, Winter told a room of management executives at the American Management Association, as scientific management.[10] Manpower offered businesses what Winter called "a new 'science' of workforce management" that through its workforce formula would allow them to create a staff of part-time and temporary workers as well as the traditional permanent.[11]

Winter's ideas were contrarian, and his speeches should be understood as sales pitches. The key parts of his prescient program were "downstaffing," "upstaffing," and "spotstaffing." Downstaffing cut staff, especially in departments where the workload was cyclical (like monthly billing or reports). Temps could be hired for just the first ten days of the month. Upstaffing, in contrast, allowed firms that "have trimmed their office staffs to a minimum" to experiment with having an additional worker in a particular role. Rather than risk a permanent hire, they could try out a temp to see if it made a difference. Spotstaffing was for onetime or yearly staffing needs like microfilming, inventories, or the holiday rush. In every case, the ideal was a much smaller core office staff, with a flexible set of temporary laborers deployed as needed.[12]

For these and other tasks, Manpower could graph the "peaks and valleys of work activity." These variations could be "forecasted; they occur on a weekly, or a monthly, or seasonal or some other regularly recurring basis." The firm would then "hold its regular staff down to a level need[ed] to handle low-load work requirements."[13]

A sign that opportunity existed, without conducting a detailed investigation of operations, could be found in a company's overtime billing. A temp paid straight time was cheaper than time and a half for a regular worker, even without factoring in benefits, turnover, and efficiency.[14] Some companies would not sign on. Kansas City Life, for example, kept workers' overtime "because they had a strong feeling that there wasn't such a thing as a temporary job. It was either a full-time job or it didn't exist, so they used overtime to get the work done."

Beyond the office, Manpower could supply industrial and retail workers. General Electric, for instance, around 1966 got a onetime order for thirty-five thousand handwired computer boards. GE had eight weeks to assemble the boards. Manpower supplied 258 people to work "three shifts for six weeks" with one GE supervisor. The boards were wired in much less than the allotted time. The supervisor told Manpower that "with our help they were able to produce more boards at less cost, and with less scrap, than ever before."[15] Retail labor could also be remade along these lines. Goldsmith's department store in New York contained the usual rhythms of retail life: "Rush hours during lunch hour; a slow period during the afternoon; another peak around 5 p.m.; a slow time during the dinner hour, and another rush before closing." Rather than protecting the core workers, Manpower enabled them to be fired. A four-hour shift of afternoon temps supplemented the now constantly busy smaller group of permanent employees, eliminating the "bored clerk standing around doing nothing."[16] Manpower took care with these arrangements, assigning an account executive to each firm to get to know its special staffing needs. Most temps could be supplied from the general pool, but some—Winter estimated 10 percent—required special training. Neiman Marcus needed temps who could run their special billing machines at Christmastime, and it simply wouldn't do, at a luxury department store, to have incompetent checkout staff.[17]

Winter was uniquely positioned to teach corporate America how to cut their workforces. "Manpower serv[ed]," Winter told the American Management Association audience, "virtually every company on the Fortune 500 list." "The largest life insurance companies, the biggest banks, the biggest retailers, the largest manufacturers" all used Manpower services.

"There is virtually no field of endeavor today that does not make some use of temporary help."[18] So if Manpower rolled out a new program to cut corporate workforces, it mattered. Every Fortune 500 company found out about Planned Staffing for Profit at once, learning how they could cut their workforces.

Consider the insurance company Minnesota Mutual in St. Paul, Minnesota.[19] New management wanted to boost profits, so they commissioned a "work measurement study done for it by an outside consulting firm," which found it was "overstaffed by some 15 percent to 20 percent." One of the reasons for this overstaffing was to compensate for the "relatively high turnover" of over 35 percent per year in the insurance industry, which "hir[ed] a lot of young girls out of high school." High turnover meant that temporary labor could help. Manpower, in conversation with Minnesota Mutual, "suggested that this vehicle [of Planned Staffing for Profit] might really accomplish their goal of operating more profitably," even though temps cost more at first glance than regular workers. Manpower suggested that the workforce be "allowed to drop—through attrition—to the level need for the slackest month of the year." High turnover would cut staff without having to fire anyone.[20] Not firing workers was as strategic as sentimental. It was difficult to know ahead of time which workers would turn over. Fire the wrong people and you would undershoot the staffing level. The most committed workers would stay. Winter acknowledged that this plan was "a radical suggestion," but Minnesota Mutual agreed to test it in two departments.[21]

Minnesota Mutual staffed 111 jobs with temps—saving the company about $4,500 a year ($34,000 in 2018 dollars) per job after including the additional cost of planned temporary labor. After three years, the plan was deemed a success, and Dave Haskins, a vice president, told the press, "I saved my company $450,000 [$3.4 million in 2018 dollars] a year through work measurement and the planned use of temporary help."[22] Cutting costs to grow profits is always easier than increasing revenues. Profit as a percentage of revenue in any healthy business is always very small, usually 5 to 15 percent. An additional dollar of revenue might only be 5 to 15 cents of profit, whereas a dollar of eliminated cost is one whole dollar of additional profit. Faced with stiff orders, cutting costs is the sure route. "A thousand dollars in savings per year," Winter said, "is worth substantially more than new product or service sales."[23] The planned staff increased the happiness and morale of the other staff, Winter claimed, because it eliminated busywork and kept them engaged in more complicated tasks. These workers, in turn, could be better paid.[24] The ideal of a real job was defended, he believed, by finding cheaper people who were not formally part of the firm to do the work.

Filling these kinds of jobs was not difficult, at least according to Bank of America's vice president of personnel relations, Frank Young. Consider Bank of America in 1965. In one branch in northern California, "two middle-aged housewives" arrived "every afternoon at two o'clock." Without much kerfuffle, they settled in at a desk and began to file checks. They worked for two or three hours and then they left. These women were part-timers, and their relationship with work was different from the temps who worked at banks. At Bank of America, about 14 percent of the workforce (3,800 of 27,500) did "spot work . . . to permit management to make the most effective use of its full-time personnel."[25] In service-oriented businesses, like retail or office work, part-timers were relatively easy to find—especially compared to manufacturing work. So while lumberyards found it difficult, banks found it easy, and the difference here was, of course, gender. Filling part-time jobs for women's work like this was straightforward. In both cases, however, whatever the ease of hiring part-timers, temps could be used for the labor since they were even easier to find and cheaper.[26] Through the postwar era, however, most firms continued to use in-house staff, seeking to fill roles permanently.

Planned staffing also allowed them to use temps anywhere outside the core operations of the firm.[27] Scheinfeld and Winter were proud of how their "customers placed greater emphasis on the use of our services to perform large-scale jobs, requiring the use of entire crews of our personnel, including supervisors." Whole units ranging in size from "20 to more than 300 of our employees" could be subcontracted.[28] For instance, the Baker Industrial Truck Company needed to take an annual inventory of its stock. To do so required shutting down the entire factory and using their own expensive people. Instead, with Manpower's help, during Baker's two-week summer vacation, three hundred temps (whose wages were more than 30 percent lower) came to the plant and took stock. Instead of shutting down for two weeks' vacation and one week of inventory, the truck company could shut down for two weeks, losing no production time. The temps did the inventory in three days; the plant staff and workers got their vacation. And Baker saved, they estimated, a hundred thousand dollars in lost production and wages.[29]

It was a short step from these one-off situations to the permanent outsourcing of noncore functions. Some corporation functions, like security and janitorial services, were already moving in that direction, but Manpower wanted to take it to the next level. They cited a Chicago warehouse that outsourced its labor to Manpower, transforming its unemployment benefits for fired workers from 2.7 percent to 0.5 percent of payroll. Since temps were not employees, the warehouse didn't have to pay unemployment insurance, and if they left, it did not have to pay their share of the workers' unemployment. Manpower, moreover, being a temporary firm, found it easier to avoid paying unemployment insurance.[30] In most states, workers needed to prove regularity of work—in pay and in hours—to claim unemployment, as well as a lack of offers of reasonable employment. The irregularity of hours made it easy for states to refuse to pay the claims. Temps, as well, could just as easily move to another temp agency. Employers with higher unemployment claims were charged more by the government, so by keeping those claims low, temp agencies could lower overall costs for clients. Proving these claims invalid—either through their own wage and hour records or through a lack of a temp applying to another agency and not getting a job—proved trivially easy, especially compared to handling laid-off workers looking for permanent work.

The possibility of subcontracting whole segments existed, especially for mailings and inventories. For specific tasks like envelope stuffing (which would occur during a billing cycle), it made sense to have Manpower do all the work. A management consultancy studied the productivity of temps and perms doing the same repetitive tasks, like envelope stuffing, transcribing, and typing. In all three common office jobs, the Manpower employee's efficiency was higher than or comparable to that of the permanent worker. Even if the cost of the permanent worker was lower per hour, the temp could make up the higher wage with higher productivity. If a Manpower temp could stuff 485 envelopes per hour, the New York Transportation Company managers must have wondered why they paid for permanent workers who stuffed only 300 envelopes per hour.[31] Similarly, temps offered advantages in repeated calculations. Statistical secretaries in many firms would do the work of a spreadsheet today: semiannual interest calculation; monthly calculations of checking account balances; stock or bond conversions; or simply tracking vacations and illnesses. While today such subcontracting appears natural, it was not so in the 1960s. Corporations had to learn how to subcontract functions like office work, and they learned how to do this through the transition to the electronic office.

Accountants Become Consultants

Accountants did not wake up one day and find themselves consultants. For the most part, they stuck to balancing the books. In the 1940s, that began to change. Under the guise of "system work," Price Waterhouse helped firms install office technology, like vertical files, to make auditing easier. Such services were narrow and only helped streamline the real business—the annual audit. Consultancies could do a much better job of helping firms conduct time studies and cut costs. With the coming of the mainframe computer to oversee accounts, firms needed much more assistance.

Consulting units popped up in the 1950s in most of the major accounting firms (like the management/accounting department at Lybrand), but they really didn't take off until firms needed to install and operate the first corporate computers. The local CPA on the corner might not know anything about computers, but those at the big firms—Arthur Andersen, Coopers & Lybrand, Price Waterhouse, Ernst & Young, and the like—developed a specialized knowledge of how to use information technology to manage account books. Accountancies helped industrial firms adapt to the new technologies, especially the new electronic technologies, while continuing the cost-cutting efficiency legacy of Frederick Winslow Taylor. More than any other factor, the adoption of new technologies, broadly called electronic data processing (EDP), drove accountancies to become more like consultancies.

Bill Holland, a CPA, recounted his early days at Coopers & Lybrand, one of the world's largest accounting firms, when he went to the IBM installation training alongside installers: "We went to the same schools . . . so I learned all about 407s and 604s and sorters and collators and whatever else they had . . . I was about to handle the system side of punch cards." Holland was learning this because Coopers & Lybrand clients wanted to use them for their payrolls, which could easily be handled by IBM punch cards. He would handle the "data processing side . . . as well as the conceptual side of what an accounting system should be and should achieve."[32] As the first mainframes came out, it was important that Coopers & Lybrand stay up to date. The world was shifting from punch cards to magnetic tape. Most of their clients still didn't have computers, so Holland consulted on how to use "electronic data processing," on installation, and on the auditing of those electronic records.[33] By the late 1950s, many accountancies began to offer technology consulting under what they called management advisory services.

Fred Herr, a former engineer from RCA who specialized in production management, joined Coopers & Lybrand in 1959 as part of this booming growth in accountants turned consultants.[34] Though he was born in New York City, he came to the firm through his old neighbor from Levittown, Pennsylvania, Felix Kaufman, whom he'd worked with at RCA. Kaufman recruited him to help with the "computer capability" rollouts for their accounting clients.[35] Before joining RCA to work on their new computer projects, Kaufman had taught college-level accounting. After RCA, he joined Coopers & Lybrand to help them use the new electronic data processing for their accounting needs.[36]

The installation of computers quickly became embroiled with questions about how best to use them to reduce costs, not only in accounting but elsewhere.[37] Building on their success with computers, Coopers & Lybrand found itself advising clients on operations, becoming more general management consultants. Kaufman explained that "in the cost reduction practice," which is what Coopers & Lybrand mostly did, "it was simple. Do more work with fewer people."[38]

Kaufman and his team "gradually . . . branched out so that [they] were also doing organizing work . . . mov[ing] out of the accounting area."[39] From advising CBS Records on installing computers (their first engagement), they were soon organizing an airplane factory for Curtiss-Wright.[40] Coopers & Lybrand was not alone. In the late 1950s, the American Institute of Certified Public Accountants (AICPA) had begun to issue guidelines on ethics and practices for CPAs, even including, by the early 1960s, "papers, books, lectures, courses and seminars" for its membership.[41] Technology consulting was becoming an extension of accounting, yet as it grew there were concerns that accountants had grown beyond their britches.

The partners on the audit side remained leery, both for reasons of professional ethics and because of financial concerns. Ethically, having the same firm spend money and then decide if that money was well spent presented an obvious opportunity for fraud and deception, or at least the appearance thereof—which was why Bower had cast it out of McKinsey. The lure of overlooking malfeasance was too tempting. The fox would be watching the proverbial henhouse.

The larger issue, however, was internal politics. When Herr pitched new work, the audit partners would look it over and tell him that he couldn't do it because it would cost the client five times the audit fee—the implication being that if he charged more, it meant that he was more important to the firm—which, of course, was correct. The consultants, to boot, got paid more than the auditors.[42]

The early consultants at places like Lybrand were CPAs who had drifted into consulting. Felix Kaufman, who hired Herr, was a CPA, as were colleague Bill Holland and most of the other consultants.[43] These consultant CPAs were, at first, subordinated to an institutional hierarchy based in auditing. Herr, lacking a CPA, was the oddity and was often accorded second-class status. So when Herr started making more than real accountants, it was not just business, it was an insurrection. As the consultants began to bring in new clients (Conrail, Pan American, Ford, AT&T), the Coopers & Lybrand audit partners grudgingly came to accept them as more than just the people who installed computers.

Because of this growth, the partners of Coopers & Lybrand—like Bower—remained conflicted over the relationship between the accounting audit and the consulting engagement. The proponents of consulting saw it as part of a suite of firm services alongside tax and auditing. Consulting offered something that auditing did not—"a continuing relationship with the top management."[44] While audits would be, at least to some degree, adversarial and engage only midlevel executives, consulting would be collegial and open the doors of the C-suite. Unlike the audit, consulting was a year-round "steady stream of work."[45] Clients would call Herr with a problem, and either Coopers & Lybrand could fix it, or he could point them toward another firm. Herr became a trusted adviser with "good relationships."[46]

The consultants forged deeper and more personal relationships than the auditors, whose relationships were transactional, often only active during the annual audit. When Herr edged out Booz Allen Hamilton for a consulting engagement with Harsco, he kvelled over his close relationship with the executive who hired him. Business was done at the office, but this executive would also invite Herr to his house, where he would "sit in the pool with him, [while] his wife [would] serve sandwiches on the patio." Lounging in the pool, the executive would ask the consultant his views on business, and Herr found that "very ego satisfying." Herr and other consultants began to become intimates with clients in a way that auditors could never do. Rather than distance defining the professional relationship, it was this closeness that became a new ideal for the consultant.

One evening in the early 1960s, Herr and Bill Holland drove back to Levittown, Pennsylvania, where they both still lived. "I think I will need to leave Lybrand," Herr said. "Why?" asked Holland. "You don't have a problem because you're a CPA. So you can become a partner. I'm not," Herr answered. "Fred, relax," Holland told him. "I don't call the shots around here, but it's very obvious to me that partners are going to have to make a decision and find a way to admit to the partner level people who are not CPAs, or get out of this business."[47] Holland was right. Herr got ahead, making partner in 1965, having demonstrated the value of a consultant within an accountancy.[48]

Though Herr installed the latest technology, he thought of technology as only a stepping-stone toward management. "You know there are very few problems in the world that are new," he later said. Problems are "not really rocket science. Only about half of it is technical . . . [and] the other half is managing change." What clients wanted was a steady hand, because "change is scary. They have a lot at risk, and they want to know who is helping them through this difficult period."[49] The opportunity was not computerization, Herr thought; the opportunity was to rethink how firms operated with computers.

Permanent Data Entry

At the dawn of the computer age, big companies everywhere in the 1960s were switching record systems.[50] Transitioning the data was framed as a special project, and such one-off projects were best carried out by temps. Boring data entry would have burdened the regular staff—especially because so much of it happened at night.

If you want to get the most bang for your buck, machines ought to be run twenty-four hours a day. Manpower's temps could fill the shifts that permanent workers could not, running data entry systems, like graveyard shift at a factory.[51] The machines to enter the data—Comptometers—were expensive. Instead of hiring more workers during the day, which would have required more machines, firms like one Milwaukee bank hired "several hundred temporaries during a short evening shift" to do the data entry. The temps worked at night and the bank "got double use out of expensive equipment," while expensive overtime was transformed into hours of cheaper temporary labor.[52] Winter, using the same kind of logic that would be used in a factory, remarked that "any unmanned work station, billing machine or computer position means a slowdown in the production and billing processes and, as a result, more capital is required."[53]

Temps made automation possible not only by running the machines at night, but by sheltering the full-timers from scut work and long hours. When "Northwestern Mutual Insurance Company decided to convert its [paper] policyholder record to IBM [punch cards]," it used Manpower labor to carry it out. To ask the permanent staff to do it would have drained morale and taken about a year. To employ workers just for this task, which was an option, "would have conflicted with a long-established policy of employment security." Better to hire temps than to hire workers for just one project, then fire them. Instead, the insurance company "lease[d] a crew of experienced key punch operators to work in the evenings," which meant that the project could be done faster with more people (who didn't need training). The office space could be used at night, so the permanent work staff would not be disrupted.[54]

The end game, for Winter, was obvious: "A machine's 'working hours' can be increased without keeping regular operators on overtime and without hiring extra regulars—who would expect to work a full shift and enjoy regular benefits—by bringing in one or more short shifts of temporaries to clean up work overloads."[55] Of course, these data migrations ended up not as onetime events, but became part of everyday office work. Data would continue to need to be entered and updated. Crews of temps were ready, even though it was a task done on an ongoing basis.

The temps who did this ongoing data entry, however, had work lives that bore little resemblance to the office staff they sheltered. Consider a temp doing data entry at Blue Cross Blue Shield. She worked in a windowless, cold room (for the machines), which was constantly dusty (because of the machines). Any complaint about the work conditions got her fired. Her assignment was for three months, working one of three data entry shifts (8 to 12, 12 to 4, or 4 to 8). Each shift had thirty women, with about "2/3 young, out of high school, maybe 1/3 black," but all with a "high turnover." Most women stayed a couple of months and then left. The job was low skill. It took "1 day to train" and "2 wks for speed to build up." If there wasn't enough work, the temp would be sent home without pay for the rest of the shift. If there was extra work, the temp would be kept but not "payed [sic] overtime just time." If the "machine [got] overloaded," as often happened, "you get sent home." The obligation was only from the temp to Blue Cross Blue Shield. While the temps were constantly aware of being temps, their checks were handed out at Blue Cross. The supervisors—"friendly"—were also Blue Cross employees. Every day temps went to work at Blue Cross and found their way to the special, unpleasant area where they worked *for* Blue Cross, but not as a *part* of Blue Cross.[56] Unlike unionized factory workers, these temps came organized by Manpower (or Kelly, or another temp agency), not the American Federation of Labor.

In the short term, corporate policy might prevent the total shift to temps in the name of employment security, but such policies were not long to last once temps' cost savings were recognized. As McKinsey consultants learned in their training, experience was always more persuasive than argument. With data entry, Manpower, Kelly, and other temp agencies showed how workforces could be planned and subcontracted. Office data processing demands would continue to rise. Good jobs, with all the promise of postwar stability, might endure, but they would be buttressed by temps running machines. The most repetitive tasks would be automated and done at night by temps, who would not disturb the real employees—that is, the employees who counted.

CHAPTER SEVEN

The Fall of the American Corporation

I n 1967, John Kenneth Galbraith, the celebrated postwar economist and intellectual, published his seminal work on the postwar corporation, *The New Industrial State*. Galbraith had spent his life considering the economy, both as a professor at Harvard and in the federal government, where he was the deputy head in the Office of Price Administration during World War II. In *The New Industrial State*, he built upon his earlier work in the groundbreaking *The Affluent Society* (1958), extending his analysis of consumer capitalism to describe what he thought was a contradiction between corporations and markets. Not only a best seller, *The New Industrial State* was lauded widely, including winning the McKinsey Foundation Book Award, and having a chapter reprinted in *McKinsey Quarterly*. Galbraith seemed to have cracked the code of the American corporation.[1]

Instead of markets, Galbraith thought, the vital center of the American economy were the five hundred industrial corporations that produced two thirds of all manufactured goods. These largest corporations, while only rarely monopolies, were often oligopolies. The barriers to entry into heavy manufacturing (capital investment, technological know-how, intellectual property) precluded new entrants. The size of these companies, Galbraith asserted, was not just about economies of scale or monopoly pricing, but stability.

Alfred Sloan's GM, the first multidivisional corporation, had become the gold standard for capitalist organization. Total control seemed possible during World War II and, after the Great Depression, necessary. At the end of World War II, a generation of executives, entranced by the logistical programs of the military and then the seeming success of Keynesian policies, had remade all American corporations along lines of long-term planning, long-term investment, and well-defined hierarchies—often with the help of management consultants.

The management "whiz kids" of the postwar years, like Robert Mc-Namara, rose to power on the promise of total knowledge and perfect planning, made possible through quantitative analysis and universal ideas of how to manage. These generalists were expected to be able to move among the government agency, the large corporation, and the university administration as a matter of course. Bureaucracy was bureaucracy. With an MBA and the ability to conduct computer-driven analysis, these executives believed that they could acquire and manage nearly any enterprise. The computer would be used to conduct planning, control, and financial and personnel management. This ideal of "total management information systems" was the apotheosis of modernist ideal—at least in business. Invoking science, both of machines and management, this new generation of managers promised a better-run tomorrow. With their forecasts would come stability, certainty, and permanence—in short, everything that Elmer Winter wanted to destroy.

This private planning by corporations—some bigger than many of the world's governments—defined postwar American capitalism. Large corporations continued to grow to stabilize their profits, not to maximize profit. Despite all the free market rhetoric, they didn't trust markets' volatility. Executives wanted stable growth, for which plans could be made. The business cycle had been tamed, and the optimistic growth that Galbraith took as normal seemed inevitable. Nothing could change it, and this new industrial state would remain for the foreseeable future.

When Galbraith wrote *The New Industrial State*, this state of affairs seemed the preordained future of capitalism. Draw a straight line from the 1950s into the 1980s (or the 2080s) and you would know the America to come. Corporate planning, not market competition, would continue to define the actual American economy. This much planning required vast managerial talent.[2] Postwar corporations recruited heavily from an expanding cadre of MBAs from American business schools to plan this world. These MBAs were not entrepreneurs, but bureaucrats. They fixated on minimizing the risk to themselves and to the corporation.

Certain profits, not maximal profits, Galbraith argued, were the goal.[3]

Corporations wanted to minimize the risk of loss, not maximize gain.[4] With so much at stake and such easy, nearly guaranteed profits, why risk anything at all? These corporations did not respond to the market; they avoided the market. Private planning made postwar American capitalism such a success.[5] Outside of "pizza merchants and dog laundries," Galbraith provocatively asked, "are the capitalist and communist industrial systems really sisters under the skin?"[6] While American politicians contrasted the free markets of the U.S. economy to the centrally planned economies of the USSR, Galbraith argued that "we have an economic system which, whatever its formal ideological billing, is in substantial part a planned economy."[7]

The Galbraith vision of the corporation was completely at odds with that of men like Winter, who thought labor, and even capital, ought to be flexible. Labor should be a variable cost, he thought, not a moral obligation. Capital should be raised in stock markets, not saved. Winter even wrote a book in 1962, *Complete Guide to Making a Public Stock Offering*, that exalted the virtues of capital markets.[8] Alongside Winter, of course, were consultants like Marvin Bower, who offered executives at a variable cost as well. In the 1960s, consultants and temp agencies offered workforce practices that were marginal, which was why Winter struggled so mightily to convince corporations that they needed his help. Galbraith, in contrast, delivered the accepted wisdom about how to run a corporation, even if it conflicted with the popular notion of free enterprise, which extolled markets.[9] Corporate executives did not trust markets.

Big businesses—planned and bureaucratic—had to be big because they had to contain all the functions that they would not trust to the market. Managers, capital, and supply chains were all internalized rather than contracted. Corporations retained their earnings instead of borrowing. They vertically integrated to control suppliers. Their payrolls swelled as they did everything in-house. Steel companies needed ore. Oil refineries needed petroleum. Sears needed appliances.[10] Large capital investments could not depend on uncertain supplies of vital materials. Corporations retained large chunks of their revenues and reinvested them. In 1965, corporations saved, in retained earnings, more than three times ($83 billion) what Americans saved in their private lives. Instead of returning dividends to shareholders, as might have been done in the 1920s, they kept a great portion of their earnings, anticipating greater capital demands in the future and resisting the intrusion of bankers into their plans.[11] These needs—for minimizing risk, for retaining managerial talent, for guaranteeing material supply, and for securing financial capital—determined, for Galbraith, the shape of the postwar economy as well as the economy to come.

Foreseeable futures, even to staggering intellects such as Galbraith's, can be shockingly short indeed. Just a few years after Galbraith wrote this book, American executives would find their faith in these corporations and their long-term plans shaken. Out of that crisis came another model of capitalism, articulated by management consultants, which did not celebrate corporate stability, but instead embraced market instability.

No firm, perhaps, embodied the arc of these changes—from M-form corporation to postwar conglomerate to lean corporation—better than General Electric.

General Electric Modernism

In 1956, Ralph Cordiner, the CEO of GE, delivered the first McKinsey-sponsored lecture series at Columbia University's Graduate Business School, in which he lent his voice to the chorus that "a great manager could manage anything," but at the same time offered an important caveat: a great business needed to be focused.[12] Part of what defined General Electric, and by extension a great corporation, Cordiner argued, was that it "grows from within." To be General Electric was to be in the "electrical industry," not any industry, and for Cordiner, being at the center of "the most sustained and dynamic growth industry of the twentieth century" was enough.[13] He famously said that "the growth curve of the use of electricity" was the best predictor of GE's future, and that was a pretty good curve to be on.[14] It did not make acquisitions, but relied on its own technical talent and capital to develop new products, which it did in droves.[15] By the late 1950s, GE had "350 distinct product lines" with 3 million unique items. With 252,000 U.S. employees (and 29,000 overseas), it earned more than $3 billion in 1955.[16] What made this growth possible? According to Cordiner, it was "a long-range point of view."[17] Innovation came from patience and stability. Corporate leaders everywhere looked to Cordiner for wisdom, and under his watch General Electric became a playbook for how to create a well-run corporation. Cordiner did not just give fancy lectures at Columbia. Perhaps more than any other executive, he sought to integrate new managerial techniques into the everyday life of GE.

From 1920 to 1939, Cordiner pointed out in his *New Frontiers for Professional Managers*, GE's sales rose from $200 million to $342 million. By 1943, its sales had risen to $1,370 million.[18] Like other industrials, GE had to decentralize, as Sloan had done at General Motors in the 1920s and Drucker had written about in *The Practice of Management*. Cordiner realigned GE around this vision and sought to develop the managers needed to bring about a modern corporation.[19] To run General Electric required an enormous pool of talent, and Cordiner believed that the best way to get that talent was to develop it internally.

While GM may have scoffed at Peter Drucker's *The Practice of Management*, Cordiner embraced it. With the help of leading consulting companies and academics, like McKinsey, Booz Allen, and Drucker, GE created its own internal management training program to disseminate Drucker's and others' ideas.[20] They brought these management ideas into its workforce at their new retreat in Crotonville, New York. Outside New York City—but not too far—managers would spend thirteen weeks (!) immersed in the new ideas of management, especially Drucker's. In 1956, four thousand managers went through Crotonville. One employee, who had served in the army, compared the training program to brainwashing. By 1959, 11 percent of the GE workforce (approximately 25,000 employees) had experienced the program. Through Crotonville, GE, one of the leading American firms, reeducated its management to think like Drucker—and his translators at McKinsey and Booz Allen.

GE was famous for its management training program. The "GE Way" was rigorous, including college- and graduate-level courses in business and engineering topics for those without an MBA. If an employee's grades flagged they could lose their job. Even more frequently than in a professional firm, a graduate remembered, "all of the trainees were evaluated every six months. If they didn't measure up, they were asked to leave."[21] The training produced a companywide vision of how management should be done.

To turn these training ideas into everyday practice internally, Cordiner founded GE's own internal consultancy—Management Consulting Services (which was later renamed Corporate Consulting Services).[22] Under Cordiner, even if the operating managers did not want consulting "support," they received it.[23] The consultants kept GE's management in line with Drucker's ideas.

These ideals did not go uncontested. As GE fine-tuned Galbraith's corporation, another kind of corporation was emerging.

The Rise of the Conglomerate

Conglomerates were a uniquely postwar flavor of the corporation. Neither horizontally nor vertically integrated, the conglomerate corporation was a hodgepodge of different industries, without any overwhelming domination by any particular product line. The conglomerate Textron, for instance, began as a textile manufacturer, which during World War II made enormous profits selling to the military. It made so much money that it began to buy other kinds of businesses.

Textron couldn't buy too many other textile companies or it would come under investigation for being a monopoly.[24] Antitrust laws, beginning with the Sherman Antitrust Act of 1890 and updated after World War II with the Celler-Kefauver Antimerger Act in 1950, have sought to defend small business against monopoly power. U.S. Steel, as the classic example, could (and did) buy out its competition and then set steel prices for the country, to its own advantage.[25] Bigness was sufficient, in many quarters, to prove insidiousness. Americans, long accustomed to equating size with concentration, did not know what to make of these megacorporations that were big but weren't monopolies. While the advantages of monopoly are obvious, the advantages of a string of unrelated business units are not. Although the Celler-Kefauver Act gave the government the power to regulate conglomerate mergers, there still needed to be proof that the merger would lessen competition. Without an actual monopoly, this could not be shown.[26]

Rupert Thompson, the head of Textron, explained that conglomerates' advantage over other corporations came from their managerial and financial acumen. Conglomerates could put money "wherever it worked most efficiently." Cash from all the Textron divisions went into a Textron bank account, where Textron management determined how to reallocate the cash across its many enterprises. A profitable but slowly growing company would not receive as much cash as a fast-growing but cash-short division. For instance, when Textron purchased Homelite, a manufacturer of chainsaws, pumps, and generators, in 1955, Homelite used Textron's greater access to capital to overcome a cash shortage in its operations and build two new factories. Homelite profits trebled as Textron's superior management and capital access helped it blossom.

The flip side of growth was death. Every division at Textron needed to achieve a 25 percent profit on invested capital or face restructuring and, eventually, sale. By 1963, the original textile division that had given Textron its name could no longer meet this bar and was unceremoniously sold.[27]

These conglomerates elicited suspicion, yet unlike monopolies they lacked the market power to set prices. Conflating mergers, monopolies, and a classic American fear of economic power over politics, the Tennessee Democratic senator Estes Kefauver declared that "through monopolistic mergers the people are losing power to direct their own economic welfare. When they lose the power to direct their economic welfare, they also lose the means to direct their political future."[28] The government, during the '50s and '60s, investigated many mergers but found just a handful of antitrust violations.[29] The threat was enough to push firms like Textron to actively avoid becoming a monopoly, yet they still needed to invest those profits somewhere.

Conglomerators asserted that they were managers of risk, not monopolists of price. Textron's 1956 *Annual Report* had only one sentence on its cover: "Stability through diversification." Conglomerators like Thompson claimed their acquisitions hedged the risk of progress. Buying one's way into high-tech industries like aerospace and electronics offset the risk that some older industries would suddenly wink out of existence. Its pages extolled the virtues of its investments in aluminum, radar antennae, and titanium fasteners, as well as its textile factories.[30] Through management, redundancies could be eliminated and economies of scale leveraged, investors believed, to turn any business profitable.[31] Conglomerators used this belief in management to justify their acquisitions. An undervalued company just needed better leadership.

In the early 1960s, conglomerates had all the hallmarks of progress: management science and technological futurism. Lammot du Pont Copeland, president of DuPont, jested that "running a conglomerate is a job for management geniuses, not for ordinary mortals like us at DuPont." He joked because managing along these lines completely broke with the traditional corporation. Yet by the mid-1960s, they seemed unstoppable.

The reality of their success, in the end, would prove less the result of leadership genius than of accounting fraud. In their fall, they took down the rest of the American corporations—even the ones that had stuck to the older Sloan/Cordiner/Galbraith model.

The real danger of conglomerates was not their power, but how their weakness perverted American corporations and helped to end the postwar prosperity.

The Rise of James Ling

James Ling was no Harvard Business School grad or Wall Street insider. Born in 1922, orphaned as a teenager, he grew up in Texas and Louisiana and attended school for only a few years after his mother died, when he lived with an aunt in Shreveport.[32] After dropping out of high school at age fifteen, he wandered during the Great Depression, ending up eventually in his hometown of Dallas.[33] He found a job as an apprentice electrician and started a family after marrying a secretary at the telephone company.[34] During the war, he worked nights at Lockheed and became a master electrician, which allowed him, in 1947, to start his own electrical contracting company—Ling Electric Company—with two thousand dollars in savings. Dallas, like much of the rest of the South, felt the influx of all those defense dollars. For the next few years, Ling's revenues exploded, from $70,000 in 1947 to $200,000 in '48 and $400,000 in '49.[35] Though uneducated, he was a natural businessman. The company rode the postwar building boom in Dallas to great profitability, and within a few years, Ling found himself the head of a prosperous contracting company.[36]

His newfound money led Ling to Dallas country clubs, where he circulated with the new financial class of the city, who, like the oilmen of Texas, were wheelers and dealers. It was with this set that Ling discovered the possibilities of high finance. From his new contacts he learned the difference between a sole proprietorship and a corporation. As a sole proprietor he was taxed the highest marginal personal rate—91 percent—but as a corporation, he would be taxed only at 52 percent. With this realization, Ling quickly turned his attention from electrical contracting to corporate finance, for which, it turned out, he also had a knack.[37]

Ling took his company public in 1955 with the sale of 1 million shares. This IPO didn't happen on Wall Street, but anywhere he could find a buyer, starting with hawking his stocks from a booth at the Texas State Fair.[38] Initially selling his company's stock door to door, he moved up to the golf course and, finally, the small-time Ling made connections with New York investment bankers White, Weld & Company, who began to issue stock and debt on his behalf.[39] Ling didn't make a lot on the stock, but it gave him eight hundred thousand dollars to work with, and within the next few years, he went on a buying spree, starting with a local electronics firm, L.M. Electronics, which made testing equipment for missiles, followed by a string of acquisitions in electronics and defense.[40] By 1959, Ling's company, now called Ling-Altec, had revenues of $48 million.[41]

Ling repeatedly bought and sold companies by issuing debt through White, Weld. Using that cash to purchase a company, he would then issue cheaper, long-term debt against the assets of this new company to retire the old debt—a totally novel financial scheme that anticipated the mergers and acquisitions world of the 1980s. In this way he turned debt into defense companies, just as the federal government's contracts remade the Sun Belt into the center of the defense economy.[42] Operational improvements were incidental to the reshuffling of debt and equity. Before the leveraged buyout became commonplace, James Ling pioneered the practice of using debt to construct an empire. Like William Durant, Ling loved finance. While other conglomerators might have had at least a passing interest in running companies or producing goods or services, Ling cared for nothing but growth. And he was not alone in these schemes.

Many of the top young MBAs were drawn to the excitement, whether with James Ling or someone like Tex Thornton at Litton Industries. Harvard MBA Charles "Tex" Thornton, like Ling, relied on the rising stock market of the late 1950s and early '60s to amass a sprawling empire of companies, ranging from small electronics manufacturers to colossal shipyards. Through the services of the investment bank Lehman Brothers, Thornton arranged stock swaps between his conglomerate, Litton Industries, and the acquired company.[43] Stockholders believed in the aura of the conglomerate and its management expertise to the extent that when a conglomerate exchanged stock with an acquired company, the value of that company's stock—now a part of the conglomerate—rose. In effect, acquired companies could trade their stock to a conglomerate for a premium, and then the conglomerate would in turn realize an additional premium from the stock market that expected the conglomerate to raise efficiency at the company. These acquisitions, financed through investment banks, required no cash, therefore no taxes had to be paid on the increased value of the stock.[44] When the conglomerates sold off portions of those companies, however, they received real cash. The difference between the paper value of stocks and the real value of cash made conglomeration possible. Acquisitions would, in the booster's view, get the benefit of that management genius, hoping that their sales would also grow at Litton's claimed historical rate of 30 to 50 percent.[45] As their stock rose, this practice enabled conglomerates to acquire boundlessly.[46]

Save for a few exceptions, the actual management of these conglomerates was nothing exceptional. The public justification for them, to those who ran and invested in them, was the newfound American faith in scientific management and in progress. In private, however, the conglomerates had little to do with managerial efficacy. Money sloshed around but created nothing of value. At the knees of these men, a generation of the smartest businessmen learned the value of clever financing.

Management science, as an ideology, legitimated conglomerates' acquisitions, but in reality, while management was trusted to smooth over acquisitions, growth came from clever corporate finance. Acquisitions were leveraged into more acquisitions. Operations within the acquired firms did not improve. Firms were not even streamlined. Since conglomerates kept acquisitions (which were usually in unrelated industries) independent, synergies—the eliminating of redundancies—could come only from the relatively small expenses of corporate overhead.

Through his own cunning Ling would build that small contracting firm, in just a decade, into the twenty-fifth largest corporation in America—and, even faster, disappear.

Ling's Zenith

By 1962, Ling's ambitions had outstripped those of White, Weld, and he decamped to the more sophisticated Lehman Brothers, who also supported Litton Industries. With Lehman behind him, he extended his conglomerate to try to buy the Dallas aerospace company Chance Vought, which manufactured planes for the navy. Initially resisting the takeover, Chance Vought executives filed a civil antitrust suit, which then was followed by a Justice Department investigation. But they could find no evidence of antitrust activity.[47] Ling renamed the conglomerate Ling-Temco-Vought (LTV).

Chance Vought, while a high-profile Dallas company, was not as asset-rich as Ling had thought.[48] He struggled for a few years. Selling off pieces of his conglomerate for cash, he wheeled and dealed his way back from the brink of insolvency, but not enough to stop his stock from plummeting to a third of its value.[49]

Luckily for Ling, federal demand resulting from the rising conflict in Vietnam took off just when LTV needed it most. Selling to the government, by 1963, LTV issued steady dividends. Yet his stock remained low, and without a higher stock price Ling could not do the stock swaps that allowed other conglomerates to grow. Focusing on the financial rather than the managerial, he restructured his stocks, exchanging higher-dividend preferred stock for lower-dividend common stock. Despite slightly declining earnings, the number of shares decreased by a third, so that the earnings per share—a key measure of a company's value—went up. While this shouldn't have affected the market value of the company at all, stock analysts on Wall Street saw a jump in the earnings per share of the company, which whetted Ling's appetite.

Ling had fooled Wall Street. In 1964, he audaciously split LTV into three separately traded public corporations whose stocks were owned by

LTV, now simply a holding company. Nothing in the earnings or operations had changed. Yet when the stocks of these three companies were sold, their combined market value increased nearly five times.[50] Over a further series of acquisitions and stock maneuvers, Ling came to be seen as a financial genius. Each additional win further cemented his reputation, and the increasing value of LTV became a self-fulfilling prophecy, allowing him to trade stock, like any other conglomerate, but at an unprecedentedly higher scale.

Ling's zenith came in his acquisition of Wilson & Company. Wilson was a diversified meatpacking company that parlayed excess pork skins into its iconic basketballs, showing just how far James Ling had come from an electrical contracting firm. Wilson was a mature company with little prospect of growth, but with the success of its restructuring, Ling thought he could divvy up its assets, issue more debt, and continue his growth. Wilson's acquisition in 1966 was a grand success.[51] The meatpacking was separated from the sporting goods, and Wall Street excitedly received the new stock offerings.

Ling had nothing but contempt for the corporate "caretakers" of Wilson as opposed to the "entrepreneurs" of LTV. "Today, in the United States," he told a convention of Southern bankers, "there are essentially two types of corporate management." On the one hand, there were the "professional caretakers who seek prestige, job security, a weekly paycheck, and good fellowship," who reveled "in their 'country club' atmosphere and [were] unlikely to welcome any new ideas." On the other hand, there were men like him, "entrepreneurial innovators who seek challenges, increasing values for their shareholders, and who are willing to put their futures on the line through equity participation in their companies."[52] His role as an innovator was to turn those caretakers out of their club and take their equity.

Ling had good reason to believe his own audacious hype. He had, in just twenty years, gone from a penniless orphan to a small-time Texas electrical contractor to the owner of the twenty-fifth largest company in the Fortune 500, bigger even than Lockheed, where he had, so long ago, taken a second, nighttime job during World War II.[53] LTV had higher sales than DuPont or Shell or Westinghouse.[54]

In April 1968, James Ling thought he had it all figured out. His backers at Lehman Brothers, and then Goldman Sachs as well, orchestrated a complicated new plan to sell various stocks, bonds, and options of his subsidiaries as integrated units on the market.[55] This sale would enable him to finance the biggest acquisition of his, or anyone else's, career.

LTV may have been the quintessential conglomerate, but it was not a monopoly. It was big, but it had no more market power than any other firm. And Ling, it turned out, was no managerial genius—he was just really good at hawking stocks.

And that, in the end, would prove Ling's downfall.

The Lure of Conglomeration: General Electric

Ling was master of a new world, but he wasn't alone. By the late 1960s, conglomerates like LTV had become a dominant new form of the corporation. Gulf and Western, Litton, and ITT—also among the leading conglomerates—dominated headlines with their rapid sales growth, achieving gross revenues in 1966 of $1 billion, $1.2 billion, and $2.1 billion respectively.[56] By 1967, 150 mergers happened each month, 70 percent of these by conglomerates—a 25 percent rise over the previous year's national record.[57]

The conglomerate grew and grew until it swept most American corporations into its wake. By the late 1960s, less than 10 percent of the Fortune 500 remained undiversified (Exxon and U.S. Steel were exceptions to the rule). Pure conglomerates, like LTV and Textron, were few and treasured, but American corporations got drunk on diversification. Through that undisciplined transformation fueled by finance, calamity ensued.

General Electric, one of the largest firms in the country, was no exception.

Fred Borch became president of General Electric in 1963, just as conglomeration became all the rage. Seeking to make his mark on what had been Cordiner's corporation, Borch radically reorganized and diversified GE, embracing the conglomerate model.

Mimicking the path of accountants everywhere, Fred Borch began his career at General Electric as a financial auditor, but rose through the ranks to become a consultant in its internal consulting practice.[58] Borch completely believed that GE possessed the managerial talent to make it in any industry.[59] Cordiner had believed in management. He had been too conservative, too protectionist, too insulated. Despite Cordiner's commitment to decentralization, corporate staff had grown tremendously. To reduce corporate staff at headquarters, Borch insisted that business units pay for corporate services, like consultants. He assumed that these services were inefficient and used only because they were free—even his own consulting unit.

Cordiner had required departments and divisions to use the consulting service, but the services were never charged for, so it was unclear if they added value or if they were just a way to control a decentralized corporation. Borch released managers from any obligation to the internal consulting practice. Instead of a free service, the internal consulting group needed to sell their services to units, just like any outside consultancy. He expected it to fail, but instead it thrived.[60] For the kind of work that the operating managers wanted help with, the consultants' inside knowledge of GE operations made them more efficient than outsiders. Borch attempted to bring the market in, and did, but that market skewed heavily to those with lower transaction costs, or in plain English, those who knew how General Electric worked. What is important here is less the role of internal management consultants than how Borch kept his eye on making GE more like independent companies, not only in their management but in their relationships. Even corporate services were charged for, as if they were acquired in the market. There was nothing sacred about being inside General Electric anymore, and nothing profane about being outside either.

Crotonville's programs under Cordiner had focused on management, not finance and strategy.[61] There was no need to grapple with strategic investment. Since a good manager could manage anything, whatever GE did, they would succeed. Borch believed otherwise, and Crotonville began to teach strategic planning alongside management.[62] Instead of thirteen weeks, the program took three and a half days.[63] In developing the new program, the staff drew on academic works as well as publications from the Boston Consulting Group, McKinsey & Associates, Arthur D. Little (ADL), and other sources.[64] Rather than just operational excellence, Borch believed that GE also needed to have strategic excellence. If managers could be strategists, GE could exceed the growth curve of electricity.[65] GE could diversify. In this regard, Borch's belief in universal management fit completely with the idea of the conglomerate, and he set out to expand GE, like those conglomerates, beyond its traditional limits, including by acquisition.

Unlike the other conglomerates (like LTV), General Electric had enough internal capital to create entire industries from scratch. Relying on an internal committee called the Growth Council, Borch targeted nine new markets in both products (nuclear energy, computers, commercial jet engines, polymer chemicals) and services (entertainment, community development and housing, personal and financial services, medical services and products, education) that were completely outside GE's traditional focus.[66] Thanks to its retained earnings and credit rating, GE could easily finance diversification both internally and through acquisition, without the need for many conglomerates' financial creativity. GE's abundant capital fostered little discipline in these new enterprises. The Growth Council and Borch overestimated GE's managerial ability to get many of these ventures off the ground, from misunderstanding the basic economics of an industry to spending millions on insignificant acquisitions. The success of these enterprises ran from colossal failure, as in computers and entertainment, to wild success—aerospace, medicine, and financial services.

As in most conglomerates—but not most M-form corporations—capital was invested with an eye to growth, not to profit. While the few successes would set a new direction for General Electric, the profusion of products encumbered GE as it had other conglomerates. Complexity overcame performance. By 1966, despite $3 billion in revenue growth, GE profits had not increased at all.[67] Moreover, five of the nine initiatives proposed by the Growth Council had failed.[68]

GE's failure to make the conglomerate model work, it would turn out, was not unique.

The Unraveling of LTV

Ling's last great conquest, the one that brought down LTV, was the takeover of one of the largest Little Steel companies, Jones & Laughlin, in 1968. His offer, $425 million (approximately $3.1 billion in 2018 dollars), was at that time the largest tender offer in U.S. history. To buy it, he had to borrow to his limit. He trusted that he would be able to spin off portions of his acquisitions to settle his debts, as he had so many times before—that the stock market would once again rally to support his empire, that the conglomerate luster would continue to shine. With his acquisition of Jones & Laughlin, LTV truly spanned the American economy.

At that same time, for the first time, a major conglomerate, Litton, reported a decline in revenue. Like other conglomerates, Litton had been buying a succession of stagnant firms in unrelated fields, like shipbuilding and office furniture.[69] For years, every quarter, it had announced higher revenues, so when it had a drop, it suddenly seemed that the emperor might not be wearing any clothes.

Business reporters and stock analysts took a closer look at the Litton miracle and did not like what they saw. Analysts began to "wonder," as the *New York Times* reported, "if the interchangeability of management skills from one industry to another truly exists."[70] Investors began to rethink what had actually happened in the past few years. How valuable was conglomerate management? Rather than miracles of management, perhaps conglomerates might only be "paper pyramids" of finance. Tactical moves like LTV's splitting into separate companies had undermined the synergy argument that justified the conglomerate.[71] If Ling expected the three companies to succeed independently, then what had been the value of the conglomerate's management synergies? SEC chairman Hamer Budge told *Time* magazine that "conglomerate financing offer[ed] only 'an illusion of security' . . . [with only] apparent improvements."[72] Complex accounting, not managerial genius, artificially improved the bottom line of these companies in a way that "many investors do not have the knowledge or patience to interpret."[73]

This public disrobing coincided with another Justice Department inquiry, this time authorized by President Lyndon Johnson. In 1968, the FTC announced that because of "growing concern" that conglomerates could "substantially lessen competition," closer investigations would begin.[74] The government attention could not have come at a worse time for the conglomerates.

As Litton's stock fell, so too did every other conglomerates', all of which were now under the microscope. Remember that conglomerates had grown, in essence, by swapping the high-value stock of the conglomerate for the lower-value stock of the company acquired. Either this swap happened directly or, after the acquisition, the conglomerate would sell off assets and more stock. If the conglomerate stock price took a dip, this pyramid of finance would collapse. After Litton's fall, stocks could no longer be swapped between companies for a premium, and the merger movement was brought to an end. For Ling, the sudden shift meant that no one bought the strange "units" from Lehman or Goldman that he needed to repay the debt that he owed to fund the Jones & Laughlin acquisition, and he found himself short of cash. A fire sale of his assets ensued, and as he sold into a declining market, LTV—and the mystique of James Ling—unraveled. In 1969, LTV operating profits fell 90 percent.[75]

The Justice Department's investigations may have put conglomerates on notice, but it wasn't antitrust prosecutions that brought them down. Justice Department antitrust chief Richard McLaren told Congress that anti-conglomerate laws were no longer needed because the stock market had done what no law could: devalued their business model. The threat of anti-trust action by the Justice Department against five major conglomerates, including LTV, coupled with the stock downturn, was enough to end the conglomerate craze.[76]

Once publicized, the financial schemes of Ling and the rest began to be denounced. Wall Street analysts and the wider public came to see the malignant growth of these conglomerates and their rising earnings per share as accounting fictions dangerous to capitalism.[77] The pressure of the government, as well as the dawning realization that these supposed geniuses did nothing to increase the underlying value of their business units, caused a sharp downturn in the stock market.[78] The 1960s conglomerate craze came to an end, like all speculative bubbles, but it brought down not just the pure conglomerates, but every corporation that had also diversified—which was nearly every major corporation. The fall of the conglomerate put the entire postwar corporation under suspicion.

By the end of the decade, then, public doubt had been aroused and conglomerate stocks had fallen much faster than even the now bearish market.[79] Between the Justice Department and the press, investors had their choice of worrying whether the government would split up the conglomerates or, even worse, whether conglomerates were nothing more than hype, whose growth in profits had come from acquisitions and accounting, not increased productivity.[80] The size of these companies might have fundamentally undermined the productivity and value of American business. For a decade, American business had burned millions in mergers with no apparent increase in value.[81] Conglomerates went from darlings to devils.

Hamer Budge "applaud[ed] such conservatism . . . [as shaped the financial practices] of us who are old enough to have lived through the Depression."[82] Budge thought that financial chicanery had been put back in the genie's bottle. He was wrong. That Depression-era generation's grip on power was already waning. The younger generation's memory was short— and there was so much money to be made. The merger-and-acquisition methods that Ling pioneered in his rise to power became essential lessons of finance, even as Ling himself fell from grace and was forgotten. Wall Street, which had slumbered since the 1920s, was back.

Architects of Change

In October 1969, Philip Shay, the executive director of the Association of Consulting Management Engineers, addressed a gathered group of consultants in New York City and began speaking in a way that would have been impossible just a few years earlier, before the collapse of the conglomerates. He saw "even our best managed institutions [as] inherently sluggish—not hungry for innovation, not quick to respond to human need, not eager to reshape themselves to meet the challenge of the times." Management, for Shay, was the center of the great "revolutions, the end of which is not apparent to sight." His question was whether "the world will change of its own accord, without human management, or whether it will be changed deliberately."[83] Nothing less than the future of capitalism was at stake, and consultants needed to make sure that the needed changes were deliberate.

Institutions that had provided stability and growth for decades would need to be torn apart. Shay believed that only management consultants could renew the growth, that "such a society cannot respond to challenge unless a serious attempt is made to redesign its institutions to adapt to and meet the problems of change in a rapidly changing world." The challenge of the 1970s would be nothing less than to remake the most basic institutions of society. "Businessmen and management consultants will continue to be architects of change and improvement in society."[84] Management consulting was not "straightening out production problems in the shop or factory," but that of corporate strategy, and at the highest level, of society itself.[85]

The American planned economy fell in 1969, a good twenty years before the Soviets' in 1989. The corporation would continue to exist in name, but that name embodied a different beast. Secure human capital, secure financial capital, and risk minimization, all features of the postwar corporation as understood in the mid-1960s, would in just a few short years be history. Galbraith's intuition and erudition, built through a lifetime of scholarship and government service in the middle third of the twentieth century, would provide little insight into the last third. In this transition, the postwar corporation focused on minimizing risk and maximizing size would disappear, and in its stead, a leaner corporation would emerge to negotiate and to create a more volatile economy. While many corporations could make this transition by embracing the market, workers and managers of all levels would find the transition more challenging, as wage inequality and job volatility rose. But while the corporation could relatively easily adapt to the unstable world, for the American workforce, this transition would be fraught, bringing back the inequality and instability that had so defined the American economy before World War II. While the names of most conglomerates have been forgotten, their financial methods were not, and it was partially through their example that finance took a new hold on American business. Not all the corporations survived, and their histories of success and defeat reveal how the corporation, as an ideal, as a belief, and as a practice, was remade.

CHAPTER EIGHT

Rethinking the Corporation

P lanners of the 1960s had expected that the '70s would be more of the same. Keynesianism would fix the macroeconomy. The corporation would fix the microeconomy. Everybody (if they were deserving white men) would have one of those good, stable jobs. "Economists were pointing to the 'soaring 70s,'" the ever wary Elmer Winter wrote, and like all alliterations, it was more fun to say than it was accurate. These predictions were, as he noted, "off by a country mile." Well-considered long-term plans went unrealized, despite the statistical accuracy of the projections and the thickness of their tomes.

Crisis after crisis began to strike at the heart of the hard-won corporate stability. The conglomerates fell. In their wake came recession and stagnation. Growth came to a halt, at least as it was experienced by regular people. Uncertainty, so long contained, had crept back in. The jolt shocked many executives into awareness that recessions were once again possible, creating a skepticism of budgets and forecasts, reminding everyone with an understatement that, as Winter wrote, "budgeting is not an exact science."[1]

These crises were not just economic but intellectual. The way that corporate leaders had understood the economy to work, it turned out, was wrong. American capitalism was at a crossroads, and no one knew what to do or whom to blame. Suddenly there was a need for new explanations. Business gurus and management consultants were happy to oblige their audiences, helpfully pointing us in a different direction.

Into this gap between reality and ideas emerged ways of looking at business and work that celebrated new virtues—like leanness, like nimbleness, like shareholder value. These ideals reinforced one another to fashion a new managerial mind-set in the 1970s. The consensus that emerged around 1970 was 180 degrees from how business had been understood since the beginning of the industrial age.[2]

"As the dinosaur skeletons in museums remind us," Gil Clee wrote in *McKinsey Quarterly*, "great size has its dangers—the dangers of dulled perceptions, sluggish reflexes, and a fatal loss of rapport with the environment." In this analogy, large firms, like the dinosaurs, are doomed by their size to extinction. Whether "great industrial conglomerate, the mega-university, [or] the government agency with a budget of billions," they would collapse under their own weight.[3] That sentiment would have been very counterintuitive to GE's Ralph Cordiner or any other corporate leader in the 1950s. Size was strength. By 1970, that connection was no longer so clear.

Although big corporations had long had critics, no one, before this moment, would have thought that smaller firms would be better run than large firms. Large firms had resources, economies of scale, professional managers, and lots of options. Yet terms like "small," "efficient," and "flexible" began to seem to refer to one another, to appear causally interconnected—as if smaller enterprise always made for a more efficient business, as if flexibility required a small enterprise, as if a flexible firm would be more efficient. The belief in size as a means to profit, sacrosanct since the days of the nineteenth-century trusts, no longer seemed to hold. Into this gap between established wisdom and turbulent experience came new beliefs about how corporations, and workforces, ought to be run.

By the early 1970s, the conglomerate craze appeared crazy—and dangerous. That firms had grown too large for anyone to manage now seemed like the inevitable interpretation of events. Lewis Young, the editor in chief of *BusinessWeek*, put it simply: "The biggest single weakness American business faces today is that the enterprise has gotten so big the management cannot run it."[4] The "focus for consultants," he intoned, was to do what the "antitrusters" could not do—"break up the big companies," and by doing that "to make the corporation more resilient and more capable of correcting mistakes."[5]

The fall of the conglomerate gave rise to a new model: the lean corporation. Today, "lean" has a very specific meaning for business scholars, but the meaning of "lean" is more fundamental than this or that management system: it is a fundamental doubt about bigness. As such, lean corporations were at odds with how corporations had been conceived since the nineteenth century. All the ways of thinking about business and work, which we are still wrestling with today, emerge out of this moment of doubt. The fall of the American corporation was not just the fall of James Ling, but in a more fundamental way, a new doubt about progress at all. To butcher an idiom: the baby of the postwar corporation was thrown out with the conglomerate bathwater. Profit, as a goal, had displaced progress. In the aftermath, business experts found themselves searching for a new way to think about the corporation now that the golden child had been shown to be made of pyrite.

These rumblings about the failure of the corporation became a roar, and with alternatives available, consultants began to actively attack all assumptions behind the postwar corporation, whether or not they were financially driven conglomerates. Instead of redoubts of invincible monopolistic power, as leading thinkers like John Kenneth Galbraith insisted in *The New Industrial State*, American corporations now appeared to be ossified bureaucracies that squandered shareholders' capital.

While futurists and gurus like Alvin Toffler and Warren Bennis came up with new ideas, it was the consultancies, like McKinsey & Company and Boston Consulting Group, that enacted these rethought corporations, restructuring firms and, in doing so, remaking how we work.

Strategy Consulting

Probably the most influential business history book ever written came out in 1962: Alfred Chandler's *Strategy and Structure*. It is a pretty good history book, but it was a watershed in business thinking. Nowadays, it is common sense that for each corporate strategy there is an ideal corporate structure, but it was Chandler's book that first showed this key insight, giving birth to what today is simply called corporate strategy in business circles. It is no coincidence that Chandler's book came out only the year before the founding of the Boston Consulting Group (BCG), today the universally acknowledged number two strategy firm after McKinsey.

Like many early consultants, Bruce Henderson had a background in engineering. He spent the first decades of his career at Westinghouse, where he rose into senior management. Leaving Westinghouse, he spent a few years at the consultancy Arthur D. Little, but left to start his own shop, at first affiliated with a little Boston bank, Boston Safe Deposit and Trust, in 1963.[6] The bank hired him to offer consulting services for their clients, but Henderson thought that the real opportunity was not in cost cutting but in revenue growing.

Henderson's reasoning was simple: competition. By the early 1960s, so-called consultants were everywhere, but most offered to help firms do time studies to cut labor costs or to help install the latest technology to replace workers. Henderson knew this well, since he had been the head of Arthur D. Little's management services, which did exactly those studies. Most of this work was done not by pure play consultancies like McKinsey but by accountancies like Price Waterhouse and Coopers & Lybrand. These accountants got into the business just as Henderson's bank had: by supporting their clients. With their existing relationships, they would usually win out over management consultancies in areas like cost cutting, where their detail-oriented CPAs excelled. But though CPAs might be good at cutting costs, they were bad at imagining new growth areas. BCG turned itself into the guru of growth.

Boston Consulting Group focused on strategy consulting—revenue growth and corporate reorganization—rather than cost cutting. Henderson realized that firms really needed help in thinking about how to organize their structure to maximize growth. Apocryphally, when batting around ideas for his new firm in the early days, Henderson suggested that it specialize in business strategy. One of the staff objected that it was "too vague." Henderson brilliantly replied, "That's the beauty of it. We'll define it."[7] Though BCG led the way, other consultancies, including McKinsey & Company, followed suit, shifting their business from the old cost-cutting time studies to new growth-strategy studies, and in the process began to remake the boundary of the firm. "The surest way to turn a client off," Henderson said, "is to come in and cold sell. We tried it in our early days. It does not work."[8] For the high-margin firms like BCG and McKinsey, the best way to sell was with innovative ideas. After the fall of the conglomerate, American executives would hunger for new ideas like never before.

The Problem of Bureaucracy

Peter Drucker had emerged as the first guru of postwar capitalism, but he would not be the last. By the early 1960s, he was in peak demand, commanding the lordly sum, then, of $500 a day. He advised GM's Alfred Sloan, GE's Ralph Cordiner, and many other heads of America's largest industrial concerns.[9] Drucker, in many ways, became the archetype of this new corporate thinker. His role was not technical, but imaginative. Business leaders described him as a "catalyst of thought," as "stimulating fresh insights," as someone who could provide a new perspective on an old problem. In short, Drucker was the first pure strategic consultant.

He believed that business success came from taking risks, from "courageous decisions," not from a bureaucracy. In a time when bigness was celebrated, Drucker was a contrarian: "Making proper decisions doesn't require adding a vice president and 50 analysts." He told *Forbes* as early as 1962, "No matter how big a business gets, only one or two people do the vital work." What corporations really needed, he thought, was to empower those one or two people and get rid of the fifty analysts. Those few could do the vital tasks and "they can go outside for the subsidiary jobs." He added, "Too many corporations staff their headquarters for everything, whether they need the job once a year or once day."[10] Drucker was not alone in thinking most bureaucrats were useless.

Warren Bennis, management guru and professor of business, wrote in 1966 that "bureaucracy, the organizational pattern born of the Industrial Revolution, still reigns supreme in the large enterprises of today . . . out of joint with contemporary realities."[11] He proclaimed the end of bureaucracy would come in the next twenty-five years. Bennis took pains to point out that by bureaucracy he didn't simply mean "those guys in Washington," or "red tape," or "faceless and despairing masses standing in endless queues," but the everyday reality of corporate America.

Bureaucracy, in the form of the organization man, was reviled by both the Left and the Right. The Left mourned the loss of the creative intellectual, while the Right mourned the death of the industrial titan.[12] The organization man, Bennis believed, masked the rise of a more important figure: the "professional man." The professional man was not tied to a job. The

professional man was "uncommitted except to the challenging environ-
ments where [he] can 'play with problems.'"[13] Like capitalism itself, these
professional men were process without purpose. They were neither fascists
nor communists, but technocrats. The professional man served a world in
which "survival is dependent on the institutionalization of perpetual
change."[14]

Bureaucracy worked, Bennis believed, in an era of stagnation, but not in
an era of change. At the core of "organizational revitalization" was the dis-
placement of hierarchy with collaboration.[15] "Fantasy, imagination, and
creativity" would define this new world and "be legitimate in ways that today seem strange."[16] In the coming years, a temporary society would displace a permanent one.[17] The organizations that would dominate that
society would themselves be temporary. If these ideas seem vague, you are
reading correctly. These thinkers tended to the gestural, rather than the
concrete.

These critiques were not unique to business gurus with ideas to sell, or
even new. Criticisms of the corporate life had proliferated for years. Sloan
Wilson's *The Man in the Gray Flannel Suit*, published in 1955, became the
touchstone for a world of conformity (although for the veteran protagonist
haunted by the war, such conformity was a comfort). *The Organization
Man* by William Whyte was published the next year and launched a thousand dissertations. Its basic ideas became so commonplace that the book is
now half forgotten. Intellectual cultural critics of the 1950s had been attack-
ing the anomie of postwar life. In the 1960s, hippie protesters and ghetto
rioters alike refused to obey. In business circles, contrarian ideas were available, but until 1969, these ideas were, if not ignored, at least not implemented. After 1969 and the collapse of the conglomerate, these criticisms
took on a new immediacy as the corporation lost not just its cultural primacy
but its apparent economic value as well.

Ad-hocracy and Bureaucracy

Alvin Toffler's *Future Shock* was published in 1970 and became perhaps the
most influential (and popular) representation of this mode of thinking. For
those who are unfamiliar with it, it would be easy to read the title today,

associate it with a vague sense of technological change, and move on. To do so would be to miss one of the most influential texts of the 1970s. Toffler was everywhere, and he was mandatory reading in every boardroom. Consultants embraced him. *Future Shock* even won a special award from the McKinsey Foundation, which was run by the directors of the firm. "The Coming Ad-hocracy," a chapter reprinted in *McKinsey Quarterly*, highlighted the relevance of Toffler, as the introduction claimed, to "top executives."[18]

These new corporate imaginings promised not only profit, but liberation from that most modern of oppressions—bureaucracy. Toffler rejected the future of the faceless bureaucracy: "If the orthodox social critics are correct in predicting a regimented, super-bureaucratized future, we should already be mounting the barricades, punching random holes in our IBM cards, taking every opportunity to wreck the machinery of organization."[19]

There was no need to mount the barricades, of course, because corporate bureaucracy was already collapsing of its own accord. He wrote, "If, however, we set our conceptual clichés aside and turn instead to the facts, we discover that bureaucracy, the very system that is supposed to crush us all under its weight, is itself groaning with change." The flexible corporation would be a liberation into "a new free-form world of kinetic organizations."[20] Toffler called this flexible corporation, in a horrid neologism, "*ad-hoc*racy."[21] Bennis called this new organization the "organic-adaptive structure." Thankfully, neither term caught on, but this vision of the firm did, set in motion by teams of consultants who brought Toffler's ideas into reality.

If Toffler's neologisms were horrible, his timing was excellent. He built on the ideas of Drucker and Bennis, pulling together many iconoclastic thinkers. Toffler's work was not only a bestseller, but also a synthetic account of the ideas about flexibility that had been circulating for the previous half decade, albeit with far more panache. These futurists were not neutral prognosticators. As they envisioned the world to come, business leaders took on their ideas of progress and of inevitability as justification for changing the world of today. You can see in Bennis, the academic; in McKinsey and BCG, the consultants; in Manpower, the temps; and in Toffler, the popularizer the same strain of thought that emphasized a flexible corporation made possible by team organization.

Words and phrases that are today banal were then revolutionary. For example, Bennis could proudly write of a future when task forces would organize around problems and "be solved by groups of relative strangers with diverse professional skills."[22] Employees would not have jobs, but would move in and out of teams. No one would have a preordained role, but would adapt to new situations. In short, as we joined teams, we would all become in-house consultants. Nothing was actually new about the existence of special task forces—aside from the stultifying sociology talk. Making teams, rather than jobs, the basic building block of the corporation was, however, nothing short of revolution.

The executive in this scheme would become the organizer of these teams. He would be the generalist who could coordinate and translate among the sea of specialists. Toffler noted the rise of "project management" as a new and distinct skill for this itinerant executive. The "'executive' thus becomes a coordinator or 'linkpin' [sic] between various task forces" rather than a fixed administrator in the bureaucracy.[23] Organizational charts, in turn, would be replaced by "project groups."

For Bennis, "the key word would be 'temporary,' there will be adaptive, rapidly changing temporary systems."[24] Both Bennis and Toffler believed that this fluid workplace would improve job satisfaction. These "adaptive, problem-solving, temporary systems of diverse specialists" would supplant bureaucracies and organization men. Bennis believed there was "a harmony between the educated individual's need for meaningful, satisfactory, and creative tasks and a flexible organizational structure."[25] These high-minded creative ideals called for nothing less than the end of bureaucracy.

Warren Bennis thought deeply about what these kinds of teams would require socially. These rapidly assembled and disassembled teams called for people who could easily fit in with strangers. Homogenous social skills—aka shared culture—would count more than ever. Individuality, at a basic level, was just as incompatible with the temporary society as it was in the bureaucracy.

Unlike in a bureaucracy, team members would need to do new jobs all the time. Routine tasks come from a stable environment, which by the end of the 1960s was no more. Each individual employee had to be able to make decisions on nonroutine tasks. The routines, in Toffler's view, were "such tasks that the computer and automated equipment do far better than men." Computers would not create the total managerial knowledge fantasized by postwar planners, but they would eliminate those planners' positions, as well as the jobs of all routine knowledge workers.

In such a firm, what would it even *mean* to work somewhere? The absence of permanent hierarchy, Toffler predicted, would reduce employee loyalty.[26] Worker's identities would become *what* they did rather than *where* they did it. In his synthesis, Toffler quotes Bennis, stating that employees would be "committed to the task, not the job; to their standards, not their boss. And because they have degrees, they travel."[27] They would not be "company men" and would have no commitments other than their careers and the current problem. In short, those able to make decisions would feel no loyalty, and those not able to make decisions would receive no loyalty.

Long-term workplace relationships would no longer be possible, but "quick, intense relationships" would replace them . . . in theory. "Living in temporary work systems . . . augur social strains and psychological tensions" that could only be relieved outside the workplace. In Toffler's incredibly sexist view, "to be a wife in this era will become a profession of providing stability and continuity."[28] Stability could be found only in the home, not in the workplace—yet there is little discussion of what that home life would look like after job security no longer existed.

This ad-hocracy would remake not just corporate work, but work identity. Employees would drift from project to project, rootless and not filling a role in a corporation. It is easy to imagine how Elmer Winter would have embraced this vision of the firm. As easily as workers could move from project to project, so could temps. The only employees who would need to be kept, who needed to be securely held, were those who made decisions in a rapidly changing world—not those who did the same thing day in, day out.

The company man, as an ideal, was dead. Loyalty and stability were anachronistic. The permanent staff, born of World War II faith in long-term planning, would no longer be needed. Those "moderately educated men" would adapt to the ad-hocracy or lose their jobs.[29] There would be no more need for middlemen. Rather than company men, employees would be entrepreneurs. The upside was that this ad-hocracy would unleash a "resurgence of entrepreneurialism!"[30] One part of this entrepreneurialism would be innovation, which is uncertain, but the other part, the individual, was clear. Employees would now be part of an organization on an individual, ad hoc basis. There would be no loyalty in either direction.

Toffler's popularity validated both the McKinsey and the Manpower labor models, which were no longer heretical but visionary. Manpower's 1974 *Annual Report* extolled the virtues of "using staff on an ad-hocracy basis—hiring the very best skills possible for a particular job and then terminating the people when the work is completed."[31] McKinsey, too, saw in Toffler a model of how work should be—that is, just like *their* work. Instead of jobs, there would be projects. Instead of bosses, there would be project managers. This *Future Shock* model mimicked the lives of management consultants, and it would be these consultants who would make that future a present-day reality.

Future Shock was not just another goofy titled book about a utopia (or dystopia) to come, it was the playbook for the gig economy—a playbook implemented by consultants.

The BCG Growth Matrix

Crucial to the remaking of the postwar corporation would be a simple yet powerful idea of Bruce Henderson's—the BCG Growth Matrix. Created in 1968 and first published in a 1970 essay titled "The Product Portfolio," the Growth Matrix redefined basic corporate strategy by combining growth and cash into one easy-to-understand schema. Imagine a 2 x 2 matrix, with growth on the vertical axis from low to high, and cash generation on the horizontal axis, from high to low.[32] Where the growth is low and the cash flow is high sits the "cash cow," a now-commonplace term. The cash cow was a mature company that had a large share of the market and generated lots of cash, but whose market was not growing.[33] Henderson's key idea was that the cash generated by this cow should be reinvested not in itself, but in new business areas with high growth. Henderson's jargony classifications for these two kinds of companies—"stars" (the high-growth, high-cash-creating companies just above the cash cows) and the "problem children" (the high-growth, low-cash-creating companies situated diagonally from the cash cows)—mattered less than the new way of viewing them. Even if a division was profitable, that did not mean that it should be reinvested in. Growth would determine investment.

The strategic brilliance of many conglomerates' industrial subsidiaries dimmed when viewed through Henderson's new matrix. Good management was concerned not just with cash creation in a particular business unit, but with intelligently reinvesting that cash in other business units. Many of the companies that comprised conglomerates neither grew nor generated cash. These "dogs" needed to be sold off or shut down, since they served no role in a successful portfolio. Cash could not be invested in them profitably and they produced no cash to invest elsewhere.

A diversified conglomerate, in this view, could have a distinct advantage over single-purpose companies—the advantage derived not just from being in different sectors, but from operating concerns in different stages of the business life cycle. Corporations were the best stewards of their own capital, not shareholders. Distributing profits through dividends, which the government taxed, destroyed the available pool of capital.[34] Society benefited from successful reinvestment of capital. The trick was putting that money where it would produce the most profitable growth. New companies in new industries needed lots of cash to grow. Old businesses in mature or declining industries could provide capital to these subsidiaries, which could use the cash productively and profitably.

Yet conglomerators like James Ling had not actually reinvested capital from the cows to the stars, they had burned it in undisciplined acquisitions. The new conglomerates may have reduced business-cycle risk, but they did not increase profitability. Ling had not conceived of his companies as a growth-oriented (or stable) investment portfolio, just a series of trophies. Finance should be at the center of the firm, Henderson believed, but not as a tool for acquisition. Finance should support the growing businesses within a firm by funneling cash from the mature businesses.

Henderson's investorcentric worldview extended deeper than a conglomerate's portfolio. Business units were now, through the help of management consultants, being seen not in black-and-white terms as profitable and unprofitable, but in relationship to capital and growth. Each business unit was evaluated as an asset, as in modern portfolio theory, with a risk and return. In the BCG Growth Matrix, growth and capital could be seen simultaneously across business units, and business units could be evaluated as investments. At every scale, it could be used to decide on reinvestment. As conglomerates began to consider the importance of all their businesses, Henderson's matrix, and other similar ideas, would help them see a path to a leaner corporation.

BCG's new framework allowed it to move from a regional start-up into a top three consultancy. While McKinsey partners thought the "growth-share matrix" and "experience curve" were gimmicks, corporations embraced them, and McKinsey lost market share. As the new postwar conglomerates fell apart, many of the older American companies that predated them but followed them in their acquisitions, like General Electric and U.S. Steel, were forced to reconsider their acquisitions. Frameworks like BCG's guided their thinking about how to carve a lean corporation out of fat conglomerates.

Drawing a 2 x 2 matrix was easier than actually reorganizing conglomerates, which is where BCG and other strategy consultants stepped in—and billed. In the wake of the conglomerate frenzy, management consultants started to help CEOs decide which parts of their businesses should be kept and which should be divested, in keeping with the BCG Growth Matrix. Later, a McKinsey partner from that era would tell *Fortune*, "We didn't renew our intellectual capital, we came to market with a dated product, and we got our ass handed to us."[35] McKinsey realized its mistake and, as its clients tried to recover from the conglomate hangover, got into the reorganization business.

Remaking corporations became the bread and butter of the top management consultancies. In 1972, about a third of McKinsey's $45 million a year was reorganizing large corporations.[36] The gap between strategy and structure was apparent, and firms turned to consultants for help. In just the three years at the end of the decade, McKinsey reported that "66 of the nation's top 100 industrial firms reported major organizational realignments." And the bigger the firm, the more likely it had reorganized: "9 of the 10 largest companies, 16 of the top 25, 27 of the top 50" were in that group of sixty-six. McKinsey alone was responsible for reorganizing a hundred firms, on average, per year.[37] Multinational conglomerates that had overreached were the most in need of McKinsey's, and other consultants', help to reorganize.

Trimming General Electric

In 1970, about the same time that the rest of America began to lose its faith in conglomerates, Fred Borch realized that General Electric could not and should not produce everything. The turning point came when he and one of his financial executives, Reginald Jones, considered buying Honeywell, a competitor of IBM, in an effort to consolidate its computer products. But instead of buying Honeywell, Jones sold GE's mainframe business, profitably and shrewdly exiting an industry in which it had no competitive advantage. Selling rather than buying was a complete cultural reversal of the growth-centered history of GE and set an important precedent.[38] Neither returning entirely to its old business nor embracing all that was new, Borch recognized his errors and set GE on a new, leaner path. As other conglomerates fell apart, GE reinvented itself.

With a little outside help from management consultants in 1971, GE developed a new strategic portfolio outlook similar to that extolled by Bruce Henderson.[39] Following Henderson's thinking, all the consulting firms produced customized matrices that emphasized cash and growth. Borch did not think a matrix with just two variables could capture the complexity of GE's operations, so McKinsey offered them a 3 x 3 matrix instead, which weighed many factors but in the end looked very similar to the BCG model.[40]

GE backed away from growth for growth's sake.[41] Instead of seeing capital as unlimited, a GE strategist from that time said that managers had to "imagine that they were making a presentation to an investment bank to get funds." Capital scarcity, as well as talent scarcity, made GE focus on these "resources be[ing] allocated to the best businesses."[42] Under this new rubric, Borch consolidated departments into strategic business units that could be classified through such a matrix.

Henderson's insights, if not precisely his model, helped set GE in a new strategic direction that was followed by his successors, Reginald Jones and, ultimately, Jack Welch.[43] With these restructurings, Borch's profitless diversification had been transformed into a profitable portfolio. Through the Jones and Welch regimes, the dogs were sold off and the cash cows were harvested for reinvestment in the stars, which turned out to be largely outside GE's original field of electrical goods, in medical devices and especially financial services.

General Electric was not alone. Illustrating just how much ideas had changed in just a few years, in 1973 Harvard Business School professor Bruce Scott published his article "Old Myths and New Realities of the Industrial State" in the *Harvard Business Review*, and it was subsequently republished in *McKinsey Quarterly* after winning the prestigious McKinsey Award for best article of the year.[44] Scott's argument, put simply, was that Galbraith and all those who saw rising corporate dominance through monopoly power were wrong. Corporations in 1973 were experiencing a surge of "market mechanism[s]" that curbed corporate power. Rather than all-powerful (and thus requiring state intervention), corporations found themselves under sharp attack on all fronts. The market had returned with a vengeance, and the postwar corporation, rather than being triumphant, was asphyxiating—and that was a good sign. Scott argued that corporations had become too insulated from markets and shareholders.[45] The managers and the workers had prioritized their own job security over shareholders' returns. That security would now be coming to an end.

Restructuring Citibank

Corporations reorganize for a variety of reasons, but according to Warren Cannon, McKinsey's director of staff, the first question that needs to be asked appears to be obvious: "What business(es) are we in?"[46] For some firms the answer might be obvious, but for most of the firms that need the services of McKinsey, the answer is not always clear, particularly after a decade of diversification. Reorganizing a firm to align with its actual strategy is hard—especially when, on a day-to-day basis, you have to run it. Consultants help firms think through the big issues while keeping track of the details.

Consider something that should appear to be straightforward: banking. Banks lend money. Yet banks in the 1960s were mutating beyond what traditional bankers understood. E. Everett Smith, a McKinsey director in the New York office, gave a speech before the American Bankers Association in 1964 in which he said that "the very nature of the industry is in flux.

Already banks have moved out far beyond the boundaries of traditional money banking into a complex pattern of service businesses."[47] By the mid-1960s, banking was becoming more heterogeneous in its practices, moving beyond commercial lending into a range of consumer banking services like CDs and credit cards.[48] While both commercial and consumer lending seemed the same—lending money—they could not have been more different. Commercial banking was based on few, well-considered deals overseen by a small staff. The profit came from the spread between the deposits and the interest. Retail banking, in contrast, turned on volume. It required more locations and more staff, whose skill level was lower and standardized. The spread margin was eaten up by transaction costs, so the profits came from fees. While both businesses involved lending money, the similarities were few. Smith suggested that "the truth is that banks are rapidly becoming conglomerates of specialized businesses."[49] If banks were hard to tease apart, imagine LTV.

Bankers heard his message in 1964, but until the late 1960s—especially after the credit crunch of 1966—had little desire, or incentive, to do anything about it. Bankers quoted Smith but did nothing. He later noted that "few banks have made serious efforts to tailor their organization structures and management practices to the sharply divergent requirements of their different businesses."[50] Even the largest banks, like First National City Bank in New York City, struggled with remaking their organization to face their new clients.

When First National City Bank (now known as Citigroup) needed to rethink its structure in 1967, it turned to McKinsey.[51] Taking a major national bank and reorganizing it in a report of a few dozen pages was an extraordinary task. Behind those pages were hundreds of pages and thousands of hours of research. The entire study began with two simple questions: "1. Is Citibank organized soundly—and for optimum profits—against the separate markets that it serves? 2. Is Citibank organized to provide sufficient top-management direction to its evolution as a financial conglomerate?"[52] The questions and answers might seem obvious or simple, but McKinsey's value was in reducing complexity to simplicity and then making it obvious.

First the team conducted a background study on Citi and the banking industry. They looked at the market data, then rethought the bank's own internal categories to make sure they were solving the right problem. Instead of the traditional two categories of banking, wholesale and retail, they identified eight different types of clients (consumers and small businesses, high-net-worth individuals, professional and service firms, moderate-size local businesses, nonprofits, government, financial institutions, and national and international businesses).[53] As they reimagined Citi, they wanted to make sure that the bank's organization paralleled those eight kinds of customers.[54] To carry this out would require creating and destroying parts of the bank, which would solve the root problem.

Consider Citi's wholesale banking operations, which provided credit to large corporations and governments. Before the reorganization, these operations were spread across different parts of the bank (the National Division, the Specialized Industries Division, and the wholesale part of the Metropolitan Division), which made it hard to grow naturally and to guarantee that clients received the best service. No product is a commodity like money, yet somehow Citi needed its bank to be different from other banks. Customer service was the way to do this, of course, and deciding between the various organizational models, McKinsey created a series of tests—"sensitivity to customer needs," "sensitivity to the environment"—to help decide among the alternatives. How should the bank be reorganized?

The McKinsey team of six men, headed by engagement manager Dick Neuschel, drew up all the different possibilities: by geography (greater New York, east, central, and west), by sector (government, finance, and insurance; extractive; industrial and capital goods; consumer goods), and even by a less cohesive set of categories (divisions that combined sector and geography).[55] Organizing by sector would be better balanced across those four areas than organizing by geography. For a bank located in New York serving national and international customers, a geographic organization did not make much sense. Borrowers within a sector would be far more similar than, say, Zenith (which made televisions) and Caterpillar (which made construction equipment).[56] Both had been in the Illinois-Wisconsin account group. Better to pair Zenith with other "durable good" manufacturers and Caterpillar with other "vehicle and heavy machinery" manufacturers.[57] Such a reorganization would help rebalance the bank, which had more than twice as many accounts in greater New York (142) than it had in the west

(65).[58] Yet the staff would need to visit those clients, who would be spread around the country, so there was a strong counterargument for organizing by geography over sector, if account managers were to visit clients on-site. The right solution would need to balance sector, geography, Citi's own bureaucracy, and, most important, client needs.

Through this transition, McKinsey worked with Citi to make sure that no accounts were lost in the shuffle. The oscillation from the details to the organization was where McKinsey added value. Consultancies helped corporations step back to see what the details meant. For every slide with a new organization chart, there was another slide showing how account management would change in this reorganization, for example. Making a new bank without putting bank customers at the center of the considerations would have been a disaster.

Could Citi executives have seen this logic themselves? Yes, of course. So why would executives look to the consultancy for help? Because McKinsey offered clean data to support the transition. In their charts and graphs, they laid out every possible alternative and systematically eliminated or confirmed alternatives. More important, McKinsey did the hard interpersonal work to convince every stakeholder, from the vice presidents on up, which alternatives were the right choices. At a midsummer working session, for instance, the McKinsey team made an interim presentation to the vice chairmen to keep them up to date and to "set the stage for the ultimate decision at the Policy Committee level by reviewing the general agreement already reached."[59] McKinsey did not issue an edict; they brought the executives along.

In the end, McKinsey suggested a structure that was mostly geographic, with a few exceptions. Financial, government, and insurance clients had their own division, as they were located mostly in New York and were so large.[60] This combination allowed for account managers to have a personal connection to their clients, but also an opportunity to see similar businesses. Assigning the individual accounts would require follow-up study. Carrying out the plan was even harder than reimagining the corporate structure. "Implementation," the executive director told the steering committee in a closed-door meeting, "will require statesmanship on the part of everyone in this room."

These same steps occurred across the bank. McKinsey teams were all over Citi, looking at every account, pulling the bank apart, and imagining how to put it back together again. Nothing was taken for granted. No job was too sacrosanct—not even the consultant's.

These same steps occurred in every major corporation. As McKinsey and other consultancies reorganized corporations, executives were re-trained to see their own firms as consultants saw them. What consultants believed about the proper way to run a business became disseminated at every major corporation. Remember that at McKinsey alone, most of the biggest industrial firms were reorganized.

For consultants like those at McKinsey, who were such hard-driven meritocrats, who had no previous experience, who were so thoroughly indoctrinated in the firm's values, what kind of work could be more effective than their own?

Short-term Profits, Long-term Consultants

In 1975, Henry Boettinger, the director of corporate planning for AT&T, gave the keynote address to a consulting conference held in New York's grandest hotel, the Plaza. The past few years had been nothing but chaos: first came "recession," then "Watergate; the Arab oil embargo; energy, capital, and raw-materials shortages; inflation riding tandem with recession. How . . . could one contemplate anything but change as the order of the times?" The most important tool in confronting this chaos was "the design of the enterprise," which, of course, pleased the roomful of consultants.[61] Boettinger pushed for a shift in consulting, from "single-shot" solutions to ongoing "retainer" contracts. Consultants would not fix an organization and move on, but become its "evolutionary solution." Instead of fixing technical "production bottlenecks," consultants would have "continuity and access" in adjusting the most fundamental aspect of the enterprise. They would become parts of the AT&T executive class, helping it continually remake itself.

Planners like Boettinger, meanwhile, would be out. Only a few hours later at the same conference, Peter Gabriel, the dean of the School of Management at Boston University, interpreted the 1970s as the end of the technocrats who had claimed to have "foresight, planning, [and] perspective" to "tame the economic system." It turned out that they had none of those things. They did not foresee the energy crisis or the depletion of natural resources or "the dangers of the 'Consumption Society' to economic equilibrium."[62] They tried to plan the economy and they had failed. Gabriel knew that most critics of "incompetent bureaucrats" meant those in Washington, but in his mind, the failure was not just public, but private. "Have our private institutions"—specifically, corporate managements—"done significantly better?" Gabriel was not alone in his doubts about planning.

Technological change, as just one example of planning, was, in the consultant's mind, impossible to predict. Citing a study from 1937, McKinsey managing director Gil Clee in 1968 criticized prognosticators who "missed not only the computer but atomic energy, antibiotics, radar, and jet propulsion, nearly all of which had been around in principle."[63] While forecasters may have failed, scientists succeeded. The postwar breakthroughs surprised, but nearly all the so-called major developments that came after 1970 (the internet, manufacturing automation, cellular phones) had been expected. One must wonder whether prediction improved in quality or, more likely, imagination faltered. Revolutionary science stopped. The shortsighted R&D of the post-1970s era produced fewer unimaginable products, and none that were based on genuinely new basic science. Correctly predicting the future means that nothing truly disruptive ever occurs. Long-term investment in R&D may not have begotten the expected products, but it did spawn unexpected products. It did create new industries that employed millions.

The turn to short-term profits changed the way American manufacturing operated. Consider Dow Corning, which, after having weathered the material shortages of 1973, then contended with capital shortages. A. William Rhodes, a vice president of engineering and manufacturing, explained that this shortage of R&D money mean[t] "delays, stretch-outs, and the cancellation of some projects."[64] Dow Corning cut back on its investment in new technology in its area of focus, the "hyper-pure silicon" that underpinned nearly all developments in electronics. These kinds of cutbacks happened across its manufacturing plant, as "economic evaluation techniques to measure return on sales, return on investment, [and] discounted cash flow" predicted too low a level of return. Cutback decisions were guided not by long-term possibility, but by the harsh metrics of profit distilled to the present. In an age of managing for shareholder profit, long-term investment faltered. Without money to invest in expanding their plant, Dow Corning turned, when possible, to "contract manufacturing," which incurred an "extra cost to seek out qualified contractors." Rhodes felt that "the return has been worth the effort."[65] This turn to contract manufacturing would not be unique. Short-term profit and production flexibility led many firms to outsource their manufacturing to third parties—first in the U.S. and then abroad.

This retreat from new products and new sectors ironically became thought of as innovation. Incrementally focusing on what they already did rather than what was possible was the essential strategic shackle that "lean" foisted on organizations. At a deep level, reducing staff went hand in hand with reducing risk. This so-called entrepreneurship was neither creative nor destructive. Without a new leading sector, these maturing firms, in an era of relative technological stagnation, used automation to displace more and more of the routine workforce.[66] The patriotic pride that GE's Ralph Cordiner could feel in the 1950s at being the head of an "American manufacturing company . . . devoted first to serving the United States" had been replaced by the pride in a rising stock price.

Firms that clung to long-term investments risked everything. While the conglomerates created bigger and bigger firms, the mergers and acquisitions activity of the 1970s was the opposite: carving up those conglomerates to reveal the lean meat of the corporation. If you ran your company in accordance with postwar values of stability and loyalty to your employees and even your product, then you were among the weak (that is, vulnerable to takeover). As Jack Vance, McKinsey managing director in Los Angeles, wrote, "If a company is vulnerable to the approach of a would-be raider . . . it may be high time for management to reexamine . . . some time-hallowed corporate policies." Low debts and stable profits made a firm ripe for a hostile takeover backed by a "velvet-clad iron fist."[67]

In short, your company could—and should—be taken away from you. To be "'oil men,' 'railroad men' or 'steel men'" was, according to Vance, a mistake. All executives should just be "profit-growth men."[68] Firms that did not adopt this viewpoint were vulnerable to takeover, and their "myopic top managements have failed to see even the most obvious seeds of their own corporate decay."[69] Managers who did not restructure risked their own jobs.[70]

McKinsey was happy to help executives save their jobs by selling off business units they didn't run or by acquiring new firms that they could run. McKinsey and other consultancies developed methods for handling post-merger management. Frederick Searby, a partner in the Paris office, explained: "Change is certain after a merger—not evolutionary change, but sudden, often traumatic change"—that is, top managers got fired so that the new owners could remake the structure of the merged firm. Managers who wanted to keep their jobs would hire consultants to remodel their own companies to prevent exactly this kind of takeover.

In the wake of the conglomerate collapse, management consultants started to take on the more strategic role of helping CEOs decide which parts of their businesses should be kept and which should be divested. In 1971, in the midst of economic chaos, only seventy-four companies listed in *Forbes* had both high growth and high return (both greater than 10 percent). What set these firms apart was their commitment, as William Hill, president of Dun & Bradstreet's management consulting division, told a conference of management consultants, to "a cohesive business concept." Focused companies, not diversified companies, did better in change, he believed. Such firms followed "fundamentals," not "current fads" like "financial conglomerates, diversification and product development with mixed results, investment in business that soon developed overcapacity, investment in land development, inappropriate mergers and public ownership." How quickly the future can be denigrated as fad! "The 1969 to 1971 recession," Hill said, "was therapeutic in removing accumulated fat in operations."[71] As the 1960s became the '70s, the commonsense answer, at least for leading consultancies, was to restructure the firm so that it was smaller, more flexible, and clearly aligned with its products.

How to decide which parts of a business to sell off, and what firms to acquire, however, was never clear. While Henderson's model was simple, and directionally correct, it did not offer any explanation about why a particular business was a dog or star. Dogs should be sold and stars invested in, but you couldn't tell beforehand which was which. How to assess an opportunity ahead of time? That answer would come from economist, professor, and consultant Michael Porter.

The Five Forces of Michael Porter

Michael Porter had received his economics PhD from Harvard in 1973, as corporate strategists were trying to figure out how to answer Henderson's question of whether an acquired business unit should be owned or divested. While it was clear that cash should go to stars, it was less clear whether a business could be turned around or if it was inevitably going to lose money. In 1979, Porter, having witnessed the fall of diversified conglomerates, offered a new answer in his concept of the Five Forces, which turned old divisions between monopolies and markets on their heads. In his model, all successful corporations were narrowly focused monopolies.

Porter synthesized competition and monopoly into one framework, allowing both to happen at once, and transformed the notion of competition from markets to supply chains. While traditional corporate strategists had considered rival companies the sole source of competition, Porter reframed competition more broadly within the microeconomic question of "capturing surplus" that was at the center of the definition of a monopoly. Porter's key insight was that the firm, at the center of the first force, market competition, is competing not only with other companies but with suppliers and customers as well—successful companies could not just wrest surplus from their competition, but had to do so from suppliers and from consumers. While other firms' rivalry still mattered, so, too, did the pressures from the "bargaining power of suppliers," the "threat of substitute products or services," the "bargaining power of customers," and the "threat of new entrants."[72] The first force may have been competition, but these four forces counted just as much.

Conglomerates may not have been monopolies, but in analyzing their fall, consultants and strategists like Porter realized that they should have been. If in competitive markets profits were impossible, then the only answer was to make sure one's business was not in a competitive market, which, Porter argued, offered the "worst prospect for long-run profitability."[73] Monopolies were the only way to get above-average profits.

Companies always occupied specific locations on a supply chain, from raw materials to final products. At each link in the chain, value was added, but who got that value depended on a balance of market power—that is, on how close they were to a pure monopoly. Companies that did not have a clear sense of their location on the supply chain, such as sprawling conglomerates, risked their investors' capital. Only by focusing on a company's core strengths, where there were barriers to entry—where the company had a monopoly—could above-average returns on capital be realized.

Porter's evidence showed that reinvestment in core businesses might be a good idea, but allowing companies to act as conglomerators—acquiring companies in unrelated fields—only eroded shareholder value.[74] CEOs made bad choices and usually paid too much, and investing in companies and operating companies required different skill sets. Porter argued that diversification as an end in itself offered little value to the buyer, unless it was in a monopoly.

Businesses in competitive markets should be divested because above-average returns were impossible. If the global wheat market was efficient and reliable, a bread company should not buy wheat farms, it should buy wheat, since farming it offered few returns beyond a competitive market.

Supply could be trusted. With reliable delivery connections, like those made possible by container ships and intermodal trucking, supply had become more reliable in the 1970s.[75] Logistics, not markets, made a leaner corporation possible. If Galbraith's postwar corporation sought to minimize exposure to supply risk, Porter offered a way to strategically consider a company's relationship within a supply chain and to profitably manage it. A bread company could just buy wheat and not worry about whether it would arrive in time.

It's a short step from there to outsourcing. For nearly any firm, the biggest "supplier" was always the workforce. The old struggle between labor and capital could be recast as just another link in the supply chain. Good corporate strategy meant outsourcing to the market everything that the firm could not monopolize—including the workforce. In the new scheme, if janitorial services are commodities that don't provide a monopolistic advantage to the firm, then they should be bought from the market. Outsourcing would become the rational solution for any product or service that could be found in a competitive market. These commodity jobs, of course, fit exactly with Winter's idea of a temporary labor force. Hiring salaried janitors instead of a cleaning company, it could now be seen, was just another way to squander capital.

With his Five Forces model, Porter answered the outstanding question of the BCG Growth Matrix: how to tell whether a business was a dog or a star by analysis and not experience. His stunning synthesis of how the economy worked got him on the fast track to a professorship at Harvard Business School and rocked the business world. At the same time, not coincidentally, Porter cofounded the Monitor Group, a strategic management consulting firm. Books, teaching, and consulting converged as a framework for disseminating Porter's ideas of the corporation. After Porter explained his Five Forces, controlling the supply chain did not matter as much as controlling the most monopolistic positions on the supply chain. Only suckers made commodities. Markets and monopolies went hand in hand in this new era of corporate strategies.

Trimming Firms, Trimming Workforces

"Management can be expected to run on a much leaner basis and be more productive with fewer 'inbetweeners.' The superstructures—vice-presidents, middle management—seemingly so necessary in the 1960s, seems now to be passé." Budgets encompassed not just people but divisions, and "the recession of 1970 has caused corporate executives to break out more accurately the various profit centers of a company," Winter wrote. "Allocations" to keep the "pets of the past" alive could no longer be kept up.[76] These pets included job security.

The achievement of economic security—if not for everyone, then for a broad swath—was pointed to as a cause of this collapse. The stable life, the achievement of the postwar world, was recharacterized by Manpower and other management organizations as "the 'galloping psychology of entitlement.'" Somehow, in just a few years, what had been an inevitable world of leisure and security had become a world of entitled whiners: "The desire for good medical care becomes the right to good medical care, and the desire for a meaningful job becomes the right to one." Whatever the source of the "increased social legislation—social security, medical care, 'portable pensions,' maternity leaves, termination benefits . . . the inevitable result is increased supplemental labor costs for employers. . . . The logical alternative," according to Manpower, was "to put on temporary staff to meet production demands."[77] Employees would need to be adaptable. The corporation would need to be flexible. The corporation as envisioned by Alfred Sloan and practiced through the postwar period would, in short, be over.

The workforce planning that Manpower had tried to sell for twenty years suddenly found a new urgency as corporations tried to find an alternative to adding someone to the payroll. Rather than the "I don't care what it costs" attitude of the 1960s, the '70s, Winter believed, would again begin to count. This "costocracy" would undo the bureaucratic expansions of the '60s that had not been checked during the growing economy.[78] "Profit improvement is something that every employee will participate in"—or they would not have a job at all.

The first article to use the term "lean organization" in McKinsey Quarterly was not published until 1985, but the term drew together these existing threads of management thought.[79] The lean revolution, whether it was called Toyotaism, Six Sigma, or Total Quality Management, was a shift in thinking that emerged from many sources, though it was a particular cadre of capitalist intellectuals—consultants and gurus—who disseminated this vision of the corporation. By the 1980s, "lean" would go hand in hand with successful business practice. Writing in McKinsey Quarterly, Stratford Sherman, an associate editor at Fortune, described what it meant to be one of "the heroes of contemporary capitalism."[80] It was definitely not being "slow and stodgy" like those big postwar firms, and yet it was paradoxically to be among the largest corporations in the U.S.—the Fortune 500. These top firms were "nimble enough to put smaller companies to shame" by "routinely treat[ing] bureaucratic considerations—who works for what division—as entirely subservient to the goal of listening carefully to their customers."[81] This ideology simultaneously valorized smallness while celebrating the largest firms. It was impossible to imagine that they could be nimble without being small. But while not small in revenues, they were increasingly small in employees.

Making the lean corporation possible meant replacing all the routine work with computers, yet in 1970, that level of automation was not possible. That permanently hired men should not do routine tasks would remain true, but it would not be computers that replaced them, but a workforce of temporary women.

CHAPTER NINE

Office of the Future, Factory of the Past

At noon, during a lunch hour in September 1979, Jane Fonda, activist, feminist, and film star, took the stage at a theater in downtown Boston.[1] She had spent the morning testifying before the Massachusetts state legislature with her husband, activist Tom Hayden, and the previous night at a benefit cocktail party at the Fan Club, but this was the main event. Before her were a thousand women office workers who had paid five dollars to hear her talk about the economic rights of working-women.[2] She had a new comedy coming out, about a housewife who goes back to work as a secretary after her husband leaves her, and as part of her publicity tour she was in Boston to support the inspiration for the film. That money would go to support the women's real-life office worker group, which had the same name as her movie—9 *to* 5. "Women office workers are underpaid and undervalued," Fonda told the crowd, "but through workingwomen's organizations . . . you can fight to win equal rights and respect."[3]

Karen Nussbaum and Ellen Cassedy, two Harvard secretaries, had founded 9to5 in Boston in 1972 to fight the scant wages and ample sexism of Boston offices. Boston had 250,000 clerical workers (about one fifth of the workforce), who were nearly all women and whose pay was among the worst in the country—only Memphis and Birmingham had lower wage rates.[4] Women's work was at the center of this knowledge economy. "Do you realize that Boston's paper economy cannot function without us?" a 9to5 speaker explained. "Office workers are to Boston what autoworkers are to Detroit."[5]

The "office of the future" had transformed office work into "assembly line jobs with clericals performing one repetitive task whose purpose the company does not bother to explain."[6] This paper economy was in the process of transforming into an electronic one. "The office of the future looks very much like the factory of the past," Karen Nussbaum would later say in *Computerworld*. "There's nothing at all new about shift work, piece work, which is what pay per line of information is," or, more generally, there was no difference between freelancing and "the cottage industries."[7]

The difference, of course, was that in the intervening decades, work in both factories and offices had become a path to the middle class, as Nussbaum knew. Now that path was becoming more treacherous, even as it was legitimated by a vague notion of progress. The "science fiction-like rhetoric," she later said, obscured the reality that "this is all pretty old stuff and maybe it's being done on new machines, but the consequences are the same for the same people who perform the work."[8]

As corporate America chose to automate its offices, those workers, unlike the ones in the factories, had little successful recourse, even as they resisted the changes. The front lines of the computer age were in the offices. As Jane Fonda ended her speech, she optimistically told the crowd, "We can win now. Our time has come."[9]

Fonda's film came out the next year, with country music sensation Dolly Parton, acclaimed comedian Lily Tomlin, and the perfectly cast Dabney Coleman (as the "sexist, egotistical, lying, hypocritical bigot" boss) and was a huge hit—grossing $103 million as the second most popular film of 1980.[10] In the movie, the workers bested their boss, and in real life Parton won a Grammy—for best country song—for the theme song.[11]

The reality for 9to5, and for women office workers more generally, was not as hilarious—or successful.

From Emergency Support to Market Discipline

As Alvin Toffler touted the glory of his ad-hocracy, Manpower was ready. Through a series of writings and speeches, Elmer Winter disseminated his own vision of ad-hocracy to clients in America and abroad. Manpower offered a trial run of seminars in six cities, for "700 management, sales, and supervisory personnel" to show them the benefits of permanent temps.[12] A "mixed work force" would combine the best of this permanent and temporary world, bringing the discipline of market forces inside the corporation.[13]

Winter envisioned a new balance in the workforce that resulted from the reality check of the recession of 1970: "Many companies will work out a personnel program which will encompass 75 percent full-time permanent employees, 15 percent temporaries and 10 percent part-time workers."[14] The fall of the conglomerate meant the reorganization not only of firms, but also of the workforces of those firms. The use of temps as a subcontracted workforce for data entry (used in one fifth of firms) proved the success of the model that Winter had long advocated. In the aftermath of the crisis, he pushed even harder for permanent temporary staffs outside of data entry.

Manpower took a hit in 1971 as its revenues shrank alongside everyone else's, but as firms began to reconsider their workforces in a systematic way, through the lean insights of the consultants, temporary workers began to take on a different character. The language Winter had deployed through the 1960s began to resonate with other voices in the business community and to be folded into a new vision of the corporate workforce.

Winter had been talking about these ideas for over a decade, but as the endless growth of the postwar era came to an end, they had a new immediacy. The lean ideal of firms led them to depend on temporary workers. The uncertainty of the 1970s, Manpower hoped, would lead them to look to "lease" workers rather than make a "permanent hire."[15]

In the face of the challenges of 1971, Elmer Winter and Manpower's senior management took the unusual tack of being interviewed for the annual report. They answered very contrived questions ("Mr. Winter, in light of current labor surplus conditions, can the temporary help industry sustain the growth rate it has enjoyed in the past?") that nonetheless spoke to the essential issues in the American workforce—especially the temporary workforce.[16] Temporary labor was not reimagined, but the contradictory ways in which Winter had previously discussed the *purpose* of temp work had a new emphasis. Winter was not alone in this vision. *McKinsey Quarterly* told its readers, slightly later than Winter, that they should think of labor as a "fixed investment" rather than a "variable cost."[17] It had become too hard to hire and fire workers. In planning the expansion of a new factory, workers had to be considered alongside machines and buildings as a permanent part of the investment.

As companies began to rehire after the recession, they would, Winter hoped, "us[e] temporary help instead of permanent staff." Temps would not be used only to fill emergency needs or to bolster a tight labor market, but would be a planned component of the corporate workforce, a cost-saving device forming a "second labor market" that "could effectively eliminate overstaffing." Winter envisioned "a more sophisticated use of our services" by managers who are "programming us into their total personnel picture on a continuing basis" as a "valuable and permanent management tool."[18] In an era of uncertainty, fixed costs could be a death knell for a business. Most firms (63 percent) considered the cost of temps as discretionary procurement rather than labor costs.[19] Long-term labor costs could be transformed into simple transactions, giving firms more flexibility.

Temps could provide a market discipline to these coddled workers. Permanent workers' security, Winter thought, made for inefficiency. While skilled workers were necessary for some tasks, those tasks rarely consumed an entire day and "nonessential work is found to keep them busy during the rest of their paid work time."[20]

The danger of white-collar work, he thought, was that it was so much harder to measure productivity than blue-collar work. The task required could expand to fill the time available. Temps provided a yardstick to measure permanent workers, by, for instance, "diplomatically demonstrat[ing] how many letters a competent secretary can turn out in a four-hour period." Over time, these norms can erode, and the "presence of short-term employees" can restore productivity. Temporary workers once existed to protect workers' vacations, but now they existed as a way to remind employees what a permanent vacation could look like.

Safe workers were unproductive workers, Winter believed. A management consultancy in the late 1960s had produced a report for Manpower that found "[permanent] workers were approximately 55 percent productive." "This means," Winter clarified, "that about half of the time the employee was at his or her desk there was a productive result."[21] The rest of the time the worker was getting paid for doing nothing. Whether this was accurate, the rhetorical effect was real, and it resonated with the honchos. A permanent worker with fringe benefits might cost more than a temp, but that could be justified by the workers' loyalty and commitment. An employee who worked half the time—a lazy employee—deserved no loyalty, and was being paid double. By employing temps, managers could remind their employees of an unwelcome alternative. Temps started to sound better every day.

Necessity, Not Choice

Annette Hopkins did not want to be a temp. She did it only because she couldn't find a permanent job, and, in fact, she blamed the proliferation of temporary firms as part of the reason for her lack of secure work. In Boston, she wrote, there were more than a hundred temporary agencies. Employers had their pick of firms and of temps. Temps were not, she said, a "small lonely band," but a large labor pool. In "the 1975 economy characterized as it is by recession, inflation, unemployment, and job discrimination," workers were forced, Hopkins wrote, to take what they could get. The fall in the value of the dollar made the need for more work very concrete. As men lost jobs to deindustrialization, women entered the workforce. Some of them broke through glass ceilings in exciting professional careers, but most of them, like most workers in general, entered offices, factories, and shops looking for a paycheck, not purpose.[22] She, and most other temps, understood that something had changed in office work. "In times of stagflation," she wrote, "client-companies find contracting with agencies for temporary workers an attractive alternative to hiring permanent employees."[23]

At the beginning of the 1970s, women office workers around the country, like Hopkins, began to try to organize themselves—most notably in 9to5. The women were ordinary secretaries, not professional union organizers. But in a few short years, they began to be effective, even creating a Service Employees International Union (SEIU) local in most major American cities.[24]

At its outset, 9to5 sought to organize university secretaries, and then it spread into the areas they thought were the most pressing for women in Boston: publishing, insurance, banking—and temporary agencies. The main committees in 9to5 focused on clerical workers with traditional jobs who could communicate with one another and have ongoing connections, if not friendships. The aim was to build worker solidarity out of women's solidarity. It was an attempt to bridge the women's movement with the labor movement. While nationally temps made up about 2 percent of the workforce, in Boston and similar kinds of cities, temps accounted for as much as 5 to 8 percent, according to contemporary experts.[25] Nussbaum and Cassedy wanted 9to5 to be more than just consciousness raising, they wanted to organize for change.[26] The need for such an organization emerged from both the changing office and the changing office worker.

The organization published reports, organized rallies, petitioned legislatures, filed lawsuits, and generally raised a ruckus—somewhat successfully.[27] Through its meetings and newsletters, 9to5 intertwined issues of wages and benefits with those of hierarchy and respect by seeking to "counter office workers' isolation from one another and hostility to unions."[28] Its greatest successes were in supporting those women who worked in traditional jobs in offices. Temps were part of their agenda, but their least successful, and their failures pointed to just how different this emerging kind of work was from traditional jobs—and how hard it would be to push back against more nebulous employers with a scattered workforce than one office in a downtown high-rise.

Temporary work for women in the 1970s bore little relationship to postwar temp work. Temps were not luxury-seeking hausfraus, if they ever were. Temping was not done to provide discretionary, additional income. For "the victims of 12 percent a year inflation and 10 percent unemployment, working for temporary agencies is an alternative to unemployment checks and/or subsistence lifestyle," Hopkins wrote to her state representative in 1975.[29] Temp work was a refuge of last resort—and temps felt treated that way, like "unhirable workers" who should be grateful for a job. "I have been unable to find an entry level administrative position, and working as a temporary gives me a flexibility in job hunting." These two facts were not unrelated. As more women entered the workforce, so, too, did the number of temp firms increase. Women who wanted a real job found that many firms were now relying on temps, especially in growing areas like data entry that were boring—not exciting.

Addressing a group of college students, a 9to5 speaker related a harsh truth: "Many of you sitting here today, if the job outlook doesn't improve, will find yourselves in the same position, and what is that? Low salaries, lack of respect and no job rights." At some agencies, most temps had college degrees, or even master's degrees.[30] With so many career paths closed to professional women, temping offered an unwanted alternative. Women worked in the 70s because the "salaries [were] vital to the support of our families, yet employers seem to pretend that women don't need as much as men."[31] Women did not just work until they found a husband. Married women worked to pay the bills.

Simply meeting women in similar circumstances was emboldening, but it was particularly important for temps. Temporary workers were usually isolated from one another, and even when they worked together they were "discouraged from discussing their relative pay rates with other temps."[32] For workers without any transparency, simply sharing information with one another pushed back on the temp agencies.

Janet Selcer, who was on 9to5's temporary committee, described temps as "urban migrant workers"—very different terms than Elmer Winter used. Selcer, who had been a temp, wanted to help other temps get the "job security, fringe benefits, [and] nearly the same pay that the regular workers have."[33] "Like the rural migrants, until recently we have had no sense of group identity," and 9to5 aimed to change that.[34] To make that happen, however, they needed facts. To understand what was happening with women temps, 9to5 organized a survey of temps and temp agencies in the Boston area. The survey of temps wasn't scientific, and the responses (about thirty) were not representative. The questions themselves were loaded. The survey said, based on 9to5's own conversations, "If you are a temporary office worker you probably are . . . an adaptable, skilled office worker . . . work for your 'bread and butter,' not just 'pin money' . . . receive none of the benefits or compensations you deserve . . . are earning less than a full-time worker." A response written on the back of one of the returned surveys, outside of any response space, simply said "ALL TRUE." The individual stories of those temps, however, confirmed other kinds of anecdotal evidence and the variety of women's experiences. The 9to5 survey revealed a reality that was inconsistent. Sometimes temps knew what they were getting into. Sometimes they didn't. Sometimes they got pressured to take a gig. Sometimes they didn't. What was constant, however, was a pervasive silence about pay, and a lack of benefits. The everyday work life of a temp did not include paid holidays, and it also didn't include paid coffee breaks or lunch breaks. It did include uncertainty about whether you would work tomorrow, and if you did, how many hours you would get, and whether you would work after that. Though the 9to5 survey wasn't exhaustive or scientific, it did reveal a world quite at odds with the temp agency brochures—a world of necessity, not choice, a world of insecurity, not flexibility.

The survey of temp agencies revealed telling patterns that confirmed most of the experiences that temps reported. Twenty temp agencies were surveyed (including all the major ones, like Manpower, Kelly, and Olsten), and their answers were largely consistent, both with one another and with the temps' responses. The agencies had no raise policies. They had no written job descriptions. They had no grievance procedures. Few (Manpower and Olsten) offered even minimal health benefits, and those only for long-term temps.[35] The most appalling finding was that none of them were regulated, which meant, 9to5 said, "that they are free to set any policies no matter how exploitative of the temporary."[36] The temp agencies treated their workers like a transaction, not a relationship.

Agencies were not opposed to relationships per se. There were no contracts with clients, at least not at Manpower, just, as the local Manpower manager told 9to5, a "gentleman's agreement."[37] But this gentleman's agreement did not hold for the ladies. While the agency and the client may have had an ad hoc relationship, the agency and the temp had a firm contract that made sure that if the temp left the agency for a client, the agency would still get paid by the employer.[38] The only lady's agreement was that ladies would have less information, less security, and less money than a full-time employee.

As temp work became less of a niche and more a standard part of the management playbook, temp work changed. The promise of temp work, for one anonymous temp, was that it would be a "learning" and "enjoyable experience," working in "several different companies over a short period of time." The reality was less appealing. The temp's life was "marred by the worries of financial insecurity." The work itself was not a learning experience but "tedious, monotonous and massive," with few incentives. The preference of temp and permanent work was made clear by the delighted exclamation at the end of one survey response: "P.S. I just got a permanent job!"[39]

While in the postwar era temps were expected to work for only one firm, by the 1970s, temps found they needed to work for multiple agencies to string together consistent work. One temp, who had been in the trenches since the 1960s, thought assignments were now too few. She currently worked "for 4 agencies in order to be kept working most of the time," but had been able, in the past, to rely on just one agency. The number of agencies had grown, and the number of people who needed temp work had grown as well.

All temps, whether or not they liked their situation, faced a reality in which they had little choice over the kind of work they accepted. In theory, a temp could refuse jobs. In practice, temps had little choice whether to accept their assignments. If they refused, as one Olsten's temp remarked, "they might not have another one for me."

The flexibility was now less for the worker than for the employer. Getting hours was everything. Temps were on the clock in a way that most office workers were not. That clock, and its hourly rate, determined their checks.[40] With so many women to choose from, temp agencies did not need to use the same people all the time. "While they offer the bogus lure of diversity [in jobs]," temp Rose Senatore of 9to5 said, "they offer no security, no benefits, and no guarantee that there will be work and a paycheck." Getting work was more like playing a "roulette wheel" for temps.[41]

Working for multiple agencies made getting enough hours to qualify for sick pay, much less vacation time (even at the firms that offered it), impossible. Agencies had few incentives to provide year-round work. Without consistent hours, it was hard to get benefits. A temp responding to the survey "knew" that Manpower "used to have these" benefits that were no longer provided, but the story was actually more complicated—and a portent of things to come for all temps, part-timers, and freelancers.

The answer to the question of whether temps received benefits was not a simple yes or no, or even, as one temp wrote, "THEY PRETEND WE DO, BUT WE DON'T!" The Boston area manager for Manpower explained to the Boston Globe that they did have a "minimal health care program" that covered only "hospitalization." Manpower offered as well "six paid holidays after working 800 hours in a 12-month period." Manpower temps also had a "week's paid vacation after 1500 hours of work, or 100 hours of work each month."[42] Olsten, similarly, offered a check for 2.5 days every 700 hours of work (in a year). If you worked 37.5 hours a week (lunch breaks taken out), that would be almost 19 weeks of solid work (about 5 months).[43] While temps could receive benefits, with an average working period of only 3 months, few did. Benefits, holidays, and health care all existed, but only if you met the minimum time requirements. Respondents liked "the idea of working temp" but "hate[d] to lose out on benefits and wages," and because hours were so hard to get consistently, at least to those active in 9to5, flexibility looked more like insecurity.

Opinions varied on whether temps were misled, and whether they were, as 9to5 asserted, "exploited." Some temps didn't expect more than what they got. "For a free-lance situation this is an excellent source of income—and consistent—without the burden of commitment," wrote one temp. The "benefits are almost non-existent; but the advantages of owning your own time far outweighs that for me," she added, echoing the arguments of a postwar temp. In response to the 9to5 provocation, "DO THESE FACTS MAKE YOU MAD? WANT TO CHANGE THEM? SO DO WE!!" she simply scribbled, "No. See other side." Office work was boring everywhere, and for some temps, the ability to leave and find other work was a real boon. A Kelly temp recounted how she just couldn't imagine "being a woman at a small desk with a calculator and a typewriter, and that's all she does all day. This is what they do year after year after year." At least as a temp there was some variety. She liked that she met new people, picked up new skills, learned about new industries.[44]

That the client paid the agency more than the temp got paid rubbed most temps the wrong way and contributed to a feeling of exploitation. Of course, all firms make money off their workers if the firm is profitable, but at a temp agency that number was precise, omnipresent, and infuriating. Temps knew that the market rate for their services was higher than what they got paid, but they didn't always know exactly how much, which was galling. Agencies took their cut, and temps knew it. For women trying to make ends meet, knowing that for every dollar that they earned that the temp agency got thirty cents was frustrating. Every temp imagined that extra 20 to 40 percent in her own pocket. Hopkins, for instance, objected that her temp firm, Office Specialists of Boston, did not provide "the corresponding pay rates and fees charged the client-companies." A temp who had

had a permanent job did know the difference between what she was paid ($3.25 an hour) and what the firm paid ($4.50) "because [she] used to be in a hiring position." The agencies, simply put, "rip us off."

Employers, in turn, complained that "one of our biggest problems with keeping a competent temporary employee is their knowledge of a less-than-standard hourly pay rate." In a national survey of employers, this result came up so often that the authors of the survey report, the American Management Society, were exasperated with its lack of specificity: "To what is the respondent comparing the rate? His own employee with years of seniority, with considerable responsibility? With union wages? With the rate *charged* by the temporary service?"[45] Likely the answer was yes, yes, and yes. The worker looked at her paycheck and imagined the paycheck of someone with a permanent job. For industrial workers, the comparison was with a union job. And all temps knew that for every hour that they worked, somebody was making a buck.

Compounding that frustration was how often temps were asked to do work outside their job description—both more complicated and more demeaning. Misclassification of temps kept client costs down. Patty Chase, a temp and 9to5 member, explained to the Massachusetts legislature that the lowest grade of temp was a "'typist' at the low pay rate of $2.75 to $3.00 an hour."[46] Upon arriving at a job, she would often find herself not doing easy manuscript typing, but "editing, filing, ordering supplies, collating, and running errands"—in short, being an executive secretary, which was a much more expensive temp position. When Chase temped at Harvard Business School, for example, she was sent there for a four-month typist position. When she arrived she "found [herself] instantly responsible as secretary to not one, but two full professors, for the operation of an entire office. I was expected to type heavy correspondence, often transcribing several tapes a day, type manuscripts for both professors, answer the phone which rang constantly, open and read mail, fetch books from the library, answer questions from students and visitors, screen visitors, make travel arrangements, often for overseas travel, keep track of numerous appointments and one professor's entire schedule, and coordinate the activities of work-study students." Chase did a lot more than type. Temps who complained about misclassification found themselves in "the agency's file of undesirables, on the 'goof list.'" "Not once," she testified, "did the actual job in any way re-semble the job that my agency described to me and paid me for."[47] Temps complained of perms who "look[ed] down their nose" at them and treated them as "second class citizens instead of an extra pair of hands to help them out of a bind."[48]

The placement counselors for the temps were not in a much better situ-ation either. At Dynamic Temporaries, a small Boston temp agency with four staff and sixty to eighty temps, the counselor made about $150 a week—only slightly more than the temps she oversaw, and about the same as a low-paid secretary.[49] She worked overtime but didn't get paid for it. She worked outside her job description, "but try not to." She had no union. But she did get life insurance and health coverage. She got regular vacations (two weeks a year). She had unlimited sick days. She did, however, "like her job."

While some at 9to5 framed this misclassification in rather conspiratorial tones, as it no doubt sometimes was a way for agencies to competitively price their workers, job classification was tricky for employers as well. Employers complained that "what one company calls a 'project secretary,' another calls a 'clerk-typist.'"[50] Firms, when satisfied, tended to stick with one temp agency. "Once a good service understands your needs," an employer wrote, "they generally do an excellent job." Getting to that understanding took time. Surveyed firms reported that a quarter had used only one temp firm in the previous two years, while 60 percent used two or three. Very few firms relied on many temp agencies.[51] For a job request, the vast majority (76 per-cent) of firms relied on just one agency at a time, using other agencies as backups. Overwhelmingly, even though they were permitted multiple an-swers, employers chose their temp agencies based on "quality of service" (76 percent) rather than "price" (12 percent).[52] For the employer, getting someone who could do the same work was paramount. Uncertain about the skills of the temp, it was easier for employers, in every case, to get a low-skill temp and push the scut work onto them.

Female temps were usually expected—like other workingwomen—to perform domestic work around the office. Employers would ask a typist to "serve coffee, run personal errands, or . . . 'clean up' the employer's private bathroom."[53] Fear of losing that job, and every other temp job, made the decision whether to serve coffee fraught with real economic fear. The temp's situation paralleled many women office workers', but with less pay and few rights. Women everywhere were starting to refuse to do "personal work," but it was so easy for a temp to be replaced, given a bad review, and then left unable to find another placement.[54] Olsten colluded with creepy bosses since it advertised in its brochures that "Olsten services cover almost every skill you can name . . . an attractive girl to serve coffee at your next business meeting."[55] Employers expected the temp to "send letters to the parents of all the boys in his Cub Scout pack" because the boss did not distinguish between his private and professional life when it came to directing women's labor.[56]

All women office workers, not just temps, faced these kinds of situations. "Sex discrimination," a temp wrote on a 9to5 survey, "goes hand in hand with secretarial work." Temps had even less recourse than regular workers. The temp agency would do nothing about it and, one temp wrote, would give "little support . . . to the girl who refuses to also play maid to the client co."[57] This temp had worked at her particular agency for two years and had seen the very real effects of women refusing to be the "maid." Refusing to "play maid" meant getting sent home, and that meant no pay.

The Failure to Regulate

From the start, Cassedy and Nussbaum had envisioned creating an "independent women office workers' organization."[58] First they had gathered facts and built a network. But they still faced serious challenges. Unions were on the decline. In the early 1970s, unions represented only about a quarter of all workers—and those were mostly men. "Labor bureaucracy," they wrote, "consists of a few men negotiating with corporations and government—not a democratic system; may not represent interests of rank and file," especially when that rank and file were women.[59] The women's movement had "increased women's consciousness of their oppression," but it had not yet created "organizational forms" to counter that oppression.[60]

The plan was straightforward. The organization would help office workers, like those at the Boston insurance company Liberty Mutual, to organize themselves. Starting with a group of "dissatisfied" women, with 9to5's support, they would make contact with a union and begin an organization

drive. When the union won, 9to5 would "get our contacts elected to the negotiating committee" and make sure that the women workers, not the
"union reps or management," were in charge. In this way, 9to5 would push
for women's voices within the labor movement.[61] Nussbaum and Cassedy
wanted to tap into women's rage, their "taste of blood," as well as achieve
"more money and benefits."

Temps would not, however, work with this plan. To unionize required
work conditions like those at large insurance companies, where "clerical
work is often performed in large offices [where] concentration of labor
makes organizing easier and its effects more significant."[62] Organizing
temps in a traditional local seemed impossible as well. As one temp wrote to
9to5, "I've thought about it some & I don't see anyway you could organize
temps—wouldn't they just shit list us? & I need the work to live." Temps
didn't have the workplace rights that other office workers had and were, by
definition, replaceable. Although 9to5 wanted to organize temp workers
alongside other office workers, the realities for temps were different. The
biggest challenge was that one agency's temps were distributed over many
different workplaces. Labor solidarity comes from group solidarity.

Temps, as 9to5 organizer Janet Selcer noted, found it "hard to meet one
another; we often have a feeling of isolation, and thus powerlessness."[63]
Temps had only the loosest connections to a particular agency and no connections to one another. Selcer was nonetheless optimistic, inspired by the
recent farmworker victories: "If the rural migrants can do it, so can we."
Overcoming that isolation through "unity and collective identity" would
prove even harder than Selcer imagined.

Ana remembered when she was eighteen and worked for a summer after
her freshman year at college, "back [when] jobs were plentiful and rents
were cheap." She and her roommate were both temps. She was hired
through Olsten to "tear carbon papers from bills of lading and stuff envelopes seven hours a day" at the Olin Mathieson Chemical Corporation on
Fifty-seventh Street in New York. In the summer heat, she wore a skirt,
blouse, and nylons to a four-story loft building where she worked in "a completely enclosed room that, except for its size, might have been a broom
closet." Eleven women worked in that room, five tearing carbon copies, five
working Comptometers, and "one watching." Though the Comptometer

work was better paid, skilled work, it was done by women who were of a lower class status than the carbon rippers, for whom the work was only a stopgap. Three of the five carbon rippers lived at home, were engaged to be married or had serious boyfriends, and would presumably quit on marriage or childbirth. Another was a temp. The other temp was a college dropout who had returned to the city after her sister killed herself. A Puerto Rican woman, Inez, was also a college dropout, looking to save money for marriage. The Comptometers were older, in their twenties and thirties, and married to "husbands [who] all worked in blue-collar jobs." Ethnically, the two groups were similar—a mix of Germans, Jews, "New York black," "Jamaican black," and Puerto Rican. The supervisor, a spinster who followed the company to New York from the South, lived in an apartment with her mother. While they were all workers in a real hierarchy, what brought them together was being women: sharing stories about successful and failed pregnancies, recipes for meat loaf, and the shows they watched on television. The work was "mindless," but for Ana, writing about it twenty years later, the "strongest image [was] of female comradery and the giggling, the tensions, and the occasional outburst of emotion." Mindlessly tearing carbon copies and sharing stories might bring people together, but abstractions like "temporary labor" did not. It might have been possible for 9to5 to organize that room, if the women had all thought of their work as long term and if they had all worked for the same company. But for temps, organization was impossible.

Instead, in 1975, 9to5 supported legislation in Massachusetts to better regulate temporary labor. They demanded transparency. The legislation called for clear job descriptions, clear safety standards, and clear rules on temp-to-perm hiring. Temps would also be able to know the "agency mark-up on her labor each hour."[64] The organization felt that workers should know not just what they earned, but what they *could* earn. Perhaps most important, if the legislation became law, temp agencies would be licensed and the state would receive and investigate complaints.[65] In short, 9to5 wanted temps to be treated more like freelancers or perms, who had more control over and information about their work conditions, rather than "exploited" employees. Some of these protections looked like the kinds that permanent employees had—safety standards, job descriptions—while others were what freelancers enjoyed—asssignment choice, wage markup. The temp occupied an uncertain middle between these two roles, with few of the benefits of either. The ambiguity of the temp's job classification led in part to their feeling of powerlessness.

Though to 9to5 temp labor meant women's office work, they had to clarify in the bill that they did not "mean any person principally engaged in the practice of law, accounting or management consulting," and did not mean an agency that supplied "a pool of industrial or day laborers or building tradesmen."[66] The slippages among these categories were already beginning to be apparent, even if 9to5 wanted only to support office workers who were mostly women.

The bill would have balanced the information imbalance between temp worker and temp agency on wage levels and job availability. Workers, moreover, would be entitled to know what the client was being charged for their time (a big no-no). It also would have prevented temp agencies from prohibiting temps from being hired into permanent roles or being intermediaries in any way. In short, it demanded that workers be allowed to contract their labor freely, with all available information, regardless of whether they had initially come to an office as a temp.

Most of these demands cut against the essence of temporary work. Temp agencies would be required to provide "written descriptions of all job categories," which was at odds with the whatever-you-need world of the 1950s, when temp agencies provided beautiful hostesess and brawny lumberjacks at the drop of a dime.[67] Unsurprisingly, temp agencies lobbied to block the bill's passage. In the course of the debate, 9to5 had to fight back against an unregistered lobbyist from Kelly Services. Massachusetts did pass a bill against unregistered lobbyists, but not a law to protect temps.

A Processed World

Chris Carlsson grew up in Oakland and Chicago, working his way through college in bookstores, where he loved to read radical literature.[68] Like few bookish dropouts, he attended late-night barroom gatherings of the Union of Concerned Commies, debating how to most effectively bring wage labor to an end. Like all bookish dropouts, he still needed to pay his rent, and for that he did what everybody did, bookish or not: he temped.

Carlsson worked a few one-day jobs and then landed a relatively long-term stint of a few months "at the Bank of America data center."[69] His job, along with two other temps, was to "produce a manual that would eventually train computer operators in Florida how to use the BofA computers systems." In other words, their temp job was to move permanent jobs to the cheaper South (which, according to branch banking laws at the time, was illegal). Temp workers like him were being employed not to support the permanent workers but to help destroy their livelihood.

In that moment, Chris Carlsson assumed the name Lucius Cabins, and the inspiration for *Processed World* was born. As *McKinsey Quarterly* reflected the world of the consultant, underground magazines—called zines—documented the world of the temporary worker. As the anti–*McKinsey Quarterly*, *Processed World* had less of a readership in the C-suites of Fortune 100 firms, but at night, when the temps had access to the copiers, these zines could spread. Imagine if the Wobblies had had Apple laptops. Writing under postmodern pen names so that they didn't lose their gigs, "Kelly Call Girl," "Dennis Hayes," "gidget digit," "ana logue," "Lucius Cabins," and the rest presented a less positive vision of the flexible corporation. *Processed World* navel gazed on San Francisco, but in the 1980s, few places in the country mattered like San Francisco and its neighbor, Silicon Valley. Cabins né Carlsson's first article, "The Rise of the Six-Month Worker," was written while working hours on the thirty-seventh floor of the Spear Street Tower.[70] On BofA computers, he composed the first issue of *PW*, and also "got most of the paper for that issue" there, stealing two reams a day.

When *PW* began in 1980, the big-*R* Revolution (at least to the editors) "didn't look so farfetched."[71] Gutter punks, nuclear activists, and radical fairies seemed to be inheriting the resistant spirit of the '60s. Then came Reaganism, the Professional Air Traffic Controllers Organization (PATCO) strike, and the sudden evacuation of real hope for labor. The proto-organizations of the '70s that held out the promise of organizing office workers (9to5, SEIU) stalled. Culturally and institutionally, the left of the '80s was not able to marshal the kind of economic (or cultural) power that had been realized in either the '30s or the '60s. While the industrial workers of the '30s formed the CIO, the temporary workers of the '80s had a harder time imagining such institutionalized resistance, partially because they were antibureaucracy.

Christopher Winks, a typical reader of *Processed World*, encountered his first issue in 1981.[72] He had just returned to an office job after a two-month break. He felt an "equal measure of disgust and relief" because of his complicity in "wage-labor in general and to the peculiar rituals of corporate life in particular." Showing up to work, he felt, was like being "somebody who surrenders to a blackmail scheme . . . despite his attempts to reassure himself that he is doing the right thing under the circumstances . . . humiliation lurks at the bottom of his stomach." Winks was not just an office worker, he was a temp, and he was immediately put to work transcribing "a tedious legal document, dictated by a disembodied individual who sounded as if he made it a habit to speak with pebbles in his mouth."

His job was terrible not just because of the transcription, but because he had no sense of why he transcribed. On some level, he transcribed, from nine to five, because he needed "money and phony security," but at a deeper level he rebelled against the lack of why.[73] "That unwritten rule obtained in every other corporation, regardless of whether this firm did management consulting, real estate speculation, or constructing nuclear power plants." You had no idea why you did what you did, and even if you did, "what difference did it make?" The work remaining for the temp was without any decision making—just as consultants had intended. The office, and the soul-crushing labor therein, appeared "permanent and unchangeable," forbidding "acts of resistance, however insignificant, that we would engage in to prevent ourselves from succumbing to resignation and boredom."

One of those insignificant acts was to print and copy zines. Winks did not overturn his cubicle. He did not organize his coworkers. All he did, he lamented, was "cope and attempt to preserve a minimum of self-respect," like "many other working people who did what they could to get by."[74] Getting by in California was becoming harder every year. The self-respect that came from rising wages and union voices was nowhere to be found.

Where office unions did exist, their ideas of workplace freedom—standardization of activities and pay—contained the seeds of their own destruction. In 1982, for instance, Blue Shield, an insurance company whose office staff had been organized by the Office and Professional Employees International Union, fired all of its staff and left San Francisco. As a temporary office worker at Blue Shield, Debra Wittley understood what had happened—and why Blue Shield could rely on temps.[75] The union had leverage over the company because of the proliferation of new forms of process claims that relied on technology that the management did not fully understand. With needed knowledge in the heads of the workers, the strike could be successful. The union was recognized. But the union push for standardization in labor processes "provided both the incentive and the means for Blue Shield to rid itself of its SF workers." Standardized work enabled automation and outsourcing. Streamlined processes—like the kind made possible by outside consultants—left offices to pick up and move.

The writings of *PW* contained no utopian alternative or even practical policies to improve the situation of temporary workers. Direct workplace action was discussed and dismissed because "the union would be blamed."[76] The rights of the few workers still protected by unions could not be endangered. Direct action had always been the source of the greatest strength for workers, going back to the Flint strike of 1936 that created the United Auto Workers. Data—the equivalent of the auto body dies of the '30s—could not be seized, because it would abrogate the union's legal rights.[77] In Carlsson's view, organized labor defended a small world that was getting smaller, leaving the rest of the working class to fend for itself. Union power had turned factory automation into better wages in the 1950s, but office workers facing automation in the 1980s had no such power. Labor laws and labor institutions failed in the face of the service economy. The traditional "methods of unions . . . [which were] limited to the traditional end-of-contract strikes, interminable grievance procedures, or lobby[ing] government for better labor legislation," as another *PW* writer wrote, could not help the office worker.[78] *Processed World* may have offered escape, not alternative—but unions didn't even offer escape.

By the 1980s, the automated office, foretold in the '60s, had come to pass, but work had not disappeared—just security and wages. "Once considered a career that required a good deal of skill," gidget digit wrote, "the clerical job now closely resembles an assembly line station."[79] Like an assembly line, she wrote, "the growing flow of paper and money" are "routiniz[ed] and automat[ed] . . . reserving the more 'mental' tasks for managers or the new machines."[80] The rising need for office workers, another *PW* writer said, to "push around the continually growing body of bureaucratic detail" meant that employers were looking for ways to "reduce costs at the office by eliminating as many clerical jobs as possible, and to gain as much control as possible over the ones that remain."[81] Factory workers were "backed by $25,000 worth of equipment, compared to only $3,000 for the average secretary," leaving an enormous opportunity for investment in the productivity of office workers. "With modern word processing equipment, one typist can do work that previously took three." The challenge of automating the office was the fear of overinvestment. Temps helped assuage that anxiety.

It was hard to sell a computer, but it was easy to fire a temp.[82]

The Temp Workforce Gets a New Name

Audrey Freedman, an economist at the Conference Board, coined the phrase "contingent worker" in 1985, and it quickly caught on, at least among the academic set, as a way to describe what the *New York Times* called "a fundamental change . . . in the American workplace."[83] Freedman, as clearly as anyone, had seen the postwar world of work disappear. From 1958 to 1973, she had been a supervising economist at the Bureau of Labor Statistics, and then had moved to the Cost of Living Council during the Nixon administration. She had seen in her numbers the rise and fall of the secure job.[84] Her phrase launched an entire scholarship of this workforce in sociology and economics. Clean categories, of course, allow for clean statistics, which social scientists treasure. Without a definition, though, measuring this contingent workforce would be impossible, and the hardest question was how to define it.[85]

Defining the contingent workforce negatively—that is, *not* normal jobs—was easy but dissatisfying. A good definition should be positive, but what kinds of nontraditional work (where traditional work really meant postwar work) should be included? Cases could be made for including part-timers, temps, freelancers, small business owners, consultants, migrants, and all the other kinds of workers who did not fit into the postwar model. To this day, the definitions of the contingent workforce are not entirely settled. What matters most, perhaps, is that this contingent workforce seemed important enough to try to measure in order to account for its mutability.

While the word "contingent" was catchy, it was a bit misleading.

Contingency, in normal usage, implies uncertainty, but for the corporations using these workforces, though the economy might be uncertain, the way in which these workers would be used—permanently—was not. For employers, of course, the appeal of this workforce was its very fuzziness. Contingency's denizens did not have the same kinds of rights as citizens of the regular working world.

By the late 1980s, temps were, as a leading office management journal described it, "a permanent part of well-planned human resources programs and staffing schedules in thousands of companies."[86] The Administrative Management Society reported in 1988 that 90 percent of businesses used temps, as Elmer Winter envisioned, to smooth workplace fluctuations. These businesses, according to the National Association of Temporary Services, budgeted for these temps, rather than treating them as an emergency expense. The "core and ring" model, as Kelly Services described it, enabled firms to "maintain a workforce that closely parallels business cycles."[87]

For managers facing restructuring and wanting to show how proactive they were, shifting to contingent work (and showing the cost reduction in benefits) was an easy move—lest they get downsized as well.

The Office of the Present

Temps and mechanization went hand in hand, but with the coming of the microcomputer and video display terminals (VDTs), all office work became more automated. Speaking at MIT in 1979, 9to5 leaders Eileen Hagerty and Joan Tighe spoke about the toll that office automation took on clerical workers. They told the story of Mary. After her office computerized, her pace had to speed up. She stared for "seven or eight hours" a day at her dark green, monochrome screen, which made her eyes burn and hurt. The computer itself whizzed and whirred with high-pitched noises that gave her headaches. Typewriters processed physical paper that human eyes were meant to look at. The VDTs seemed otherworldly. Secretaries like Mary began to feel like robots themselves, wondering whether their "once-prized secretarial skills [were] obsolete."[88]

Job loss and/or job degradation seemed like the only possible consequence. Automation would increase productivity, and there would be either more work to do or fewer workers.[89] Rather than reduce drudgery, 9to5 believed that it would increase routinization. Workers would be adapted to the machine. The only liberation that would occur would be of the profits of corporations as they could let office workers go.

"A conscious choice is being made," Hagerty and Tighe told their MIT audience. "Business is choosing to automate the office as a way of cutting costs while preserving corporate profits." Sometimes management would simply automate and then not hire, rather than cut staff, but the positions were being eliminated. The office of the future looked more like the factory. Jobs were broken into tasks, and the unpleasant ones were sent to the word-processing center. The results weren't always what was intended. In a Los Angeles bank, after it created a word-processing center, the split in work collided with the social meaning of secretaries. "All we did was concentrate the drudgery," a vice president of the bank said, "and give others more time to run for coffee. It just didn't work according to the IBM grand plan."[90] The failure here, IBM said, was not the technology but the people or, more accurately, the job security that some people had.

In 1979, however, Mary and other clerical workers felt "lucky to have a job at all."[91] Automation threatened all clerical work. "Office workers, like factory workers," 9to5 said, "are practically interchangeable." As all work became routinized and mechanized, everyone could be replaced.[92]

Hagerty and Tighe ended their speech by invoking the old Wobbly bard, Joe Hill: "Don't mourn—organize, office workers shouldn't waste time mourning the passing of the office as we know it today. They should be organizing to prevent job loss and job degradation in the office of the future." They told the audience that "the boss doesn't give a damn whether clerical jobs become routine, narrow, boring or speeded-up." If office workers could come together, "then maybe the new technology of office automation will benefit all of us, and not just the boss."[93]

That did not occur. Instead, the coming of the microcomputer exacerbated what had already been happening in the workforce—what had been planned and carried out for two decades.

At an executive committee meeting of Coopers & Lybrand in 1977, Felix Kaufman came to the front of the room with a silver tray cloaked in a white sheet. "Gentlemen," he said to the room, "this is the future!" Pulling off the sheet, he revealed an Apple II computer. Kaufman believed that, more than anything else, his legacy at Coopers & Lybrand was the remaking of the workplace to use these new forms of technology, from IBM punch cards to Apple microcomputers, bringing technology consulting, and the new kinds of labor that made it possible, to firms across the country.[94]

The revolution, when it came, would be computerized.

CHAPTER TEN

Restructuring the American Dream

R onald Reagan and the neoconservatives may have celebrated supply-side economists, but it was the interpretation
sold by McKinsey consultants that became best-selling bibles on how to restructure American business.[1] Consultants offered solutions for what was,
from a postwar perspective, an upside-down world where the Japanese
made the quality products and American cars didn't run. Whether your
firm was broken up because of a hostile takeover, a court order, or Asian
competition didn't really matter. You would still hire McKinsey, or BCG, or
Price Waterhouse, or Coopers & Lybrand to put the pieces together again.
The old promises of the postwar era had no claim on this new world, which
looked very different than postwar Americans had imagined it would.

"Some time during the 1970s," business guru Peter Drucker declared in
1980, "the longest period of continuity in economic history came to an end. At
some point during the last ten years we moved into turbulence."[2] The economic crises of the 1970s—stagflation, inflation, wage stagnation, oil crises—
were not aberrations but had become a new normal, what the chairman of the
Federal Reserve Alan Greenspan would later famously call the age of turbulence. For most Americans, it was hard to feel like they were still on top. American business was losing ground to countries that, a generation earlier, the U.S.
had beaten in war. Germany and especially Japan were once again ascendant.
While Americans had voted for Reagan's optimism instead of Carter's pessi-
mism, for those who worked outside of Wall Street, Reagan's America was not
a new morning, but a drawn-out dusk—except in one place: Silicon Valley.

The agricultural economy was born between two great rivers, the Tigris
and Euphrates; the digital economy was born between two great highways,
U.S. 101 and I-280. Connecting San Jose to San Francisco, these roads

define the eastern and western borders of what we now call Silicon Valley, which had, until the 1950s, been fruit orchards. In the '60s, as the electronics industry grew, those trees were cut down to make way for factories and offices. Although today Silicon Valley is known for software, in the '70s and '80s it was still a place where hardware—first transistors and then whole chips—were made. By the '80s, electronics was the largest manufacturing industry in the U.S., and Silicon Valley's factories left Detroit's far behind. As the rest of traditional American manufacturing—and those good jobs—began to dry up, we looked to Silicon Valley as the lone place where American industry could once again deliver the good life.

Moore's law famously predicted (accurately) that twice as many transistors could be crammed on a chip every eighteen months, for the same price. While this pace of miniaturization was astounding, it also made it impossible for firms to earn much money on their products before they had to shrink their components. This punishing cycle drove electronics firms to seek flexibility in labor and capital in a way that no other industry ever had to do. Airplane plants worked on the same production schedule for decades, car plants for years, while electronic plants had only months. For the first time, industry truly had to be flexible. Investments in electronics factories had horizons measured in months, not years or decades.

Short-term investment and flexible production found their natural home in the early electronics start-ups, and Silicon Valley became a model of success for the rest of the country. While Detroit faltered, San Jose thrived. Japan might make better cars, but we made better computers. If American manufacturing was successful, it was in Silicon Valley. The electronics industry validated new thinking about capitalism since, unlike any of the previous leading sectors, it depended on short-time, flexible workforces. Unions were nowhere to be found. Sporadic organizing campaigns in the 1960s, '70s, and '80s had all failed.[3] Silicon Valley became the laboratory for a lean American capitalism.

Robots and Migrants

Postwar Americans had imagined that the future would be a time of leisure, when robots relieved the tedium of our lives. Working just a few hours a week, our greatest challenge would be figuring out what to do. If any industry would be automated, it would reasonably seem, it would be the high-tech world of electronics. Apple, that iconic Silicon Valley firm, bragged in 1984 that the factory for its new computer, something called the Macintosh, would be the most automated in the world. Yet Apple's factory, like all the other electronics factories, was shockingly old-fashioned. In 1986, only two industries in the entire world, according to *McKinsey Quarterly*, accounted "for 80 percent of installed robots . . . aerospace and automaking."[4] The flexibility of electronics production in Silicon Valley, despite all the technical wizardry, came from workers, not machines.

Apple never produced the good life for its line workers like General Motors did. The story of flexibility in Silicon Valley is not just about the insecurity of the workers on the bottom, but the success of the workers on the top. Venture capitalists moved from start-up to start-up. Software engineers hopped from project to project. From top to bottom, Silicon Valley defined a new flexible model of business even though its own industry—electronics and then software—was unique.

As much as politicians wrung their hands over the disappearing jobs in Detroit, they were largely oblivious to the kinds of jobs being created in Silicon Valley. When Democratic vice-presidential candidate Geraldine Ferraro spoke at Apple's headquarters in 1984, she told them, "People in your industry have been told for years that the problems in the auto and steel industries are not your problems . . . but that's a narrow gauge of view . . . a strong manufacturing base is essential to a healthy technological base."[5] The irony, unbeknownst to Ferraro, was that there were more robots in Detroit than in Palo Alto.

Ferraro was not alone in contrasting a tech company with a manufacturing company—and this rhetorical distinction helped Silicon Valley employ workers in ways that never would have happened in postwar Detroit. Machines made Apple workers more productive, to be sure, but defining these machines as "robots" was a very important cultural sleight of hand: humans use machines, while robots work autonomously. Emphasizing automation hid the humans who were, by their gender, race, and origin, incompatible with the national imagination of its workforce. In Detroit, the autoworkers were white men, and unionized; in Silicon Valley, the workers were not. Those autoworkers counted as factory workers; the tech workers did not.

To understand the electronics industry is simple: every time someone says "robot," simply picture a woman of color. Instead of self-aware robots, workers—all women, mostly immigrants, sometimes undocumented—hunched over tables with magnifying glasses assembling parts, sometimes on a factory line and sometimes on a kitchen table. Though it paid a lot of lip service to automation, Silicon Valley truly relied upon a transient workforce of workers outside of traditional labor relations. Twenty percent of electronics firms had no production automation, and 94 percent of firms had less than half.[6] By 1984, only 30 percent of the *official* Silicon Valley workforce was in production. Managers made up 13 percent, of the workforce, professional/technical staff made up 43 percent, and other office workers made up the rest.[7] Those numbers should seem odd for a manufacturing industry—and they were.

Subcontracted workers still did the work—they just weren't officially counted as employees of those leading firms. If they were white and native born, they were temps, and if they weren't, then they were laborers who worked by the day or by the piece. Tech firms outsourced labor to temp agencies and subcontracted to sweatshops and overseas factories. If the faces of Silicon Valley were the technologists of Stanford, then the bodies of Silicon Valley were the assemblers of Fremont, the undocumented workers of San Jose, and the temps of San Francisco.

Migrants had long been at the bottom of the Santa Clara workforce. The fruit pickers of Santa Clara County over most of the twentieth century had been a hodgepodge of Mexicans, Asians (Chinese, Filipino, Japanese), Europeans (Italian, Spanish, Portuguese), and, after the Dust Bowl, midwestern climate refugees. Migrants from everywhere, of every nationality, found their way to the plum groves and orange orchards of the peninsula. After World War II, that composition began to change. Europeans and white Americans went to the canneries of the coast. Long-standing Chinese and Japanese families bought their own farmland. The existing Anglo planters looked, then, to more desperate migrants to pick their fruit. Over the course of the 1970s, the number of legal Mexicans in Santa Clara County rose from 15,000 to 227,000 in 1980. As the electronics industry took off, it took off in the context of an immigrant workforce in what had been the countryside.[8] These "factories in the country," as historian Glenna Matthews has called them, were one of the secrets of why "the high-tech industry contains almost no unions."[9] Just as Toyota looked to the rural Aichi Prefecture town of Koromo to build its docile factories, IBM looked to cities with no history of organizing, like San Jose. Just as with San Jose, Koromo grew into a massive city. Koromo was renamed Toyota, as greater San Jose, more or less, was renamed Silicon Valley. Electronics was not the same, of course, as fruit picking. As a leading industrial sector, electronics defined one of the profit centers of the national economy. Its dictates defined what the American economy meant at the most fundamental level. Yet just like the earlier fruit economy, it, too, depended on workers with precarious lives.[10]

In Fremont, Apple opened its flagship Macintosh factory, but here also GM partnered with Toyota to open the first U.S. factory based on Japanese lean manufacturing principles—the NUMMI plant (New United Motor Manufacturing Incorporated, where Tesla now builds its cars). In Fremont, worlds—GM and Apple—collided as lean production methods reinforced the new flexible ideas of the corporation. In San Jose, undocumented workers did the jobs that were too toxic for Americans to do legally.

Temps, meanwhile, managed the logistics and paperwork of these new industries. The flexibility of the workforce was in the offices as well as the factories. A spokesperson for the Silicon Valley temporary agency association said, "When you're dealing with volatile industries like semiconductors and electronics the role of the temporary has changed to a detached workforce actually planned for by personnel departments."[11] The largest users of temp labor in Silicon Valley were, of course, the largest firms: Hewlett-Packard, IBM, and Control Data Corporation. Hewlett-Packard even had its own subsidiary temp firm. "The general consensus," he continued, "for a lot of high-tech companies is to have ten to fifteen percent of their labor force temporary." The temps were a "buffer zone," as the executive president of the National Association of Temporary Services described it. With a slowdown, "you don't have those layoffs that put you on the front page."[12] IBM and Hewlett-Packard could claim never to have had layoffs only because firing a temp was not like firing a real worker.

Unlike any previous industry, crucial work in electronics happened outside the firm. From high-paid programmers to barely paid assemblers, software and hardware were built by workers who were not themselves employees. The short-term electronics product cycle could be generalized to all "correct" corporate organization and capitalist investment in industries that did not have the same production demands as electronics. The organizational success of electronics "proved" the lean management ideas being sold by consultants and gurus.

In Silicon Valley, the big firms, like Hewlett-Packard, looked to Mc-Kinsey for help in becoming even more flexible. In Fremont, California, across the San Francisco Bay from Palo Alto, two American companies—Apple and GM—would experiment with new kinds of lean manufacturing, as well as flexible workforces. Theories and sales pitches made since the postwar period finally, in the 1980s, became a reality. This rise of Silicon Valley, however, played out against a backdrop of a country in decline.

Falling Down the Marble Staircase

Fred Herr, though he was a consultant at Coopers & Lybrand, felt like "part of the family" at his longtime client AT&T. The future chief financial officer, Bob Kavner, upon his promotion had invited Fred and his wife to visit him and his wife in his new office at AT&T headquarters. The Herrs took an elevator and then ascended a "huge marble staircase" to "this huge office" that took up a quarter of a floor. Kavner joked to them that "there's a big hole in Vermont somewhere where this building came from." But even as he reveled in the trappings of power, harking back to Rome, Kavner confided to Herr that this kind of corporation could not last. AT&T had to "become more competitive." They could "no longer live with this . . . this kind of structure." The Kavners and the Herrs then left the marble-clad office, walked down the grand staircase, and went to dinner. The evening was "enjoyable," but also foretold what was to become of AT&T, consulting, and the American corporation.

AT&T typified the old inflexible corporation, and its breakup was mandated by an antitrust decision in 1982, but Ma Bell restructured like any other corporation—with the help of consultants. It had long been a client of Coopers & Lybrand, so when the court decided to break it up, Coopers & Lybrand was there to help.[13] Herr thought of the AT&T moment as the most challenging of his career, "unbelievably complex." AT&T was so "highly structured [that it was] almost like a civil service structure."[14] More than a hundred partners worked on figuring out how to restructure Ma Bell into its many regional components. And Coopers & Lybrand was not alone at AT&T. As Ma Bell gave birth to the Baby Bells in each region, consultants remade every part of the corporation. One Baby Bell, Pacific Telephone & Telegraph, alone hired ninety firms to help them with the transition.[15] Management Analysis Center consultants helped with the "corporate culture." Coopers & Lybrand promoted an "entrepreneurial spirit." McKinsey, ADL, Booz Allen, and every other firm tried to get a cut of the action, not only at PacTel but everywhere. McKinsey developed Michigan Bell's marketing strategy. Lippincott & Margulies rechristened New York Telephone Company and New England Telephone & Telegraph as the simple NYNEX Corporation. While AT&T workers wondered if their jobs would survive, consultants worked like never before.

AT&T was perhaps the most public restructuring, but it was not unique in being broken up or in becoming a feeding frenzy for consultants. In many ways, it was typical of the ways that corporations and conglomerates were broken up in the 1980s—except for the court order. As the Justice Department reveled in how it had broken the evil, monopolist AT&T, the real horror for Americans was in how their restructured workplaces eliminated jobs. Those with marble offices would not feel the squeeze. Behemoths like AT&T would become more flexible, but this flexibility would come from the increased insecurity of their two million workers, not the Bob Kavners.

Permanent Consultants

The terror of restructuring, while scary for workers, was good for the consulting business. As executives cut workforces, management consulting grew.

The crisis of capitalism in the early 1970s had also been a crisis for consulting—even McKinsey. Revenue per partner fell. Monthly billings fell. McKinsey cut the number of associates. Net operating profit, even with the inflation, fell by half. As Alonzo McDonald, McKinsey's managing director, addressed its shareholders in Freeport on Grand Bahama Island in 1976, he conveyed a feeling of relief. The crisis seemed to have abated. Profits were two and a half times their level in 1972. Associates were being hired again. Once more, McKinsey was growing. Their last meeting had been in London, two and half years earlier, and in a very different world.[16] Oil and food shortages had disrupted the global economy just as badly as inflation and bearish stocks. Currency fluctuations had played havoc with global trade. And somehow, McKinsey and its clients came out the other side. Partners and directors had "agonized" with them; they had "lived with our clients" to make sure that they had "new responses and solutions." McDonald told its shareholders, "In the face of a threatening storm, the Firm acted as a superb center of positive direction, cool reflection and analysis, and a source of confidence for our clients."[17]

The resurgence of McKinsey, however, did not come from its existing clients. McDonald noted, in his opening speech, that the firm was not as reliant on the old industries. It had a "new forward momentum" in forward-looking areas such as operations management, threshold companies, compensation, telecommunications, and technology. The "entire Insurance Group with Phil Dutter and Dick Neuschel leading the way" received a special acknowledgment.[18] The aim was, by 1980, to have industrials be reduced to "half to two thirds" of the client base, with the rest made up mostly of "service/transportation/financial institutions (20–30 percent)."[19]

The new profits also came from increased billings. Associates were being worked harder and team sizes had been increased, which together accounted for a third of the increase. The other two thirds came from simply charging more money (even after adjusting for inflation). McKinsey's elite status kept the associates and clients coming in, despite the more intense working conditions for the associates and the higher prices for the clients.[20]

This push for growth meant compromises. Ron Daniel, a long-standing McKinsey director, gave the closing speech to the shareholders' meeting in Monte Carlo the following year. The studies, he had noticed, had become understaffed in an effort to cut costs, which "create[d] tremendous pressures on our team to perform under what are sometimes impossible conditions and with unrealistic client expectations."[21] McKinsey consultants, he acknowledged, were "achievement-motivated and task-oriented," so that "it is hard for us to not work hard: we always have and we always will." But this ethos had crossed a line. "This pressure," he continued, "grows out of an

ill-founded desire to secure assignments, and to secure them at any cost."
This shift, he believed, came out of the "serious worldwide recession and
great uncertainty," and it left a mark on the firm's culture. He hoped that the
firm would "find a more reasonable balance between running scared and
behaving like competent, secure professionals."[22] If the switch from security
to fear was evident at McKinsey, imagine how it was in the rest of corporate
America. Moving from growth to stagnation was economic, but it was also
emotional.

The team room, with that particular musk of takeout and young men,
was, by 1980, never empty. As large corporations became more flexible in
their organization, they had also become dependent on expensive external
consultants to, as one author in the *Harvard Business Review* put it, "patch
these cracks."[23] By the 1980s, the most powerful American corporations
typically had a continual set of consultants advising them on matters of
business strategy, whether from McKinsey, BCG, or—the new kid on the
block—Bain & Company, which had split off from BCG in 1973. Consultants did not simply come in, do a time study, and then leave. A senior Bain
partner complained of McKinsey that "they have these deep relationships
with senior management that lead companies to return to McKinsey, un-
questioned, time and time again."[24] Consultants were the business strategists
for the corporations, instead of the corporation's senior leadership.

The *Harvard Business Review* and other business journals and newspapers published articles to advise their readerships on the best ways to use
consultants. In the case of a small project requiring specialized knowledge,
the consultant's fees might be justified, but the main question was how to
weigh the "benefits of in-house development against a possible dependency
on a consultant."[25] If executives can't plan and carry out long-term plans
without assistance, one business writer suggested, then "a new management team, not a surrogate, is needed."[26]

Skeptical business journalists, like *Forbes* writer John A. Byrne, could
not understand why management even needed consultants—at least for
strategy. Byrne complained that "executives at big companies everywhere
can't pay the bills, hire employees, reorganize, launch new products or plot
strategy without outside help." "A small industrial," he wrote, might be

"better off asking for help in selling its one consumer product than in hiring a full-time marketing director," but the constant presence of consultants at big corporations made no sense. Byrne was troubled when "outsiders get too involved in a company's basic business." GM, in his example, might need help with real estate but should not need to ask for any help with cars. Consultants were not useless, but they were overused. Instead of just help in "narrow, technical areas," managers used consultants for "the very heart of their business."[27] Managers who don't make decisions, after all, aren't really managing, they are just paying consultants.

Detractors may have questioned the value of fresh-faced MBAs telling twenty-year veterans how to run their businesses, but it was clear that for the executives, the gains appeared incontrovertible. In a remarkably angry op-ed in the *Boston Globe*, Bruce Henderson of BCG denounced the "punk business magazine reporters" who were critical of consultants simply because they found out that "such a young genius is often paid a multiple of a reporter's pay."[28] Business reporters and management professors, Henderson said, lampooned consultants, blaming them—unjustifiably—for the collapse of firms and the demise of industries. Consultancies' accomplishments—and growth—spoke for themselves. *Forbes* might cite example after example of consultants failing, but billings just increased. Exposés of consulting could come out every few years, showing how they had given bad advice, but firms kept coming back for more. McKinsey still didn't need to advertise.

That managers used more consultants when the economy became more volatile was not a coincidence. With so many shaky corporations, executive jobs were at risk in a way that they had not been in the postwar years. A simple explanation was that the more insecure jobs felt, the more managers needed consultants to shoulder blame if something went wrong. If something went wrong, instead of firing the executive, Byrne observed, "the refrain merely becomes 'Never hire Glutz & Co again.'" The more investors pushed for restructuring, the more frightened executives looked to consultants for safety.

A client might have an ongoing relationship with a partner, but never an associate. The job of partners at big firms was, and is, to sell business and then farm it out. New associates got worked hard, and then most of them were let go. The head of a midsize firm complained that as he used the consulting services of a "Big Eight accounting firm," he met a "very bright young man who was gone in twelve months," only to be replaced by another "bright young man who was also gone in twelve months."[29] Part of the turnover was physical—the result of long hours and exhausting travel. The lifestyle still favored the young. Consultants, McKinsey managing director Fred Gluck told *Fortune*, peaked around forty-five, slowed down around fifty-five, and needed to transition out around sixty. Bower's own life set the model for the firm. But the churn also came from the business model of up or out. Consultants themselves were temps, and they had to reconcile themselves to a worldview that accepted that truth.

The growth of the consulting firms depended, in multiple ways, on turnover. "Firm lore" held, *Fortune* reported, that "McKinsey is a very kind place. McKinsey is a very cruel place." Everyone, from raw business analysts to slick engagement managers to veteran partners, was constantly being evaluated. The head of the New York office told the magazine, "It's a rigorous, constant microscope that we have everybody under. It's impossible to feel secure here." And that was by design. By the 1990s, only one in five associates made partner, and only half of those made director (the position where, finally, there was no up-or-out policy.) To enable this culling, McKinsey overhired. Gluck said that they "hire[d] ten times the number we need."[30]

He also said, "All I know is that every consulting firm anybody talks to always says they're second to McKinsey."[31] While that may have been true in terms of prestige, it was not true by most metrics of influence. McKinsey boasted the highest revenue per consultant ($280,000 in 1986), but it was not the largest firm. The leader in terms of business was not the elite McKinsey, but the ubiquitous Arthur Andersen. While top-shelf strategy firms like McKinsey and BCG offered books and frameworks, in the 1980s, it was the accountancies that did most of the actual consulting business. In 1982, McKinsey earned $145 million, but Arthur Andersen earned $218 million. BCG, which earned $50 million, may have popularized the 2 x 2 matrix, but Price Waterhouse, which earned $57 million, and Coopers & Lybrand, with $79 million, implemented it. Andersen's 3,400 professional consultants dwarfed McKinsey's 800. The Big Nine accountancies captured one third of all management consulting revenues.

While the auditing business was profitable, it could not keep pace with the consulting practice. On average, consulting earned 21 percent of revenues for accountancies by 1987, double what it had been in the 1970s. At Andersen, by 1987, consulting was one third of the firm's revenues. As Andersen grew its consulting business through the 1980s, tensions continued to rise between the accountants and the consultants. Computers could automate audit work but not consulting work. Audit hours fell as all those computers boosted productivity, while the demand for consultants proved insatiable—and stubbornly time intensive. No computer could replace a consultant. And as the money from all that consulting piled up, the professional quandaries of men like Marvin Bower could easily be forgotten.

In Search of Excellence

In the midst of Jimmy Carter's malaise, Thomas Peters and Robert Waterman, two directors at McKinsey & Company, had launched a new study of what made the top companies succeed. They were "bored working for big, okay companies that would pay big money, accept our recommendations, and then do a half-assed job of implementing them," and wanted to find out what made their excellent clients so excellent. Their research, underwritten by McKinsey and published in 1982, became a number one bestseller and business classic: *In Search of Excellence.* The book presented a new model of how corporations ought to be restructured to compete in the increasingly globalizing, automating economy—and the answer was by cutting staff. *In Search of Excellence* called for "simple form, lean staff." More than technology, success came from organizational change. Successful firms were moving toward a new kind of workforce that looked more like ad-hocracy than bureaucracy.

McKinsey offered new norms—tight limits to the scope of the firm and even tighter limits on the staff—for how a business ought to be run. *In Search of Excellence* was a primer on the new ways to think about the proper ordering of the corporation outside of the politically charged language of

Reaganomics. Like good consultants, Peters and Waterman drew on the best practices of their clients and disseminated them through the economy. For most readers, the ideas were startling, but *In Search of Excellence* merely synthesized what McKinsey had already been telling its high-paying clients for years.

Peters and Waterman called this the "rule of 100": even the largest firms did not need more than a hundred people at corporate headquarters. Citing numerous corporations with tens of thousands of employees and billions in revenues, they gleefully reeled off how workforces had been reduced from 500 to 100 without a change in the success of the organization. At Wal-Mart, Sam Walton told them that "he believes in empty headquarters" because the answers are in the field. At Intel, Peters and Waterman claimed that there was "virtually no staff. All staff assignments are temporary ones given to line officers." What does it matter, then, whether the temporary assignment comes from a line officer or a McKinsey consultant? At Ore-Ida, where they, as consultants, put together "one of the most thoughtful strategic plans we've seen," the only staff they worked with were the CEO's secretary and part-timers from the CEO's department and division manager. Though Ore-Ida, a major subdivision of Heinz, was one of America's largest consumer packaged goods companies—a classic postwar industrial company—the CEO "has no staff, let alone a planning staff."[32]

The postwar middle management and the executive planning staff that oversaw them were no longer necessary. Peters and Waterman lauded Ford president Donald Petersen for cutting 26 percent of his middle management and believed that Ford would continue. "Reductions in the neighborhood of 50 percent or even 75 percent . . . are not uncommon targets when businessmen discuss what they could honestly do without." This temporary corporation, except for the actual machines that made all those delicious Ore-Ida french fries, would leverage the ad hoc insights of a constantly recombining planning staff of super-senior executives and management consultants.

The only necessary employee, in this model, was the CEO.

Searching for Excellence at HP

Silicon Valley arguably began in the garage of Bill Hewlett and David Packard, and HP's founders were as committed to job security as any other postwar industrialists.[33] As they steered the company from the postwar through the 1970s, they continued to try to protect their workers (yet, at the same time, resisted any kind of unionization). In the '70s, instead of firing workers during a recession, HP reduced employee hours. Executives voluntarily cut their pay. Employees shared work and kept their jobs.[34] Twice, this enabled HP to avoid layoffs.

While AT&T, GM, and GE may have reveled in cutting their workforces, companies like HP had a harder time reconciling their values to the new lean ideal, struggling, for as long as possible, to preserve job security. Job security at HP was so entrenched that human resources had to remind managers that it was okay to fire people. "There is," a memo said at the time, "a prevalent misconception that HP never terminates an individual's employment involuntarily."[35] To prove the point, they cited the sixty people who had, over the last six years, lost their jobs due to absenteeism, job performance, and gross misconduct. Firing ten people a year, in any normal corporation, was inconceivably low. HP bent over backward to avoid layoffs. If you got hired, you rarely got fired.

While *In Search of Excellence* may have promoted a corporation with only a hundred people at corporate headquarters, somebody still needed to do the real work. At the top there might have been teams of consultants, but for the paperwork—which, despite the office automation, still existed—there was a growing army of temps. In the downturns of the 1970s, cutting-edge firms used temps as a buffer for their employees. By the '80s, using temps as a buffer workforce was becoming the norm. If temps were let go in a downturn, companies could proudly tell the press that they had never laid anyone off—and technically that would be true. Firms that struggled to protect their work forces in the '70s and '80s, like Hewlett-Packard, eventually gave in. If HP could be restructured for flexibility, then any firm could. That moment would come after founder Bill Hewlett passed on the company to John Young.

Though he had an engineering background, Young also had an MBA.

He spoke the language of business as fluently as the language of electronics. In the recession of 1982, he seized the opportunity to force HP to break its commitment to its employees. Instead of cutting jobs this time around, HP shifted into creating a more flexible workforce. For such a fundamental shift, Young looked to McKinsey for help.

Robert Waterman, before he became famous with *In Search of Excellence,* had consulted at many firms across the world, including Hewlett-Packard's computer group, where he had met the soon-to-be CEO Young. Waterman and Young spoke the same language. McKinsey helped HP automate their offices.[36] Waterman, in particular, tried to reorient HP away from focusing on engineering to the exclusion of marketing. HP, in their view, should be more business than products.

In 1984, Young invited Waterman to give a speech at the annual management meeting, laying out HP's strengths and weaknesses as part of the run-up to a McKinsey-led reorganization of HP.[37] The number one asset of HP, Waterman said, was its culture of "innovative technical, entrepreneurial spirit."[38] Engineers could find their own problems and solve them. Unlike Digital Equipment Corporation (DEC) or IBM, HP was a place that "set people free."[39] This freedom was made possible, he thought, by the "security of employment policy, which lets you move people from division to division and across functions without people feeling particularly threatened by it." Security allowed "mobility" and "flexibility" that Waterman had never seen in a firm, "except maybe in Japan." He lauded HP's "technical strength," "can-do attitude" and brand image as well, but before all of that came HP's peoplecentric policies.

Those policies, Waterman thought, were also HP's greatest possible weakness. The job security insulated HP from "competitive analysis."[40] The focus on technical innovation—resulting from that security—increased their "cost position." HP was good at inventing machines, but it was "surprisingly naïve at business fact accumulation and analysis." HP leadership believed in engineering, not management. "HP is terrific," Waterman concluded his speech, "and I think that's the biggest single danger."

John Young, however, believed in management. He reorganized HP in line with Waterman's vision, taking it in a new direction. McKinsey oversaw the fieldwork of the reorganization, consulting with a group of sixty senior HP executives.[41] McKinsey interviewed HP clients and staff, examining every part of the business. The executives weighed McKinsey's problem statements to find possible alternatives, deciding, in the end, on a new strategic and organizational path for HP. While the press saw a power struggle at HP, internal memos claimed there was only unity. Certainly McKinsey and Young saw eye to eye as they launched the restructuring of one of Silicon Valley's signature brands.

Planning for Flexibility at HP

At the 1987 annual general managers' meeting, John Young revealed his disappointment over the past few years. HP had not become the company he had hoped it would be after the McKinsey-led 1984 reorganization. The problem, he felt, was "<u>not</u> poor planning or strategy, it was simply weak execution." Their strategy had not been wrong; HP had just not gone far enough. He called for the theme of 1987 to be "excellence in execution," invoking Waterman's speech in 1984. The practical policies were manifold but focused on cutting costs, consolidating operations, limiting hiring, and "developing a 'buffer' workforce." New products were nowhere mentioned. The workforce would need to become even more flexible.

Hewlett-Packard's internal HP Temps Pool had begun in the late 1970s, positioning itself as an alternative to temporary agencies. These temps could circulate like the temps of the postwar years, filling in for sick or vacationing administrative assistants.[42] Often retirees, they knew "HP's style and procedures," as a helpful HP circular explained to employees. Apple, similarly, created its AppleCorps in 1985 with just three people. A hundred temps would come in every day, and many didn't even know how to use a Macintosh, much less understand how Apple operated.[43] Then Apple had a reorganization, as AppleCorps head Gary White recalled, and suddenly they had thirty people filling all the gaps created by the reorganization but not having their own full-time jobs. Some of the internal temps found jobs in the new organization, but not all did. White believed that AppleCorps created "a cost-effective manner of fulfilling Apple's temporary administrative needs *internally*." The roles that these internal temps filled were like those at HP: more independent, sometimes verging on project management. They even replaced people who went on vacation. White dismissed the notion that temps did "menial labor performed by peasants."

Internal temps at HP and Apple did provide an important service, but only in those areas that looked like old-time postwar emergency replacement. The reorganizations used external temps for exactly the peasant work that AppleCorps would not do, which was why these kinds of services could complement, but could not replace, temp agencies. AppleCorps had a couple dozen employees. At HP, internal temps were not quite the same as regular personnel, since they were classified as internal temp employees, like interns. Personnel, through the early 1980s, may have requested managers to use the internal pool whenever possible, but these requests were frequently ignored. For instance, in 1983, at just the corporate offices, HP used 22,580 hours of external temp labor compared to a mere 7,675 hours of HP Temps Pool labor. Like consultants, temps had become a permanent part of the new corporate structure created through the waves of restructuring. Peasant work was outsourced.

The point of temps, by the 1980s, was no longer emergency replacement. It was cyclical replacement. In the face of demands for higher quality, lower cost, and workforce flexibility, the desire for job security and marketplace success were incompatible (at least in the minds of HR professionals). After a hiring freeze in late 1981 and an encouragement to reallocate the existing workforce, HP personnel sent a memo around chastising managers for a 56 percent increase in the use of temp workers.[44] In the first quarter of 1982, the main buildings in Silicon Valley billed 75,848 hours of temp labor, or about a hundred temps per day. Managers simply evaded the hiring freeze by using temporary labor.

In 1987, an HP task force reexamined the problem of job stability at HP.[45] Though HP made use of temps extensively in manufacturing, its office staffing was still 99 percent regular workers. And that was a problem. An internal workforce that was "99 percent fixed" could "not allow a timely reaction to a slowdown in the economy." Those who were already part of the HP workforce needed to be protected from the market. "Flexibility" coming from using "more agency temporary employees" would allow HP to "hold full-time regular positions open until excess employees are available for placement."[46]

New kinds of temps, who didn't get benefits, whose children were not eligible for HP scholarships, were needed. The task force recommended that the company focus on hiring "external and new internal resources instead of hiring regular full-time employees." To that end, HP rolled out pilot sites to find "alternative staffing practices."[47] At HP, they called this the Flex Force.

In 1988, HP extended their Flex Force to create two additional job categories, "on-call" and "on-contract," to help strengthen the wall between the permanent workers and the temp market. On-call workers could work only up to 1,400 hours a year, and contractors could work on multimonth contracts, renewable up to two years. These employees would be like temps, working for short periods. They would be paid directly by HP, but not as W-2 employees; they would file 1099 independent contractor forms for their taxes. These workers would not receive the generous benefit and pay package for which HP was famous. Contractors would "only receive legally mandated benefits" and have "no employment security."[48] By the end of 1988, Flex Force had created, between temps, on-calls, contractors, and consultants, the flexible workforce that HP leadership wanted.

Through Flex Force and similar programs, CEO John Young looked for ways to become leaner. He cut layers of management out of the company in an effort to improve accountability and flexibility. With fewer middlemen, Young hoped that employees would take more ownership of their work. The flexible labor force remained a buffer, but as time went on, the lines between the temps and perms blurred, especially in the minds of high-level corporate strategists. Young told his general managers in 1989 that "managing headcount is a priority." HP would need to "manage headcount by function, including flex-force employees."[49]

Yet HP's needs for flexibility quickly exceeded even its internal pools of on-demand workers. HR representatives pestered managers to reserve "on-call flex force" workers weeks in advance. By 1991, HP entered contracts with two temp agencies, Manpower and Volt Services Group, for its temporary needs. Assignments varied from "several weeks, three to six months, or longer."[50] The placements were in "administrative, manufacturing, and technical functions." "Manpower and Volt," an internal memo related, "are able to provide external temporary workers for all of HP's job profiles." These external workforces would be cheaper. HP estimated that they would save $20 million a year through these contracts. At two large manufacturing sites alone they would save eight hundred thousand dollars.[51] In short, Manpower and Volt could supply any job position for any length of time for any area of the company.

A representative from each of the agencies sat in the headquarters, "providing an on-site coordinator to facilitate the hiring ... and to relieve HP personnel from this function." Manpower's representative was Mary Hoffman. Her cubicle was in the staffing office, along with all the rest of the HR department. As "Mary [was] beginning to set up personal interviews with managers who [were] larger users of temporary workers," how could they not imagine that something fundamental had changed at the company? Still, they would know that their jobs were safe. With an expandable workforce of temps, HP would not have to worry about real layoffs.

The Flex Force at HP started as a buffer but became part of the normal head count and acted as a rehearsal for permanent temporary positions procured through staffing firms like Manpower. In the midst of the recession of 1991, HP offered voluntary early retirement, shedding thousands of workers. The workforce discipline took its toll on morale, but Young warned that they "need[ed] to protect the investment we've made in getting employment down. If we don't make good on that investment, we'll have to pursue even more aggressive measures next year."

Japanese Management

The explanation for the need for restructuring was not just a competitive market, but a competitive *global* market, by which Americans meant Japan. In the 1980s, Americans widely blamed the Japanese for their industrial misfortunes. While Carter failed to convince Americans of their own cultural failings, Americans were more than willing to credit Japanese success to the Japanese culture. In 1964, Toyota began exporting to the U.S. Starting with only four thousand vehicles, exports rose tenfold in three years, to forty thousand. In 1966, Toyota introduced the Corolla, which was a small car aimed at a mass market. Riding the doubling of the average Japanese income by the mid-1960s, Corolla was a total success and, by 1974, the best-selling car in the world. With global oil prices rising, the gas-efficient Corolla turned heads, not only in Japan but everywhere. By 1980, Japanese imports accounted for 20 percent of all cars sold, and all the Big Three U.S. companies lost money. Special tariffs to keep out Japanese cars, or even to adjust the value of the yen, did little to assuage autoworkers who saw Corollas displace Cadillacs. Business leaders accustomed to decades of a particularly stable, U.S.-centric way of doing things confronted a new world order that they did not understand. Consultants offered answers.

Yet for all the anti-Japanese sentiment, the basic elements of restructuring were American—even in Japan. The insights that allowed for Japanese quality and Japanese efficiency had come from the U.S. as part of the postwar rebuilding program. In the aftermath of the war, Japanese industrialists had sought new ways to think about their economy. While American observers lauded the leanness of Japanese just-in-time manufacturing methods, the inspiration for this supply-chain management was American. In charge of managing supply for his division in the 1950s, Toyota manager Taiichi Ohno considered the American supermarket. The supermarket had no inventories in the back, only shelves in the front. Customers could take exactly what they needed, when they needed. Instead of vast heaps of car parts, what if suppliers provided the parts as needed to Toyota, just like a supermarket did to its customers? This just-in-time system would vastly reduce inventories, which would reduce working capital, which would allow for better investment elsewhere in Toyota.

All the way down Toyota's supply chain, this system spread through the Japanese economy, increasing efficiency and integration. Toyota reduced costs and reinvested their capital in ways that allowed them to produce cheaper, better cars. The success of Japanese manufacturing had nothing to do with an ancient Asian culture; it was managerial. It had nothing to do with samurai, unless there happened to be an American samurai named Edwards Deming.

Deming began his career as a mathematical physicist, working in both academia and in government. After the war, as a U.S. government consultant, he lectured in Japan on statistical controls for manufacturing quality. His lectures were collectively published as *Elementary Principles of Statistical Control of Quality*. Deming was not alone, but he became the most visible of American engineering evangelists. He donated the profits from his lectures back to the Union of Japanese Engineers and Scientists; the union, in turn, created the Deming Prize in quality management. Deming's ideas quickly circulated in Japan, placing him alongside Frederick Taylor in the Japanese managerial imagination. While Japan could not compete with the U.S. on the cutting edge of technology, they could make sure that what they did make worked well. Deming's lessons on "scientific quality control techniques" were disseminated widely in the 1960s in Japanese engineering circles, and by the time that Japanese firms began to seriously export in the '70s, their products were excellent.

Deming brought American management to Japan, but Kenichi "Ken" Ohmae brought it back to the U.S. At the height of American anxieties about Japan, Ohmae, who managed the Tokyo office of McKinsey, emerged as a leading translator of Japanese management. Ohmae, who had grown up in Japan, had come to the U.S. in the late 1960s to get a PhD in nuclear engineering at MIT, after which he joined McKinsey. When the firm opened its Tokyo office, Ohmae moved back home.

Ohmae managed the office through the 1970s and '80s, becoming an intimate, in the way that only a consultant can, of the leading businessmen of Japan. With his perfect knowledge of Japanese and American management, he became a leading translator of Japanese managerial thought for McKinsey and the first widely read author-consultant to emerge from the firm. In 1975, he published his first management book, *The Mind of the Strategist*. Dozens of books would follow. McKinsey, through Ohmae, acted as a bridge, in many ways, for Japanese organizational ideas to move to North America and then to Europe. While he denounced the exoticization of Japan, he also took advantage of it as much as he could, as Japan's ascendance terrified and fascinated American businessmen.

Japanese firms had a mystique that in some ways was antithetical to the increasingly flexible workforce of the U.S. corporation. Rather than short-term profit, Ohmae wrote in *McKinsey Quarterly*, the Japanese valued the "perpetuation of the enterprise." The stability of the career ladder was essential to that perpetuation. Japanese firms focused on long-term investments and guaranteed jobs for life. Employees were not variable costs, but "fixed assets."

Ohmae emphasized that this peoplecentric capitalism with long-run goals was not an "ancient cultural heritage"—as so many in the West liked to imagine Asia—but a "pragmatic institutional arrangement" that arose out of the scarcity of the postwar years, when older communalist values resurged in Japanese life, just as they did in European countries.[52] Confronted by this scarcity, the corporations took on a different flavor. Stockholders in Japan were not seen as "owners" but "moneylenders," like bondholders. The real corporation was the people who worked there. While Toyota, Sony, Mitsubishi, and other Japanese firms advanced short-term product design and manufacturing, they continued to focus on long-term employment and investment. This difference in Japan stemmed, in Ohmae's view, from a continued focus on "the corporation's long-term well-being" with a "real commitment" to business excellence, rather than "strictly financial objectives with only the stockholders in mind."[53] "Stockholders," according to Ohmae, do not matter more than "bankers" or "factory workers." While written by the head of McKinsey's Tokyo office, the quote reads today like something from *The Nation*. For Ohmae, American firms had lost track of maintaining long-term profits—and that was where American capitalism had gone wrong.

Executive leadership in Japan was based on seniority, not cleverness, which produced a different kind of corporation. While corporate planners in American firms "were so smart that they had to spell out every detail of a corporation's strategy for three to five years into the future," in Japan there were no such firm divisions between the "smart people" and the "dumb people [who] never got the big picture."[54] Like John Galbraith, Ohmae was convinced that postwar Western corporations, with their top-down military organization, were more like "communist and socialist regimes . . . [whose] detailed long-range planning . . . is a remarkably effective way of killing creativity and entrepreneurship."[55] The Japanese corporation, "less planned, less rigid," was more able to adapt to changing circumstances—an essential quality for the age of turbulence. Western corporations were choked by "too much strategic planning."[56]

In Japan, new college graduates did not earn more than machinists, unlike the bright young things who got MBAs at Harvard Business School. Because everyone worked their way up the corporate ladder, all employees were thought to have useful insights—unlike in the hierarchical U.S. corporation. The source of this top-down approach, he believed, stemmed from the "McNamara syndrome." Robert McNamara famously was one of the whiz kids who brought World War II military planning to post–World War II corporations, like Ford.[57] Described by an "auto man" as "bookish and rather impractical," he became president of Ford at the young age of forty-four, for his knowledge not of engineering, but of logistics. Ohmae believed that those of McNamara's stripe thought that they were smarter than other people and thus should set rigid guidelines and plans. Respect, however, was not the same as democracy.

As Toyotaism swept the managerial establishment, Ohmae pushed back against American misunderstandings. "Having worked as a consultant with many of Japan's best known companies," he wrote in 1982, "I often wonder where people get the idea that bottom-up decision making is a hallmark of Japanese corporations." Simply put, he said, "They are wrong." Toyota may have had a suggestion box, but that was not the same as bottom-up control. For three generations, at that point, control of Toyota had passed from father to son. Toyota and other firms had the same top-down management as U.S. firms, if not more so. The difference was in how they thought about their workers. Ohmae said that the corporate truism that "people are our most important asset" was actually believed in Japan, while in the U.S. it was just "pious rhetoric."[58] In Japan, workers were assets, not costs.

These workers didn't have control, but they did have a voice. Japanese employees, even the line workers, who were "of high and fairly even quality," gathered a few times per month to discuss how they made their products. Their ideas were shared and disseminated. They were not managers, but their managers supported their experimentation with methods. With some ideas coming from them and not just from the management, workers were more willing to change how things were done. Developing quality circles took time. While American managers scrambled to implement *kaizen* (continuous improvement), they failed to notice that it was "this philosophy, not the mechanism of QC circles" that produced Japan's "enviable results."[59]

Looking to overcome export restrictions, Toyota opened its first auto plant in the U.S. in a joint partnership with GM in 1983—the NUMMI plant in Fremont, California. The plant had been one of GM's worst performing, and presumably they felt like they had nothing to lose. Ohmae told the *New York Times*, "It's a smart thing for Toyota to go into the U.S. with a partner."[60] It is difficult to imagine that Ohmae, in McKinsey's Tokyo office, had nothing to do with that smart decision. At the NUMMI plant, the GM way was dismantled. Detailed contracts and job descriptions were eliminated. Workers were put on teams instead of into slots. Teamwork and flexibility reduced boredom and increased commitment. Absenteeism fell from 25 percent to 2 percent. Quality rose to nearly match that of Japanese counterparts. Japanese management approaches, because they were not cultural, could be exported as well.

Toyota had come to America, and not just for car production. The language of Toyota production began to infuse American business—*kaizen*, *kanban* (just-in-time scheduling). As James Abegglen, who was vice president in BCG's Tokyo office, said, "GM's upside was to see how Toyota runs a factory."[61] GM and other American industrial firms struggled to learn from the competition. In the 1980s, then, there was a flood of assistance in translating these American-cum-Japanese ideas back into English. Ohmae, McKinsey, and other consultants were there to help, bringing ideas of quality and leanness into American corporations.

The world was global, and McKinsey moved ideas around the world. Mobility was, at the same time, foundational to the "one firm" concept. The managing director in 1977 celebrated that the partner who oversaw "the Firm's relationship with the H. J. Heinz Company in Pittsburgh" lived in London. Ken Ohmae oversaw studies in Italy and Spain, and Bob Waterman did the same in Japan.[62] Consultants, like capitalism, had to be global. Having "roots," as the managing director said, was antithetical to "mobility."[63] On the one hand was "individual drive and entrepreneurship" and on the other hand was "collaboration and support." Like professional work trading off with personal lives, these binaries, which would not have been framed as such by Bower, did define the globalized, professional world of work that was emerging.[64]

Nowhere were these ideas taken up with as much fervor as at Apple, which opened its first Macintosh factory right across the street from NUMMI in 1983.

Manufacturing Apple

During the Super Bowl's third quarter in January 1984, millions of Americans watched an arresting commercial: rows of gray bald men marched and then sat while listening to the ideological drone of a great leader on an oversized television. Evoking *1984*, the dystopian George Orwell novel, the ad compared the monolith of IBM to a repressive totalitarian state. A woman running in Olympic shorts then spun a sledgehammer into the television's screen to smash it and free the minds of the drones. That hammer was, the commercial told us, the Macintosh computer. "On January 24th, Apple Company will introduce Macintosh," the voice-over said. "And you'll see why 1984 won't be like *1984*."[65] The liberation of the consuming masses, Apple said as well, would come through individual computers. "We tried to capture the computer age's worst nightmare," Apple said, "where machines control people, and show that our alternative empowered people and set them free."[66] During Steve Jobs's first public presentation of the Mac, it showcased its now iconic voice synthesizing ability, joking that "I'd like to share with you a maxim I thought of the first time I met an IBM mainframe: NEVER TRUST A COMPUTER YOU CAN'T LIFT!"[67] The crowd, of course, went wild—not only for the talking computer, but for the price of that talking computer, which was about $9,000 in today's dollars. The personal computer was to be a tool of business, but also a tool of individual liberation.

Explaining why every desk needed a computer, rather than a mainframe in a big room, took some convincing. Jobs turned to historical analogues. The personal computer was to the mainframe as the VW was to the train, or (more obscurely) as fractional horsepower motors were to "huge motors." In each case, the smaller version allowed individuals to go where they wanted (VW) or to do what they wanted (smaller motors). Jobs claimed that the personal computer would do in the 1980s "for the individual as the big computers did for the corporation in the '60s and '70s." Jobs invoked none other than Alvin Toffler, calling the personal computer a "third wave" tool, like the hoe of agriculture (first wave) and the motor of industry (second wave). This "third wave tool" would "help every individual deal with the complexities of modern life."[68]

Apple's previous hit, the Apple II, could be used by normal people who knew nothing about programming, but it still worked, more or less, through a command line interface. Like IBM computers, they were overwhelming. The "average computer user," Apple said, took "over 20 hours just to get comfortable with this new tool," and Apple "knew that office workers were terrified, not overjoyed, by the new devices." The Macintosh was the attempt to reinvent the computer, so the interface ("file folders, clipboards, a trash can") used familiar objects rather than arcane computer terms.[69]

The first Apple computer to use a point-and-click interface, the Lisa, had been far too expensive—$10,000 in 1983 ($25,000 in 2018 dollars).[70] Retailers couldn't sell them. Software companies, in turn, wouldn't develop software for such a niche market. So when Apple thought about designing its next computer, they tried to remake the Lisa "smaller, cheaper, and better . . . at a competitive price."[71] As they designed this next computer, the Macintosh, they did so with an eye toward its production to keep the price down.[72] The most automated, most robotic factory would make that low price possible. Investing $20 million in the Fremont plant, they consolidated all U.S. production in one place "to create the most highly automated factory in the western world"—what Apple called a Robot Factory.[73] Behind that consumer freedom, though, was the new regime of work and machines that made the Macintosh possible, but that was less freeing.

Jobs told Apple shareholders at the 1984 meeting that their new factory in Fremont was the "computer industry's first automated factory."[74] "The factory is based on the ideas of just-in-time delivery and zero defects parts," he said, "which allows extremely high volume production of extremely high quality products." What made this possible? A promotional video shown to shareholders told them the secret, and it wasn't the workforce—it was, as with Toyota, the relationship with vendors. Quality parts plus automated manufacturing equaled the Macintosh. The secret to Apple's manufacturing success was the same as with other '80s firms—drawing a bright line between the supplier and the firm. All Apple needed to know was that the vendor's part was there when it needed it, not how it was made.

Using that vendor's part required a factory for assembly. A small team of engineers designed the computer, coordinating the work of many other teams. The factory to build the Macintosh was designed alongside the machine itself. Jan Grappel, who had come to Apple from RCA, designed the production line for the Fremont factory, automating the line wherever possible, aiming for a thousand computers per shift.[75] "A Machine Builds Machines," touted Apple about its "Highly Automated Macintosh Manufacturing Facility."[76]

At Apple, the actual builders of the computers were being reorganized. Debi Coleman, head of worldwide manufacturing, had shifted production from earlier factories in Dallas, Texas; Garden Grove, California; and Mill Street, Ireland; to new facilities in Cork, Ireland; Singapore; and, most important, Fremont. She had gotten her start at Apple as the project controller for the Macintosh in 1981 and, with Jobs's support, been promoted to head of worldwide manufacturing. Though she had studied literature at Brown as an undergrad, she had become disillusioned during the Nixon administration, turned from "you-have-to-change-the-world," as she said, to "screaming market share! Market share!" A twenty-month finance program through General Electric, and then an MBA at Stanford, taught her how to think in ways that Vladimir Nabokov—the writer on whom she wrote her thesis— never could have imagined. She joined Hewlett-Packard, where she learned about technology manufacturing, but her promotion was limited by her lack of an engineering background. At Apple she thrived, with Jobs sponsoring her quick advancement.[77]

At Fremont, her secret was simple: Toyota's *kanban* just-in-time production. The just-in-time system rewarded vendors who could provide products at the right time, at the right price, and at the right quality. Coleman viewed "vendors as extensions of our own factories. People said it couldn't be done—that you could not make vendors into partners," but she did. Those who did not become partners lost their contracts. Coleman reduced the vendor list from eleven hundred firms to three hundred. Firms that met requirements found they had more orders.[78] During the tumultuous 1985, Coleman reduced Apple's inventories from $261 million to $107 million, freeing up all that capital to be used elsewhere.

The first few months after the Macintosh was introduced were not the success that Apple had hoped; 1984 was a slump year in the computer industry. In April, the Fremont plant was closed for a week as excess inventory was sold. In Dallas, where Apple manufactured the Macintosh XL, the workers were all laid off.[79] At the corporate offices, Apple's president, John Sculley, reorganized the company from product lines (Lisa, Apple II, Mac) into functional lines (products and marketing). In the reorganization, twelve hundred employees were let go. By the end of the year, though, Apple was planning for growth. The Fremont factory installed equipment intended to double its capacity from forty thousand computers per month to eighty thousand.[80] During the downturn, Sculley's approach was straightforward: "centralize, consolidate, streamline, and organize" to increase flexibility.[81] Coleman decided to close the factories that could only produce single products. She kept the ones with the "most flexible machinery." "To be world-class," she said, "[Fremont] would have to handle multiple production in varying volume." "With flexible automation," Coleman continued, "you have robotics with sensors you can reprogram, so you can produce eight to twenty-four products on one line."[82] The flexibility manufacturing system project at Apple, as Coleman said in 1988, was about "reinforc[ing] a focus on automation, on future thinking, on flexibility, and on quality."[83] The new tracking system, done through a Mac, allowed the same person to assemble multiple products on the same production line.

The following year, Steve Jobs was pushed out of Apple as part of Sculley's reorganization of Apple away from products to functions. The intense competitive atmosphere between different products (Lisa, Macintosh, Apple II, etc.) was detrimental to the business. At first the split seemed mutually amicable (Jobs was starting another company), but it quickly soured as Jobs poached top talent for his new company. He succinctly lashed out in a full-page ad in the *Wall Street Journal*: "The personal computer industry is now being handed over from the 'builders' to the 'caretakers'; that is, from the individuals who created and grew a multi-billion dollar American industry to those who will maintain the industry as it is and work to achieve marginal future growth."[84] Reorganizing Apple in this way was exactly what he feared most: "Companies as they grow to become multibillion-dollar entities somehow lose their vision. They insert lots of layers of middle management between the people running the company and the people doing the work."[85] Jobs's complaints parroted, almost verbatim, the text of *In Search of Excellence.*

According to Jobs, the people "doing the work" were him and

(sometimes) cofounder Steve "Woz" Wozniak, but it was another 140 people—mostly women, mostly immigrants—who actually put the Macintosh together. These workers showed up at 5:45 A.M. to spend the day assembling, putting together the same sets of connectors, regulators, and capacitors for an entire shift.[86] Sara Trujillo inspected circuit boards before they were baked in the oven.[87] Hung Troung put the computers in boxes. When the line shut down, workers like Therese Deering used those same Macintoshes to track problems in spread sheets. "This is something new to me," Deering said, but she felt "like I'm contributing something the supervisors need to know."[88] Assemblers tracked the line, just as their Japanese analogues would have done.

On the Mac's fifth anniversary, John Sculley congratulated the factory's workforce on making the Macintosh, which he proclaimed a "new concept in computing" with its "focus on the individual—not on the organization."[89] After the congratulations, a few issues later, the cover story of Apple's *Fremont Flash*, the employee newsletter, featured Joe Mendoza and Dolores La Fauci, two "aces" from the assembly line, smiling broadly. They weren't featured for their skills or their smiles, though. They were featured because they had gone to Singapore for a month to train thirty local assemblers to "build the same products we build."[90] Mendoza was proud that his "fine-tuning tricks" increased production from "400 to 550 units a day." Apple invested deeply in Singapore in 1988, some $38 million, producing all of the new IIGS, IIe, and IIc computers there. Like Fremont, the plant was heavily automated, and had 380 employees. Like Fremont, it adhered to just-in-time principles, with only four hours of small inventory and one hour of bulky inventory. While the plant was kept busy with variants of the Apple II, the market for that computer was petering out. The Apple IIc was in production for only three months a year, to prepare for school season. In 1988, Fremont was preparing to produce Macintoshes.[91]

Apple was not alone in moving its employees around to train their overseas replacements. Tech companies could bring their overseas workers to the U.S. for training under a B-1 visa.[92] Seagate Technology, which made disk drives and other storage technology, had fired eight hundred employees in 1984, when they opened a factory in Singapore. In 1986, they brought a hundred workers from Singapore to San Jose to "train" in their factory, while actually doing some production work.[93] While the workers were there,

Seagate officials took their passports, put them in houses—ten to a house—and gave them a small weekly stipend. Once workers were trained in the manufacturing, those jobs could be shipped back to Singapore. Whatever the cost here, the end goal was to have these workers, who earned about $1.00 an hour, do what was now being done in California for $4.40 an hour.

As the 1980s wore on, the tech firms of Silicon Valley prepared for a day when hardware would no longer be made there.

Commodified Temps

Unlike gold, which created the first California rush, silicon is everywhere. Every grain of sand is silicon dioxide. Making that cheap silicon pure enough for electronics, however, costs a lot of money. To do that, there can be no errors—even a slight bit of dust can ruin a batch.

Achieving this purity requires extremely clean rooms, which are called, suitably enough, "clean rooms." The fully contained hazmat suits ("bunny suits," in industry parlance) are not to protect the workers wearing them, but to shield the silicon wafers from the impurities of the human body. Smooth, controlled airflow likewise ensures that the environment is perfect for the silicon wafers' growth. After the growth stage, however, wafers need to be altered—etched with acids, reacted with chemicals—and in this next stage, the hazmat suit is no longer needed.[94] Semiconductors and electronics, then, need to be thought of as consisting of two main parts—the hypercontrolled first part, in which the semiconductors are created, and then the second part, in which they are assembled. If the first part is about machines, the second part is about labor.

The first part was done in semiconductor fabrication plants (fabs), and their clean rooms were extremely expensive, requiring massive outlays of capital as well as highly skilled engineers to oversee them. The skilled staff and the large investments meant that they could not be overseas, but they could be built in Texas or Colorado, where everything was less expensive. In making the chips themselves, firms were limited in how much they could cut costs.

When it came to putting the components together, however, high-tech firms had more options. In the production facilities that remained in Silicon Valley, the goal was to keep a very lean workforce that could be supplemented by temps. No more layoffs were possible—at least for the skilled workforce. As one corporate HR manager said, "We're running so lean right now that we can't afford to go out and say . . . I need five people to go in and layoff. It becomes more cosmetic than anything else."[95] The core skilled technicians of the fab plant could not be let go, but the other workers, who assembled, packed, and tested, were more interchangeable. The work could be done in-house, or, as we will see, could be subcontracted.

Firms that did assembly in-house looked to stay flexible. The so-called full-time staff did not have much certainty, either; they had only six-month contracts.[96] Temps were an even better option. By 1984, Santa Clara County, with its 180 temp agencies, had the highest density of temps in the country (1 in 60 workers).[97] In Silicon Valley, Manpower supplied more temps for production work and electronic assembly than any other tasks.[98]

Temp assembly workers could be ramped up or ramped down, but it is perhaps surprising how consistent their numbers were. Most semiconductor firms got about 10 percent of their production staff through temp agencies. Rather than going from no temps to some temps, firms, like one chip plant, would go from "95 temps to as much as 150 temps." This pattern was "fairly predictable," said a plant manager. "Every quarter, I can tell you exactly."[99] Temps were a "buffer zone," as the executive vice president of the National Association of Temporary Services called it, for the permanent workers, but they were now becoming a permanent part of that workforce as well.[100]

Firms had standing contracts with temp agencies. If they needed those extra temps for the end of the quarter, they could just call them. For the ninety-five temps who were always there, the firm could arrange a "pay-rolling" system, where employees were shifted to a temp agency. With an average markup of 34 percent, even the more expensive wages of the temps were cheaper than the average cost (benefits, payroll, etc.) of 42 percent above wages that firms paid at the time for full-time workers.[101]

Electronic assembly was not hard. At Convergent Technologies, a computer manufacturer in Santa Clara, about 30 percent of the workforce was temporary, but that number could shift rapidly. From June to September 1984, the number of temps went from 370 to 627, out of 2,200 total workers.[102] These temps were "screwing in disk drives or taking boards and placing them in the chassis of the computer," the kind of work that requires a screwdriver and five minutes of training. Larger firms used temps in the same way. Also in 1984, HP spent $5 million on temps, using about half of them in assembly. These firms took pride in "never having a layoff," but that was made possible by temps.

The first part of production was straightforward: build an expensive machine and turn sand into semiconductors. The second part of production, though less technological, was far more complicated organizationally. To cut costs and stay flexible, firms became extremely creative about finding cheap workers willing to do toxic work.

Unclean Rooms and Undocumented Workers

After dropping out of his PhD program in sociology in 1980, Dennis Hayes came to Silicon Valley and started temping, working in the assembly room of a leading audio equipment manufacturer—Ampex.[103] While Blondie and the Bee Gees touted their products, the glamour somehow didn't make its way back to the assembly room. Hayes may have hated temping, but he knew he didn't have the worst job in Silicon Valley. Unlike most of the rest of the *Processed World* writers, Hayes noticed that this futuristic economy rested on a very old idea: give the dirty, dangerous work to people who had no alternative.

Though Hayes worked on the floor of the assembly room, he didn't put anything together. The room, like most assembly rooms in Silicon Valley, contained all women, mostly women of color. Automation was not an option because the products changed too quickly to recoup the investment in machinery.[104] The tools the women used were primordial—older than transistors, older than screwdrivers, even older than the ax—their fingernails. They grew "two or three strategically long nails" on each hand so that they could more easily maneuver the components onto the circuit boards.[105] Tongs were an option, but fingernails worked better. Some production technologies in Silicon Valley were as much ancient as futuristic.

Ampex was not unique. The much-heralded flexibility in manufacturing in most industries came through low-cost labor, not through autonomous machines. Some of those workers were in Asia, but just as many were immigrants, also from Asia, who now lived in California, where they worked alongside Mexican immigrants in the subcontractor shops that supplied the electronics manufacturers. The low-end workforce of Silicon Valley mimicked the populations that did assembly work overseas—Taiwanese, Filipinos, and Vietnamese—as well as a large Latino population of 320,000.[106] While electronics firms had their headquarters near Stanford, they had their factories wherever they could find their preferred workers.

Silicon Valley was the most visible part of the electronics industry, but these same work conditions were found elsewhere, especially in Southern California. In the 1970s, more electronics factories were built in Anaheim (464), Los Angeles (367), and San Diego (123) combined than in San Jose (339) or San Francisco (151). Other top cities included Dallas (276), Chicago (224), and Houston (204).[107] The pattern in these cities was not particularly different than in Silicon Valley.

Investigations in the mid-1980s found that among legally employed electronics production workers most were women (64 percent) and most were Hispanic (57 percent), even though the population of Southern California was only about one fifth Hispanic. Of those Hispanics, about half were foreign born. Foreign-born Asians also made up a substantial percentage of the workforce (10 to 20 percent). Managers, as they told interviewers, preferred foreign-born workers for being "diligent, hardworking, and loyal."[108] Black workers, they felt, were less reliable, more resistant, and prone to unionization. Help-wanted ads posted phone numbers for Spanish- and English-speaking applicants. On the English line, there were no jobs available, while on the Spanish line, there was always room for new applicants for low-wage assembly positions.[109] Managers wanted obedient employees—preferably immigrants. While technical knowledge, and venture capital, was lauded for the valley's achievements, that success was made possible by a hidden underworld of flexible, poorly paid labor.

Apple did not run a sweatshop. Inside the highly visible Apple factory, the workforce was legally employed. Workers got paid the minimum wage (or more). The production regimes followed OSHA regulations. Apple made protective safety equipment available. Yet about 40 percent of electronics firms subcontracted to small independent firms, whose production in less visible spaces, while essential, looked very different than in those high-profile factories.[110]

Not all firms were as aboveboard as Apple. In the competitive world of electronics, corners were cut. In 1982, Fermina—not her actual name—had worked for about three years at an electronics assembly plant in Tijuana, where she earned sixty-five cents an hour "soldering gold filaments to nodes neatly marked on printed circuits." She peered hour after hour through her microscope, bonding semiconductors. Then the peso destabilized, and Fermina crossed the border to stay with relatives and look for work. After looking in the newspaper, she called a number to inquire about jobs like the one she had left behind—and she could even do it in Spanish! She found her old job, bonding semiconductors, but this time it was in an assembly plant in San Diego that made parts for personal computers. Instead of sixty-five cents an hour, she now got five dollars. In the plant, hundreds of Mexicans worked alongside Fermina, many of them undocumented just like her. For Fermina, it was a good paying job. For the firm, Fermina and those like her led to great profits. In 1983, it was the fourth largest supplier of personal computers in the U.S., with sales of $75 million—and profits of $13 million.[111]

When an INS raid occurred in November 1984, Fermina hid in a supply closet, terrified. She escaped, but fifty of her coworkers, nearly all Mexican women, were put in vans for deportation.[112] "I came to this country to work hard but now I live torn between duty and shame," she told an interviewer.[113] Fermina was not alone. Other high-profile INS raids found firms had employed, on average, about half their assembly workforces illegally. Scholars estimated that a hundred thousand—many undocumented—Hispanic women worked in electronics just in Southern California.

Back in Silicon Valley, Hayes's job at Ampex was not to put the components together but to drop off and gather chassis panels, nuts, and screws made in Ampex's factory from subcontractors who processed them in "metal shops in Silicon Valley." High-end audio at Ampex was made possible by low-end subcontracting. "They'd just give me an address and a car," Hayes said, "and I would go out and get this stuff."[114]

Hayes drove to a "a dirt-floor Quonset hut in Santa Clara," inside of which "were Hispanic workers in rubber boots, gloves, and aprons—and without respirator masks." The toxic labor of electronics manufacturing was outsourced. Chip fabrication had to take place in clean rooms, but electronics assembly could take place nearly anywhere.[115] The front and back doors of the hut were open, and some passively turning fans were on the ceiling, but otherwise there was no ventilation. The workers "moved about quickly, stoking fires beneath vats of chemicals, climbing up and down the jerrybuilt platforms that gave access to the vats. Some of them boiled; others, untouched by the fires, yielded the smoke of chemical reaction." The subcontracted workers dipped metals and printed circuits into their vats. Hayes, only there for minutes at a time, wrote, "the foul metallic odors made me want to hold my breath." He never talked directly to the workers, only to the boss, who spoke to him in English while commanding the workers in Spanish.

In the early 1980s, there was a dawning awareness of the health risks of working in the semiconductor industry. Investigators found that occupational illnesses were three times higher in semiconductor manufacturing than in other manufacturing industries.[116] Today, Santa Clara County has more EPA-designated Superfund sites—twenty-three—than any other county in the United States.[117] The most illustrious names of Silicon Valley—Fairchild, Intel, Raytheon, Teledyne, Westinghouse, National Semiconductor—dot the EPA's map of toxic waste sites. Clean-room employees, over the years, began suing their companies. Environmental and labor groups with long acronyms staged protests.[118] This formal workforce certainly suffered, but the informal workforce, less documented, less studied, probably suffered much worse.

Subcontracting avoided American wage laws, but also American safety laws. The tort-liable work was outsourced, with a network of temps to act as intermediaries. No permanent employee of Ampex delivered or picked up the panels, nuts, and screws, so no official employee of Ampex could ever *really* know the conditions under which the chemistry took place. Ampex was not alone.

In Silicon Valley, the clean rooms of high-end technology were built atop a foundation of poisonous Quonset huts. Never in one place for too long, these left no Superfund sites—except of course for the workers themselves. If there was a legal problem at one hut, it was easy to disappear into another anonymous shop—or even a home.

The bottom rung of the electronics industry was not in a small factory or a Quonset hut, but a kitchen. Investigators found that somewhere between 10 and 30 percent of electronics firms subcontracted to "home workers."[119]

Like garment workers taking in sewing, electronics workers could assemble parts in their kitchen. A mother and her children gathered around a kitchen table putting together components for seven cents apiece.[120] These little shops put together the boards that went to big companies.[121] California labor inspectors turned a blind eye:

> A Mexican or a Vietnamese can take home a thousand coils for wiring one evening, and put every close neighbor and family member to work, and return the next day to the plant. . . . It's not even worth our time trying to wipe it out. When there are people eager to work for pennies, you can expect that kind of thing to happen.[122]

While the image of Silicon Valley was futuristic, its methods harked back to the nineteenth century. The component assemblers of the 1980s—poor immigrants—would have been hard to tell apart from piecework seamstresses of the 1880s living in tenements. These homeworkers offered firms a cheaper labor force, but their real appeal was, of course, flexibility. Chip processing fluctuated.[123] Like with cars, computer demand varied through the year for consumers (holidays and new school terms) and as a result of changes in technology (new chips). As demand went up and down, firms had no obligation to their homeworkers.[124] So kitchen and Quonset-hut workers would open and close shop as needed.

The exact numbers—how many firms, how many chips—are hard to pin down precisely because it was a subterfuge. Behind the big, expensive plants were vast networks of other workers. Tellingly, more firms in the various surveys subcontracted to homeworkers than to offshore plants.[125]

Hayes was not the only one to notice the relationship between undocumented labor and electronics.

The INS Comes to Silicon Valley

In 1984, John Senko, an eighteen-year veteran of the INS, opened its first office in San Jose and began to oversee immigration issues in Silicon Valley. The INS believed that as much as 25 percent of the Silicon Valley workforce (approximately two hundred thousand workers) was undocumented.

Senko's task was simple and yet impossible: eliminate illegal labor in Silicon Valley. The office had only four investigators and was chronically under-resourced. He said, "It's difficult to make people realize that because of the nature of the industry, illegal aliens are working here." Because "high technology is a sophisticated industry," it was easy, Senko said, to believe that no part of the production process was unskilled.[126]

The INS at first broadly investigated the use of illegal labor in electronics by raiding Quonset-hut operations and even large factories. General Technology, for instance, had 10 percent of its workforce (forty-six people) seized by the INS in a raid.[127] It turned out, according to their arrests, that the actual number of undocumented workers was much lower than the 25 percent initially believed, and was in fact closer to about 8 percent.[128] What mattered, of course, was not the percentage, but the way in which some segments of the electronics industry relied so heavily on undocumented labor.

The INS encouraged companies to cooperate. At Circuit Assembly Corporation in San Jose, the INS asked for the names of its noncitizen employees. Of the 250 names, the company thought that "20 or 30 of them could be using forged papers."[129] The actual number was 187. The company, because it cooperated, received no sanctions or penalties, and, according to Senko, replaced those 187 with legal workers.

The San Jose local government pushed back against the INS in the name of defending "Chicano citizens" against harassment, passing a resolution against "the unwarranted disruption of the business community."[130] Harassment was all too real. Over the first year and half of Senko's administration, the INS raided not just workplaces but neighborhoods. In Menlo Park, just near Stanford, INS agents blocked the streets and removed "Hispanic males" from cars and from homes, checking them for proof of citizenship. In Santa Cruz, the INS went door to door checking Hispanic citizenship.[131] Senko and his agents believed that they did not need warrants that named names ahead of time.[132] They were "surveying."

San Jose, Senko complained, "didn't want us weeding out illegal aliens anyway."[133] The city didn't, but it wasn't just to defend the rights of San Joseans. The city attorney tried to stop the raids. Police refused to cooperate with the INS. In 1985, a San Francisco district judge issued an injunction to stop the raids, requiring the INS to have the names of illegal aliens ahead of time. In December of that year, San Francisco declared itself a sanctuary and directed its police and officials not to assist the INS in finding "law-abiding" but "undocumented" migrants.[134] In 1986, though a judge in the Ninth Circuit ruled that the INS could conduct its "surveys" without naming warrants, the INS and Senko were still blocked politically. Senko, due to a lack of staff, was not "going to rush out" to conduct workplace raids.[135]

This local resistance did not, however, improve the working conditions of those Chicano or Vietnamese or Filipino or Taiwanese laborers. The INS surveillance quickly became just another instrument of worker repression, as Hayes noticed at the time. Business owners could selectively check green cards against an INS database or simply hand over "troublemakers." Attempts to organize the electronics factories proved unsuccessful. The spokesperson for the International Association of Machinists explained that whenever they tried to organize, the company "threatened to have anyone who joined the union deported."[136]

Deportation hearings did not happen the next day, but could take place months, and sometimes years, after someone was arrested.[137] Those who agreed to deportation could leave quickly, but those who appealed could languish in detention for months. Mexicans, on average, left within a few days, while those from Central America stayed longer, since they were less eager to return to the civil wars going on back home. While the INS operated seven main detention camps, it also subcontracted detention to a thousand different companies, with names like Corrections Corporation of America or Behavioral Systems Southwest. These detention facilities varied from overcrowded hotel rooms to overcrowded jails. The miserable conditions encouraged the detainee to agree to deportation without a hearing.[138]

Unprotected Workers, Undocumented Workers

"This economy," former INS head Leonel Castillo told a newspaper, "was built on the assumption and reality of a heavy influx of illegal labor."[139] Castillo was referring not just to the electronics industry, but to the entire economy of the American west. California conducted a study in 1979, using scientific sampling methods, that found that 81 percent of Hispanic garment workers and 75 percent of Hispanic restaurant workers were undocumented.[140] The *Wall Street Journal* estimated that in Houston by the 1980s, one third of all construction workers were "illegals, doing jobs that nowadays most citizens refuse: lugging pots of hot tar to rooftops, pulling nails from concrete forms and clearing debris." INS agents, on just one random Thursday, could stop by a Ryan Homes site to get "three dry-wallers," and then that same day, only a short drive away, pick up "three illegals pouring a sidewalk for No. 4-ranked U.S. Home Corp." After that, they made two more arrests, then went to have barbecue for lunch. They arrested another undocumented worker from behind the counter.[141] Undocumented workers were everywhere—not just the fields.

Legal workers could demand rights that illegal workers could not.[142] A subcontractor who was supervising an undocumented crew explained: "Whenever there's an accident on the site, the Chicano (Mexican American) will stay home and ask for worker's compensation. The Mexicans, they work."[143] Undocumented aliens still had the right to join unions and actually had most other labor rights as well, like minimum wage and overtime laws. They could bring suit in courts. Of course, if they were discovered, then they could be deported. As much as undocumented aliens were protected in theory, they were not protected in practice.

For women, legal status sharply divided the Mexican American workforce, especially for those who were born in the U.S. Undocumented workers did not compete with native-born Chicanas as much as they competed with recent legal immigrants, especially women. Mexican women who were undocumented or legal immigrants were six or seven times as likely to work in electronics as native-born Chicana women, who tended, like most Americans, to work in retail.[144] Among the estimated undocumented in Los Angeles in the 1980 census, 29 percent worked as "textile sewing machine operators" and 33 percent worked as "other machine operators, assemblers, and inspectors." Native-born women rarely did these jobs, working instead (51 percent) in "administrative support occupations, including clerical." Only 1 percent of native-born women worked on a sewing machine. While legal immigrants also worked on sewing machines (27 percent), fewer worked in the more capacious "other machine operators, assemblers and inspectors" category (18 percent). The competition for these jobs was between undocumented and legal migrants, not with native-born Chicanas.[145]

Native-born Chicano men faced competition from both legal and illegal migrants.[146] For men, the occupational distribution was much more similar across legal statuses. Most common were "machine operators, assemblers, and inspectors" for undocumented (38 percent), legal immigrant (32 percent), and native-born citizen (21 percent), as well as the construction trades (7.4 percent, 5.6 percent, and 9.8 percent, respectively). This competition, however, did not mean that Chicano men earned less than women. Undocumented men had incomes roughly half ($8,485) that of the average Angelino ($16,875). Legal immigrant and native-born Chicanos had roughly comparable incomes ($12,047 and $13,185), which, while lower than average, were not half. Perhaps explaining why Hispanic women worked less than Hispanic men, undocumented women ($4,774), legal immigrants ($5,881), and native-born ($6,492) women all earned less than even undocumented men and less than the average Angelina woman ($8,438).[147]

A more satisfying solution to illegal employment would be to penalize the employers who seek to subvert our laws and exploit those without recourse. This plan was first tried—and failed—in California in the early 1970s. Knowingly employing illegal aliens in California, after November 1971, when Governor Ronald Reagan signed the Arnett Bill, became illegal. Employers faced sanctions (between two hundred and five hundred dollars per offense). In reality, however, this law failed. In the decade after its passage, no one in California was prosecuted under the law.[148] As Gaylord Grove, of the San Diego office of the Labor Commission, told an interviewer in 1982, "Oh, we don't enforce that law. . . . It's a dead law."[149] After the law's passage, instead of increasing enforcement funding, the number of California Labor Commission field investigators dropped from twenty to six.[150] The commission, as immigration scholar Kitty Calavita noticed, cut funding for eighty positions. With so few staff (the entire Central Valley had but one investigator, nicknamed the "Lone Ranger"), the law was born dead. Its passage was purely symbolic. Employers, whether agricultural or industrial, had no incentive to obey a law that was clearly not being enforced. No employer was ever successfully fined under the law.

The failure of the California statute went unnoticed. The logic of employer sanctions, with its moral high ground, became a model for national policy, starting with President Carter in 1977. From the early 1970s through the mid-1980s, employers resisted the passage of such laws—ostensibly because of fears of going to jail for simple clerical errors. Arnett, who had sponsored the California bill, himself doubted the ability to enforce the law. He feared that the law, by depending on Social Security cards, would allow employers to be "harassed" and liable for employees with fake papers, since Social Security cards were "so freely issued, [so] easily forged."[151]

Mexican Americans feared that rules against hiring *indocumentados* would simply mean "turn[ing] away," as California senator S. I. Hayakawa said, "all those with brown skin instead of going through the process of checking the credentials of a possible employee." Sanctions would not actually pass Congress until 1986, as part of the Immigration Reform and Control Act (IRCA). But there was little to worry about. Thanks to the lobbying of the contracting associations (as they proudly told their memberships), the law contained so many loopholes that no one would be going to jail—for anything.

IRCA combined the approaches of both Castillo and Chapman, of Carter and Ford. Employer sanctions came along with a broad citizenship amnesty intended to finally seal the border, apply universal labor laws, and improve the lives of the undocumented. Studies of amnesty applicants after IRCA would, for the first time, provide an accurate picture of undocumented life in the U.S. and then the effects of amnesty on the undocumented. The studies confirmed what Chapman had claimed in the 1970s: the undocumented filled in the gaps in the service economy. Only a handful (5 percent) of undocumented immigrants had worked white-collar jobs. Most (55 percent) had worked blue-collar jobs—as laborers (15 percent), factory operatives (25 percent), and craft workers (15 percent). Only 19 percent worked on farms. Even just considering undocumented Mexican migrants, still only 27 percent worked in the fields. The agricultural rhetoric regarding the undocumented migrant simply wasn't true.

At Apple, for instance, HR vice president Kevin Sullivan was committed to complying with the new immigration law—but only for official employees and contractors. Before anyone got paid, Apple had to "receive proof of a new hire's (or independent contractor's) identity and right to work."[152]

Sullivan issued a memo to that effect, and half of it regarded independent contractors, who were an increasing part of the Apple workforce. The independent contractor needed to make sure that the "Human Resource liaison" had the verification information. Equally important, Sullivan pointed out, Apple did "not discriminate against foreign nationals." No one was to be asked about their status "until a job offer has been accepted." Outside parts suppliers, of course, were not part of this careful system.

It was a brief victory. In the first few years, cases against employers rose to a peak of about seventeen hundred a year in 1989, but then fell—quickly. By 1994, IRCA sanctions numbered a thousand a year, crashing to fewer than two hundred by 2000. The law was rarely enforced. IRCA had almost no effect—it neither reformed nor controlled immigration. Employer sanctions were supposed to end the flood of illegal laborers, but they did almost nothing. It did not even particularly help those who received amnesty. They were still part of the same economy as before. On average, wages of formerly undocumented migrants went up a little (approximately 10 percent), but not as much as advocates hoped.[153] Understanding the wage increase, moreover, required looking past the averages. Skilled workers benefited the most from legalization. Uneducated or unskilled workers hardly benefited at all. For new undocumented migrants, the pull of *el norte* remained, and employers had very little difficulty in hiring them. The undocumented workforce may have lived in the shadows, but their work was part of the legal economy.

In theory, IRCA affected every business with more than three employees, but in practice it had little effect. In Houston, the celebrated Ninfa's Mexican Restaurant told the *Houston Chronicle* that it had no trouble at all, despite its "mainly Hispanic workforce," for the same reason that any large employer in Houston had no problem: the law applied only to new workers.[154] Ninfa's had a "stable workforce." Only workers moving in and out of work, or the firms that employed them, would have difficulty with the new law. And then, of course, they could simply turn to subcontractors.

Following the letter of the law was safe, but actively discriminating against noncitizens was not. "Employee," it turned out, excluded "independent contractors." As long as the workers were at arm's length, the employer could not be held responsible for their immigration status. Congress, under pressure from contractors, adjusted the law so that employers could be held liable only when they hired subcontractors "to obtain the labor of an alien in the United States knowing that the alien is an unauthorized alien." Hiring in this way made employers safe.

In April 1987, the leading white-shoe Houston law firm, Fulbright & Jaworski, gave a presentation to the Associated General Contractors of Houston to apprise them of "employer responsibilities under the Immigration Reform and Control Act of 1986."[155] The law made it easy—though it was not stated as such—to hire undocumented workers. Employers were not liable unless they knew they were hiring an alien unauthorized to work. Penalties for first offenses were light—"$250 to $2000 per unauthorized alien"—but rose, by the fifth offense, to up to six months in jail. Even then, employers had many ways around the law. Only new employees were affected by IRCA and any worker employed before 1986 could still be employed. In fact, Fulbright & Jaworski counseled, "discharge because of non-citizenship may violate civil rights laws." In every market that employed undocumented workers, these kinds of legal seminars took place.

At the end of one of the AGC's many Q&As on the new immigration law, a simple question was asked: "What if I decide just to give up and have no one in my business other than independent contractors and leased employees?" The answer was equally simple: As long as you did not knowingly hire "leased employees from an agency which you knew was utilizing illegal aliens" you would be free and clear.[156] Avoiding the immigration law was as simple as subcontracting your entire labor force.

For John Senko, his time in San Jose was "the worst three years of my life."[157] He came to believe that if he was actually successful in deporting undocumented workers from Silicon Valley "we'd have a revolution."[158] In 1987, he transferred from San Jose to the border for what would be, he thought, a lower-stress job. He preferred, he said, businesses to cooperate rather than to have to raid them, but that missed the point. The low cost of the undocumented, as well as their willingness to work in illegal conditions, made them too valuable to the Silicon Valley economy.[159]

No Company Is Safe

In Search of Excellence was such a successful book that it eventually drove Peters and Waterman out of McKinsey, when they refused to share all the earnings with the partnership. Waterman, who had spent twenty-one years in the firm, joined a chorus of detractors: "McKinsey thinks it sells grand strategies and big ideas, when really its role is to keep management from doing a lot of dumb things. They do great analysis, but it won't get your company to the top."[160] By the end of the 1980s, despite a decade of restructuring and leaning, it was not clear what exactly would get any company to the top. Thomas Peters wrote another bestseller, *Thriving on Chaos: Handbook for a Management Revolution*, though it was only on the bestseller list for a year this time.[161] It opened with a grim epigraph from the *Financial Times* that simply said "Can America make it? A huge trade imbalance, a sliding currency, falling real wages and a dismal productivity record."[162] Unlike his earlier work, Peters said, "There are no excellent companies. . . . No company is safe. IBM is declared dead in 1979, the best of the best in 1982, and dead again in 1986." Chaos had become the new order. While *In Search of Excellence* had a well-measured argumentative arc, *Thriving on Chaos* was a spastic series of examples and aphorisms in what he called "prescriptions for a world turned upside down."[163] In part, he had helped turn that world upside down by embracing the new lean model of the corporation.

As nowhere before, electronics' flexible labor propelled an industry. This "itinerant worker," Dennis Hayes wrote, could be a "temporary worker, the immigrant worker, even the skilled 'professional'" moving from product to product at different companies. We should not be surprised that coincident with the rise of temps and the ideology of lean corporations, the labor movement, at least in the private sector, precipitously collapsed. As much as good union jobs defined the postwar era, the absence of unions defined the age of turbulence. Easily replaced workers don't demand higher wages. They don't organize. The *indocumentados* were Americans, if only temporarily. Some went home every year, like the braceros, but millions stayed on, at the margins of society and at the bottom of the economy. For American industry, these workers formed a key component of the new flexible labor regime, without benefits and without workplace safety. At the intersection of these three worlds of consultants, temps, and undocumented laborers would be a new kind of capitalism, where the borders of the firm were more porous than ever before. Just-in-time production promised parts when you needed them for the assembly line, and at the same time, the ability to ignore where those parts came from. Just-in-time workers could similarly be used and ignored as needed.

"Silicon Valley's labor practices," Peters wrote, "except for engineers, often make Detroit's look humanistic."[164]

CHAPTER ELEVEN

Permatemp

E xecutives used the recession of 1991 as a cover for yet one more corporate transformation. Lean, in the 1990s, was not only applied to the line but to the cubicle. The restructuring of the '80s became the "corporate reengineering" of the '90s. While AT&T (and GM and GE) may have reveled in cutting their workforces, other companies had a harder time reconciling their values to the new lean ideal, struggling, for as long as possible, to preserve job security. "Consultants spread the new concept like bees in summer pollinating flower after flower," Price Waterhouse's William Dauphinais told the *New York Times*.[1] In the recession of 1991, as downsizing became a household word, the cuts that had hit the working class in the '80s finally came for the middle class. College-educated workers, long thought untouchable, were laid off like industrial workers had been since the '70s. The economy, from top to bottom, was suddenly revealed as more insecure than ever before. Economic growth, measured through gross domestic product, returned, but jobs did not. Even as the stock market again began to boom under President Clinton, wage stagnation continued.

Only during the 1991 recession did Americans begin to realize that the postwar boom was well and truly over—for everybody. Downsizing and outsourcing accelerated over the 1980s, but it had hit factories harder than offices. During the recession, the "finality," as *Fortune* termed it, hit home. In 1992, James Swallow, a vice president with A. T. Kearney, said that those who "walk out of these management positions [would] never see these kinds of jobs again." *Fortune* told its readers that "the new shape of corporate America will present all kinds of opportunities for consulting, temporary management, and new business niches," but to take advantage of that world we would need to give up security. For those who, as a futurist quoted by *Fortune* said, possessed "initiative, creativity, and mastery of technology," there would be "challenging new opportunities in a restructured world." For those who did not have those skills, from supervisors to executives, the managerial class was collapsing. The American Management Association told its members that "these jobs are not coming back." Even the now broken-up Ma Bell embraced this vision. The senior vice president of human resources at AT&T contrasted a world of "AT&T: A Job for Life" with the new reality: "That's over. Now it's a shared kind of thing. Come to us. We'll invest in you, and you invest in us. Together, we'll face the market, and the degree to which we succeed will determine how things work out."

The postwar prophecies of office automation finally came to fruition in the 1990s, but they gave us downsizing instead of leisure. White-collar workers soon faced the same consolidation, as one manager's spreadsheet could replace a room of analysts and a word processor could replace the entire secretarial pool. Call centers, accounting, and many other formerly internal functions could be outsourced to the lowest bidder, often with the assistance of HR consulting firms. Middle managers were becoming extinct. The recession of the early '90s marked the first time that when employees lost their jobs, those jobs never came back—even though the work itself did, in the guise of lower-cost contractors, who sometimes were the same people who had been laid off. Instead of investing in higher productivity, corporations looked to cut costs.[2]

The temporary world truly blossomed in the recession of 1991. In that year, more than 3.5 million people worked as temps. Downsized office workers looked for work at the temp agencies or struck out on their own as independent consultants, a phrase that took on a slippery new meaning and did not usually signify a globe-trotting high-wage McKinsey man. Even in the midst of recession, temporary services, with 20 percent annual growth, were in the top three fastest growing industries (only exceeded by computers and health care).[3] This new contingent workforce grew as a motley mix of independent contractors, leased temps, and other jobs, as firms drew even deeper lines between the firm and the market. While many of the downsized called themselves consultants, they often worked for the same boss whom they had had before they were downsized. Legal challenges erupted through the 1990s as workers looked to the government to enforce the postwar employer-employee relationship. A few Pyrrhic victories did little to alter the direction of the economy. Big corporations like Microsoft were happy to pay whatever legal fees were necessary in order to rearrange their workforces as they liked.

The recession of 1991 was unlike prior recessions because it marked not a cyclical downturn, but a break with the past. GDP began to rise at the end of the recession, but few jobs were added. The wealth of the entire country concentrated at the top, but that wealth, when invested, did not produce good jobs. This investment failure signaled the end of the virtuous cycle of capitalist investment. The jobless recovery after 1991 would be the first, but not the last.[4] Since 1991, this pattern has marked the business cycle. Every downturn has meant a permanent loss of jobs. The workforce was being disposed of, replaced by cheaper temps and automated machines. The use of temps as a buffer to provide security to the core workers was not new, but the use of temps to enable permanent workforce reduction was.[5] Firms planned not for growth, but for fluctuation. Throughout the '90s, even as the U.S. GDP surged under the Clinton administration and the tech boom thrilled the stock market, American workers felt ever more insecure.

HR and IT

The recession had represented a big opportunity. The big ideas may have come out of strategy, but the big paychecks came out of operations, especially human resources and information technology (IT).[6] IT and HR consulting drove the expansion of consulting in the 1990s as firms adapted to the new technology, reduced their workforces, and outsourced their operations.[7] Operations firms, like Andersen, helped firms downsize (HR) and automate (IT). Some firms, like Towers Perrin (with $1.1 billion in revenue), could oversee the entire outsourcing transition.[8] Their profit margins—and prestige—weren't as big as the strategy firms', like McKinsey, but their revenues grew much more rapidly. While IT got the headlines, HR consulting grew quickly as well. Estimates put growth at 15 percent per year in the 1990s.[9]

For accountancies like Andersen, the 1990s represented the long-feared turning point. By 1992, consulting engagements (under which HR fell) earned more than tax audits, and sometime in the summer of 1995, consulting edged out auditing as the highest revenue segment of accountancies.[10] More money was made selling ideas than was made keeping corporations honest.

The rising profits of consulting were remaking Andersen just like the other accountancies—only Andersen was the biggest. The division between technology/accounting consultants and strategy consultants paid off handsomely for Arthur Andersen. A McKinsey consultant, at a very public consulting convention, said, "Andersen is looking like a Goliath to everyone, including McKinsey."[11] Forty percent of its profits—about $1.1 billion—came from consulting, and unlike tax and audit, it was growing at 20 percent a year.[12] Consulting practice partners—650 worldwide—"grumbled" about sharing their profits with the stagnant auditing partners, who numbered 2,100.[13] After splitting their business units in 1989, the consulting arm, especially the "information systems consulting practice," of Andersen really took off. Average computer system overhauls ran $25 million to $40 million, with some over $100 million.[14] Over the course of the recession, it grew into the largest consultancy in the world, with nearly thirty thousand consultants and revenues of $3.5 billion.[15] Though the two practices split, they initially remained as part of one overall company.[16] But not for long.

The lure of high-margin engagements drew industrial firms like GE and IBM to consulting. For those firms, the appeal of consulting was obvious: profitability. In 1997, the average pretax profit margin for the S&P 500 was 9.3 percent. For consultancies, it was 27.3 percent.[17] It is difficult to imagine a world where GE would have been number one or two in consulting, but the opportunity was too high to dismiss. In its 1996 *Annual Report*, GE claimed that "our vision for the next decade is a GE that is a 'global services company that also sells high-quality products.'"[18] Helping other firms cut jobs through technology, GE believed, offered a lucrative new market for its in-house consultants, who had been so successful in downsizing its own workforce.[19]

AT&T also drifted into consulting. From 1989 to 1994, AT&T spent a half billion dollars in consulting fees, with the largest share going to Monitor ($127 million), McKinsey ($96 million), and Andersen Consulting ($76 million).[20] After spending hundreds of millions during the 1980s and '90s on restructuring, they realized how much money could be made. With all their experience in restructuring and outsourcing, they lured Victor Millar from Unisys to build a consulting practice arm of AT&T—AT&T Solutions. In 1996, AT&T Solutions earned $70 million in revenue. Millar left after only a couple of years and was replaced by "25-year AT&T veteran Richard Roscitt," who had been the managing partner of AT&T's worldwide out-sourcing practice.[21] AT&T claimed that it was moving its consulting "out of incubation." In 1996, Roscitt claimed to the *Wall Street Journal* that he planned to grow to thirteen thousand consultants and $1 billion in revenue over the next year—a truly bewildering number. Moving from outsourcing to full-on consulting was harder than AT&T expected. Clients might want help setting up a call center, but they would not turn to AT&T for general consulting. By 1999, it appeared to have folded. Finding the next low-cost vendor didn't offer the same kinds of returns as breaking up a corporation. Yet these big industrials invested their capital and their time in transitioning from making things into consulting—only to find that there was no future there.

Meritocracy's Levers

McKinsey hired ten times the number of associates that they needed.[22] The associates, the engagement managers, and then the partners who remained were those who, in the end, could survive the harrowing. A brutal lifestyle became a filter for becoming a successful consultant. An associate noticed that the partners "that seem to have adopted a reasonable lifestyle appear to be on their 2nd marriages, having sacrificed their 1st in order to become a partner at McKinsey."[23] Hours were unreasonable, with "11 and 12 hour days" the norm, along with weekend work. Most of the work was seen as unneeded.[24] The New York office added an overnight "Visual Aid" night shift so that consultants could, twenty-four hours a day, revise their charts. Spouses, children, and lives needed to be sacrificed in this process. The people who reorganized corporations, by this filter, had little respect for sta-bility. The lifestyle was, at a basic level, acceptable to them. When consul-tants left the firm, it was often because they "didn't want to live the kinds of lives that I saw our partners leading."[25] Ron Daniel, speaking to the shareholders, put it bluntly: "Many of our associates are feeling used and exploited. They see wide variations between our aspirations and our accomplishments."[26]

Perhaps it is hard to marshal sympathy for the overwork of overpaid graduates of Harvard Business School. Yet the larger point is this: these consultants oversaw the restructuring of the American workforce. They believed that the long hours, the tensions, the uncertainty were all a perfectly reasonable way to work. Professional workers of all stripes in the 1990s found themselves working harder than their counterparts in the '60s, and some of that came from the partners hired to reorganize their firms. These partners were rewarded for more studies and more billings with more intense hours.

Some of these complaints were not unique to McKinsey. Plenty of professors got divorced on their way to tenure. For the professional class everywhere, work was much more intense than it had been during the postwar years. Whether in a firm being downsized or in a consultancy doing the downsizing, job security and quality of life took a backseat to meeting goals. Most associates agreed that they felt like "just a number around here," and about a third felt that "my office manager couldn't care whether I live or die, just so long as I work."[27] "The entry-level associate," one said, "was frequently regarded as a 'raw Army Private and often treated like an idiot,'" despite coming through an extraordinary selection process and graduating from a top school.[28] *Consultants News* suggested that firms try to convert their "sweatshops" into "spas" if they wanted to recruit the best talent.[29] The irony was obvious, as *Consultants News* pointed out: "high-end consultants don't like the notion of being considered 'contract workers.'"[30]

Bower probably saw some of this through the tinge of nostalgia for a time when consultants simply served clients, but partially it was real. A generation of hard-charging achievers ran McKinsey, and this is what meritocracy looks like. If associates only did their job correctly, there would be no problem—or so the analytically gifted believed. Publishing "guiding principles" like Bower's would do little to solve the underlying problem: if you hire ambitious, analytic meritocrats, they will bear out the rewards of meritocracy. Their belief about themselves, and the world, rested on this hierarchy of achievement. Those who failed deserved what they got, and not compassion.[31]

Rajat Gupta, who became the managing director of McKinsey in 1994, was born in the globalized world that Marvin Bower had helped create. Like Bower, he had attended Harvard, though instead of starting in Cleveland, he had come from New Delhi.[32] While Bower believed in meritocracy, Gupta had lived through it and been rewarded by it. As the first non-American managing director, his vision of the firm was more global and more diverse. By the 1990s, most partners and associates were not American. Most offices were overseas.[33] In a world of consultants, he had risen to the top. Gupta believed in "living and modeling McKinsey's values every day," and that included the belief in this meritocracy of up or out. These values of instability, these experiences of indifference, were brought everywhere that consultants went.

Apple: Logistics, Not Innovation

When Apple employees came to work on May 20, 1991, and booted up their Macs, they found a letter from John Sculley, now the CEO, and COO Michael Spindler posted to the internal bulletin board system, HotLinks, telling them that layoffs—about "10 percent of . . . 15,600 employees and contractors"—were coming.[34] The previous year, Apple had begun to cut its prices in a bid to build market share. The computer was becoming a commodity, as the letter told the employees, which meant competition on price for products that could not be told apart. Macintosh was first to market with a usable interface. Microsoft had introduced an early version of Windows in 1985, which Bill Gates hoped would close the usability gap between PCs and Macs. It wasn't until the 1990s, first with Windows 3.0 and then Windows 95 (released, oddly, in 1994) that the point-and-click mouse fully integrated with the PC. Alongside easier operating systems came easier word processing. As Steve Jobs pointed out in 1985, "Some people are saying that we ought to put an IBM PC on every desk in America to improve productivity. It won't work. The special incantations you have to learn this time are 'slash q-zs' and things like that. The manual for WordStar, the most popular word-processing program, is 400 pages thick."[35] By the '90s, PCs embraced the mouse, and with a graphical user interface, the "incantations" were not as necessary. Without the dark arts of arcane codes, computers became usable for ordinary office tasks without having to memorize a 400-page manual. But instead of that computer being a Mac, it was a PC.

Mac had been first, but once Jobs left, its innovation stagnated. Operating systems went unfinished. New products, like the early personal digital assistant, the Newton, foundered in product development (and then foundered in the market when released in 1993). Luxury brands succeed only when they are truly different. Apple, by the early 1990s, was not different. Layoffs and restructuring, to get costs to match the lower profit margins, seemed inevitable. Apple provided extensive transition services for these employees—severance packages, loan extensions, employment services—in the attempt (which was costly) to blunt the blow. The first round of layoffs, when nine hundred employees lost their jobs, came a month later.[36]

During the ongoing restructuring of 1992, Apple announced that it would shift to an operations center model, in which Mac production would now be in Sacramento, where Apple coordinated its global supply chain. Fremont would be closed. Of the seven hundred employees in Fremont, four hundred were offered jobs in Sacramento, but the other three hundred would be laid off. Jim Forquer, then the vice president of worldwide operations, posted to HotLinks that his own "personal feelings about this are mixed." The Fremont plant, of course, had been the flagship plant, had "led the way in innovation," and had met "every commitment."[37] And still nearly half the Fremont employees were losing their jobs.

Forquer believed that the choice made "the best sense for Apple" because it allowed final assembly to integrate with distribution. The lower cost of living also meant that workers could be paid less. Low-cost logistics, not technical innovation, was the wave of the capitalist future. Audrey Freedman argued that this logistical turn meshed with the new realities of the contingent workforce. "Using the Japanese term [kanban] for just-in-time delivery and no stockpiling or inventorying of resources" was the right way to describe the new approach to labor, she thought. "Management is trying to make employment far more fluid and adjustable," she wrote, "to make labor costs even more variable."[38] Workers were now treated like commodities in a supply chain, so it was natural to call it, as she noted, "*kanban* employment."

Disposing of the Workforce

As the recession ended but the jobs didn't come back, it became clear that something had gone wrong in the American economy. The rising consciousness of the contingent workforce—both temps and contractors—gave rise to a backlash, especially after the recession. Government hearings ensued. Senator Howard Metzenbaum, a Democrat from Ohio and head of the Senate labor subcommittee, called the rise of the contingent workforce "insidious" and "un-American."[39] Downsizing, in 1993, was on everyone's mind. Most days, when Metzenbaum held hearings on these developments—bleakly titled "Toward a Disposable Workforce: The Increasing Use of 'Contingent' Labor"—1.6 million people reported to a temp job.[40] Manpower alone employed 560,000 workers (compared to GM's 370,000 and IBM's 330,000).[41] While all those temps earned $19.7 billion, temp agencies earned even more—$28.4 billion in revenues.[42] The hearings emphasized the root cause of these transformations, which, as the Department of Labor's Delores Crockett explained, were the "lean staffing" of corporations supplemented by "contingent workers who can move in and out of firms as needed and at a lower cost than permanent workers."[43] Unions, like the Office and Professional Employees International Union (OPEIU), tried to push back, as they had since the beginning of the 1980s, and with similar failure. Richard Delaney, a representative of the OPEIU, testified that "we are witnessing today a fundamental restructuring of the jobs of American workers . . . not a cyclical phenomenon." These "new jobs perform the same work as the old," he said, "but now the jobholders are simply disposable workers."[44] Law seemed the last hope to stop the transformation of the American workforce.

While Metzenbaum's hearings revealed the experiences of members of the contingent workforce, no one truly knew how big this workforce was. Not until 1995 did the Bureau of Labor Statistics conduct the first serious survey of contingent workers in the United States, as a supplement to its monthly Current Population Survey. The headline BLS numbers were low—between 3 million and 6 million Americans, or about 1 percent of the workforce. The definitions that they used limited who would be included.[45]

Part of the problem with the BLS surveys of the 1990s was the implicit understanding of the role of temporary workers in the economy. A job was defined as temporary if "the person was working only until the completion of a specific project, temporarily replacing another worker, being hired for a fixed period, filling a seasonal job . . . or if other business conditions dictated that the job was short term." This defines temporary work in the postwar sense, of replacement, rather than as an auxiliary part of the labor force. If a job, like a secretarial position, was filled by an unending number of temps, then the job would not be counted. If Manpower supplied a shift of assembly workers every day for a year, that job would not be counted as temporary, although from the position of the worker, it was a temp job. Work is understood only as an individual experience rather than as a corporate plan.[46] If leased staff planning was the growth area of temp firms (which it was), then the BLS data did not reflect that.

Using the same data from the same year, if you included all independent contractors (8.3 million), on-call workers (2.0 million), and temps (1.8 million), you could also say it was 12.1 million, or 10 percent of the workforce.[47] The difference turned on questions like whether temps could expect to be temping in a year and whether it was a "personal choice." If so, they were not really contingent. The narrow definition took no account of the variation in the short run (a temp might be temping in a year but not next week).[48] A later BLS study, in the same vein, could comfortably contain the (self-contradictory) phrase: "Only 24 percent of temps were contingent."[49]

Economists seemed to go out of their way to show that temping was a choice, not an unwelcome necessity. The impossible divisions in the survey on whether the choice to temp was economic or noneconomic revealed a blindness to how people lived their lives—and how businesses remade their workforces. These small numbers turned on the expectations of the contractors and temps, not on the reality of what happened. Somewhere between 1 percent and 10 percent of the workforce lived uncertain working lives in the last decade of the twentieth century, but employees everywhere knew that being replaced by a temp was not just a possibility, but part of the workforce planning at their firm.

These definitions reinforced a vision of the economy based on common stereotypes but not lived experiences. Reading the BLS documents and survey data, one would have no idea that temporary work was anything but a marginal part of the labor force. The BLS definitions defined this work as marginal only because economists missed the ways that temps had become a permanent solution. Beyond the numbers, stories still mattered.

Temp Slaves in Postrecession America

Jeff Kelly had for the past year worked as a temp in the mailroom at an insurance company in southern Pennsylvania's Lehigh Valley. For generations, Bethlehem, Allentown, and other nearby towns had been the foundation of the American steel industry, but by 1994, Kelly couldn't find work in those plants, or even a full-time job. He was a temp. And he found out, shortly before Christmas, that the temp job he had been told would become full time was instead being cut.[50] This was, as he said, "my introduction to the brave new corporate future of the disposable workforce." For the next two weeks, he wrote about his experiences as a temp and, in the tradition of *Processed World*, made the first issue of *Temp Slave!* under his pen name, Keffo, on an "old computer located in a messy bedroom" and copied it at work when his boss went on a break.[51]

The zine quickly developed an underground following and, by zine standards, had a large circulation of a few thousand copies (that were, naturally, hungrily passed from one temp to another). Like those for *Processed World*, the writers wrote about their own lives, often under assumed names, detailing acts of workplace resistance. Jack Kear, for instance, temped in the General Electric finance office doing data entry on the status of customers' home mortgages: "paid in full, delinquent, or rejected." His job was just to type data, but he could also "read the explanations for why they were late with their payments, whether it was due to a divorce, a job layoff or an out-of-control medical bill." Since he was the one doing the data entry, he decided that the hard-luck cases got their status changed from delinquent to paid in full. He had been given a "monkey wrench" and "damn if [he] wasn't going to throw it!"[52] He never knew if GE even found out, but he knew for sure that "some poor Joe out there had at least a month of unexpected freedom from the debt grip." And he also knew that his job would last only a month, so what did he care?

While some stories in *Temp Slave!* celebrated acts of defiance, most simply testified to the ennui of the office or the mistreatment at the worksite. More often than *Processed World, Temp Slave!* recounted the experiences of industrial temps, who made up about a third of all temps.

Jeff Kelly himself worked on the remodel of a department store at the local mall, where he installed shelves and carted off demo scraps. He was a temp laborer. His foreman was also a temp. At one point during the remodel, fifty temps worked on-site. Yet the real construction (it was in Pennsylvania) was being done by unionists—electricians, carpenters, and painters. Kelly was both in awe of these guys—"slow workers, time thieves, and thus the smartest workers of the whole lot of us"—and also aware that his temp job meant something had gone wrong. One day, when he was hanging drywall with a sixty-four-year-old carpenter, he wondered "why was his union so chicken shit that they allowed non-union laborers like me on their site?"[53] The older man then went on a long, expletive-laced rant about how "the American people are the most fucking ignorant people in the world! All they do is cry about unions but it was the fucking unions who got them all the benefits they enjoy. Even a fucking 8-hour day for most of 'em. But, to answer your question," he continued, "the reason we are so chicken shit is because we are weak. When Reagan fired the air traffic controllers the whole country should have gone into revolt. But what'd we do? We wanked ourselves."[54]

Keffo was not romantic about straight white male unionists, even as he admired their ability to stick it to the bosses. Kelly thought these guys were "sexist, racist, and arrogant" with their catcalling, homophobia, and racial slurs. The unionists he saw were not powerful bastions for the working class. To see organized labor in this way filled him with despair, just as it did the old carpenter. Fixing shelves in the mall, the unionists were earning 60 percent of their standard rate. "Today we take any old thing that comes our way," he said, "and we can't do a thing about it."[55]

Like those in *Processed World*, the writers in *Temp Slave!* advocated sabotage and delinquency, but by the 1990s, the inevitability of disposable workers seemed overwhelming in a way that it had not in 1980.

Delinquency seemed sad. Sabotage just seemed futile. "Resistance can be fun, and at least it is good practice," Keffo wrote—but it would not produce change. In a mournful tone, Kelly described his temping as a kind of death: "Some people have made it a cottage industry to describe just how rotten work is. . . . Utopian alternatives are offered up as an exotic dish to be looked at but never feasted on. . . . The kind of life the prophets of the no-work school only talk about is the kind of life I ache for. Every single atom in my body aches to be free. Every single second I spend working is a denial of the kind of life I really want to live. To work is to deny life."[56] Certainly for the kind of work that he had—little choice, little purpose, little respect—that was true. Kelly was not alone.

The Slack(ers)

More than slackers—as young Gen Xers of the 1990s were disparagingly called—temps were the slack, the leftovers in a downsized economy.[57] Temp work of the '90s was largely involuntary. Most temps, before they were temps, were employed full time. According to a survey by the National Association of Temporary Services, these temps optimistically thought of themselves as "in-between jobs."[58] For a substantial minority of temps, their optimism was justified. Many temps (38 percent) had been offered permanent positions in the past year. So it is not surprising that so many of those who remained (39 percent) wanted to be temps indefinitely.[59] The temps who wanted permanent jobs, and were offered permanent jobs, stopped being temps (and thus were not included in any survey).[60] For this minority, temping was just a transitional period. For the majority (62 percent) of temps who had not been offered a full-time job and did not want to temp forever (61 percent), this betweenness was more like purgatory, waiting for some opportunity—any opportunity—to happen. For them, the phrase "temp slave" made the involuntariness of their job less like hyperbole.[61]

Yet the postwar narrative of temping as a choice for housewives lingered. In official government writings, it overwrote the new numbers. The Bureau of Labor Statistics attributed the discontent among temps to external factors; they were "mothers with small children, people going to school, and people taking care of family members," which according to their own survey did not describe the motivations of the temps or, in the case of school, even a large fraction of the temporary workforce.[62] Rather than the working housewife with disposable time, then, the temp was a long-term unemployed American trying to get back in the workforce—with varying levels of success.

Although the 1990s temp is often thought of as a white college graduate, reality differed. African Americans made up 13 percent of the workforce, but they made up 33 percent of all agency-supplied temps. College graduates were 25 percent of the workforce, but they made up only 15 percent of temps. Most temps, 57 percent, were high school graduates with no college. This number was about 15 percent higher for temps than for the general labor force.[63] Rather than overeducated, entitled white kids, temps were those more often excluded from traditional jobs—and those temps found it harder to move to a permanent job.

One silver lining: temp work does seem to have offered a space where women and African Americans encountered more wage parity than in the permanent workforce—though equally low wages should hardly be the ambition of racial and gender progress. Close studies of the temps' wages found that they were consistently below permanent workers' wages, even if they had the same role.[64] Those wages were lower, but somewhat more equal. The median earnings for men who worked as temps and were over twenty-five was $378 a week. This is about 40 percent less than the median earnings for similar men with permanent jobs, $657. For women, the difference was smaller—$346 for temps and $493 for perms—but it was still 30 percent lower. Though meaningful, the gender difference between temps (9 percent) was much less than perms (25 percent). It is not terribly surprising that women earned less than men, but what should be surprising was that African Americans—$354—earned more than white temps—$338.[65]

Temp agencies thought of themselves as doing these stranded workers a favor. In this downsized world, temp agencies, as the executive vice president of NATS, Sam Sacco, testified to the Senate, provided a "critical safety net."[66] Temp agencies "help[ed] ease the burden on individuals during this period of restructuring." Perhaps these slackers would have been "unemployed" without the availability of temp jobs—as a Bureau of Labor Statistics paper sensitively put it.

Perhaps, alternatively, without the rise in temp work, employers would have had to offer them regular jobs.

Weighing the Future

In July 1993, Apple published a very special issue of their employee magazine, 5 *Star News*, titled "Weighing the Future."[67] The issue came out as former COO Michael Spindler had become CEO and launched a massive round of layoffs.[68] The explanation for these layoffs was on the cover of the magazine: the future.

The cover collage showed workers and computers, in factories and in offices, but they paled (were literally washed out) compared to a male office worker stylized as a balance. On one side were "reorgs, layoffs, resource constraints, job insecurity, salary freeze, dropping margins," and on the other, more heavily weighted, side were "making a difference, challenge, minimal bureaucracy, products, people, compensation, company pride." The implication was that Apple was at a crossroads and needed to balance out those opposite weights. The weight of the "good" side was heavier than the "bad" side, but the articles inside the magazine seemed to have a different measurement of mass than the picture on the cover. As the editor's note said, the purpose of the issue was "the acknowledgment of some major organizational and personal pain, and to employees' decisions about whether and how to recommit to our work at Apple." The recession had remade Apple, like other firms. The tech giants (IBM, Sun, DEC, Dell) were hurting but so were U.S. firms more generally. Apple workers considering leaving saw "that the grass is pretty much brown wherever you look."[69]

Laying off the permanent workforce and hiring temps, as the title on the next page explained, were part of "The Changed Nature of Workers and Work." Articles like this one explained to Apple's workforce that in the future, firms would no longer be loyal to them. This "Changed Nature" where "more and more companies are laying off permanent staff and relying on contract workers and outsourcing to carry out their business" was not a choice, but a trend that was "a predictable evolution." Corporate cutbacks, downsizing, and restructuring were inevitable. "The successful worker in the next generation," the Apple article continued, "will no longer be able to choose a single skill or company." In the employee magazine, intending to placate remaining workers, Apple told them that "the emerging workplace has a head and no body. It centralizes free-floating talent resources as necessary to meet current needs, and changes size from moment to moment as the marketplace dictates. Every one of us becomes a separate but networked company, responsible for marketing our resources, trying to remain in-demand, and making leveraged use of each other's skills."[70] The article's author, the cryptically initialed "MDG," framed these changes as the "fu-ture." "Future" at a tech company was not a neutral signifier of time. "Fu-ture" fused together "inevitable," "progress," and "good," but to the actual employees, this future must have seemed anything but positive.

The present, to Apple workers, seemed to have gone terribly wrong be-cause of management's choices, not because of some inevitable future. Posting on an internal electronic bulletin board ("the 'Can We Talk' discus-sion folder on HotLinks") employees questioned those corporate choices. "Can someone please explain to me," a poster wrote, "where in corporate America's history, quarterly earnings became all important [?] I think this quarter-to-quarter way of running corporations causes many problems in America." Layoffs had happened just a couple of years earlier, and at the time, they were to be a onetime event to make Apple's "lean, mean goal." That goal line, however, kept moving. When Apple was "rolling in money" a few years earlier it spent lavishly, but then "competition" and layoffs came. Planning instead, in "five years chunks," an employee speculated, might make Apple "less stressful!"[71] That long-term planning, of course, was in-compatible with this new vision of the instant on–instant off workforce.

Apple restructured and laid off workers throughout the 1990s—in 1990, 1991, 1993, 1996, and 1997—in a desperate bid to improve profits through cost cutting as its innovation stagnated. In the '80s, Apple enjoyed high profit margins (approximately 50 percent) on every computer sold, but by the mid-1990s those margins were less than 20 percent.[72] Margins kept falling, and by January 1996, even though net revenues had grown, margins were now only 15 percent.[73] Layoffs began again, with Apple cutting "1,300 employ-ees, temps and contractors," or about 8 percent of its workforce. What is noticeable here is how employees, alongside temps and contractors, were laid off. The temps and contractors were not a buffer for bad times anymore. The so-called permanent staff was as vulnerable as the temps.

While Spindler reengineered Apple for a few years, the pressure for cheaper computers only intensified. And then Microsoft's Windows 95 made the PC operating system (OS) as easy to use as a Mac—or at least good enough not to justify the much higher costs of a Mac. In 1996, Spindler was replaced by Gil Amelio as CEO, and in the popular press, Apple's future—as a fading luxury brand—was all but sealed.

Amelio confronted a "cash crisis," "a quality crisis," and an "OS crisis"—not to mention a "management crisis."[74] He told the employees that now they had the "strong managers that can lead the turnaround." He name-checked "great products" in the middle of one sentence, but what he really thought would save Apple was "a direct, easy concept: simplification." The solution for Apple was yet another reorganization.

Unlike the first small, multitalented team that had designed and built the Mac, manufacturing and design and marketing were now completely siloed.[75] No great products happened. Apple sputtered along, waiting for a savior to bring them great products again.

Yet even when Steve Jobs came back to Apple in 1997, ousting Amelio, the jobs at Fremont were gone forever. Jobs would pioneer more portable computer products: the iPod, the iPad, and, most important, the iPhone. These unique computers would bring back the margins and resurrect Apple. What Steve Jobs did not do, however, was bring back American jobs. These machines would be designed in California, but they would all be made overseas. Even when innovation eventually returned, the work did not.

Gaming Misclassification

The blurring of lines among freelancing, contracting, and consulting was often the point for employers. The classification of an employee, of course, had enormous ramifications for pay, benefits, and workplace rights. Generally called misclassification, the problem was not just HR making an error, but employers and employees gaming those categories. Step inside the employee box, and you had an enormous body of law to support you at work.

Outside the employee box, you were just another contractor struggling in the market. Contract workers came to be known as 1099ers—by the IRS form that they received, Form 1099, as opposed to the W-2 received by ordinary employees. Full-time permanent employees would still enjoy all the stability, benefits, and legal protections that Americans expected from their work. And that was exactly why firms turned to contractors. Temps formed a bridge to the subcontracted workforce, but remained covered by the tenets of labor and employment law. Contractors did not. In the 1980s and '90s, temps surged as part of the workforce, but other kinds of contingent workers rose even faster, as work-arounds to labor law. As a result, legislating employer-employee relationships proved harder in the '80s and '90s than ever before, especially, but not uniquely, in the technology industry.

Buying the right systems, and training employees on them, was a boom industry for technology consultants. Consultants could, and did, offer guidance on hardware, software, installation, and training. Consultants would be aware of little details, like the need for updated power requirements to run computers as opposed to typewriters.[76] Terrence Arter, for instance, a computer consultant in Chicago, made the case for firms hiring him on a temporary basis instead of as a permanent hire. When firms were in a technological transition, they could hire Arter for help with "conversions, peak loads, large project implementations, installation of new hardware or technology, or to fill a gap which is delaying implementation of a cost-saving application."[77] Billing his clients at forty-five to sixty dollars an hour, he estimated that he would still be cheaper over the few months it would take to do any project. The boundary between computer consultant and computer contractor had always been blurry. Members of the Independent Computer Consultants Association coded when they consulted. They weren't doing the same work as McKinsey. These "consultants" were just short-term, but highly skilled, temps.

Some tech consultants' roles might not be temporary at all. Jimmie Ruth Daughtrey expected to live a classic postwar life. She lived in Chattanooga, Tennessee, where she stayed at home, raising five children, while her husband worked. In 1976, when she was forty, she and her husband divorced, and she had to get a job. She clerked, but at night she attended Chattanooga State Community College, where she learned computer programming.

She didn't get a degree, but she learned enough to land a job coding at Honeywell in 1978. She received good evaluations and good raises, and even oversaw some other programmers.[78] She felt like a real "Honeyweller."[79]

Then, in 1986, Honeywell was reorganized and everyone in her department was laid off. She looked around for another job at Honeywell with no luck. She searched for another programming job, but "high-tech companies did not seem too interested in hiring a 50-year-old grandmother without a college education as a computer programmer."[80] That is, they didn't want to hire her at the price she had previously cost. Honeywell, it turned out, still needed programmers, but instead of a full-time employee position, they offered her a role as a so-called consultant. In this role, she "did the same sort of work" she did before, with the "same schedule," and even worked "side by side with most of the same people."[81] Those same people, it turned out, had also been rehired as consultants. As a "consultant" she received no benefits and would have to pay the employer's share of Social Security. She got no health insurance. She received no pension. She worried that this consultant role would not turn back into a real job, as her former supervisor had told her it would. Her fears were well founded.

A year and half later, she and the rest of the "consultants" were fired. She filed a lawsuit, citing the illegality of hiring her as a consultant in order to avoid benefits, and also age discrimination. The judge dismissed her case because she was not a real employee. For Daughtrey and many other Americans caught up in this shift, the law offered little recourse, as "employee," her lawyer told her, had a "very technical legal meaning." All Daughtrey knew was that she was, once again, out of a job, and this time, there weren't even consultant jobs available to her. She said, "If Congress does not make clear that federal employment rights protect people like me, pretty soon there will be no employees. There will be only consultants, independent contractors, and other kinds of workers, with no rights and no protections."[82]

If only workers could be properly classified, these critics believed, then the law could restore the postwar economy.

William Storey had owned a garment manufacturing plant just south of Dallas since 1958, shortly after leaving the military. The company, W. R. Storey, grew over the decades, from twenty-five workers at the start, peaking at five hundred by the early 1980s, when the business began to unravel.

Buyers rejected his bids, telling him that they were too high. While, no doubt, his firm faced challenges from globalization, Storey didn't blame foreign competition, but competition down the street. Talking with other Texan manufacturers, he found that they were in the same situation, and for the same reason: manufacturers who used misclassification to avoid paying payroll taxes. Employers with regular workers had to pay taxes for every worker—Social Security, unemployment, workers' compensation—taxes that did not have to be paid for contractors. Manufacturers without employees, only subcontractors, had much lower overhead and so could offer much lower prices.

In Dallas, Storey's competition had begun sending out cut garments to be sewn by subcontractors. These subcontracted employers paid no payroll taxes, and paid their workers less. "It is impossible," he said, "to produce these garments at these prices and obey all required laws."[83] The model was broken. After years of selling his own assets to keep the business afloat, he finally closed shop in 1988, and those five hundred workers, with their medical insurance, paid vacations, child day care, incentive pay, and, most important, security, lost their jobs.

Similar stories abounded in the Dallas area as new firms popped up, subcontracting their sewing. Many of these Dallas firms supplied the big Dallas buyer: J. C. Penney. Janis Flynn was one of these suppliers. She hadn't been in business as long as Storey, but had run a small sewing company in Dallas, employing forty workers, that is, until 1992, when J. C. Penney began to cut back its orders, though she met deadlines and quality standards. Like Storey, as Flynn talked with other manufacturers, she found out about the subcontracted workforce, with which she could not compete. She closed in 1992, and most of her employees were still unemployed a year later. "These illegal contractors," she said, "and home sew operations destroyed my image of what the American Dream should be."[84]

As part of the broad 1986 Tax Reform Act, Congress enacted Section 1706, which created "20 common law tests" to distinguish between true contractors and misclassified employees.[85] The tests pulled apart whether a worker was independent or not, based on the employer's control over how the work was done, and how permanent the relationship was. If a worker controlled the product of the work and the way that the work was done, then the worker was probably an independent contractor. The tests were simple, in and of themselves. For example, if you got paid in a lump sum, you were probably a contractor, but if you got paid by the hour, you probably were not. If you had your own shop or office, you were probably a contractor. These easy rules, covering everything from pay to tools to customers to "helpers," were intended to clarify the muddy waters of the restructured corporation. Firms like HP issued long flowcharts and checklists to help managers understand if a worker was an employee or a contractor, but that ambiguity created value for the firm. Using independent contractors like disposable employees was just too convenient.[86]

The new rules did not erase an older IRS ruling from 1978—Section 530—that created a "safe harbor" for employers accused of misclassification.[87] Employers could claim exemption from IRS penalties if they had "consistently treated the workers . . . as independent contractors," filed 1099 forms, and "had a reasonable basis for treating the workers as independent contractors."[88] Defining what was or was not a reasonable basis was as simple as claiming that "a significant segment of your industry treated similar workers" in the same way.[89] So if the industry was misclassifying workers, then legally misclassification became acceptable. Moreover, if the IRS had audited the employer in the past and not found a misclassification problem, the employer could not be audited for the same issue again. These two sections of the IRS code—one analytical (1706) and one historical (530)—contradicted each other. In all this uncertainty and contradiction, employers, and their lawyers, could easily defend themselves over these classification issues—or comply and watch their businesses disappear.

Leased Employees

The National Association of Temporary Services (NATS) supported an alternative to these independent contractors—the leased employee—that fit within existing employment law. Temporary agencies took in a company's full-timers and moved them all onto their payrolls. If the leased temps worked enough hours, then they might have benefits—but at best these were the bottom-of-the-barrel benefits haltingly offered by temp firms, not gold-plated office worker corporate bennies. The line between the firm and the market would be clear. "Leased employees" provided firms with an alternative to having a workforce at all.[90]

Leasing could be framed as a smart and humane alternative to rebuilding workforces after the recession. A popular management journal, *The Office*, noted that as the economy recovers, "an employer can even hire back former employees by simply placing them on the temporary service company's payroll."[91] Temp agencies were there to help, and "confer[red] with the human resources departments at leading companies on a regular basis to help plan for anticipated long-term needs" in temporary staffing.[92]

NATS attributed the growth in leasing to the leaning of corporations— "from 1982 to 1988 Fortune 1000 companies reduced employment by 4 million"—as well as the regulatory hurdles faced by small businesses.[93] At a conference, NATS featured a conservative think tank intellectual, William Styring III, who articulated the position of NATS (which was reprinted in their trade journal). The jobless recovery happened, he argued, because small businesses could not grow to include the unemployed. Small business owners faced regulatory "trip wires" that made incremental hiring prohibitive.[94] These trip wires were not economic but legal. Hire more than a certain number of workers and new legal requirements kicked in. If you had fourteen employees, your business was not subject to the Civil Rights Act, but hire employee number fifteen and businesses suddenly found themselves regulated. At twenty workers, the Age Discrimination Act kicked in; at twenty-five, the Americans with Disabilities Act; at fifty, the Family Leave Act; at one hundred, the Business Closing Law and more EEOC paperwork. None of these legal issues arose if the workers were contractors or temps.

Styring illustrated his point. He had been studying deregulation and taxis in Indianapolis for its mayor (echoing shades of an Uber economy to come). Styring asked the head of Yellow Cab, "'How many full-time employees do you have?' He said, 'I don't have any. I haven't had any for a couple of years. All my cab drivers are independent contractors. They lease the cab every day from me for $70. They lease the license and the insurance on the car. The gas is on them. They pay me the first $70 each day; the rest is theirs."[95] No small business owner, like a taxicab company, actually wanted to have employees.

In California, for instance, some Bank of America employees found that during their corporation's reengineering their jobs became part time or even temporary. For these employees, the only choice they had, if they wanted to keep their job—if it could now be called that—was to accede. Those workers moved to temp payrolls kept doing the same job, at the same desks—just with meager benefits and with lower pay. Even for those who remained part-time employees, Bank of America kept their hours low enough to avoid having to pay benefits, retirement, sick leave, or holidays.[96] Costs were minimized, whether the workers were kept in the firm or leased from temp firms. The granddaughter of Amadeo Giannini, the founder of Bank of America, denounced the changes, saying that "her grandfather would not have dealt with the workers that way."[97]

Government agencies, as well as corporations, embraced leasing. Staff leasing allowed these entities to take advantage of more flexible labor while still appearing to defend their "core" workforces. Consider the heavily unionized New York City government. Processing parking tickets, one would think, would be a job done by a civil servant. But those civil servants, with their municipal unions, can be expensive. In July 1987, Chemical Bank won a contract with New York City to process the payment of parking violations. Payments could be dropped off in a lockbox at the bank, and the payment would be credited to the city's account.[98] There are a lot of New Yorkers, and a lot of New York City parking tickets—about twenty-five thousand payments a day, totaling, in 1987, about $750,000. Of course, if you missed the deadline, the payment increased, so keeping track of all the payments, and their dates, was crucial. Chemical Bank got the final go-ahead from the city only ten weeks before it was supposed to take over the payment operations.

Facing a need to hire and train dozens of workers, Chemical Bank decided to staff the entire project with temps. The bank turned to a management consulting firm, Charles Brooks Associates, to organize the temps' training. Temps were trained to categorize the payments, to decide on the correct return correspondence (there were twenty-six types), to enter the data, and to confirm correct payment. No one temp did every step. The processing was broken down into very small, very narrow tasks. At first, the amount of correspondence was overwhelming, but over time the temps increased, as the ABA *Banking Journal* described it, their "stamina." Seventy temps started, but "if a temp was dissatisfied or proved to be a weak performer, a replacement could be brought in easily and quickly."[99] Working two shifts a day of five and four hours, temps were carefully overseen by the consultants as the program rolled out. Eventually, the number of temps was reduced from seventy to fifty, further increasing productivity. The error rate with this system was extremely low (1 in 500,000, or about one error every few weeks).

Temp leasing helped companies explore other ways to replace their workers through external firms. It was a short step from leasing employees in the office through a temp agency to sending that work out of the office to an entirely different company. Arthur Andersen found, in a year-long 1995 study, that 85 percent of all firms were "outsourcing all or part of at least one business function."[100] Most firms outsourced financial functions like pension management/tax/payroll/asset appraisal and evaluation. Data entry, the standby temp job of the 1980s, could be done off-site. As this outsourcing gained currency, both as a practice and as bizspeak, temp firms realized that they didn't need to go to the work. The work could come to them. A "national temp agency headquartered in Atlanta," Norrell Corporation, offered to "handle most or all of its client companies' data-entry needs at its own Memphis, TN, facility."[101]

The jobless recovery thus spawned an explosive growth in "managed services," or outsourcing. Robert Fell, a vice president of Kelly Management Services, which was the outsourcing unit of Kelly Services, wrote in 1998 that "the best economy ever is even better than we thought."[102] Outsourcing was growing at 20 percent a year, and he estimated that it would be a "$280 billion industry worldwide by the year 2000." Kelly Services, as well as the other major temp agencies, wanted to be at the center of that new world. The staffing insiders saw themselves as possessing natural advantages. Customers, Fell said, wanted one vendor for all their "office services, administrative services, transaction processing operations, distribution services and customer service operations."[103] Fell counseled their clients that "any support function they can 'draw a box around' . . . [Kelly] can take ownership of."[104]

Any commodifiable service could be outsourced, just as Porter's Five

Force model would have predicted. Kelly could provide these services, but so could new kinds of specialized professional temp services, like Accountemps. Accountemps could offer these services because an "unprecedented number of highly qualified, able-bodied employees were retired early during the first half of this decade because of mergers, increased competition and severely depressed markets in many areas."[105] This pool of trained professionals, "involuntarily retired," as Kelly put it, made it possible for Accountemps, Accountants on Call, and other specialty firms to exist. And, of course, the elimination of their permanent positions in the first place created a demand for these temporary ones.

Microserfs

The workforce divisions became most visible at the world's largest software firm—Microsoft, where contractor misclassification and employee leasing became notorious.

Donna Vizcaino coordinated the production of user manuals at Microsoft. With such an office job a generation earlier, she would have had health benefits and paid vacations, and looked forward to a sufficient if not luxurious retirement funded by a company pension. In 1992, Vizcaino had none of those things. She went to work every day there and used Microsoft equipment and sat in a Microsoft cubicle where she produced Microsoft user manuals, but she was not a real Microsoft employee. She was a contractor.

Larry Spokoiny answered "a Microsoft employment ad," thinking it was for a regular position. Instead he became a permatemp, working for a temp agency with no benefits, even though he tested Microsoft Word software side by side with regular employees.

In 1990, after an IRS ruling demanded that Microsoft clarify the line between employees and contractors, Microsoft pushed many of its long-term contractors and many of its new workers into joining temp agencies as leased employees. These permatemps worked at Microsoft, but were not of Microsoft.

Barbara Judd, for instance, had been hired through a temporary agency as a "business systems analyst at Microsoft." She worked as "part of a team creating a new tax software program." Judd liked the work, but didn't like "feeling like a second-class citizen." Temps and contractors could easily be distinguished by their "different color badges," which meant they could not, as at HP, attend "seminars and parties."[106] Temps and contractors had orange badges. Regular employees had blue. Temps could not shop at the company store. Social lines were drawn, just as Elmer Winter envisioned, but also economic lines. These relatively high-end temps and contractors did not complain as much about the pay as about the lack of stock options and benefits. Leased through a temp agency, Judd had to pay three hundred dollars a month in health insurance fees, which, in the 1990s at a high-tech firm, would have been nearly free.

Vizcaino, Spokoiny, and seven other contractors filed a lawsuit against Microsoft in 1992, demanding compensation for their insurance payments and all the other trimmings that regular employees enjoyed. In 1993, the U.S. District Court for the Western District of Washington ruled that not only would Microsoft have to deal with these former contractors, all Microsoft contactors could form a class-action suit against the company.[107] The lawsuit was less about what Microsoft promised the contractors than what Americans believed corporations owed office workers. Some of the perma-temps worked through temp agencies. Some of them were contractors. None of them felt like they were given the respect, or benefits, that they were due. The case became the bellwether for the future of the subcontracted high-tech workforce.

While the suit wended its way through the courts, no firms stopped using contractors. The machinery of law chugged along, but in the meantime, work continued, begging the question: does law matter if it cannot be enforced quickly and widely? Microsoft and other firms simply drew the lines even more clearly between temps and perms.

Guidelines for Managing a Temporary Workforce

Coming out of the recession of 1991, John Young was finally satisfied with HP. The "new organization is working well," he told the HP managers. "The results speak for themselves."[108] The company was finally moving, he thought, in the right direction. David Packard may have disagreed, having recently denounced the "micro management from the top" as a sign that

HP was becoming his anathema, a "bureaucracy."[109] He feared that HP was no longer innovative, and that "increasing the bottom line with tax benefits, stock buybacks, or other financial shenanigans really does no credit to the tradition of our company."[110] In Young's mind, however, he was destroying the bureaucracy and saving the company that he had inherited. He was cutting management layers and, more important, transforming the workforce. "The themes of renewal," Young said, were "accountability and flexibility," "improved processes," and "operating results."[111] While Packard fixated on innovative products, Young focused on the business.

In 1995, codifying their embrace of employee leasing, HP issued a manual called *Hewlett-Packard Guidelines for Managing a Temporary Workforce*, which instructed its management in the best ways to use temps.[112] The manual reassured managers that hiring temps was the new normal in America, as "since 1983 approximately 20 percent of this country's new jobs have been temporary in nature." The "largest employer in the United States today is a temporary agency," and that employer, Manpower, supplied Hewlett-Packard. Even at HP, they made up "about 10 percent of our U.S. workforce." Temps fulfilled a wide variety of jobs, from "fill-ins, special projects, anticipated closures or consolidations, balancing the hiring over peak-and-valley business cycles, and staffing unpredictable businesses." The manual reassured the manager that these temporary employees "protect the jobs of HP employees." The differences between temps and HP employees helped HP be a "leader in employee benefits and working conditions," but employees sometimes questioned why HP hired temps at all. The *Guidelines* openly encouraged managers to acknowledge the "dilemma" but to remind the employees that their security was contingent on the insecurity of the temps.

Part of the difficulty for HP might have been that "76 percent of all [temps were] looking for regular full-time positions," but HP made it a policy to restrict hiring temps to full-time positions.[113] Managers were told to look to "company excess employees" and "internal candidates" for more staff. HP was already overstaffed, and it was better for morale to move people around than to hire temps. This lack of prospects was supposed to be kept secret because "experience has shown that if they are encouraged in their hope and then don't secure a full-time job, their trust and frequently their motivation is totally undermined." While many temps thought of their jobs as a "trial period," HP was clear that its managers should encourage temps to "go through the normal employment process for external openings." To keep the lines between temp and perm clear, HP human resources would not allow more than "20 percent of external hires" from temps. There could not be, for most temps, a path to permanence.

Managers, while treating "temporary workers with dignity, courtesy and respect," should not treat them the same as regular HP workers. HP created charts for managers to help them understand how to keep contractors (and temps) from appearing to be actual HP employees. This eligibility matrix had a checklist that included practical matters, like not being on an org chart or phone list or having HP-provided safety equipment, as well as social matters— no sports league, no social events, no recreation areas. Managers were reminded that "there should be a clear distinction between an HP employee and a non-HP employee." The lines between the temps and the perms were hard to maintain. Memos went out yearly to remind managers that no temps could come to company events. At the bottom of this document, scrawled in blue pen: "no pot lucks—conflict of co-employment issues"—showing both the incompleteness of a list intended to draw lines between coworkers and how central those activities, like potlucks, were to the HP workplace.[114]

While some temps worked only for a couple of weeks and could care less about softball, temps might work at HP in this way for up to two years. They could come to work every day to process the same paperwork as the person in the next cubicle, but knowing that they were not really part of HP, much less its softball team. Christmas parties would come and go, but they would never attend. For a company that had prided itself on its job security, there was doubt about why HP hired temps at all. Temps would never be the same as regular employees, but HP reassured its managers that the temp program was "something we can honestly stand behind and say is socially responsible."

The decision to use permatemps at HP and elsewhere was not entirely financial. Few managers enjoy laying off workers during a downturn, and over the previous two decades, those downturns seemed to have been happening all the time. In the auto industry, for instance, temps were used to meet cyclical changes and structural adjustments. A general manager said that he liked to use temps because he knew that everybody understood that the job would not last forever—an idea impossible to imagine for a postwar UAW member.[115] In Manpower's hometown, Milwaukee, W. H. Brady Company, for instance, relied on "temporary workers for flexibility in meeting production schedules." Brady's recruitment service manager did not "want to build an infrastructure of employees and have to turn around and lay them off."[116] Temps could be disposed of without any consequences. Hiring permatemps avoided the emotionally fraught reality that those "real" jobs were disappearing every day.

Mergers and Breakups

When Coopers & Lybrand and Price Waterhouse agreed to merge in 1997, they were positioned to become the world's number two consulting service and the largest accountancy/consultancy. With $12 billion in revenue, 135,000 employees, and 8,500 partners, this juggernaut was intended to crush the competition. Unlike the accounting consolidations of the 1980s, this one focused on consulting. Consulting in each firm was growing at a breakneck 25 to 35 percent per year, compared to 10 percent for audit and tax. Their strengths were complementary: Price Waterhouse installed technology; Coopers & Lybrand handled change management.[117] Streamlining back-office operations was obvious, but more lucrative was the opportunity to cross-sell complementary services. IT and HR would now both be available in one shop.

While PricewaterhouseCoopers (PwC) merged, Arthur Andersen finally broke up. Freed of its accounting arm, Andersen consultants believed they could have greater freedom—and even more money. In 1996, the consulting unit—which was much more profitable—paid the accounting unit $100 million, or about $88,000 per partner. In December 1997, the thousand-plus partners in Andersen Consulting voted to break away from the Andersen parent company and, at the same time, the accountants.[118] In the months after the vote, the breakup turned messy. The head of the consulting unit, George Shaheen, and the accounting unit, Jim Wadia, had a very public feud, so that by 1998 the New York Times could wonder, "How the Andersens Turned into the Bickersons."[119] Between 1989, when the two units were divided, and 1996, the ostensible accounting arm had grown its own consulting practice to revenues of $953 million.[120] They refused to turn this consulting practice over to the "consulting unit" of Andersen. In short, nobody wanted to be left without the profits of consulting. No one wanted to just be an accountant.

As the size of the accountancies/consultancies grew ever larger, regulatory fears grew. The Securities and Exchange Commission continued to push accountancies to regulate themselves. In 1997, the American Institute of Certified Public Accountants created a joint task force (the Independence Standards Board) with the SEC to create standards on the intersection of consulting and auditing. It is hard to say no to money. The SEC's chief accountant, Lynn Turner, said that "a $2 million fee is a $2 million fee, regardless of whether it includes fees for consulting contracts or is entirely for the audits."[121]

Spokespeople for the five largest accountancies denied that there was any conflict of interest. PricewaterhouseCoopers' Robert Herz, leader of professional, technical, risk, and quality services, sternly stated that "no individual client could provide the firm with enough revenue to influence an audit, and the penalties are a deterrent."[122] Herz, speaking in 1998, should have known better, because the penalties had not stopped Andersen from doing exactly that at Waste Management, Inc.

Andersen had audited the books for this large Chicago-area trash company since 1991, and had even formally classified them as a "high-risk client" who "actively managed reported results."[123] In other words, Waste Management was cooking the books. In 1994, Andersen initially refused to certify their financials after Waste Management misstated $128 million in earnings. The company pushed back and threatened to find another auditor—and consultancy. While Waste Management capped the audit fees they would pay Andersen, the additional "special work" was not capped.[124] More money could be made from consulting than from overseeing the books.

Through the mid-1990s, for every dollar in audit fees, Andersen billed $1.57 in "special work" (tax consultations), and Andersen Consulting billed an additional 80 cents. Of the $25.3 million in billing, only $7.5 million came from the audit fees. SEC investigators pushed, in 1998, for Waste Management to restate its earnings, reducing them by $1.43 billion—the largest restatement to that point in U.S. history. Andersen ended up paying a paltry fine of $7 million for their role in enabling Waste Management's underreporting. Andersen and Waste Management were not alone. They were part of a failed system of incentives.

An SEC investigation in 1999 found eight thousand "independence violations" that came from "serious structural and cultural problems" in the consulting sector.[125] The SEC pushed for a revision to "auditor independence rules" in 2000, which would have been the first since 1983.[126] Despite all the bluster, the new SEC rules did not really alter nonaudit services. They actually loosened regulations in November 2000.[127] The same firm could still audit and consult, even on the underlying IT of the financial control system.[128] The kinds of transformations that happened most visibly at Waste Management, and later at Enron, happened throughout the U.S. economy during the 1990s as auditors competed with consultants inside accountancies.

"We Began to Lose Our Identity"

The most visible consequence of these developments was the rise and fall of Houston's Enron. Enron's story has been retold many times, but in short, those at the top of the firm cleverly cooked the books.[129] Instead of an economic dynamo, Enron was, in reality, a debt-ridden dud. Like James Ling and the other Texans of the conglomerate era, Enron used accounting tricks to inflate its apparent profits.

Consultants remade Enron from an energy supplying company to an energy trading company. Jeff Skilling was hired directly from McKinsey in 1990 to develop Enron's complex financial strategies, which ultimately destroyed what had been a well-run energy company.[130] McKinsey consultants freely roamed the halls of Enron, where the firm billed over $10 million every year, dispensing advice on everything from personnel management to energy markets. Enron valued talent in the way that the McKinsey authors of *The War for Talent* suggested all corporations behave—ruthlessly firing and hiring both inside and outside the firm.[131]

The notorious division of Enron that eventually brought down the company, Enron Capital and Trade, emulated McKinsey in its hiring practices, "decid[ing] to bring in a steady stream of the very best college and M.B.A. graduates . . . to stock the company with talent."[132] The best were rewarded and given free rein. But even these geniuses didn't operate in a vacuum. At every step of development, McKinsey was there, guiding these young executives in their plans to control American energy markets. No one had a long-term, permanent interest in their work, or even in the firm.

McKinsey left the building only when Enron collapsed in 2001, but McKinsey was not alone in that building, or elsewhere. This breakdown happened everywhere that accountants mixed with consultants. Like all large firms, consultants from all the big players roamed the halls at the big firms at the same time. Enron's accounting firm, Arthur Andersen, was also its financial auditor, and Andersen also consulted at Enron—and was competing with McKinsey for its business. This contradiction, and a certain cleverer-than-thou arrogance, was at the core of the Enron collapse. Just as the auditors and consultants had worked together to remake AT&T, the old walls between them were torn down as well. "We began to lose our identity," Fred Herr had remembered, "as auditors and consultants."[133]

Risk management had assumed a new centrality in auditing in the late 1980s and early '90s, as it did in finance more generally. Despite a lot of talk, the failure of the audited savings and loans in the '80s brought a fresh look at the lack of accounting standards but no real reform. Firms like Coopers & Lybrand began some soul-searching over what they called the "expectation gap" between "what people expected" and "what [they] delivered." Accountants began to be aware, for a moment, of the larger significance of accountants' "responsibilities to society . . . responsibility to markets."[134] But the incorporation of these ideas into everyday practice in accounting meant something different than the adoption of a risk model in investment banking. Accountants, after all, determined what was a real risk. Their standards were the foundation upon which all the rest of business rested. When the largest accountancies got together and developed legislation that became securities act reform and securities litigation reform in 1995 (Private Securities Litigation Reform Act) it set the stage for a new way to value securities of all sorts.[135] The collaboration between accountants and the SEC to set up the Independent Standards Board in 1997 clearly did not help either. While the partners in the firm believed that they were restoring professional standards—"fix[ing] its own internal house," as one Coopers & Lybrand partner, Vincent O'Reilly, remarked—to the field, they were, in fact, undermining those standards.[136]

The failure to separate the incentives of consultants and accountants would be crucial to the fall of Enron, but also in the fall of Arthur Andersen.

Enron, Andersen, and McKinsey were not alone. The problem was structural: many of the corporate failures of the early 2000s resulted from this same contradiction—the failure of the corporate audit function, often in the context of simultaneous consulting. In the aftermath of Enron, reform bills, like the Sarbanes-Oxley Act, sought to clarify the relationship between accounting and consulting, creating a wall much like the Glass-Steagall Act had erected between commercial and investment banking. Sarbanes-Oxley increased the paperwork, but the profit was still there. This essential check on the behaviors of corporate managers, the audit, could still be entrusted to the same firms that provided consulting services.

Criticisms of consulting, and accounting, continued. Regulators once again called for reform. Books like *Dangerous Company* and *The Smartest Guys in the Room* focused on high-end exposés of failure and fraud rather than on the day-to-day decision making that created the circumstances that enabled that failure and fraud. These salacious tales piqued interest, but quickly faded into the background amid a steady churn of corporate IT and strategic needs. The real scandal lay not with any particular incident, but with the way that corporations lacked the ability to adapt to the 1990s without outside assistance and, in turn, spat their workforces out into a harsher world while searching out get-rich-quick schemes.

While the media looked for a few evil geniuses to blame, the real cause was amoral bizspeak. Corporate common sense regarding how to run a business had shifted over the years from long-term reinvestment and worker obligations to short-term returns. The ex-McKinsey men of Enron were cleverer, but not different from those at Andersen. While McKinsey or Andersen might have helped lead any one company astray, the real culprit was more insidious: the erosion of honest investment.

As the Enron scandal unspooled, Arthur Andersen's reputation collapsed. Prosecutors discovered that Andersen, responsible for checking Enron's books, had failed to do so, and had, in fact, destroyed documents. McKinsey's reputation, meanwhile, continued unabated. KPMG bought up Andersen accounting's consulting practice overseas.[137] Ernst & Young bought up Andersen's audit practices in various cities. The venerable firm was sold off at fire-sale prices. While Andersen's accounting collapsed, Andersen Consulting took off.

The dangers of mixing consulting and accounting became clear—but consulting profits had not dimmed. As all firms needed hardware and software, tech firms believed they could offer consulting services. In late 2000, HP and PwC even talked over merging their consulting arms. HP, at that point, had about six thousand consultants, or about 7 percent of its workforce. PricewaterhouseCoopers sold its tech consulting business to IBM in 2002. The move was not unique. IBM, Dell, Microsoft, Sun, and many others grew their consulting wings.[138] In a year-end issue of *Consultants News* in 1996, the editors had joked, in a fake New Year's prediction, that "Bill Gates will buy McKinsey to help Microsoft sell more product under the guise of 'consulting services.'"[139]

While that specific event never happened, the broader joke, that technology firms would spread into technology consulting, certainly did. As the millennium turned, venerable IBM—on the losing side of the PC clone wars—transformed itself from a hardware company into a technology consulting company. Technology was not about the machines, but about the machines replacing and de-skilling workers, making them interchangeable and standardized—in short, making them into robots. Consultants, computers, and contingents went hand in hand. The tech boom made the IT investments of PricewaterhouseCoopers, Andersen, and the rest finally pay off. In the 1990s, every smarter player knew IT was the key to the future of the corporation, yet just like their analogues in the 1960s, they did not know how. The one exception was Andersen Consulting, which rebranded as Accenture and grew quickly through the 2000s, riding the surge of Internet 2.0 into the Cloud era. Oriented to technology, Andersen Consulting was primed for success.

Permatemps All

The Microsoft permatemp case was not resolved until 2000. Microsoft had to pay $97 million to the now former contractors in the class-action suit. Of Microsoft's forty-two thousand employees, in 2000, five thousand to six thousand were temporary or contract. Since the lawsuit began, Microsoft had actually taken steps to transition some of its permatemps into actual employees, hiring three thousand into full-time roles. Yet the lines between permatemp and employee remained. The distinctions were too valuable.

While the suit compensated temp workers at Microsoft going back to 1987, no actual policies changed as a result of the case. For a company that in 2000 alone earned $22.9 billion, paying out $97 million, or 0.4 percent of revenue, to keep their permatemps must have seemed like a bargain.[140] Contractors and employees continued to work side by side in the technology sector. Microsoft and other firms simply drew ever clearer lines between temps and perms. Barbara Judd might have been delighted to receive her share of the class action settlement, but if she ever worked at Microsoft again she would still be treated like a second-class citizen.

By 1997, on an average day, two and a half million Americans, or about 2 percent of all workers, worked for a temp agency. That percentage had doubled since the 1991 recession.[141] Most of these temps, 56 percent, came to temping through events over which they had no control, like having their positions eliminated, or a company bankruptcy or plant closing. Only a quarter had quit their previous job.[142] Most (55 percent) had had full-time jobs immediately before becoming temps.[143] The consultants had helped remake the American workforce, and the jobless recovery had set a precarious tone for the decade.

For many Americans who weren't themselves part of the contingent workforce, the *Microsoft* decision alerted them to a fundamental shift in the economy. Surprising numbers about the contingent workforce began to appear in mainstream media. By the millennium, even the Bureau of Labor Statistics estimated that roughly 10 percent of the American workforce was doing some kind of contingent work.[144] Of the workforce, 6 percent were independent contractors, 2 percent were on-call, and another 2 percent were supplied by an agency.

During the 1991 recession, Americans broadly worried about downsizing. Now they knew where all those downsized workers had ended up. The office of the future during the 1990s became the battlefront for corporations that wanted to crack the formula that brought together flexible workforces, office automation, and globalized production.

By the time that Carly Fiorina became the CEO of HP in 1999, bringing massive layoffs (six thousand employees) that drew the media's attention, the die had been cast for a decade. Though she was denounced as destroying a company committed to lifelong job security, Fiorina made visible a shift at HP that had already happened in secret, but in other companies had happened quite openly. HP distributed a Q&A to its employees explaining the layoffs. One of the questions was simple and harked back to an older Hewlett-Packard: "Why is HP doing workforce reductions while continuing to use ETWs [external temporary workers], consultants and contractors?" The answer was simple: "All companies, including HP, will have a portion of their requirements met by temporary workers or contractors . . . even during pressing economic conditions."[145] While workers' jobs were not protected by the use of temps, the company's image was. As the Q&A explained, "ETWs, consultants and contractors are not employees of HP and were not included in the six thousand."

The fundamental intellectual step, imagining a blended workforce of external and internal employees, had already happened, even at the firms, like HP, that were most committed to job security. Key corporate functions were outsourced from top to bottom. In the years during the rise of the internet economy, the American corporation was restructured to align to a leaner model that could compete in a global marketplace. These reforms had more to do with ideological change than technology. The technology itself was neutral, but deployed to solve the problems created by a flexible workplace.

While the reframing of work from permanent to temporary was ideological, the next step, the gig economy, would accelerate the deployment of this workforce model through a combination of the internet and a new kind of distributed computers called smartphones. The digital economy would make visible what had been hidden, as the realities of the 1099-driven workforce entered the public consciousness. The work practices pioneered in Silicon Valley would be baked into the next iteration of the digital economy, for everyone. The digital gig economy, born when Craig Newmark turned his Bay Area email service into a website called Craigslist, would herald a new vision of work that no one, except Alvin Toffler, could ever have imagined.

CHAPTER TWELVE

Flexible Labor in the Digital Age

I f you walk into the headquarters of Upwork in Mountain View, California, the first thing you notice is that the lobby is empty, except for a couple of modernish chairs and a reception desk with the company name hanging on the wall. But the lobby has no people. I don't mean no visitors. I mean no receptionist.

Atop the reception desk is a monitor mounted on an easel, with the face of a receptionist, who, it turns out, lives two hours north of Chicago. Her name is Faith. She can see you through the tablet's camera and can, through the tablet's speakers, ask you to sign in. She can ask you to sit down while you wait for your appointment with the CEO, and even offer you water (which is under a side table). If the future of the economy is online labor, then the future of corporate organization is Upwork.

Upwork is the world's largest digital labor platform. Every year, over a billion dollars of knowledge work is transacted through its online marketplace of buyers and sellers. If you want to hire an Android app developer, Upwork can make that happen in under an hour. If you want a translator, a transcriber, a consultant, an editor, or nearly any knowledge service that can happen on a computer, you can hire an Upworker within a few hours. Any office worker whom a temp agency could provide can be found with a click of a button, but so can the services of accountancies and consultancies. The business model is as simple as the interface: Upworkers set their own price, and for every dollar you pay the Upworker, Upwork takes ten cents. Staffing an entire firm could take place in an afternoon. If you don't want to hire people yourself, you can hire someone on Upwork to hire *other* people on Upwork. If you don't want to manage your own workforce, you can hire Upwork project managers to oversee Upwork programmers. A whole company can be assembled from around the world in a matter of hours. Upwork practices what it preaches. About three fourths of Upwork's own workforce neither live in Mountain View nor receive a W-2, since they are, in fact, just individual contractors hired through the Upwork platform.

Upwork, like many of the new on-demand work platforms online, shares the same structure: workers are contractors, the online service is a middleman, and all work lacks security. For those in Silicon Valley, this gig economy appeared to come out of nowhere, popping up in the aftermath of the Great Recession of 2008 and made inevitable by new technology, but apps only accelerated what began that day Elmer Winter couldn't find a secretary. As Stephane Kasriel, the CEO of Upwork, told me during our interview (which is why I was in the Upwork lobby that day), "There is nothing new here. Firms have been subcontracting to other firms for decades." Upwork was simply the logical extension of Manpower onto the internet. Technology solved for what was already happening.

The internet did not cause this shift, but it did make it more visible. In 1995, the first web browser, Mosaic, was released and the world appeared to be born anew. For the first time, the internet, which had been an odd mélange of text interfaces (Gopher, Usenet) and technologist communities (the Well), became easy to access. No one knew what the World Wide Web would mean. In the first few years, businesses, usually without viable revenue models, appeared everywhere, funded by Silicon Valley venture capital desperate to cash in on what appeared to be a new gold rush. Delivery services appeared to be the big play, as firms offered online food delivery (Webvan), online books (Amazon), and even online pet food (Pets.com). Physical distribution turned out to be hard, and these firms, flush with cash, ineptly invested in infrastructure that demand could not sustain. While Amazon limped through the tech crash, most of the other firms disappeared.

Flexible workforces and flexible firms had been growing for forty years, but computers and other technologies reinforced these changes, just as the steam engine accelerated the industrious revolution. Reorganizing people made industrialization possible. The first factories were just buildings. The first assembly lines were just slides. Businesses then developed technology to take full advantage of these new ways of organizing people. Technology, in turn, became intertwined with this reorganization, becoming the most visible part of the epochal change. Observers confused cause and effect.

The application of the internet to the flexible workforce was no different.

The digital platforms developed over the last twenty years provide flexible workforces, now catchily called "liquid workforces," to employers with a click. At the same time, however, these platforms might contain the seeds of an alternative to the corporation, which, if realized, would be a truly radical break in the economy. It is unclear that any of the plaforms discussed in this chapter will exist in a few years, but what is apparent is that the digital platform, as a way to coordinate work, is unlike anything ever before.

Flexible workforces are nothing new. But that workers might truly be able to be independent from employers, without temp agencies or consulting firms—that is what has become possible with the new platforms. Workers can now do on their own what just a few years ago required participation in a corporation: manufacturing globally, selling globally, shopping globally, working globally. The corporation might no longer be necessary. The office certainly will not be, as the remote work revolution is finally here. Today, the same information technologies that allow capital to manage labor in new ways might also enable labor to collaborate in new ways. With the death of the employer-employee relationship—and the industrial economy—workers certainly need an alternative.

Craigslist and Gig Labor

In the first tech boom of the late 1990s, most of the capital-intensive companies that sought to bridge the digital and the physical worlds failed. The success stories, like eBay and PayPal, were inventory-free middlemen who made it easier to buy, sell, and pay for goods and services. In the first dotcom rush of the late '90s, and then the internet 2.0 2000s, delivery services largely flopped. Social media exploded, but jobs in the real world, moving real things, was hard. Amazon barely scraped by, eking out years without profits as it struggled to run its warehouses efficiently. While eBay charged by the transaction, and Facebook sold ads, Craigslist remained free.

Craig Newmark had come to San Francisco in 1993, looking for work as a contract programmer, and found a pre-web internet community—the Well—of fellow geeks and artists. The list was a way to keep some friends, and then friends of friends, informed about event information, stuff swapping, and the odd roommate situation. With the tech boom, San Francisco housing was starting to get trickier. When the list got to 240 people, around 1995, his email program, Pine, couldn't "cc" anymore. He realized he needed to expand the list somehow. Craig had planned to call the list "SF Events, since," as he said, "as a nerd, I'm pretty literal." His friends told him that the list already had a name—Craig's list—and that it was a brand. "And after that," Newmark said, "they told me what a brand is."[1]

At the time, Newmark was himself a gigger, moving from contract to contract, coding Perl and HTML for the early stages of the World Wide Web. Bank of America hired him as a contractor to build their second website, and he taught himself Java along the way. So, savvier than most, in the middle of 1995, he programmed a way to automate the conversion of emails into web posts. Over a few years, he developed his email list into a website—Craigslist. It had his name on it, and he wanted to "keep it quirky and personal." By 1997, he was getting a million hits a month.

The website started in the Bay Area but began to spread by 2000, first across the U.S. and then the world. In its wake, newspapers lost one of their main revenue streams, classified ads, but consumers gained a free way to buy and sell anything locally and without transaction fees—even work. In 1998, Craigslist started charging job posters for ads, which allowed Newmark to hire some staff. While Craigslist let companies post regular full-time jobs, it also allowed for gigs—one-off (or strange) situations—stemming from Newmark's own experiences as a temp and contractor. Early on, one of the job categories was simply called "freelance services 1099." Later it was called "gig labor." For the first time, it was cheap to hire somebody for a transactional, informal labor relationship. Most of the gig jobs—moving, lawnmowing, cleaning—required no particular skills.

Craiglist was free. Craigslist was endless. But Craigslist wasn't slick. After the first smartphone debuted in 2007, new firms rushed in to carve out Craigslist into individual apps and slicker interfaces. Users were willing to pay (a little) for a better user experience, and more certainty about what, exactly, they were buying. Personals became Grindr and Tinder. Arts and crafts became Etsy. Sublets became Airbnb. The gigs section of Craigslist became TaskRabbit and Upwork. TaskRabbit provided one-off services, mostly IKEA assembly, but Upwork provided more sophisticated knowledge work that allowed businesses, not just consumers, to mesh their flexible and permanent workforces seamlessly.

Upwork and Digital Temps

Upwork began as two different companies, oDesk and Elance, that had similar origin stories. Both were started by a pair of immigrant engineers who noticed that in Silicon Valley there was a huge demand for great engineers, and back home, in India and Greece, there were engineers but few opportunities. At first, both firms did the same thing: One person here went from firm to firm seeing if they would hire engineers remotely. Back home, the partner looked for engineers. The firms expanded through the 2000s, diversifying from programming into other knowledge-based fields. Instead of matching candidates with jobs by hand, they both created online platforms to coordinate buyers and sellers. In 2013, Elance and oDesk merged into Upwork.

There were two different value propositions at Elance and oDesk, which represented two visions of the future of the global workforce. The first was a global cheap labor model where one would seek out, for instance, the cheapest person in the world to transcribe an interview. The job would be like the gig section of Craigslist. The second model, which Kasriel thinks is the future of Upwork, is the global best labor model. Consider Upwork's own employment history. Of the first fifteen engineers oDesk hired in 2003, twelve still work at Upwork. One of the lead database programmers lives in Greece. The guy who oversees the release process lives in Jakarta.[2] One of the best back-end engineers lives in Siberia. The main benefit of Upwork, Kasriel argues, is not price, but quality. All the best programmers cannot live within ten miles of Palo Alto. Less than half of the contributions on GitHub (a computer code host) come from the U.S., much less Silicon Valley. Working at Upwork is the "best possible job these guys [in Siberia] can get." Without moving, programmers far away, whether abroad or even in Alabama, can be part of the exciting technological developments of Silicon Valley, rather than coding at the local telecom. High-end technology firms, desperate for talent, need to look globally. Kasriel calls Upworkers "insourcing" rather than outsourcing. Upworkers are remote, not second class. Stable, long-term global labor makes up about 40 percent of the work on the platform.

Upwork's two models are both simultaneously possible. For Americans without skills, who can only type and speak English, the competition is global. A transcriber in India will work for four dollars an hour. A secretary in Thailand will work for three dollars. The biggest comparative advantage Americans have is simply being American. The growth area on Upwork is foreign firms that want to sell here. Only Americans can really sell to Americans. We may not be great programmers but we at least know our own culture.

Upworkers are far more educated than the American, or the global, population—75 percent have a college degree.[3] For underemployed and educated workers, it offers an alternative. Upwork will certainly improve the paychecks of high-skill workers—but for the rest of the workforce, the two thirds of American workers and nearly everyone in the developing world who never went to college—Upwork alone cannot be the answer to their problems. Just as different corporations sell different products, platforms will sell different kinds of workforces.

Uber as the Waste Product of the Service Economy

The digitally dispatched car service Uber, despite regulators' protests, quickly dominated every city it entered. Most cities had a well-regulated taxi system, which limited the number of cars on the road at any time and guaranteed the quality of the drivers. In New York, for instance, taxi drivers were required to comply with a long list of qualifications—"A knowledgeable driver who speaks English and knows City geography"—but mostly a regulated price. In the era of GPS and cell phones, knowledge of city geographies no longer mattered, and the regulated price created an opportunity for price competition. In the aftermath of the Great Recession, as Americans were desperate for work, Uber came to the forefront of the debate over the gig economy. Founded in 2009, the on-demand car service quickly spread from San Francisco around the world in just a few years. A regulatory regime designed for an older world could not cope.

The criticisms of Uber, Google, and tech more generally had little to do with the services themselves. Google was free. Uber's app was convenient. What galled people was how much money was being made by so few. While wages stagnated, IPOs created instant billionaires. Rising wealth inequality and declining economic security made tech the lightning rod for the left. Uber became shorthand not just for car services, but for what appeared to be an entirely new on-demand market economy, where nothing was secure. Like jobs, even prices—with the advent of surge pricing—were no longer stable. Firms like TaskRabbit, Instacart, Seamless, Grubhub, and many imitators flooded the market, seeking to be the intermediary between smartphones and retailers. Unlike Upwork's jobs, jobs on these platforms did not require specialized skills, but commodity skills. Nearly all Americans knew how to drive, and nearly all owned a car. Subcontracting that skill and that tool made rapid expansion possible.

The sharing economy, as Uber was first called, had begun in the early 2000s with Zipcar, which offered an alternative to car ownership. Instead of owning a car or even renting one for a day, you could subscribe to a service that allowed you to easily pick up a vehicle conveniently located in different places around whatever town you were in. For urbanites, the Zipcar offered an easy way to trek out to a big-box store in the suburbs. Zipcar, for a certain niche, was successful, but it didn't displace rental car companies, much less taxis, and certainly not private cars. What Zipcar did do was offer a new model of temporary ownership, otherwise known as sharing, that pushed entrepreneurs to rethink what the economy could look like. The barriers to entry for Zipcar-like businesses were high: you needed capital to actually own all those cars, or power tools, or whatever you were sharing, which retarded the growth of these firms. Zipcar could not be everywhere, and if its cars were idle, they lost money. The trick with Uber, like Manpower before it, was in being capital light.

Unlike the early internet companies, like Webvan or Zipcar, that owned their fleet and employed their workers, the Uber-of-X companies expanded without owning anything. The sharing economy might be better described as a zero-capital-investment economy. Like temp agencies of the postwar, these Uber-of-X firms grew rapidly because their revenue was nearly pure profit and their growth required no fixed investments.

The debates over the on-demand economy weren't about whether taxis should be delivered by app, but about what such work meant in a postrecession economy. Uber expanded quickly because the service was great. Uber drivers liked the flexible hours. Uber customers, especially black customers who had always had a hard time getting a cab at night, liked the convenience. Surge pricing, while sometimes annoying, did mean that supply and demand were more nearly aligned. Criticisms of Uber were not about Uber, but about the meaning of Uber in the larger economy. The laws that seemed to keep the dream of the postwar era alive were well and truly defunct. Who were these unregulated drivers? If the government couldn't even regulate taxis, how could it enforce all the rest of the labor laws?

Uber provided work, it seemed, to those who were most in need of a paycheck. While early drivers for Uber were students, as the service expanded it appeared to be the case that the drivers were more desperate than digital. Drivers might like the easy money, but critics worry that drivers didn't take account of the cost of gas or car depreciation. Uber drivers wear out their cars, but then again, so do Domino's (and all other pizza delivery) drivers. The difference between Domino's and Uber, of course, is that Domino's workers receive a W-2 and some benefits, and Uber drivers get a 1099 and that is it. Since they are contractors, Uber drivers can deduct their car's depreciation. Domino's workers actually get a worse deal.

The anger here was not about tax deductions but about an assumption of what kind of person did what kind of work. In the 1980s, teenagers who needed extra money delivered pizza, not adults trying to support a family. By the time that Uber came around, however, adults and teenagers alike were delivering pizza and, through Grubhub, any other kind of restaurant meal. The outrage at Uber was about deteriorating income. The problem for Uber's drivers is not the work itself, but that they have no alternative to that work.

Uber did not cause this precarious economy; Uber was possible because of a precarious economy. It is the waste product of the service economy. The choice for these drivers is not between driving for Uber or working on a unionized assembly line. It is between Uber and slinging lattes. Uber is possible because shift work, even with a W-2, is so bad.

The anxiety over the on-demand economy, then, was rooted more in the precariousness of the work than the technology. Ubiquitous gig work seemed to be the final nail in the coffin of economic security. Uber made that coffin visible. For very few, apps would create instant wealth, and for the rest, they could only look forward to spending their adult lives delivering pizza (and sushi), standing in line for building permits, or creating graphs and spreadsheets for consultants on the other side of the world. The anxiety surrounding Uber and the rest of the digital economy was that it seemed to be a poor substitute for those good manufacturing jobs of yesteryear.

For those at the top, the winners of *The War for Talent*, who were ambitious, smart, and entrepreneurial, the digital economy was just shorthand for opportunity on a global scale. Energetic entrepreneurs could have an idea, assemble a team through Upwork, and bring a product to market with few barriers. For everybody else, the digital economy was a grind. Labor laws offered few protections, designed, as they were, for an industrial age. Employers, given a chance, evaded wages and benefits through 1099s and twenty-nine-hour caps. Labor laws and labor unions may have solved the problems of the factories (uncontrolled overtime, no breaks, workplace injury, etc.), but they were unable to grapple with the new workplace relationships. Office work no longer felt like a path to the middle class. Professionals and managers could easily imagine being outsourced or downsized. Factory workers knew that foreigners, whether in the U.S. or overseas, were doing their jobs. Robots and computers could replace everybody. Uber drivers hated the low wages and lack of choice but lamented the coming of driverless cars, which promise to eliminate even that last refuge of commodity skill. Self-driving cars would not be the first step toward a futuristic utopia, but the last step off the plank into the sea of turbulence. Unless a new way to make the flexible economy work for everyone was found, it was hard not to see this new world as a dystopia, where a few were rich and the rest were replaced by robots.

Uberification portended a future of winners and losers, of insiders and outsiders, of differentiated employees and commodity workers. Interchangeability was the core of the workforce problem. Just as Michael Porter pushed firms in the 1970s to find their own monopoly niches, workers in the twenty-first century need to find monopoly skills. For the rocket scientists and visionaries, this requirement is not a problem, but for the rest of us, who are more or less human, commodity workforces can't help but seem like a race to the bottom.

Instacart: Blended Business

And then it hit retail markets, literally. Instacart, when it started in 2012, seemed like any of the dozens of grocery delivery firms that had come and gone on the internet since the early days of Webvan. Through an app, drivers would receive a list of groceries, buy them, and then deliver them to a customer. This model worked, but it was expensive. To make money, customers had to be charged more than in the store, pay a delivery fee, and then pay a tip. The key move for Instacart was realizing that these purchases were not just cannibalizing existing sales, but were extra.[4] After Instacart demonstrated to grocers like Whole Foods Market and Safeway that customers would not have spent as much money in their stores, the entire business model changed. Grocers had an incentive to support Instacart. Whole Foods, for instance, now provides a staging area, complete with freezers and refrigerators, where Instacart workers can bag orders. Individual stores have dedicated Instacart shoppers and dedicated Instacart cashiers. Whole Foods updates Instacart every night on current store inventories, nutritional information, and pricing. Because the revenue is additional, Whole Foods charges Instacart customers the same price as in the store.

Altogether, this retail-delivery partnership results in a blended workforce of 1099 and W-2 employees, much like at Upwork. The delivery drivers are still 1099, but instead of shopping they just deliver, picking up tips and fees at every stop instead of just one. In the stores, Instacart employs W-2 workers to be shoppers, baggers, and cashiers. These workers, while interchangeable at first, became differentiated as they learned the products of the store. Skills, after all, can be universal (knowing how to program in Python) or they can be specific (knowing where the quinoa is). To be successful, Instacart needs the specific knowledge of its workforce. While the workers are still part-time W-2s, it suggests a way for low-skill workers to reframe their commodity status: experience. Workers cannot be easily replaced, and if they can't be replaced, they have power. Instacart's profits will rely on the economics of scale of being in-store, but it will need to contend with a workforce, unlike its drivers, that cannot be temporary.

Etsy: Women in Microbusiness

When Etsy began in a Brooklyn apartment in 2005, its goal was to sell handicrafts over the internet. While Amazon could offer mass-produced goods, Etsy could sell the unique. After the Great Recession, it grew quickly, as sellers, most often women, found the platform to be a way to earn some extra cash.

With rapidly growing revenues approaching $200 million, Etsy decided to go public in 2015. At the time of their IPO, 1.4 million sellers offered crafts every year. That number probably underestimates the number of workers who participated in Etsy-related crafts, since many of the sellers operated their own small manufacturing operations.[5] A quarter of sellers employ other people to assist them. Etsy calls these sellers microbusinesses and believes that, as Etsy grows, they will increase in number.[6] In 2016, Etsy retailers sold $2.84 billion in goods, growing at about 19 percent per year. It is a drop in the bucket compared to big retailers, but compared to their stagnant growth (or contraction), it suggests an alternative in the making.

If Uber is the all-male digital job (86 percent men), then Etsy is the (nearly) all-female gig shop. Etsy sellers are mostly women (87 percent) and think of themselves as businesswomen.[7] While the media worked itself into a frenzy over Uber and taxi drivers, few challenged what Etsy was doing to traditional small-time retail. It is hard not to see the gender of the male drivers and female sellers as the deciding difference in the public hysteria: men deserve real work while women do not. For the women of Etsy, their microbusinesses are a better option than whatever else they have available. A third of these sellers live with Etsy as their sole income. About half (52 percent) work independently, using Etsy as a part of their portfolio of income. Only a third also have a traditional job.

These digital labor (Uber) and selling (Etsy) platforms created alternatives for workers pressed by the precarious economy. The scale of this income volatility is almost impossible to believe. Most (55 percent) of average American households in 2014 had month-to-month fluctuations in their income of 30 percent.[8] Imagine trying to budget—for anything—with that kind of income swing. For those at the bottom, in the lowest quintile, three quarters had these month-to-month swings. Households didn't lose or gain jobs—they just got paid different amounts every month.[9] Shift work was unreliable. A small amount of the variation did come from switching jobs (14 percent), but nearly all of the pay swings happened to workers who kept the same job.

The income volatility, both with and without a job, is truly staggering. For those with uncertain income, the idea of driving a car for a few hours to make some extra cash seems like a good alternative. About 60 percent of Uber drivers have another job. Three quarters of Uber drivers cite the instability or uncertainty of their sources of income as a main reason for driving.[10] Access to digital-labor jobs, like Uber, means stabilized incomes. When other income dips, they just drive Uber for more hours.[11] Putting together multiple streams of income, including digital, helps households offset those swings. Etsy sellers are not alone. Combining multiple income streams into a portfolio of income is becoming more common. A Federal Reserve study found that 22 percent of earners combined multiple sources.[12]

Equally compelling is that Etsy sellers do not need to be in expensive cities. A third of sellers live in rural areas.[13] Ninety-nine percent of U.S. counties have Etsy sellers, showing how a distributed, digital economy might take root, as Kasriel suggested, outside of Silicon Valley or other big cities. For rural women left behind by deindustrialization, the digital platforms could not come quickly enough, because those jobs, despite the promises of President Trump, are not coming back.

Managed by Algorithms

It is very easy to get swept up in the technology and neglect the most important truth: digital workers are not choosing between online work or not working. They are choosing to do this digital work rather than (or in conjunction with) traditional jobs. For middle- and working-class hourly workers, the alternative is shift work—retail, restaurants, the low end of the service economy. A fifth of the U.S. workforce has on-call or rotating schedules, which makes planning for the rest of life onerous (and don't forget the low wages). The alternative to Uber is not a union job at GM, but a part-time job at Starbucks (and the Gap and Subway).

Understanding the 1099 gig economy requires recognizing that even those who receive W-2s aren't living in a world of stable employment. The labor law cuts both ways. Especially for those in retail, the legal line between part time and full time—twenty-nine hours per week—created perverse opportunities for employers. For hourly workers, employers cap schedules at twenty-nine hours to avoid paying benefits. Legally time and a half is required for those who work over forty hours, but with new scheduling software, like Kronos, firms are careful to keep the hours down. Software schedules workers to be in the store as needed, but without giving workers too many hours. These algorithmic bosses optimize for store profits, not employee needs.

Managed by algorithms, workforces are kept lean but subject to uncertain week-to-week scheduling and a more volatile income. De-skilled work made for commodity workers. Schedules can change from week to week unpredictably, as the software balances the strange number of hours against employers' needs, making a second job, much less childcare, a nightmare. Missing a shift means getting fired, and workers at the bottom can always be replaced. For these part-timers with unpredictable schedules, having another source of income to fill out their weeks would be attractive. This other job would have to be scheduled around their part-time hours, over which they have no control. Digital jobs are the only kind of work that can be combined with this scheduling uncertainty. Instead of one good job, the best that the working poor of today can hope for is a portfolio of work that, overall, reduces income volatility. Keeping track of all those jobs, of course, can be a job in itself.

The problem of "algorithmic bosses" exposes one of the key choices we have, between banning or embracing technology. The postwar labor accord happened because it helped both workers and employers—not because of laws. A reactionary path would be to pass laws to guarantee workers hours and limit algorithmic optimization of the lean workforce. Such laws, resisted everywhere, would keep some workers employed, but not provide them more flexibility. Flexibility in the workplace these days is mostly the worker being flexible for the employer—but it does not need to be that way.

An alternative would be to think of how to make algorithms that support both workers and employers. Workers want pay security but also flexibility. Employers want to match customer demand with employee hours. Instead of a one-sided optimization for the employer, Kronos (or some other scheduling software) could optimize for both the worker and the employer. Workers could tell Kronos (or some other software that communicated with Kronos) their other jobs, as well as the hours they did not want to work (in order to take care of their children, for instance). The algorithm could match workers not only at Starbucks, but also at Subway. The algorithm here would no longer be the boss, but the secretary, helping the worker schedule her day—balancing the needs of her employers and her paycheck. Technology can't do everything, but it is very good at solving scheduling problems. Using algorithms in this way today would be analogous to using the assembly line to create prosperity for both workers and employers in the postwar era. It would be a win-win.

Digital Migrants

While the 2016 election brought home how enraged Republican voters were about the undocumented, 2016 also marked the first year that technology might render migrant labor—at least with migrants coming to the U.S.—a thing of the past. If knowledge work has long been outsourced, physical work might, for the first time, be as well. As before in Silicon Valley, low-paid workers from other countries became a transitional workforce to a more automated economy.

In the spring of 2016, I visited a cutting-edge robotics lab at the University of California, Berkeley. On YouTube, I had seen this amazing video of a robot folding towels. Now, a towel-folding robot doesn't sound that impressive, because as humans we have great vision (and lots of experience folding towels). But folding a towel is a very difficult problem for a robot. Simply *seeing* the edges of the towel is tricky using computer vision. In bad paintings, fabric looks flat, while in the paintings of the best Dutch masters the fabric flows in convoluted colors and shadows. Reality, it turns out, is even more complex than Rembrandt. Clump a towel on a table and you will most likely stump a robot.

Once the robot found the edge, folding the towel was still hard. The folds had to be done in a particular way that could not be programmed ahead of time. This robot was using something called machine learning. Machine learning is simpler than you might imagine. Teaching robots to fold towels (or move around a room, or do anything) is simply a question of giving them the proper incentives. If the language of machine learning sounds surprisingly like that of economics (or video games), it is not a coincidence. Both use optimization (getting the highest value) as their fundamental driver of human (and robot) behavior. Programmers don't need to directly program the robot to fold towels, just to create a scoring system that rewards a folded towel. The hard part for programmers is developing that scoring system. Robots that need to avoid walls (or people) need to create a map (using their robot cameras) every moment and decide what is a wall, a person, or a floor. Robots that need to fold towels need to decide what is a towel and what is a table, and whether that towel is in the right position.

The genius of this lab was to teach robots how to find the edges of a towel using machine learning algorithms that created a scoring system simply by showing examples—lots of examples. Like most of the machine learning revolution coming down the pipeline, the towel-folding robot is not directly programmed to fold towels. It is shown how. A graduate student puts a towel in front of the robot and moves its pincers to grab and fold the towel— over and over again. I was told they had to do it about a hundred times for the robot to start to be able to fold the towel. Through this process, the robot slowly builds up a mental map of what it thinks its task is. No one directly tells it how to do it, or even what the goal is. Every time is a little different (just like towels), but the robot can adapt. If you want to see this, just go on YouTube and search for "towel robot." It is pretty neat. I was excited to see it in action.

Yet for an hour, I sat there as a very patient graduate student put the towel on the table and hit the button, and the robot attempted to fold the towel. Again. And again. The attempts took forever. The towel, after that hour, remained unfolded. Though it worked sometimes, it didn't work that day. Something was off about the towel. Given enough training, the robot could have folded the towel every time, if it had seen enough examples—just like we learn to fold towels. Although the robot was cool, I had no fear of robots replacing towel-folding people anytime soon.

And then another graduate student offered to let me play with the robot using the new virtual reality rig that she had just gotten. It was an HTC Vive, and this was weeks before either it or the Oculus was in stores. I put on the goggles and grabbed the controls, and suddenly I was looking through the eyes of the robot at the table with the towel. Though I had never used a VR control before, I reached down with the robot's arms, grabbed the towel, and folded it. My speed was limited only by the speed of the robotic arms. What the most advanced robot could not do, a human could do nearly instantly—remotely.

This changes everything. Machine learning works best when a robot can see more examples, and while a grad student can move a robotic arm a few hundred times (or maybe even a few thousand times), they can't do it a million times. With millions of examples even complex tasks become machine learnable. Let me clarify.

In 2016, Tesla, the electric car company, announced that its "autopilot" had driven customers over 200 million miles. That is a truly astounding number for a project that was launched only two years earlier. Meanwhile, Google's program, started over a decade ago, has driven paying customers an equally astounding *zero* miles. Why was Tesla able to advance so quickly while Google, with all its money, brains, and headstart, seems unable to catch up? The answer is important not just for self-driving cars but for the future of work in general. From millions of miles of human driving, the car's eyes recognized what successful driving looked like. This machine learning is how Tesla could scale up its autopilot so quickly. Google tried to train its cars directly, with employees driving around Mountain View. It took years. Tesla simply sold its cars with the sensors built in. Tesla owners drove the cars while the sensors watched. Instead of years, Tesla's autopilot took months. While traditional programming relies on deductive logic, machine learning relies on inductive logic. The more examples the better.

I realized, in that towel-folding moment, that VR operators could train robots to fold towels as drivers had trained Teslas.[14] But why would anyone use VR to control a towel-folding robot when low-wage workers (especially migrant workers) are so cheap? As with office automation in the 1960s, the choice is not temp or machine, but both temp *and* machine.

Sometime in the next few years, some clever entrepreneur will realize that while programmed robots can't do household or workplace tasks, robots operated by people (with VR) can. This entrepreneur will realize that in the U.S., Europe, and the Arab states are vast markets for service labor (the International Labor Organization estimates that 71 percent of all migrant workers are in the service sector).[15] At the same time, those citizens want fewer immigrants in their countries. A robot who can replace a migrant laborer will have a clear value proposition, both economically and politically. With VR goggles, those workers don't even need to be in the same time zone. Bangladeshis, Mexicans, and every other migrant population could, from their home country, fold towels in Miami hotels through robot bodies. These robot bodies will be able to do any task a human can do, but unlike a human worker whose body and mind come bundled together, the mind of the robot can be replaced with a click of a button. Workers who don't perform can be replaced instantly.

All those physical jobs that "can't be moved overseas" will be moved overseas. As these overseas workers drive the robots, the machines will learn. Instead of one hundred towel folds, robotic operators will fold towels millions of times. Eventually the machine learning built into the robots will learn how to fold towels perfectly. The first tasks will be repetitive, simple tasks that require really good visual recognition, but as those get mastered, the need for actual humans to drive the robots will decline. Fewer humans will manage more robots, taking over the task only when the robot is uncertain what to do. When a towel can't be folded, a human will intervene. Over time, that uncertainty will go away.

Productivity will accelerate. Robots will be able to do what low-cost migrant service labor does now. With the rise of VR, robot bodies will be the cars that people drive. But instead of owning the car, overseas workers will be operating in robotic bodies that they do not own. These overseas workers will be digital migrants, training the robots to replace them.

This feedback loop of VR/machine learning/cheap labor will rapidly bring self-working robots into our lives in a way that without those millions of hours of training could never happen. Robots will get trained for free, like a Tesla. Our debates over migrant labor will be moot as Americans and Europeans opt for domestic robot bodies and foreign human minds. Robot bodies will "solve" the migration problem—at least from the perspective of Americans and Europeans. For the migrants abroad and the service workers here, the solution might be less appealing.

Through VR and the internet, our robots will be as smart as people from the get-go, and only over time will AI take over from humans. This path is inevitable. But what is not inevitable is what we choose to do with all those people who were formerly consigned to tasks that a machine could do. That question is not economic, but political. Just as in the industrial revolution, we will have a choice over whom to include in this new economy.

Nothing to Lose but Your Blockchains

While these early digital platforms were for-profit, they were not all the same. Etsy and Kickstarter have ridden the wave of corporations becoming "B corporations" that have pledged to elevate stakeholders' needs alongside those of investors.[16] These firms try to differentiate themselves from the short-term-profit mind-set of recent corporations and "be the change we seek in the world."[17] This B-corporation model, while heartwarming, has no binding qualities. There is no law enforcing it, just a set of voluntary guidelines. Indeed, Etsy's board pushed out its CEO in early 2017 to make it more responsive to the interests of its shareholders over its employees and customers.[18] In response, many Etsy sellers left the platform. Similarly, in 2017, Uber and other tech firms faced waves of allegations of sexual harassment. The #deleteuber campaign caused the platform to lose an estimated two hundred thousand users, most of whom switched to its rival Lyft.[19]

What mattered here was how easily customers and workers could switch from one platform to another—once they knew these options existed. As sellers and buyers learn how to use digital platforms, it will become as easy for them to switch "jobs" as it is for us to switch from Macy's to Bloomingdale's (or to Amazon). Uber might not exist in five years, but some on-demand car service will. Etsy might not exist, but some platform for authentic crafts will. Upwork might not exist, but some platform for knowledge work will. The question is who, in the long run, will own these platforms. The corporation has been the primary mechanism for the consolidation of capital over the past few hundred years, and we might be living through its end days—or at least the emergence of a truly viable alternative.

The platform cooperativist movement is pushing for worker-owned cooperatives as an alternative to the privately owned platforms. Digital labor and selling platforms make their profits from a cut of sales or wages, just like Manpower. Upwork, Uber, and Etsy all take a percentage or a fee from every sale. Worker-owned platforms, instead, could return those fees to those who labor or sell through the platform. Imagine a temp agency owned by the temps.

Where digital cooperatives might be different from temp agencies is in the ability to start cheaply and to coordinate decision making. Open-source platform software makes it easier than ever to set up a platform. In the past, the challenge for all co-ops was capital. Most businesses require capital to start and capital to grow. Marketing cooperatives, like orange growers, or procurement cooperatives, like grocery stores, don't actually make operational decisions. They make selling and purchasing decisions. For drivers, sellers, and laborers, different kinds of platforms could help them find customers—without extracting a stiff toll like the current platforms (or temporary agencies). Running a cooperative is a challenge, because no one, in many cases, is in charge. And that is part of the point. New technology, developed for other purposes, might be able to solve the governance issues.

Blockchain, the much-hyped technology behind bitcoin, allows for a kind of decentralized knowledge that enthusiasts believe could liberate us from the need for state or corporate record keeping. Bitcoin works because the verification of balances (a kind of information) does not rely on a central bank for verification of its authenticity. This kind of decentralized data verification could work for all kinds of data—medical, property, intellectual property—as well as labor and sales records. For libertarians, this technology could even eliminate the need for state enforcement of contracts. Building on this idea, the Ethereum Project offers not just inactive data, but active programs encoded on a blockchain—so-called smart contracts. With ethereum, two parties can agree to a contract, then encode that contract on a blockchain for all to see. When the contract is satisfied, an event occurs, like a payment from one party to the other. With the contract encoded rather than just written down, one of the primary functions of the state is eliminated. Blockchains, and the platforms built atop them, appeal to those who imagine a system of perfect public rules encoded so that no one can privately alter them. Blockchain technology, in theory, should prevent any one party from cooking the books or seizing control, since the assets, and the rules governing those assets, are encoded in publicly visible algorithms.

Operating outside existing legal regimes, how these anarchic spaces operate is still being decided. The possibility of true stateless economies is catnip to the technolibertarians.[20] Equally appealing is the notion of a post-corporate capitalism. Worker-owned cooperatives would ensure that the value created by workers would return to the workers themselves. This peer-to-peer economy would offer an alternative to the corporate value capture of the past. We would all be individuals contracting with one another. Peer-to-peer work systems, in this view, allow workers to control the fruits of their own labor. The code of our ethereum contracts would be supreme over any other kind of law.

Bitcoin and ethereum have already had several high-profile failures in those perfect, impregnable records. There was a hack. There was a divergence in values between two blockchains. These events led to a series of community-approved "hard forks" in the record.[21] Forking the data meant that there were now two nearly identical copies, except for that one event. Who would decide which had value and which was worthless? Blockchains were manually rolled back. Despite the idealization of decentralized anomie, a pseudostate is still required to decide on these hard forks, which allows communities to decide on who gets the underlying property. Ethereum has already seen a collapse in its operations from these blunders, both technical and social, but something incorporating the underlying idea of smart contracts will soon be with us, and its meaning will always be less about making hard, coded laws than about the assumptions built into who, when, and how those codes are unmade.

Those who can write and unwrite rules, who can break rules, are the ones who will, in the end, have the power.

The Second Time as Farce

Since the 1970s, workers who found themselves outside the core work of the economy had also found themselves with less power. Organizing temps, since the days of 9to5, had proved hopeless. Traditional labor unions, for the most part, saw temps as a threat, not an ally. But as temp work morphed into the gig economy, the first inklings of change began to emerge. In the 1990s, Jono Shaffer, with the SEIU, organized successful Justice for Janitors campaigns in many cities by targeting the companies that subcontracted janitorial services. In the 2000s, in New York City, Sara Horowitz, a former labor organizer, began to think about how to empower the freelancers of her hometown by organizing portable health-care plans. In the 2010s, meanwhile, Michelle Miller and Jess Kutch, after leaving the SEIU, started a website, coworkers.org, to create a forum for workers' voices that successfully fought back against Starbucks and other shift employers. These new kinds of labor organizations were not alone. Whether in real life or over the internet, precarious workers of all stripes began to find one another. Portable benefits mattered, because jobs were so precarious, but so did workplace respect. Few traditional unions took part in these developments, though most of the founders of these new organizations came out of the labor movement, especially the SEIU. Traditional organizing methods failed in the face of a distributed labor force, but slowly, workers and their organizers found new ways to connect in the flexible world.

The digital economy was organized through an earlier vision of total flexibility for the employer and total pliability for the worker. Yet the new tools of the digital age, especially cooperative platforms and digital organizing, offered new alternatives to the jobs that no longer existed. With all job growth occurring in the contingent workforce, Americans began to find new ways to work.

While most of us work in the old economy, all the new jobs are in the flexible economy. Those who found jobs after the Great Recession, when the only new jobs were contingent, have had a very different experience than those who started working just ten years earlier. Our feeling that something is changing—especially for the young among us—is entirely correct.

The end of the postwar prosperity in the 1970s may have been tragic, but handwringing over today's jobs is farce. We are all terrified that the coming of Uber means the end of security, but we shouldn't fear that: it is already gone. We already live in that world.

We should not mourn the passing of a regime, moreover, that compelled us all to be afraid. Secure work began to erode the minute that Elmer Winter began to sell temporary labor. For some Americans—migrant laborers, African Americans—precariousness has always been part of the labor market. For white women, security was contingent on marriage to white men. Only for working-class white men, and even then not all of them, was job security a reality. Even for the high-paid executive, the office was a place of anxiety, and then possible downsizing. For decades, in ever more insidious ways, employers have found means to make workers disposable. For decades, this flexibility has benefited the employer, but for the first time, we are in a digital world where the flexibility might finally benefit the worker, who might, in the end, not need an employer after all.

What should organized labor learn from Uber? Over the last few years, we have watched city after city, state after state, try to put the genie of ride sharing back in the bottle—and fail. Uber was not legal when it started, but through economic power, it made itself legal. Enough riders, and drivers, and lawmakers wanted Uber that it became legal. No amount of legal handwringing could stop it. On-demand law, like labor law, could manage the margins of the new economy, but it could not stop it—any more than law could stop industrialization. Cities like New York could create requirements—like licenses and background checks—but could not stop the expansion of the new services.

Industrial labor unions did the same thing in the 1930s. Was it legal for the autoworkers to occupy and shut down a GM factory? Clearly not. But the power that they seized made it legal, and in the aftermath, there were enough people, including lawmakers, who sanctified the power of this new kind of union. The laws of the 1930s legitimated the new labor relations, but it was the unions that made it happen. Laws can tweak how a particular workplace arrangement plays out, but laws can never substitute for power. Faced with industrial corporations, workers organized their own counter-bureaucracies. Postwar unions mirrored the corporate bureaucracy and provided a stable workforce for firms and good jobs for the workers.

In today's economy, workforces are more distributed and firms more subcontracted. If workers are to succeed in this iteration of capitalism, they once again need to learn from capital's own innovations how best to demand their fair share.

CHAPTER THIRTEEN

The Second Industrious Revolution

For there is nothing mysterious about the foundations of a healthy and strong democracy. The basic things expected by our people of their political and economic systems are simple. They are:

Equality of opportunity for youth and for others.
Jobs for those who can work.
Security for those who need it.
The ending of special privilege for the few.
The preservation of civil liberties for all.
The enjoyment of the fruits of scientific progress in a wider and constantly rising standard of living.

—President Franklin Delano Roosevelt, State of the Union Address, 1941

The recent election unearthed an enduring debate about American capitalism: what exactly is a good job? For a long time, we need to remember, the very idea of a "good" "job" was a contradiction. Until the twentieth century, it was self-evident that there was nothing good about a job. What was good was being independent, which usually meant being an artisan, a retailer, or, most commonly, a farmer.

While we often discuss the American dream in terms of consumption, there is another American dream that is more visceral: control over one's work. This older dream, the Jeffersonian vision of independent farmers, was promoted by the federal government in the nineteenth century by providing farmland to citizens. Rising industrialization had threatened to turn us into a nation of wage earners dependent on a boss. Low earnings were part of the problem, but wage labor itself, in which one did not have freedom to control one's own work, was the real dilemma. The postwar economy may have provided for good living, but it did nothing to make us free from bosses.

The postwar economy provided millions of households with steady paychecks, but we should not romanticize how protected people were during that period. For the people excluded from those jobs, especially women and African Americans, the economy was not so glorious. Even for white men who had the "good jobs," working on an assembly line or in a mine is dehumanizing, backbreaking, and, most important, soul-breaking work. Humans should not do the work of robots. The challenge for the twenty-first century will not be defending our robotlike jobs, but discovering what is valuable in being human.

For a hundred years, we learned how to work like robots, so why should we be surprised when robots finally arrive to take our jobs? The point is not to be better robots than robots, but to have more human work than our ancestors—creative, caring, curious. By treating people like machines, we are squandering lives. At Google they have, in some areas, stopped measuring projects by dollars and begun to measure them by how many engineers' working lives they will consume. I don't think Google engineers' lives matter more than anybody else's. I suspect you don't either. The highest and best use of a human life cannot be towel folding. If that is the only opportunity that someone has, something has gone wrong with our society.

The longing many Americans feel for owning their own business, the celebration of entrepreneurship in our culture, and our homesteading heritage are not just about money—or buying houses. Yet for several generations we have made it easy to own a home, but hard to own a business. The rise of the new economy, as the last election showed, has left many people, especially rural people, behind. This new reality of our decentralized, digital economy, however, offers the possibility of returning to our core American values of security and independence. The gig economy might have the best of both worlds: the autonomy and independence of an economy before wage labor, but with *individuals* possessed of the productive capacity of an industrial economy.

There is more than one path to supporting an independent workforce. One option is radical individualism: each person has portable benefits that are contracted through private firms, with each temporary employer chipping in, alongside wages. We refresh our laws to account for independent workers that are neither W-2 nor 1099.[1] Another, more collective path would be toward a universal benefits system (like every other industrialized country possesses), where workers could change jobs without worrying about losing their benefits. Risk takers could become entrepreneurs and create jobs for other Americans. A still more radical path would be a citizen's share. Whatever course we take, we need to make choices. The economy has changed, but our institutions, and our needs, have not.

The Conservative Path

The most powerful tool of the New Deal was its recognition of how to channel private capital for a public purpose. As of May 2017, U.S. banks had a reserve requirement of $127 billion, which sounds like a lot of money sitting idle, until you realize that on top of that they have $2,075 billion, or $2 trillion, more dollars sitting idle on top of that, with nowhere to go.[2] All that capital is money that is not invested. That uninvested capital is the sound of capitalism stalling out. We ought to look to the investment innovations of the New Deal, overseen by the Reconstruction Finance Corporation, to inspire us to invest in our most basic needs (like the Federal Housing Administration), our infrastructure (like the Rural Electrification Administration), and our futuristic industries (like the Defense Plants Corporation). We need broadband in rural America today, just like we needed electricity in the 1930s. Our far-out technologies that will create millions of jobs (climate jobs, green transportation) need capital.

At the same time, we should empower small- and medium-size businesses that are less sexy but still necessary—like plumbing supply companies. These kinds of firms—with steady profits—might not be disruptive, but they still create jobs and growth. The Small Business Administration's flagship lending program, 7(a), accounts for only 0.65 percent of all small loans. It is, in effect, a rounding error. Yet the financial institutions that could lend so much more to small business are awash in excess funds at an inconceivable level of over $2.5 trillion.

As always, the federal government's power to rechannel private capital outweighs its power to spend. Our federal insurance programs have made it easy to lend for consumption, as with a home mortgage, but not for business investment. Banks that can easily resell a mortgage find it cumbersome to securitize a business loan—even though it is small business that drives our economy. Let's rebalance the lending incentives to make it as easy for Americans to own their work as to own their houses, using private capital for small business just as we did with houses. Channeling capital into business, rather than consumer debt, will create an unprecedented boom, not only in economic growth but also in quality of life.

The federal government gave away homesteads to create stability and self-reliance in the nineteenth century. Most Americans today don't need farmland, but they do need other kinds of support—health insurance, skills education, maybe even a basic income—to take the risks upon which success depends. A minimum safety net enables maximum risk taking, unleashing the true growth potential of capitalism. Rather than thinking of these as the last gasps of a defunct welfare economy, we should instead see them as the first steps toward an independent economy. In place of seeing benefits as a cost to taxpayers, we ought to see benefits as an investment in our collective future. Only with the knowledge that their families are safe can entrepreneurs and inventors recreate capitalism anew. Portable benefits seem the perfect solution for many of the flexible worker's needs. Just like the 401(k) divorced pensions from a job, we need to find a way to divorce all other worker benefits from a workplace: health care, childcare, etc. Yet a better term than the currently trendy "portable benefits" might be "universal investments." Americans need life security, not job security. The trillions in untapped capital in corporate coffers and on bank balance sheets need to be invested, if not in business enterprises, then in creating the context for bold new ventures.

As a first step, we should divert the money we have used to support homeownership into supporting work ownership. Mortgage deductions are predicated on the idea that a worker would live in the same place, working at the same office or factory, for his career. We know that worker immobility hurts income opportunities. We also know that mortgage subsidies create pricing distortions that might raise homeownership rates, but not wealth.[3] We can start by diverting the tax benefits (about $175 billion per year) for home ownership into the new safety net, to empower the new flexible workers, who can, with their own money, buy houses if they want them. Home mortgages, as the financial crisis has shown us, do not create stability. We can expand health insurance and higher education, and even edge our way toward a guaranteed minimum income.

For those who still have jobs, labor and employment laws need to be changed so that the laws help solve the problems of workers, rather than create problems for workers. American labor law, more or less, is a product of the 1930s, designed for a different set of problems, for a different age. Then, workers needed to be protected from involuntary overtime on an assembly line. Workers needed guarantees to have a lunch break, much less a bathroom break. The twenty-eight-hour part-time worker is an artifact of a legal regime that sought to differentiate male breadwinners from female dependents, in an era when working-class jobs were industrial jobs.

We need to construct a new set of regulations and benefits to empower workers and employers in the flexible economy. Laws to protect the interests of flexible workers are needed, and they cannot just force 1099ers into a W-2 box. We need to debate how labor law for a digital economy ought to look rather than try to gerrymander our workforce into tax forms that reflect an older kind of employment.

If the only way to make an Uber job viable is through the use of tax deductions, then we need to make sure that all the Uber drivers know that. Today there are limits on what kinds of tax services Uber (or any other firm employing 1099ers) can offer their subcontractors without violating labor law. Suggestions for a new legal category of independent worker, combining the qualities of W-2 and 1099, would be a step in the right direction. Such workers are not truly entrepreneurs, and we are deluded in thinking that individuals will find it as easy to be contractors as employees. We need to recognize that workers of the future might not be categorized as employees, but they will still require the protections and empowerments of labor law.

For industrial workers today, especially in those factories where the workforce may or may not have U.S. citizenship, such protections are vital. As we recast labor law for a new century, we need to be sure that everyone, citizen or not, is safe at work. The two-tier system has provided protections for citizens, but not denizens, of this country, to everyone's detriment. Employer sanctions remain a good idea (though not enforceable). What is an even better idea is actually protecting migrant workers in the United States. If we want to protect our native-born workers from wage competition, the best course is to protect migrant workers. The gaps in those laws, with a third of our workforce in the freelance economy, become more glaring every year.

Providing life security, while not inhibiting this second industrious revolution, will therefore be the labor challenge of the twenty-first century. Flexible workers need to have a safety net to allow them to pursue their ambitions. Freed of some of their fear, people could find out what they can do. Even today, only a third of Americans go to college. Most of us haven't had the chance to truly find out what we are capable of. Not all will succeed. Yet a safety net that allows someone to try to find rewarding work matters much more than, say, helping that person mortgage a house. It can help assure not just material comfort but spiritual success, something that our nineteenth-century ancestors fought unsuccessfully to preserve as they moved into dehumanizing factories and offices. Many will find they can do nothing particularly impressive, but my suspicion is that there is far more untapped talent than we can imagine.

The Radical Path

At the same time, we could remember that the corporation itself has a history. Before the mid-nineteenth century, the corporation existed as a way to carry out risky but publicly needed ventures: building bridges, founding universities, and trading overseas. Our legislatures had to approve every corporation, because giving individuals the opportunity to act in our society, but without shouldering the full responsibility for those actions, was a special dispensation. Today anybody can form a corporation for any purpose, yet we as a society still bear some of that risk and have, through our shared heritage, made that venture possible. When our corporations fail, it hurts us all, yet when they succeed, we do not get compensated for our risks. American corporations, as it is often said, socialize risk and privatize return.

I would suggest that as we synthesize the agricultural and industrial models of capitalism, we also revisit how we think about the corporation. The B corporation is a step in the right direction, highlighting priorities beyond the shareholders. Yet it does not go far enough. Every time a worker is replaced by a machine, that worker gets no benefit, and we, as a society, support that person. What would it be like if every time someone was laid off, we all benefited? Not as much as the corporation itself, to be sure, but in some measureable amount.

Instead of thinking of a universal basic income as just another tax, let's think of it instead as a citizen's share.[4] We create a holding company that, whenever stock is issued, gets some fraction of it. Every American, in turn, has one share in the holding company. As our businesses create value, it flows to us all. This model of shared wealth can be seen as an extension of sovereign wealth funds, like the Alaska Permanent Fund. Instead of oil wealth flowing to all of us, it would be our shared heritage of good governance and mutual investment that has allowed corporate capitalism to flourish, even at the expense of our technological and organizational unemployment. This citizen's share has the advantage of being framed as something we already own, which fits with all of our values, rather than a redistributive tax, which, for many Americans, does not. We all have a right to our national parks; why not our corporations?

In return for this shift, we could consider rolling back some of the industrial-era laws that hobble our businesses, no longer truly benefit workers, and burden the federal government. In this way, we give all of our citizens the equivalent of farmland, which can give them, at least, the basics of life. A citizen's share would rapidly promote corporate investment in productive technologies, displacing workers but not turning them out to starve. As a society, we could have an important and robust conversation about what we think humans should do in the twenty-first century. Just as few of us are farmers or miners anymore, or would want to be, we should not force humans to work jobs that can be done more efficiently by machines simply because it is cheaper.

Whatever the path forward, we need to stop fixating on propping up a world of security that is tied to a job. In this way, the flexible economy can finally be true liberation: from bosses, from a cubicle, from monotony.

Those benefits will mean nothing if the cost of that liberation is fear: of eviction, of illness, of poverty. Just as the assembly line did not necessarily lead to immiseration (as many critics predicted) because we made a political choice to distribute that productivity widely, we must return to an economy that produces income for the middle, not just for the top. At stake is nothing less than our democracy. We have already seen the warning signs of what inequality can do to our polity.

American Work for All Americans

Supporting the independent workforce means supporting it everywhere in the country. Rural America has been devastated in the last forty years. While our cities boom, our countryside has withered, producing a populist backlash as strong as that of the 1880s.

Whether we implement portable benefits (which I think is politically feasible) or a universal basic income (which I don't), our policies need to support rural Americans in this transition. The frustrations that fuel nostalgia for Main Street are understandable—and long-standing. From the beginning of our country's history, rural and small-town Americans have been on the losing side of a rising market economy. You can draw a straight line from the Jeffersonians in the late eighteenth century to the agrarian populists in the late nineteenth century to President Trump's voters, all of whom have felt that the city hornswoggles the country. The rage that arose in the 1880s, as rural incomes fell and farm mortgages defaulted while city bankers got rich, does not feel so distant today.

If the only answer to rural downward mobility is to turn everyone into software engineers, then there is no hope. The idea that every truck driver or coal miner can, or should, become a member of the modern professional class is closely related to the belief that unless you have those particular skills, you have no value—which isn't the case. No one wants to feel like they are a waste product or have nothing to contribute.

Many rural Americans, sadly, don't realize how valuable they already are or what opportunities presently exist for them. It's true that the digital economy, centered in a few high-tech cities, has excluded Main Street America. But it does not need to be this way. Through global freelancing platforms like Upwork, for example, rural and small-town Americans can find jobs anywhere in the world, using abilities and talents they already have. A receptionist can welcome office visitors in San Francisco from her home in New York's Finger Lakes. Through an e-commerce website like Etsy, an Appalachian woodworker can create custom pieces and sell them anywhere in the world. It seems bizarre, but in a long-tail, global marketplace, niche producers can make a living. In a digital economy, the work can come to the worker, where they already live, solving a huge chunk of the employment crisis. These microbusinesses need capital, they need educational support, and they need respect as "real" businesses.

Americans, regardless of education or geographical location, have marketable skills in the global economy: they speak English and understand the nuances of communicating with Americans—something that cannot be easily shipped overseas. The United States remains the largest consumer market in the world, and Americans can (and some already do) sell these services abroad. Right now we are too fixated on upskilling coal miners into data miners. We should instead be showing people how to get work via platforms like Upwork and Etsy with their existing skills. We should also be empowering people to create platforms for the other skills that they already have. What's novel is that today, the underlying values of Main Street—living and working with autonomy in your own small community—can be attained, as long as you are willing to find that work online.

Everyone has something to offer. We just need to find a way to reach everyone. In the digital era, connecting people is easier than ever before. While the flexible workforce and the flexible firm brought insecurity in the last forty years, we can turn them around now and make them work for us. Technology will make it possible, but what will make it happen is collective will to finally achieve the real American dream.

Technology creates new possibilities, but only we determine our future—or at least we have every time before in human history. The wage connected to a job might just be a passing moment in our economic past, a contingent part of the industrial economy, a footnote to history. This distributed digital economy may reduce workplace relationships, just as Alvin Toffler predicted so long ago, but it will also force us to rediscover other communities around us. Our jobs should not be all that we are, even as work can give our

lives meaning. Defined as purposeful action, work will always be an enduring part of the human experience. Caring for one another. Making for one
another. These acts make us human and make us a society. In that society,
no one is disposable, and we all deserve a measure of security so that we can
find out what we can truly become. As we confront the inequities of the digital economy, let us not make the same mistake we made in the 1930s. This
time around, everybody's security, everybody's dignity, should count.

Embracing the new reality of flexible work, rather than fighting it, we
can find a way to provide a new American dream that is, in essence, the
oldest one of all—to declare our independence.

ACKNOWLEDGMENTS

Though there is only one name on the jacket of this book, it truly was a collective enterprise. I never could have written it without a wide range of support—institutional, professional, and personal.

The ILR School of Cornell University is the reason that this book exists. *Temp* was written at the intersection of multiple kinds of history, and it would have been possible only in such an interdisciplinary place. Without its welcome and support over the years, I never would have been able to work so long (permanently, it seemed at times) on a book about temporary labor. In a moment when labor history no longer seems to be particularly fashionable, my colleagues at ILR supported this project. Verónica Martínez-Matsuda showed me the ropes and has always been a generous colleague and inspiring friend. Nick Salvatore will always and forever have a place in my heart for offering a job to a historian of labor who happened to write his first two books on the history of business. I am certain that was not an easy sell. Jeff Cowie encouraged this project all along and kept me laughing the whole time. Deans Harry Katz and then Kevin Hallock have been generous in supporting my research trips, as well as in giving me support when I was offered opportunities outside of Cornell.

Outside support also made this book possible. A Gilder Lehrman Fellowship from the New-York Historical Society supported early-stage research in New York City archives. An Andrew W. Mellon Foundation Fellowship at the Center for Advanced Study in the Behavioral Sciences at Stanford provided me with a year to fully immerse myself in the archives and culture of Silicon Valley.

The research for this book was also supported by many stupendous research assistants at Cornell: Alex Caruso, Emily Busch, Emily Coombs, and Rebecca Tally. Jessica Stewart worked with me for years on this project, from hunting down sources to editing the endnotes. Ellen Fitchette, the world's great admin, has kept my teaching and my travel from making me crazy. Sara Edwards helped me adjust to my new position at the Institute for Workplace Studies in an incredibly supportive way that allowed me to continue to write. I also need to thank the many archivists and librarians who supported this project, especially Cheryl Baredo, Catherine Bezman, Patricia Bouteneff, Suzanne Cohen, Curtis Lyons, Aliqae Geraci, Richard Gomes, Anna Mancini, and Patricia Sione.

The book benefited immeasurably from businesspeople willing to be interviewed either on or off the record, as well as from the organizations that opened their archives. I deeply appreciate their participation. Business and labor history can't be written without archives and interviews.

Various groups read and debated chapters of this book, pushing the arguments to be more expansive: the History of American Capitalism Seminar (Johns Hopkins), Greater Bay Area Modern Political Economy Group (Berkeley-Davis-Stanford), History of Capitalism Workshop (Stanford), Urban History Conference, Business History Conference, Organization of American Historians (OAH), and Labor and Working-Class History Association (LAWCHA). I also benefited enormously from the campers who attended the History of Capitalism Summer Camp.

Too many friends and colleagues have supported this work, either through drinks or drafts, to be listed in this already too-long book—except for a few who went above and beyond. My colleagues in the History of Capitalism Initiative—especially Ed Baptist and Larry Glickman—have been an enduring source of intellectual vitality. Julilly Kohler-Hausmann and Victor Pickard were touchstones of bourbon, humor, and political economy. Margaret Levi has been a generous mentor and supportive friend. Paul Fleming, Eli Friedman, Tom McEnaney, and George Spisak talked through the Foucauldian foundations of the book, often while enjoying the pleasures that only Monday nights can provide. Mike Manville helped me articulate a central theme and kept me in touch with what grumpy microeconomists might say. Margaret O'Mara reaffirmed the importance of Silicon Valley's history. Diane Burton showed me how to balance writing with professing. Daniel Rodgers gave some early chapters a deep read, in that way only he can do, and I am grateful for his clarifications. Tim O'Reilly opened his proverbial Rolodex and made nearly all of the interviews possible—and, more important, shared his ability to be critical without being cynical. Ben Waterhouse provided amazing criticism and support. Adam Miner shared his infectious enthusiasm for the futuristic. Natasha Iskander talked through ideas, dropping her expansive knowledge of all things migratory. Julia Ott has been my intellectual comrade in arms for many years, and I hope for many more years to come. Mentors may not have had a direct hand in a project, but their guidance over the years makes everything else possible. Thank you to Gwen Hyman, Eric Foner, Betsy Blackmar, Sven Beckert, Niall Ferguson, and Liz Cohen.

Eric Lupfer is the best agent that a historian can hope for. He supported this obvious commercial hit—"I want to write a labor history book about temps!"—from the start. His intellectual engagement and narrative sensibilities made this book possible.

Viking has been a dream come true. Georgia Bodnar has kept the whole project on track and provided invaluable editorial ideas. Jane Cavolina copyedited this manuscript to a level that I did not think was possible, and slightly terrified me. My dream editor, Wendy Wolf, has a passion for labor history that is exceeded only by the ferocity of her uncompromising editorial perspective. Without her vision, this book would have been unreadable. If this book made any sense, thank Wendy, if it did not, the blame is all mine.

My family has been extremely supportive during this process. My brothers, Eli and Noah, did not read chapters, but we had a good time anyhow. Patty and Greg provided love and support, as did Kath and George. My sister, Rachel, read numerous chapters and debated the ideas therein, drawing on her own experiences working in tech. When I doubted it would ever end, or that it mattered at all, she told me to keep working.

Most important to me, as I carried out this temp project, was my permanent love: Katherine Howe. She lived with this manuscript as much as I did, even while writing her own (much more fun) books. I dedicate this book to her.

NOTES

Archives

APL Apple Computer, Inc., records 1977-1998, Special Collections, Stanford University, Palo Alto, CA

AGC Associated General Contractors of Houston, Houston, TX

CITI Citigroup Archives, New York, NY

EWP Elmer Winter papers, Jewish Museum of Milwaukee, Milwaukee, WI

HP Hewlett Packard Enterprise Archives, Palo Alto, CA

MBM Research materials about Marvin Bower and McKinsey & Co., 1901-1984, Baker Library, Harvard Business School, Allston, MA

9to5 9to5 papers, Schlesinger Library, Harvard University, Cambridge, MA

PWC PricewaterhouseCoopers Records, 1891-2000, Columbia University, New York, NY

USCIS Immigration and Customs Enforcement Library, Washington, D.C.

Introduction: **How We All Became Temps**

1. Elmer Winter, "Speech for Europe," April 1, 1960, 4-7, folder 5, "Speeches, 1958-1961," box 12, EWP.

2. Manpower, "Corporate Fact Sheet 2017," www.manpowergroup.com; Walmart, "Company Facts," corporate.walmart.com/newsroom/company-facts.

3. Emmanuel Saez and Gabriel Zucman, "Wealth Inequality in the United States Since 1913: Evidence from Capitalized Income Tax Data," *Quarterly Journal of Economics* 131, no. 2 (May 2016), http://elsa.berkeley.edu/~saez/#income.

4. Lawrence Katz and Alan Krueger, "The Rise and Nature of Alternative Work Arrangements in the United States, 1995-2015," March 29, 2016, Alan B. Krueger, Princeton University, https://krueger.princeton.edu/sites/default/files/akrueger/files/katz_krueger_cws_-_march_29_20165.pdf.

5. Upwork and Freelancers Union, "Freelancing in America 2015," https://fu-web-storage-prod.s3.amazonaws.com/assets/pdf/freelancinginamerica2015.pdf.

6. See Gerald Davis, *The Vanishing American Corporation: Navigating the Hazards of a New Economy* (Oakland, CA: Berrett-Koehler Publishers, 2016). Davis confuses the drop in the number of publicly traded U.S. corporations for the net global rise of corporations, but certainly in the American case, which I am mostly concerned with, he is correct.

7. Daniela Retelny, et al., "Expert Crowdsourcing with Flash Teams," in *Proceedings of the 27th Annual ACM Symposium on User Interface Software and Technology* (New York: Association for Computing Machinery, 2014), 75–85.

8. Discussed more expansively in Louis Hyman, "The Myth of Main Street," *New York Times*, Sunday Review, April 8, 2017, www.nytimes.com/2017/04/08/opinion/sunday/the-myth-of-main-street.html.

9. From the 1980s through 2008, the wage stagnation of the middle class was largely hidden by rising asset prices (stocks, housing) as well as by expanding consumer credit. See Louis Hyman, *Borrow: The American Way of Debt* (New York: Vintage, 2012).

10. Emmanuel Saez, "Striking It Richer: The Evolution of Top Incomes in the United States" (updated with 2012 preliminary estimates), UC Berkeley, http://eml.berkeley.edu//~saez/saez-UStopincomes-2012.pdf.

11. Olga Khazan, "Why Are So Many Middle-Aged White Americans Dying?" *Atlantic*, January 29, 2016, www.theatlantic.com/health/archive/2016/01/middle-aged-white-americans-left-behind-and-dying-early/433863.

12. Blackwater, now known as Xe Services, is a private military that uses independent contractors instead of employees. During the writing of this book, I have been excitedly asked by many academics why I did not write more about adjuncts. Today, about 70 percent of professor positions are adjunct positions without the job stability (or workplace freedoms) of tenured faculty. As a professor, I think this shift is important, but I also think it has been well analyzed by other scholars. I hope my fellow academics' excitement over the plight of the adjunct extends to other workers' lives transformed by the temporary economy. My favorite analysis to date is Marc Bousquet, *How the University Works: Higher Education and the Low-Wage Nation* (New York: NYU Press, 2008).

13. George R. Boyer, "Robots and Looms: If Today's Robots Are Just the Automated Looms of the 21st Century, Then Expect a Couple Decades of Wage Stagnation, Declining Living Standards, and Civil Unrest" (original essay prepared for the 2013 Employment & Technology Roundtable, Cornell University, ILR School, April 12, 2013, New York City), www.ilr.cornell.edu/sites/ilr.cornell.edu/files/Robots_and_Looms.pdf.

Chapter One: **Making Company Men**

1. Julie Greene, *Pure and Simple Politics: The American Federation of Labor and Political Activism, 1881-1917* (Cambridge, UK: Cambridge University Press, 1998), 139.

2. Alfred Chandler remains the greatest historian of business in this period. See Alfred D. Chandler, Jr., *The Visible Hand: The Managerial Revolution in American Business* (Cambridge, MA: Belknap Press, 1977). See also Olivier Zunz, *Making America Corporate, 1870-1920* (Chicago: University of Chicago Press, 1992). Many different corporate models emerged in this period, and while Chandler certainly promoted a particularly teleological model of corporate development (checked by other historians like Zunz and Robert Sobel), he nonetheless pointed to the models that later became dominant.

3. Naomi Lamoureux, *The Great Merger Movement in American Business, 1895 to 1904* (New York: Cambridge University Press, 1985), 1.

4. Ibid., 3.

5. This account of Durant is based on Chandler and on Alfred P. Sloan, Jr., *My Years with General Motors* (1963; repr., New York: Doubleday, 1990), 4–16.

6. Ibid., 5.

7. The ins and outs of the financing of this shift are too detailed to cover here. See Alfred D. Chandler, Jr., and Stephen Salsbury, *Pierre S. du Pont and the Making of the Modern Corporation* (New York: Harper & Row, 1971).

8. Sloan, *My Years*, 18.

9. Ibid., 18–19.

10. Ibid., 23.

11. The stock was actually in United Motors Corporation, which would be absorbed into General Motors in 1918. This kind of sprawling acquisition was very Durant.

12. Sloan, *My Years*, 25.

13. GM's role in the development of the modern corporation is well documented. For the broad overview see Sloan, *My Years*. Also see H. Thomas Johnson, "Management Accounting in an Early Multidivisional Organization: General Motors in the 1920s," *Business History Review* 52, no. 4 (Winter 1978): 490–517.

14. DuPont's accounting methods set the pattern for many other firms, but it was Sloan who truly set the road map for the industrial firm. For more on early management accounting see H. Thomas Johnson, "Management Accounting in an Early Integrated Industrial: E. I. du Pont de Nemours Powder Company, 1903–1912," *Business History Review* 49, no. 2 (Summer 1975): 184–204; and Johnson, "Management Accounting in an Early Multidivisional Organization: General Motors in the 1920s."

15. This section on Sloan is based on Chandler, *Strategy and Structure*.

16. Interview with Glenn Petty, 34143.txt, box 36, unpaginated, PWC.

17. Chandler, *Strategy and Structure*, 10–11.

18. Marvin Bower, *Perspective on McKinsey* (New York: McKinsey & Co., 1979), 38.

19. Elizabeth Haas Edersheim, *McKinsey's Marvin Bower* (Hoboken, NJ: John Wiley & Sons, 2004), 7; Bower, *Perspective on McKinsey*, 1.

20. Edersheim, *McKinsey's Marvin Bower*, 8–9.

21. Bower, *Perspective on McKinsey*, 2.

22. Ibid., 2–3.

23. Curt Schleier, "Consulting Innovator Marvin Bower: His Vision Made McKinsey & Co. a Pioneer," *Investor's Business Daily*, November 9, 2000, 4.

24. Bower, *Perspective on McKinsey*, 5.

25. Edersheim, *McKinsey's Marvin Bower*, 19.

26. Schleier, "Consulting Innovator Marvin Bower," 4.

27. Ibid., 15.

28. Ibid., 23.

29. Ibid., 20.

30. Edersheim, *McKinsey's Marvin Bower*, 2.

31. Bower, *Perspective on McKinsey*, 25.

32. Ibid., 26–29.

33. Ibid., 35–36.

34. Ibid., 37.

35. Ibid., 40.

36. Edersheim, *McKinsey's Marvin Bower*, 23.

37. John Huey, Joyce E. Davis, and Jane Furth, "How McKinsey Does It," *Fortune* 128, no. 11, November 1, 1993, 56–81.

38. Arthur Schlesinger, *The Coming of the New Deal, 1933-1935* (New York: Houghton-Mifflin [1958], 2003), 98.

39. Ibid., 139.

40. The term "unskilled labor" has an enduring controversy since it is often used to describe work that is low paid, like that done by immigrants, or unpaid, like the care work typically done by women. Its use is seen as offensive because the work done is often skillful. The term, then, contains a hidden assumption: skilled work is defined by what kind of wage it commands in the market. Today, discussions of "upskilling" contain similar overtones.

41. Typically, labor leaders, like the AFL founder Samuel Gompers, pointed to the rise and fall of the Knights of Labor. Certainly the AFL rejected the radical industrial organizers of the 1910s, like the Industrial Workers of the World (IWW), who were better known as the Wobblies.

42. *A. L. A. Schechter Poultry Corporation v. United States*, Oyez.org, www.oyez .org/cases/1900-1940/295us495, accessed November 27, 2017. The Supreme Court case turned on whether it was constitutional for the NRA codes to regulate the killing of chickens, in this case by a kosher butcher in New York. Though NRA officials had increasingly tried to withdraw from regulating such small trades with community ties, the case had begun before the change in policy. Through its decision, upholding the right of Schechter to conduct its business as it wanted, the NRA codes were all struck down. The judges decided the case on two grounds. First, it was unconstitutional for Congress, to which the constitution gave the power to regulate interstate commerce, to unrestrainedly grant that power to the executive branch. The executive had no constitutional right to regulate interstate commerce. Second, the NRA code in this case was not about interstate commerce. The chickens may or may not have been brought in across state lines, but the code regulated the killing and selling of chickens locally, which was not within the domain of the interstate commerce clause. The court, in framing its decisions broadly and declaring the entire NRA in violation of the Constitution, was going against a narrow tradition of slowly accumulating decisions. The Court was warning the executive and the legislative that it was no longer going to brook the expansion of executive power. While labor leaders decried the decision, conservatives applauded it. More important, Congress, in which support for the NRA had already flagged, took this as a sign to stop support.

43. More accurately, some body dies were also at a factory in Cleveland. But controlling Flint was sufficient to bring down the supply chain.

44. *National Labor Relations Board v. Jones & Laughlin Steel Corporation*, Oyez .org, www.oyez.org/cases/1900-1940/301us1, accessed November 27, 2017.

45. These actions dovetailed with the transformative social and cultural practices of the 1930s, as shown in Lizabeth Cohen, *Making a New Deal: Industrial Workers in Chicago, 1919-1939* (New York: Cambridge University Press, 1990).

46. Matthew Sobek, "Major Industrial Groups of Labor Force Participants—All Persons: 1910-1990," Table Ba652-669, in *Historical Statistics of the United States, Earliest Times to the Present: Millennial Edition*, eds. Susan B. Carter, Scott Sigmund Gartner, Michael R. Haines, Alan L. Olmstead, Richard Sutch, and Gavin Wright (New York: Cambridge University Press, 2006), http://dx.doi.org /10.1017/ISBN-9780511132971.Ba652-103210.1017/ISBN-9780511132971 .Ba652-1032. Calculations by author.

47. Kitty Calavita, *Inside the State: The Bracero Program, Immigration, and the I.N.S.* (New York: Routledge, 1992), 20.

48. Quoted in Deborah Cohen, *Braceros: Migrant Citizens and Transnational Subjects in the Postwar United States and Mexico* (Chapel Hill: University of North Carolina Press, 2011), 145.

49. Ibid., 201.

50. Ibid.

51. Calavita, *Inside the State*, 20-21.

52. Glenna Matthews, "The Fruit Workers of the Santa Clara Valley: Alternative Paths to Union Organization During the 1930s," *Pacific Historical Review* 54, no. 1 (February 1985): 51-70.

53. Ibid.

54. Ibid., 51-70, 66.

55. Ibid.

56. Ibid., 51-70, 57.

57. Calavita, *Inside the State*, 28.

58. Ibid., 24.

59. Cohen, *Braceros*, 29-30; see also Mireya Loza, *Defiant Braceros: How Migrant Workers Fought for Racial, Sexual, and Political Freedom* (Chapel Hill: University of North Carolina Press, 2016), 73. Historians have excluded the slippage from braceros to undocumented workers from historical narratives because of political concerns. Official histories, as historian Mireya Loza writes, like those offered by "NMAH [National Museum of American History], the Bracero Justice Movement, and policy makers thus have engaged in the solidification of a 'bracero' identity that purposely divorces itself from that of the undocumented laborer. But, acknowledging that the flow of Mexican temporary workers was intricately tied to that of undocumented workers, or how easy it was to move in and out of these categories, would have made creating a cohesive narrative about bracero history difficult." Inclusion of legal braceros, she points out, is an important step toward a broader narrative of the United States. Nonetheless, excluding the undocumented people who did the labor that made our economy possible seems to me a gross gap in the historical narrative, however inconvenient it is for an uncomplicated story.

60. U.S. Congress. Senate Subcommittee on Labor and Labor-Management Relations, 1952, 743, quoted in Calavita, *Inside the State*, 39.

61. Otey Scruggs, *Braceros, "Wetbacks," and the Farm Labor Problem* (New York: Garland Publishers, 1988), 307, quoted in ibid., 34.

62. Nelson Lichtenstein, "Auto Worker Militancy and the Structure of Factory Life, 1937-1955," *Journal of American History* 67, no. 2 (September 1980): 335-353, 341.

63. Ibid., 341.

64. Racial and gender integration on the shop floor proved more difficult than simply issuing an order. While the AFL and the CIO tried to contain their workers and maintain the no-strike pledge, wildcat strikes still broke out, at least fifty in 1943 and '44, over shop-floor integration, using 2.5 million man-hours. White men refused to work with black men. White women refused to work with black women. White men wouldn't work with white women (unless they were limited in number and paid less for the same work). Some strikes were led by black workers, as whites would be given better work. White workers, in turn, would strike over integration. In Detroit, twenty thousand white workers at Packard walked off, contributing to a citywide race riot a week later. In Baltimore, white women walked out of the Western Electric plant, demanding racially segregated bathrooms. This back-and-forth, more often with white workers going on a short wildcat strike, continued through the war. Most manufacturers, if forced to hire black workers, tried to keep them separated from the whites, especially black women. By 1945, white workers had largely, if reluctantly, accepted that black workers would work in plants but still wanted shop-floor segregation. If the Wagner Act and FLSA defended the importance of industrial white men, the federal government, in wartime, celebrated white women and somewhat supported black men and women. Black men and women remained the last hired and first fired. With the end of the war, this socially precarious integration came undone, as did the industrial peace of wartime. The UAW, which was perhaps the most racially progressive union, did not support the seniority claims of black women as the war came to an end. While some white women might have wanted to return to "normal," for black women—married or not—normal was working, though at lower wages. Industrial work paid better than being a maid (and had the benefit of union and FLSA protections). James Wolfinger, "World War II Hate Strikes," in *The Encyclopedia of Strikes in American History*, eds. Aaron Brenner, Benjamin Day, and Immanuel Ness (New York: Routledge, 2015), 126; Megan Taylor Shockley, "Working for Democracy: Working-Class African-American Women, Citizenship, and Civil Rights in Detroit, 1940-1954," *Michigan Historical Review* 29, no. 2 (Fall 2003), 125-157, 144; Todd Michney, "Civil Rights Strikes," in *Encyclopedia of Strikes in American History*, 118; Lichtenstein, "Auto Worker Militancy," 347; Karen Tucker Anderson, "Last Hired, First Fired: Black Women Workers During World War II," *Journal of American History* 69, no. 1 (June 1982): 82-97.

65. The best account of Reuther's life and times, upon which this narrative is based, remains Nelson Lichtenstein, *The Most Dangerous Man in Detroit: Walter Reuther and the Fate of American Labor* (New York: Basic Books, 1995).

66. Lichtenstein, "Auto Worker Militancy," 351.

67. Ibid.

68. At Ford, starting in 1947, the foremen were, as historian Nelson Lichtenstein points out, "put on salary, told to wear ties and white shirts, given desk and special

parking privileges, and indoctrinated in the management-oriented 'human relations.'" Drawing a line between workers and management was not just legal but
organizational and cultural. Dressing like management, parking like management, and being paid like management were all of a piece to align the interests of
foremen and management. Ibid., 349.

69. Ramon C. Sevilla, "Employment Practices and Industrial Restructuring: A Case
    Study of the Semiconductor Industry in Silicon Valley, 1955-1991," PhD diss.,
    UCLA, 1992, 154.

70. Peter F. Drucker, introduction to Sloan, *My Years with General Motors*, v-vi.

71. Ibid., v.

72. Peter F. Drucker, *Concept of the Corporation* (New York: 1946; repr., Rout-
    ledge, 2017), 149-50.

73. Ibid., 227-28.

74. Ibid., 226.

75. Drucker, introduction to Sloan, *My Years with General Motors*, v.

76. Drucker, *Concept of the Corporation*, 5, 8.

77. Ibid., 21.

Chapter Two: Temporary Women

1. Sociologist Erin Hatton has done extensive work on the ways that temp agencies
   used gender to shape the early temp industry. Where her work and mine diverge is
   that she focuses much more on the discourse and advertising of temporary labor
   rather than the way it interweaves with the workplace. See Erin Hatton, "The
   Making of the Kelly Girl: Gender and the Origins of the Temp Industry in Postwar America," *Journal of Historical Sociology* 21, no. 1 (2008): 1-29, and Hatton,
   The Temp Economy: From Kelly Girls to Permatemps in Postwar America (Philadelphia: Temple University Press, 2011). The works of Leah Vosko are more concerned with political economy, but also from a sociological rather than a historical
   perspective. They are, nonetheless, required reading for an international context.
   Leah Vosko, *Temporary Work: The Gendered Rise of a Precarious Employment
   Relationship* (Toronto: University of Toronto Press, 2000); Leah Vosko, *Managing the Margins: Gender, Citizenship, and the International Regulation of Precarious Employment* (New York: Oxford University Press, 2011).

2. Elmer Winter, *A Woman's Guide to Earning a Good Living* (New York: Simon &
   Schuster, 1961), 58.

3. Elmer Winter, *Your Future as a Temporary Office Worker* (New York: Richard
   Rosens Press, 1968), 10.

4. Winter, *A Woman's Guide*, 58.

5. Ibid., 59.

6. Definitions of postwar work could not be conceived independently of gender and
   marriage. Historian Robert Self has recently argued that "male breadwinning
   was so taken for granted that it was not even acknowledged as an ideology, as a
   choice." Gender was the most basic way in which work was structured, and male
   work was intended to provide stability in the paycheck and authority in the home.
   Workers, in the aftermath of the Depression and war, did not just want the

highest wage, but a certain wage as part of a "secure future." As one personnel administrator explained, "The people who remember the early thirties won't forget those days in a hurry." Workers "laid off through no fault of their own," who had "lost face," were "ashamed and perplexed by the economic situation." Job security mattered not just for wages, but for a sense of self-worth. Robert Self, *All in the Family: The Realignment of American Democracy Since the 1960s* (New York: Hill and Wang, 2012), 18; Albert Hendrickson, "Human Relations in Business," *Proceedings of the National Office Management Association*, 1948, 52–53.

7. Other parts of this book show the rise of this belief about long-term work and long-term investment in the postwar corporation.

8. Other factors would include deindustrialization, offshoring, globalization, antilabor laws, technological stagnation, etc. Most of the literature focuses on the fall of unions or the movement of capital. Few historians examine alternative labor models. The only major historical work on temporary labor is Hatton, *The Temp Economy*, and her book focuses on the cultural reading of women without connecting it to changes in corporate organization or even to the larger contradiction of male temps. For a few books in this literature, see Jefferson Cowie, *Capital Moves: RCA's Seventy-Year Quest for Cheap Labor* (New York: New Press, 2001); Jefferson Cowie and Joseph Heathcott, eds., *Beyond the Ruins: The Meanings of Deindustrialization* (Ithaca, NY: Cornell University Press, 2003); Judith Stein, *Pivotal Decade: How the United States Traded Factories for Finance in the Seventies* (New Haven, CT: Yale University Press, 2010); Tyler Cowen, *The Great Stagnation: How America Ate All the Low-Hanging Fruit of Modern History, Got Sick, and Will (Eventually) Feel Better* (New York: Penguin, 2011); Kim Phillips-Fein, *Invisible Hands: The Businessmen's Crusade Against the New Deal* (New York: W. W. Norton & Company, 2010).

9. Winter, *A Woman's Guide*, 3.

10. Ibid.

11. R. H. Coase, "The Nature of the Firm," *Economica*, New Series 4, no. 1 (November 1937), 386–405. Manpower and temporary labor made possible a new way to think about labor and the firm. Only ten years earlier, in 1937, the economist Ronald Coase had published what would become an influential essay in which he argued that the only reason why firms existed at all, as opposed to every person constituting a company of one, was because market-based relationships were too expensive. In a world where connections cost nothing, we could all buy and sell commodities and services directly from one another. The cost of creating a firm in this imaginary frictionless market would prohibit its formation. Only in a world where the transaction costs of interacting with a market were high could the cost of a firm be justified. Coase conveyed this idea most simply in a 1932 letter to a colleague: "Think of the inconvenience (increased cost) if every time someone worked with someone else, there had to be a market transaction." Quoted in Coase, "The Nature of the Firm: Origin," *Journal of Law, Economics, & Organization* 4, no. 1 (1988): 4. Manpower sought to overcome this inconvenience by providing temporary, flexible labor as needed by the firm and as desired by the worker.

12. Winter, *A Woman's Guide*, 4.

13. Classified Ad 9, *Daily Tribune* (Chicago), June 21, 1948, B12; see Gunter Peck, *Reinventing Free Labor: Padrones and Immigrant Workers in the North American West, 1880-1930* (Cambridge, UK: Cambridge University Press, 2000).

14. Elmer Winter, *Cutting Costs Through the Effective Use of Temporary and Part-Time Help* (Waterford, CT: Prentice-Hall, 1965), 7.

15. Manpower, *Annual Report*, 1960, 12, folder 1, "Manpower, *Annual Reports*, 1959-1964," box 11, EWP.

16. "Manpower Proves Staying Power," *Milwaukee Sentinel*, April 1, 1996, folder 7, box 11, EWP.

17. Manpower Prospectus, September 29, 1959, 9, folder 1, box 11, EWP.

18. Winter, *Your Future*, 78.

19. Winter, *Cutting Costs*, 12-13.

20. William Kelly founded Russell Kelly Office Service in 1946 but didn't offer temps at clients' locations for a few years after that (www.kellyservices.com/global/about-us/company-information/background). Which temp agency was first, though, is not a particularly interesting question. What is interesting is that these services developed in the midst of the development of the postwar corporation. This book could have been written with Kelly at its center, save for the availability of Elmer Winter's archive. Manpower, moreover, was the bigger firm for many decades.

21. "Temporary Hiring Climbs Up the Ladder," *BusinessWeek*, July 15, 1961, 17.

22. Kelly Girl had roughly half the revenue of Manpower throughout the postwar period. The key difference between the firms was that Kelly Girl did not franchise, which allowed Manpower to grow much more rapidly, as will be discussed later. See ibid.

23. Irwin Ross, "For Rent: Secretaries, Salesmen, Physicists, and Human Guinea Pigs," *Fortune*, October 1968, 164, folder 7, "Speeches, 1971-1973," box 13, EWP.

24. Winter, *Your Future*, 27.

25. Winter, *Cutting Costs*, 70-71.

26. Manpower, *Annual Report*, 1961, 5, folder 1, "Manpower, *Annual Reports*, 1959-1964," box 11, EWP.

27. Break-even calculation by author.

28. Winter, *Cutting Costs*, 3.

29. Ibid., 70-71.

30. Elmer Winter, "Remarks Before the New York Society of Security Analysts," January 26, 1961, 4, folder 7, "Speeches, 1971-1973," box 13, EWP.

31. Winter, *Your Future*, 24.

32. Ibid., 26.

33. Ibid., 43.

34. We will return to this distinction between jobs and tasks later in the book. It is an essential part of how we should be thinking about the usefulness of artificial intelligence.

35. Winter, *Cutting Costs*, 94.

36. Ibid., 95.

37. Winter, *Your Future*, 51.

38. Ibid., 109.

39. Winter, *Cutting Costs*, 33.
40. Ibid., 84.
41. Ibid., 90.
42. Joyce Brothers, *So You're Thinking of Returning to Office Work* (n.p: Manpower, 1966), 5, Special Collections, Schlesinger Library, Harvard University, Cambridge, MA.
43. Winter, *Your Future*, 37.
44. Brothers, *So You're Thinking*, 7.
45. Ibid., 15.
46. Ibid., 16.
47. Winter, *Cutting Costs*, 17.
48. Winter, *Your Future*, 123.
49. National Manpower Council, *Womanpower: A Statement by the National Manpower Council with Chapters by the Council Staff* (New York: Columbia University Press, 1957), 4.
50. Elmer Winter, "To Californian Stockbrokers on November 12, 1962," folder 12, "Speeches, 1962," box 12, EWP.
51. Manpower, *Annual Report*, 1962, 1.
52. Winter, "Before the New York Society of Security Analysts," January 26, 1961, 13, folder 7, "Speeches, 1971-1973," box 13, EWP.
53. Winter, *Your Future*, 34.
54. Ibid., 51.
55. Ibid., 55.
56. Manpower, *Annual Report*, 1962, 1, folder 1, "Manpower, *Annual Reports*, 1959-1964," box 11, EWP.
57. Winter, *Your Future*, 46.
58. National Manpower Council, *Womanpower*, 103.
59. Brothers, *So You're Thinking*, 23.
60. National Manpower Council, *Womanpower*, 103.
61. Winter, *Cutting Costs*, 44-45.
62. National Manpower Council, *Womanpower*, 81.
63. This observation is not new, but it is important to reiterate. See bell hooks, *Feminist Theory: From Margin to Center* (Boston: South End Press, 1984).
64. Brothers, *So You're Thinking*, 24.
65. Winter, *Your Future*, 70.
66. Ibid., 96.
67. Ibid., 123.
68. Ibid., 119-121.
69. Ibid., 69.
70. Ibid., 70. The categories used by the Manpower survey are frustratingly open-ended at the top and bottom, like many postwar surveys. The salary of $100 a week is roughly $32,000 a year in 2015; $200 a week is roughly $64,000 in 2015. This calculation was done using the Consumer Price Index and assuming year-round work.
71. Ibid., 20.
72. Ibid., 91-93.

73. Ibid., 21.

74. Winter, "Before the New York Society of Security Analysts," January 26, 1961.

75. Winter, *Your Future*, 64.

76. The argument here is very similar to today's debates on "choice" versus "necessity" in freelance labor.

77. Agnes Ash, "Job Agency in a Station Wagon Offers Part-Time Office Work," *New York Times*, May 28, 1957.

78. Winter, *Your Future*, 99.

Chapter Three: **Consulting Men**

1. Elizabeth Haas Edersheim, *McKinsey's Marvin Bower* (Hoboken, NJ: John Wiley & Sons, 2004), 60.

2. McKinsey & Company, *Supplementing Successful Management* (1940; repr., New York: McKinsey & Company, n.d.). The version I have is an undated copy that I believe is from around 1970. The inside cover has the card of San Francisco partner John Neukom, so I believe it must have been a gift to a prospective client; Marvin Bower, *Perspective on McKinsey* (New York: McKinsey & Co., 1979), 136.

3. Bower, *Perspective*, 55. *Top Management Notes* lasted only a few years but the spirit was resurrected in 1964 with *McKinsey Quarterly*. In the intervening years, firm members penned various articles and essays to send to clients. *McKinsey Quarterly* initially was intended as a compendium of reprints, but would become a signature reputation-building instrument for the firm. Ibid., 137-38.

4. John G. Neukom, *McKinsey Memoirs: A Personal Perspective* (New York: self-published, 1975), 10-11.

5. Ibid., 34.

6. McKinsey & Co., *Supplementing*, 8.

7. Ibid.

8. Bower, *Perspective*, 143.

9. Ibid., 142; David Ogilvy, *An Autobiography* (New York: John Wiley & Sons, 1997), 136.

10. Edersheim, *McKinsey's Marvin Bower*, 80-81.

11. Ibid., 20.

12. Association of Consulting Management Engineers (ACME), "Interviewing and Testing Techniques Used in Selecting Management Consulting Personnel" (self-published, 1961), 1.

13. Ibid., 2.

14. Today, consultant interviews are so standard that there is a book, *Case in Point*, which every McKinsey hopeful totes to Starbucks to study. See Marc P. Cosentino, *Case in Point: Complete Case Interview Preparation*, 9th ed. (Santa Barbara, CA: Burgee Press, 2016).

15. ACME, "Interviewing and Testing Techniques," 9.

16. Consulting was, like other jobs, structured around a breadwinner model but, unlike other jobs, with the breadwinner absent for long periods of time. Some firms went so far as to interview the applicant's wife "for all key jobs and for all men sent out of the country. Sometimes at their home; sometimes at our home."

Interviewers looked at a wife's ability to "manage a household without her husband's constant presence." Consultants would, of course, be traveling. Ibid., 12.

17. Ibid., 3.
18. Ibid., 4.
19. Bower, *Perspective*, 202.
20. Ibid., 200–202.
21. Edersheim, *McKinsey's Marvin Bower*, 95.
22. Bower, *Perspective*, 180.
23. Edersheim, *McKinsey's Marvin Bower*, 85.
24. Neukom, *McKinsey Memoirs*, 58–60.
25. McKinsey & Co., *Supplementing*, 9.
26. Ibid., 59.
27. Bower, *Perspective*, 254.
28. Ibid., 189.
29. Ibid., 185.
30. Ibid., 309.
31. Ibid., 207.
32. Edersheim, *McKinsey's Marvin Bower*, 55.
33. J. E. Ellsworth, "Management Consulting in the Smaller Company," *Conference Board Record*, July 1969, 27.
34. McKinsey & Co., *Supplementing*, 24.
35. "How We Work on Studies: Orientation Material for New Professionals: Training Coordinators Meeting," *The Strategic Approach to Consulting*, October 1985, 10, box 7, folder 9, "Research Materials About Marvin Bower and McKinsey & Co., 1901–1984," MBM.
36. Bower, *Perspective*, 172.
37. Ibid., 137.
38. Ibid., 130.
39. Ibid., 131.
40. The problem of professionalization in consulting is treated exhaustively in Christopher McKenna, *The World's Newest Profession: Management Consulting in the Twentieth Century* (New York: Cambridge University Press, 2006).
41. McKinsey & Co., *Supplementing*, 13.
42. Bower, *Perspective*, 121.
43. McKinsey & Co., *Supplementing*, 16.
44. Bower, *Perspective*, 182.
45. Ibid., 124.
46. Ibid., 181–83.
47. Ibid., 237.
48. Ibid., 253.
49. Ibid., 241.
50. Michael Barratt, "The Change Makers," *McKinsey Quarterly* 5, no. 4 (Spring 1969): 27.
51. McKinsey & Co., *Supplementing*, 9.
52. Ibid., 11.
53. Ibid., 255.

54. Neukom, *McKinsey Memoirs*, 27.
55. Ibid., 62.
56. "How We Work on Studies," 7.
57. Neukom, *McKinsey Memoirs*, 62.
58. Ibid., 15.
59. Ibid., 5.
60. ACME, Subcommittee on Professional Reports, "Survey Report Practice," Spring 1954, 4.
61. Ellsworth, "Management Consulting in the Smaller Company," 29.
62. Neukom, *McKinsey Memoirs*, 57.
63. "How We Work on Studies," 9.
64. McKinsey & Co., *Supplementing*, 10.
65. Ibid., 304.
66. Ibid., 214.
67. Ibid., 222.
68. Ibid., 220.
69. Ibid., 223.
70. Ibid., 58–59. CPI calculation by author.
71. Ibid., 222.
72. Ibid., 213.
73. Ibid., 222.
74. John Miner, "The Management Consulting Firm as a Source of High-Level Managerial Talent," *Academy of Management Journal* 16, no. 2 (June 1973): 263.
75. Bower, *Perspective*, 213.
76. Ibid., 224.
77. Edersheim, *McKinsey's Marvin Bower*, 62.

Chapter Four: **Marginal Men**

1. Manpower Prospectus, September 29, 1959, 3, folder 1, "Manpower, Annual Reports, 1959–1964," box 11, EWP.
2. Willard Kelly, "The Wetback Issue," *I&N Reporter*, January 1954, 37.
3. Ibid.
4. Argyle Mackey, "Highlights of 1953," *I&N Reporter*, January 1954, 35–36.
5. INS, *Annual Report*, 1955, 14–15, USCIS.
6. Ibid.
7. INS, *Annual Report*, 1962, 61–62, USCIS. Added "Aliens Deported" and "Aliens Required to Deport" from Tables 24 and 24A. One could add an additional 12,610 Mexicans who were sent under "direct required departures under safeguards," and who were "chiefly Mexicans who entered without inspection," to make the total approximately 30,000. The larger point remains the same.
8. INS, *Annual Report*, 1962, 53.
9. INS, *Annual Report*, 1964, 8, USCIS.
10. Manpower, *Annual Report*, 1961, 18.
11. Elmer Winter, *Cutting Costs Through the Effective Use of Temporary and Part-Time Help* (Waterford, CT: Prentice-Hall, 1965), 10.

12. Manpower, *Annual Report*, 1960, 1, folder 1, "Manpower, *Annual Reports*, 1959–1964," box 11, EWP.
13. Winter, *Cutting Costs*, 9.
14. Ibid., 9.
15. Irwin Ross, "For Rent: Secretaries, Salesmen, Physicists, and Human Guinea Pigs," *Fortune*, October 1968, 238, folder 7, "Speeches, 1971–1973," box 13, EWP.
16. Elmer Winter, "Managing Temporary Employees for Maximum Cost-Control," *Human Resource Management* 2, no. 1 (1963): 7.
17. Ross, "For Rent," 238.
18. Elmer Winter, "To Californian Stockbrokers on November 12, 1962," 9, folder 12, "Speeches, 1962," box 12, EWP.
19. Elmer Winter, "Multiple City Franchisee Seminar Closing Remarks," November 17, 1967, 23, folder 8, "Speeches, 1967," box 12, EWP.
20. "Decisions and Orders of the Board," 157 NLRB No. 1, 1734 (1966), 1731–32.
21. "Decisions and Orders of the Board," 164 NLRB No. 1, 1194 (1967), 287.
22. Elmer Winter, "A Challenge to the People of Milwaukee: Presented to Greater Milwaukee Committee October 11, 1965," 1–2, folder 7, "Speeches, 1963–1965," box 12, EWP.
23. Elmer Winter, "Speeches 1968," 2, folder 1, box 13, EWP.
24. Carl Rowan, "City Youths Need Job Help," *Pittsburgh Press*, June 2, 1970, 22.
25. "Found! Summer Jobs for Teen-agers," *Better Homes and Gardens*, May 1965, folder 8, "Youth + Equal Opportunity Council," box 11, EWP.
26. Karl Detzer, "There's No Job Too Tough for Youthpower," *Reader's Digest*, June 1966, folder 8, "Youth + Equal Opportunity Council," box 11, EWP.
27. "Found!," *Better Homes and Gardens*.
28. "Youths Work to Find Work for Youthful Work Seekers," *Milwaukee Sentinel*, August 24, 1968.
29. "Youthpower Beacon for Self-Help," *Milwaukee Sentinel*, August 12, 1965, folder 8, "Youth + Equal Opportunity Council," box 11, EWP.
30. "Found!," *Better Homes and Gardens*.
31. Ibid.
32. Judith Martin, "Manpower Without Women; It Turns to Youthpower," *Herald Tribune*, May 24, 1966, folder 8, "Youth + Equal Opportunity Councel," box 11, EWP.
33. "Job Campaign Started to Aid Disadvantaged," *Milwaukee Sentinel*, February 20, 1969, folder 8, "Youth + Equal Opportunity Council," box 11, EWP.
34. "Part-Time Jobs Are on the Rise for Women," *Washington Post*, May 19, 1966.
35. "Teens Offer Jr. Dial-A-Job," *Chicago Tribune*, August 6, 1967.
36. "Young Job Seekers Find a Friend," *BusinessWeek*, July 6, 1968, folder 8, "Youth + Equal Opportunity Council," Box 11, EWP.
37. Ibid.
38. Winter, "A Challenge to the People of Milwaukee," 7.
39. Winter, "untitled speech," 4, folder 1, "Speeches, 1968," box 13, EWP.
40. Winter, "A Challenge to the People of Milwaukee," 6–7.
41. Winter, "untitled speech," 15, folder 1, "Speeches, 1968," box 13, EWP.
42. Ibid., 15.

43. Winter, "A Challenge to the People of Milwaukee," 13; paraphrase from a quote in Bernard W. Harleston, "Higher Education for the Negro," *Atlantic Monthly*, November 1965, 139-43.
44. Winter, "A Challenge," 9.
45. Elmer Winter, "The Business of Business Is America—the Businessman's Role in Overcoming the Urban Crisis," November 19, 1968, 2, folder 1, "Speeches, 1968," box 13, EWP.
46. Winter, "untitled speech," 10, folder 1, "Speeches, 1968," box 13, EWP.
47. Winter, "The Business of Business Is America," 8-9.
48. "Summer Job Problem," *Chicago Daily Defender*, June 20, 1966.
49. "Youthpower Inc. Extends Operation to November," *Chicago Daily Defender*, October 3, 1967, 6.
50. Ibid.
51. "Youthpower Inc. to Get Summer Jobs for Teens," *Chicago Daily Defender*, June 8, 1968.
52. "Youths Work to Find Work for Youthful Work Seekers," *Milwaukee Sentinel*, August 24, 1968.
53. "Youthpower: Jobs, No Frills," *Chicago Tribune*, April 28, 1968.
54. Winter, "Multiple City Franchisee Seminar Closing Remarks," 20-21.
55. "Young Job Seekers Find a Friend," *BusinessWeek*, July 6, 1968, folder 8, "Youth + Equal Opportunity Council," box 11, EWP; all dollar adjustments are CPI-weighted with BLS data. These numbers should be considered rough estimates. By limiting the number of significant digits, I hope to emphasize the roughness of the CPI adjustment. https://data.bls.gov/cgi-bin/cpicalc.pl.
56. "Firm Ends Your Job Plan Role," *Milwaukee Sentinel*, April 24, 1975.
57. Ross, "For Rent," 238.
58. Elmer Winter, "Statement to National Alliance of Businessmen, June 14, 1968," 1, folder 1, box 13, EWP.
59. "750 File for Jobs with Youthpower," *Milwaukee Sentinel*, June 13, 1972.
60. Mary Spletter, "Youth Summer Job Outlook," *Milwaukee Sentinel*, April 4, 1970.
61. INS, *Annual Report*, 1966, 72, USCIS. Calculation by author.
62. INS, *Annual Report*, 1965, 8, USCIS.
63. INS, *Annual Report*, 1966, 11.
64. Ibid.
65. INS, *Annual Report*, 1967, 11, USCIS.
66. INS, *Annual Report*, 1966, 27.
67. Leonard Chapman, "Ladies and Gentlemen," 1974, "JV6455.C3C Chapman, Leonard F., Collection of Addresses, Testimony, Speeches, etc.," vol. 1, 1, US-CIS. (These speeches are in two sequentially arranged binders by date).
68. Leonard Chapman, "Naturalization Ceremonies, Washington D.C.," May 11, 1976, "JV6455.C3C Chapman, Leonard F., Collection of Addresses, Testimony, Speeches, etc.," vol. 2, USCIS.
69. Leonard Chapman, "American Legion National Commanders Banquet," May 5, 1976, "JV6455.C3C Chapman, Leonard F., Collection of Addresses, Testimony, Speeches, etc.," vol. 2, USCIS.

70. Leonard Chapman, "Statement by Leonard F. Chapman, Jr." September 24, 1975, "JV6455.C3C Chapman, Leonard F., Collection of Addresses, Testimony, Speeches, etc.," USCIS.

71. Leonard Chapman, Immigration and Naturalization Service, "The Impact of Illegal Aliens in the Southwest: Briefing Before Members of the House of Representatives Who Represent Congressional Districts Along the Southwest Border," December 10, 1974, 12, "JV6455.C3C Chapman, Leonard F., Collection of Addresses, Testimony, Speeches, etc.," USCIS.

72. Chapman, "American Legion National Commanders' Banquet," 3.

73. Leonard Chapman, "Houston, Texas, January 23, 1975," 11, "JV6455.C3C Chapman, Leonard F., Collection of Addresses, Testimony, Speeches, etc.," USCIS.

74. Leonard Chapman, "Remarks Presented at Outreach Program Ceremonies Good Shepherd (El Buen Pastor) Church, Washington, D.C., Thursday, April 28, 1977," 4, "JV6455.C3C Chapman, Leonard F., Collection of Addresses, Testimony, Speeches, etc.," USCIS.

75. Chapman, "American Legion National Commanders' Banquet," May 5, 1976, 9.

76. Ibid.

77. Leonard Chapman, "Ladies and Gentlemen," 11.

78. Community Research Associates, *Undocumented Immigrants: Their Impact on the County of San Diego, May 1980*, 33, USCIS.

79. "1966 Negotiation with the Common Laborers Union in Houston, Texas," 1, folder "Union Historical, vol. 2: f-q," box 11126, AGC.

80. "AGC-CEA Joint Negotiating Committee," August 8, 1966, 1, "Union Historical, vol. 2: f-q," box 11126, AGC.

81. Interview with Leonel J. Castillo by Oscar J. Martinez, 1980, "Interview no. 532," 2, Institute of Oral History, DigitalCommons@UTEP, University of Texas at El Paso.

82. Ibid., 8.

83. Ibid., 11.

84. Ibid., 75.

85. Interview with Leonel J. Castillo by Kerry Wince, September 29, 2006, Houston Oral History Project, http://digital.houstonlibrary.org/cdm/singleitem/collection/oralhistory/id/17.

86. Interview with Leonel J. Castillo by Oscar J. Martinez, "Interview no. 532."

87. *Chispas* literally means "sparks," but in this context it means "unexpected raindrops," as in the Americans would leave at the first sign of rain.

88. Interview with Leonel J. Castillo by Oscar J. Martinez, "Interview no. 532," 33.

89. Leonel Castillo, "Commonwealth Club of California," June 8, 1979, 7, "JV 6455.C14C Collection of Addresses, Testimony, Speeches, etc.," vol. 2, USCIS.

90. Leonel Castillo, "Illegal Aliens and Your City Budget," "Attorney General's Management Seminar, FBI Academy, December 15, 1977," 2, "JV 6455.C14C Collection of Addresses, Testimony, Speeches, etc.," vol. 1, USCIS.

91. Leonel Castillo, "La Raza National Lawyers Association Convention," August 6, 1977, 2, "JV 6455.C14C Collection of Addresses, Testimony, Speeches, etc.," vol. 1, USCIS.

92. Leonel Castillo, "Attorney General's Management Seminar, FBI Academy, December 15, 1977," 1.

Chapter Five: **Temporary Business**

1. Marvin Bower, *Perspective on McKinsey* (New York: McKinsey & Co., 1979), 58-59.
2. Ibid., 67-70.
3. Ibid., 74.
4. Ibid., 77-79.
5. Manpower Prospectus, September 29, 1959, 3, folder 1, "Manpower, *Annual Reports*, 1959-1964," box 11, EWP.
6. Ibid.
7. Elmer Winter, "Before the New York Society of Security Analysts," January 26, 1961, 13, folder 7, "Speeches, 1971-1973," box 13, EWP.
8. Irwin Ross, "For Rent: Secretaries, Salesmen, Physicists, and Human Guinea Pigs," *Fortune*, October 1968, 238, in folder 7, "Speeches, 1971-1973," box 13, EWP.
9. Winter, "Before the New York Society of Security Analysts," 3.
10. Manpower Prospectus, September 29, 1959, 5.
11. Ibid.
12. Ibid. Calculation by author.
13. Manpower, *Annual Report*, 1971, 7. (After 1971, Manpower annual reports are from the Mergent digital archive, Mergent.com.)
14. Manpower, *Annual Report*, 1961, 12, folder 1, "Manpower, *Annual Reports*, 1959-1964," box 11, EWP.
15. Elmer Winter, "Before the New York Society of Security Analysts," 3.
16. Manpower, *Annual Report*, 1962, 1.
17. Manpower Prospectus, September 29, 1959, 3.
18. Ibid., 1.
19. Ibid., 9.
20. Winter, "Before the New York Society of Security Analysts," 4.
21. Ibid., 11.
22. Manpower Prospectus, September 29, 1959, 5.
23. Bower, *Perspective*, 214.
24. The earlier version of the partnership had also developed obligations to retired partners, who received a fraction of the earnings of the firm. The reorganization eliminated that obligation.
25. Bower, *Perspective*, 272-73.
26. Ibid., 214.
27. Ibid., 215.
28. Ibid., 216.
29. Curt Schleier, "Consulting Innovator Marvin Bower: His Vision Made McKinsey & Co. a Pioneer," *Investor's Business Daily*, November 9, 2000, 4.
30. Bower, *Perspective*, 270.
31. Ibid., 83, 279.

32. John G. Neukom, *McKinsey Memoirs: A Personal Perspective* (New York: self-published, 1975), 49.

33. Philip Shay, *Management Consulting in the 1970s and Beyond* (n.p.: Association of Consulting Management Engineers, 1971), 5.

34. Elizabeth Haas Edersheim, *McKinsey's Marvin Bower* (Hoboken, NJ: John Wiley & Sons, 2004), 7; Bower, *Perspective*, 93.

35. Bower, *Perspective*, 84.

36. Ibid., 88.

37. Ibid., 86–87.

38. Hugh Parker to Marvin Bower, October 29, 1994, box 11, folder 38, Shell—various pieces, MBM.

39. Conference Board, *Organizing for Global Competitiveness: The Matrix Design* (1994), 28, box 11, folder 38, Shell—various pieces, MBM.

40. Hugh Parker to Rajat Gupta, October 29, 1994, box 11, folder 38, Shell—various pieces, MBM; Carl Motished, "Shell Hires McKinsey to Review Group Structure," *New York Times*, September 19, 1994.

41. Bower, *Perspective*, 91.

42. Ibid., 88.

43. Ibid., 89.

44. Ibid., 93.

45. Per Berg Anderson, "Build Firm: Becoming International," 6, box 11, folder 38, Shell—various pieces, MBM.

46. Marvin Bower, "On Our Firm's History & Guiding Principles," 28, box 9, folder 12, 1997-2000—Oral History Interviews, 1997, MBM.

47. Christopher McKenna, *The World's Newest Profession: Management Consulting in the Twentieth Century* (New York: Cambridge University Press, 2006), 177.

48. Bower, *Perspective*, 97.

49. Ibid., 96.

50. Ibid., 103-10.

51. Ibid., 186.

52. Peter Drucker, "Global Management," in *Challenge to Leadership: Managing a Changing World*, Conference Board (New York: Free Press, 1973), 232-33, quoted in Bower, *Perspective*, 300.

53. Bower, *Perspective*, 95.

54. Neukom, *McKinsey Memoirs*, 24, 46.

55. Bower, *Perspective*, 117; Neukom, *McKinsey Memoirs*, 25.

56. Bower, *Perspective*, 94.

57. Hugh Parker, "The Change Makers," *McKinsey Quarterly* (Spring 1969), 26.

58. Elmer Winter, "Remarks Before the National Association of Investment Clubs," October 21, 1961, folder 7, "Speeches, 1971-1973," box 13, EWP.

59. Ross, "For Rent," 238.

60. Manpower, *Annual Report*, 1962, 1.

61. Ross, "For Rent," 164.

62. "European Businessmen Seen as Shirking Social Responsibilities," *Milwaukee Sentinel*, October 22, 1968, folder 7, "Speeches, 1971-1973," box 13, EWP.

63. Quoted in Manpower, *Annual Report*, 1974, 5, Mergent.com.
64. Ibid.
65. Ross, "For Rent," 238.
66. Manpower, *Annual Report*, 1974, 15.
67. Ross, "For Rent," 238.
68. Manpower, *Annual Report*, 1971, 7.
69. Ross, "For Rent," 164.
70. Elmer Winter, "This Is Manpower's 'Happening,'" July 8, 1968, 2, folder 1, box 13, EWP.
71. Bower, *Perspective*, 271.
72. Hugh Parker, "Marvin Bower Tribute—Boca Raton," 12, box 9, folder 12, 1997–2000—Oral History Interviews, 1997, MBM.
73. Andy Pearson, "Marvin Bower Tribute—Boca Raton", ibid., 9 (Eisenhower's inauguration, to be exact).
74. Bower, *Perspective*, 230.
75. Ibid., 287.
76. Ibid., 290.

Chapter Six: **Office Automation and Technology Consulting**

1. Arthur Gager, "Determining the Need for Office Machines," *Proceedings of the National Office Managers Association*, 1952, 27.
2. Elmer Winter, *Cutting Costs Through the Effective Use of Temporary and Part-Time Help* (Waterford, CT: Prentice-Hall, 1965), 81.
3. "There's Profit in Using Temporary Help," *Bankers Monthly*, August 15, 1965, 40.
4. Ibid.
5. "Temporary Hiring Climbs Up the Ladder," *BusinessWeek*, July 15, 1961, 17.
6. Elmer Winter, "A Speech on Planned Staffing," c. 1968-1969, 7, folder 9, box 13, EWP.
7. Elmer Winter, "You Have to Be Twins," March 25, 1964, 2, folder 7, "Speeches, 1963-1965," box 12, EWP.
8. Elmer Winter, "Speech for Europe," April 1, 1960, 4-7, folder 5, "Speeches, 1958-1961," box 12, EWP.
9. Elmer Winter, "Before the New York Society of Security Analysts," January 26, 1961, 9-10, folder 7, "Speeches, 1971-1973," box 13, EWP.
10. Winter, "A Speech on Planned Staffing," 6.
11. Manpower, *Annual Report*, 1972, 5, Mergent.com.
12. Elmer Winter, "How to Effectively Purchase Services from a Temporary Help Service Firm," n.d., 3, folder 9, box 13, EWP.
13. Winter, "A Speech on Planned Staffing," 7.
14. Ibid., 22.
15. Winter, "A Speech on Planned Staffing," 6.
16. Elmer Winter, "Managing Temporary Employees for Maximum Cost-Control," *Human Resource Management* 2, no. 1 (1963): 8.
17. Winter, "A Speech on Planned Staffing," 19-20.

18. Ibid., 4.

19. Now known as Securian Financial Group but still in St. Paul.

20. Winter, "A Speech on Planned Staffing," 7. Emphasis in original.

21. Ibid., 10.

22. Ibid.

23. Ibid., 18.

24. Ibid., 17.

25. Winter, *Cutting Costs*, 11.

26. Ibid.

27. This question of "core" corporate functions will be further developed elsewhere in the book, but here it is essential to show that temporary labor enables that question to be asked.

28. Manpower, *Annual Report*, 1962, 1, folder 1, "Manpower, *Annual Reports*, 1959-1964," box 11, EWP.

29. Elmer Winter, "To Californian Stockbrokers on November 12, 1962," 4, folder 12, "Speeches, 1962," box 12, EWP.

30. Manpower, *Annual Report*, 1961, 9.

31. Winter, *Cutting Costs*, 70-71.

32. Interview with Bill Holland, n.d., tape 2, 4, folder "Interviews & Bios He-Hz," box 7, PWC. This archive of material was collected when Price Waterhouse and Coopers & Lybrand merged in 1998. Interviews, though undated, are from around then.

33. Interview with Felix Kaufman, n.d., tape 1, 1-24, folder "Interviews & Bios J-Ke," box 7, PWC.

34. Interview with Fred Herr, n.d., 1, 34142.doc, box 36, PWC. The exact names of the firms involved are not entirely correct. There were many mergers over this period that are only incidental to the story. The core firm was Lybrand, Ross Bros. and Montgomery (1898), which merged in 1957 to form an international consultancy named Coopers & Lybrand, which in 1998 merged with Price Waterhouse to form PricewaterhouseCoopers (PWC). For narrative's sake, during this period I am referring to the firm as Coopers & Lybrand. Though the collection varied, the Big Eight accounting firms, as of the 1970s, were Arthur Andersen; Arthur Young; Coopers & Lybrand; Ernst & Ernst; Haskins & Sells; Peat, Marwick, Mitchell; Price Waterhouse; and Touche Ross. As outlined by federal investigations and published as *The Accounting Establishment*, these firms controlled the organizations (the American Institute of Certified Public Accountants, Financial Accounting Foundation, and Financial Accounting Standards Board) that the SEC recognized as the arbiters of accounting standards, which they then applied to the Big Eight. The Big Eight defined accounting. *The Accounting Establishment: A Staff Study* (Washington, D.C.: U.S. Government Printing Office, 1976), 3.

35. Interview with Fred Herr, 2-3.

36. Interview with Felix Kaufman, n.d., 1-15, 3296-1.doc, box 36, PWC.

37. Ibid., 1-17.

38. Interview with Felix Kaufman, tape 1, folder "Interviews & Bios—J-Ke," 1-24.

39. Kaufman, 1-17.

40. Lee Engel, "CPA as a Management Adviser," *The Office*, July 1969, 14.
41. Ibid., 4–15.
42. Interview with Bill Holland, tape 1, folder "Interviews & Bios He–Hz," box 7, PWC.
43. Interview with Fred Herr, 36.
44. Ibid., 8.
45. Ibid., 9.
46. Ibid., 8.
47. Interview with Bill Holland, tape 1, folder "Interviews & Bios He–Hz," box 7.
48. "Firm Council Candidate, Fred C. Herr," n.d., 4, folder "Interviews & Bios He–Hz," box 7, PWC.
49. Interview with Fred Herr, 27.
50. Winter, *Cutting Costs*, 6–7.
51. Winter, *Your Future as a Temporary Office Worker* (New York: Richard Rosens Press, 1968), 90.
52. Ibid., 29.
53. Manpower, *Annual Report* 1974, 5.
54. Winter, *Cutting Costs*, 4.
55. Winter, *Your Future*, 126.
56. "Temporary Survey," (c. 1974), folder 951, n.p., folder 951, series IV, Industry-Based Committees, 9to5.

Chapter Seven: The Fall of the American Corporation

1. John Kenneth Galbraith, "The Future of the Industrial System," *McKinsey Quarterly* (Summer, 1967), 26.
2. John Kenneth Galbraith, *The New Industrial State* (Boston: Houghton Mifflin Company, 1969), 57.
3. Ibid., 167.
4. Ibid., 189.
5. Galbraith, "The Future of the Industrial System," 26.
6. Ibid.
7. Ibid., 6.
8. Elmer L. Winter, *Complete Guide to Making a Public Stock Offering* (Englewood Cliffs, NJ: Prentice-Hall, 1962).
9. Elizabeth A. Fones-Wolf, *Selling Free Enterprise: The Business Assault on Labor and Liberalism, 1945–60* (Champaign, IL: University of Illinois Press, 1994).
10. Galbraith, *The New Industrial State*, 28.
11. Ibid., 81.
12. William Rothschild, *The Secret to GE's Success* (New York: McGraw-Hill, 2007), 102. Rothschild was a corporate strategist with General Electric, where he worked from the 1950s to the '80s.
13. Ralph Cordiner, *New Frontiers for Professional Managers* (New York: McGraw-Hill, 1956), 43.

14. Ibid., 11.
15. Rothschild, *The Secret*, 102; Cordiner, *New Frontiers*, 29.
16. Cordiner, *New Frontiers*, 43.
17. Ibid., 44.
18. Ibid.
19. Rothschild, *The Secret*, 108.
20. Ibid., 103.
21. Ibid., 112.
22. Ibid., 162.
23. Ibid., 143.
24. Ralph Winter, "Miscellany Corp.," *Wall Street Journal*, January 31, 1967, 1. Some profitable corporations looked to buy companies with losses so as to reduce their taxes, rather than give their windfall profits to the U.S. government. Textron enjoyed exemption from federal taxes until 1964 due to these "tax carry-forward" losses. One interpretation of the rise of the conglomerate points to this tax avoidance as their origin. The problem with this interpretation is that the Federal Trade Commission, in a 1948 investigation, sought out these new conglomerates but could find only one in the country, despite an enormous rise in mergers during and after World War II. "The Celler-Kefauver Act: The First 27 Years," *A Study Prepared by Willard Mueller for the Subcommittee on Monopolies and Commercial Law, Committee on the Judiciary, U.S. House of Representatives*, 95th Congress, 2nd Session, December 1978 (Washington, D.C.: U.S. Government Printing Office, 1978), 7; Robert Sobel, *The Age of Giant Corporations: A Microeconomic History of American Business, 1914-1992*, 3rd ed. (Westport, CT: Praeger, 1993), 196.
25. For the best history of U.S. Steel, see Kenneth Warren, *Big Steel: The First Century of the United States Steel Corporation 1901-2001* (Pittsburgh, PA: University of Pittsburgh, 2001); Willard Mueller, "The Celler-Kefauver Act: Sixteen Years of Enforcement," Staff Report to the Antitrust Subcommittee of the House Judiciary Committee, October 16, 1967 (Washington, D.C.: U.S. Government Printing Office, 1967), 3. Mueller wrote the report while he was the director of the Bureau of Economics at the Federal Trade Commission.
26. Max Ways, "Antitrust in an Era of Radical Change," *Fortune*, March 1961, 128-31.
27. Winter, "Miscellany Corp.," 1.
28. Senator Carey Estes Kefauver, 96 Congressional Record 16452, quoted in U.S. House of Representatives, Committee on the Judiciary, "Investigation of Conglomerate Corporations," 91st Congress, 2nd Session, serial no. 91-23, Part 7, 3.
29. Mueller, "The Celler-Kefauver Act: Sixteen Years of Enforcement," 4. Between 1950 and 1967, the federal government launched 801 antimerger cases but without any big conglomerate breakups. Ways, "Antitrust in an Era of Radical Change," 128-31.
30. Textron, *Annual Report*, 1956.
31. Harvey Segal, "The Urge to Merge," *New York Times Magazine*, October 27, 1968, SM32.

32. Stanley H. Brown, *Ling: The Rise, Fall and Return of a Texas Titan* (New York: Athenaeum, 1972), 44-49. Ling also was not Asian American (he was German Catholic), though business correspondents who had never met him sometimes thought so.

33. Ibid., 79; "Business: The Conglomerates' War to Reshape Industry," *Time*, March 7, 1969.

34. Brown, *Ling*, 49.

35. Ibid., 51.

36. Robert Sobel, *The Rise and Fall of the Conglomerate Kings* (Fairless Hills, PA: Beard Books, 1999), 80.

37. James Tanner, "Road to Riches," *Wall Street Journal*, May 16, 1960, 1.

38. Brown, *Ling*, 56; Sobel, *Rise and Fall*, 81.

39. James Tanner, "Ling's Empire," *Wall Street Journal*, August 18, 1967; Sobel, *Rise and Fall*, 81.

40. Brown, *Ling*, 57.

41. Sobel, *Rise and Fall*, 83.

42. For more on the relationship between the South and the defense industry—what Bruce Schulman calls Fortress Dixie—see Bruce Schulman, *From Cottonbelt to Sunbelt: Federal Policy, Economic Development, and the Transformation of the South, 1938-1980* (New York: Oxford University Press, 1991).

43. Sobel, *Age of Giant Corporations*, 199. This example of conglomerate financing is drawn from Sobel's work.

44. Terry Robards, "FTC to Study Rights to Be a Conglomerate," *New York Times*, July 14, 1968, F1.

45. "Corporations: Into the $1 Billion Club," *Time*, August 20, 1965.

46. Lee Burton, "The Merger Surge," *Wall Street Journal*, September 19, 1967, 1.

47. Brown, *Ling*, 86-87.

48. Ibid., 97.

49. Sobel, *Rise and Fall*, 87.

50. Ibid., 92.

51. Ibid., 95.

52. Brown, *Ling*, 154-55.

53. "1969 Full List," Fortune 500, *Fortune* archive, http://money.cnn.com/magazines/fortune/fortune500_archive/full/1969/, accessed April 10, 2010.

54. Brown, *Ling*, 4.

55. Sobel, *Rise and Fall*, 97.

56. Ibid.

57. "Corporations: Double the Profits, Double the Pride," *Time*, September 8, 1967; David Jones, "F.T.C. Will Study Major Mergers in Mixed Fields," *New York Times*, July 9, 1968, 59.

58. Rothschild, *The Secret*, 127.

59. Ibid., 157.

60. Ibid., 144-45.

61. Ibid., 157.

62. Ibid., 158.

63. Ibid., 160.

64. Ibid., 159.
65. Cordiner, *New Frontiers*, 11.
66. Rothschild, *The Secret*, 129.
67. Ibid., 151.
68. Ibid., 153.
69. Brown, *Ling*, 166.
70. John Abele, "Conglomerate Mergers Get Spotlight," *New York Times*, July 10, 1968, 51.
71. Segal, "The Urge to Merge," 142.
72. Ibid.
73. "Business: Cooking the Books to Fatten the Profits," *Time*, April 11, 1969; Charles Stabler, "The Conglomerates," *Wall Street Journal*, August 5, 1968, 1; "Memories of the Roaring Twenties," *Wall Street Journal*, February 28, 1969.
74. Jones, "F.T.C. Will Study Major Mergers," 1.
75. "Corporations: Ling Sticks with Steel," *Time*, March 2, 1970.
76. Ibid.
77. "Business: The Conglomerates' War to Reshape Industry," *Time*, March 7, 1969.
78. Ibid.
79. John Abele, "Market Place: Analysts View Conglomerates," *New York Times*, August 26, 1969, 54.
80. Sobel, *Age of Giant Corporations*, 208.
81. Economists point to the 1970s as the moment when productivity cratered. The well-respected macroeconomist William Nordhaus believed that this occurred because of the oil shocks. Yet in his wide-ranging literature review, his own graphs show a decline in productivity beginning in the early 1960s. William Nordhaus, "Retrospective on the 1970s Productivity Slowdown," NBER Working Paper No. w10950, December 2004, 5.
82. "Memories of the Roaring Twenties," 10.
83. Philip Shay, *Management Consulting in the 1970s and Beyond* (n.p.: Association of Consulting Management Engineers, 1971), 1–2.
84. Ibid., 3.
85. Ibid., 38.

Chapter Eight: **Rethinking the Corporation**

1. Elmer Winter, "What We Should Have Learned from the Early 70s," n.d., folder 9, box 13, EWP.
2. In the interest of readability for those not inclined to academic theory, I am using words like "worldview" and "common sense" to substitute, in a one-to-one fashion, for the more technical term "episteme" as used by Michel Foucault in *The Order of Things*.
3. Gilbert H. Clee, "The New Manager: The Man for All Organizations," *McKinsey Quarterly* 4, no. 4 (Spring 1968): 2–12.
4. Lewis Young, "Coping with Change: The Challenge to Consultants," *Proceedings of the North American Conference of Management Consultants* (Spring 1975): 29.
5. Ibid., 31.

6. Thomas C. Hayes, "Bruce Henderson, 77, Consultant and Writer on Business Strategy," *New York Times*, July 24, 1992, www.nytimes.com/1992/07/24/us/bruce-henderson-77-consultant-and-writer-on-business-strategy.html.

7. Boston Consulting Group, BCG Perspectives, "Bruce Henderson," www.bcgperspectives.com/classics/author/bruce_henderson.

8. "The Consultants Face a Competition Crisis," *BusinessWeek*, November 17, 1973, 72.

9. Peter F. Drucker, "Top Adviser to Top Brass," *Forbes*, February 15, 1962, 34.

10. Ibid.

11. Warren G. Bennis, "Organizational Revitalization," *McKinsey Quarterly* 5, no. 2 (Fall, 1968): 43. (Note: the title of this article is misspelled in the EBSCOhost database as "Organizational Revitilization.")

12. Warren Bennis and Philip Slater, *The Temporary Society* (New York: Harper & Row, 1968), 11.

13. Ibid., 12.

14. Ibid.

15. Bennis, "Organizational Revitalization," 47–48.

16. Ibid., 52.

17. Bennis and Slater, *The Temporary Society*, 74.

18. Alvin Toffler, "The Coming Ad-hocracy," *McKinsey Quarterly* 8, no. 1 (1971): 2.

19. Ibid., 3.

20. Ibid.

21. Ibid., 7.

22. Ibid., 52.

23. Ibid.

24. Ibid.

25. Ibid.

26. Ibid., 12.

27. Ibid., 13.

28. Bennis and Slater, *The Temporary Society*, 90.

29. Ibid., 10.

30. Ibid., 13.

31. Manpower, *Annual Report*, 1974, 2, Mergent.com.

32. The curious inversion of the axes has been maintained by writers on management strategy despite running counter to how all other graphs are made.

33. Bruce D. Henderson, "The Anatomy of the Cash Cow," in *Perspectives on Strategy from the Boston Consulting Group*, eds. Carl Stern and George Stalk (New York: John Wiley & Sons, 1998), 200.

34. Henderson, "The Corporate Portfolio," in *Perspectives on Strategy*, 203.

35. John Huey, Joyce E. Davis, and Jane Furth, "How McKinsey Does It," *Fortune* 128, no. 11 (November 1, 1993), 56–81.

36. Figure from "The Consultants Face a Competition Crisis," 70; Warren Cannon, "Organizational Design: Shaping Structure to Strategy," *McKinsey Quarterly* 9, no. 1 (Summer 1972): 26.

37. D. Ronald Daniel, "Reorganizing for Results," in Roland Mann, *The Arts of Top Management: A McKinsey Anthology* (New York: McGraw-Hill, 1971), 66.

38. Ibid.

39. Ibid., 159.

40. Pankaj Ghemawat, "Competition and Business Strategy in Historical Perspective," *Business History Review* (Spring 2002): 46.

41. John Seeger, "Reversing the Images of BCG's Growth/Share Matrix," *Strategic Management Journal*, 5, (1984), 93–97, 96.

42. William Rothschild, *The Secret to GE's Success* (New York: McGraw-Hill, 2007), 163.

43. Welch's famous rule of thumb—if you aren't number one or two in market share, you should exit—is just the BCG matrix without a chart. Jack Welch later took credit for GE's renaissance in the 1980s, but his ideas were already in the works when he took control of GE.

44. Bruce R. Scott, "Old Myths and New Realities of the Industrial State," *McKinsey Quarterly* (Summer 1974): 41–65.

45. Ibid., 43.

46. Cannon, "Organizational Design," 30.

47. E. Everett Smith, "Bank Management: The Unmet Challenge," *McKinsey Quarterly* 3, no. 4 (Spring, 1967): 29.

48. Ibid., 31; see Louis Hyman, *Debtor Nation: The History of America in Red Ink* (Princeton, NJ: Princeton University Press, 2011).

49. Smith, "Bank Management," 34.

50. Ibid.

51. McKinsey & Company, "Reorganizing the Investment Management (Trust) Banking Group to Improve Profitability," n.d., folder Reports, Recommendations by McKinsey, Item #508, CITI.

52. McKinsey & Company, "Progress Report on Phase I Findings," n.d., 1, FNCB, RG2/FNCB, CITI.

53. McKinsey & Company, "Citibank's Customers Fall into Eight Groups…," n.d., 1, folder "First National City Bank Reorganization Steering Committee," folder 13, RG2/FNCB, CITI.

54. McKinsey & Company, "Organization Planning Steering Committee, Meeting Minutes, May 16, 1968," 2, folder 13, RG2/FNCB, CITI.

55. McKinsey & Company, "Proposed Initial Structure—Wholesale Bank," n.d., 1, folder 13, RG2/FNCB, CITI.

56. McKinsey & Company, "The Resulting Broad Customer Group…," n.d., n.p., folder 13, RG2/FNCB, CITI.

57. McKinsey & Company, "The Scope of Most…," n.d., n.p., folder 13, RG2/FNCB, CITI.

58. McKinsey & Company, "The Concentration of Present…," n.d., n.p., folder 13, RG2/FNCB, CITI.

59. McKinsey & Company, "Working Session on Organizing the Wholesale Bank," n.d., 3, folder 13, RG2/FNCB, CITI.

60. McKinsey & Company, "Organization Planning Steering Committee," June 6, 1968, n.p., folder 13, RG2/FNCB, CITI.

61. Young, "Coping with Change," 1.

62. Ibid., 23.

63. Clee, "The New Manager," 4.

64. Young, "Coping with Change," 39.

65. Ibid., 40.

66. On relative technological stagnation, see Tyler Cowen, *The Great Stagnation: How America Ate All the Low-Hanging Fruit of Modern History, Got Sick, and Will (Eventually) Feel Better* (New York: Penguin, 2011).

67. Jack O. Vance, "Is Your Company a Take-Over Target?," *McKinsey Quarterly* 6, no. 1 (Fall 1969): 35.

68. Ibid., 40.

69. Ibid., 42.

70. In a fundamental sense, the logic of capital had shifted. As Georg Lukacs noted a century ago, the bourgeois who does not act in accordance with the logic of capital is very quickly no longer in the bourgeoisie.

71. William Hill, "New Dimensions in Corporate Strategy," *Proceedings of the North American Conference of Management Consultants, New Horizons for the Management Consultant*, 2nd meeting, January 23, 1973, 83.

72. Michael Porter, "How Competitive Forces Shape Strategy," *Harvard Business Review*, March–April 1979, 137.

73. Ibid.

74. Ibid., 48.

75. For more on postwar trucking, see Shane Hamilton, *Trucking Country: The Road to America's Wal-Mart Economy* (Princeton, NJ: Princeton University Press, 2008); on the shipping container, see Marc Levinson, *The Box: How the Shipping Container Made the World Smaller and the World Economy Bigger* (Princeton, NJ: Princeton University Press, 2006).

76. Winter, "What We Should Have Learned from the Early 70s."

77. Manpower, *Annual Report*, 1974, 18.

78. Elmer Winter, "Your Work Force—1976 Style," n.d., 1, folder 7, "Speeches, 1971-1973," box 13, EWP.

79. The first reference I can find is Stratford P. Sherman, "Eight Masters of Innovation," *McKinsey Quarterly* no. 4 (1985): 22-31. My point is not simply to move "lean" from the 1980s to the '60s, but to 1) show that these ideas were organic to the transformation in the American economy at the moment when the postwar system began to break down; and 2) show how, as part of an intellectual history, these later "breakthroughs" rested on an assemblage of insights and keywords.

80. Ibid.

81. Ibid., 23.

Chapter Nine: **Office of the Future, Factory of the Past**

1. "Jane Fonda Speaks to Office Workers: 9to5 Hosts Event," September 28, 1979, folder "1979 convention," box 5, 9to5.

2. "Schedule: Tom Hayden, Jane Fonda," September 6, 1979, box 5, 9to5.

3. "Jane Fonda Speaks."

4. "Office Work in Boston: A Statistical Study," 1972, 1, folder "Office Work in Boston: A Statistical Study," box 1, 9to5; "I'm Here Today to Tell You About 9to5 . . . ," 1, folder "Speeches 1975-1980," item 719, box 1, 9to5.

5. "Man Comm Guter Lunch June '76," 1, folder "Speeches 1975-1980," item 719, box 1, 9to5.

6. "I'm Here Today," 6.

7. Bruce Hoard, "9 to 5 President Raps Office Automation, Says It Deskills, Devalues Office Jobs," *Computerworld*, May 3, 1982, 53.

8. Ibid.

9. "Jane Fonda Speaks."

10. *9 to 5*, directed by Colin Higgins (1980; Los Angeles: Fox), DVD. Quote from Judy Bernly (Jane Fonda), www.boxofficemojo.com.

11. IMDB, *9 to 5*, Awards, www.imdb.com/title/tt0080319/awards?ref_=tt_awd.

12. Manpower, *Annual Report*, 1974, 5, Mergent.com.

13. Elmer Winter, "Managing Temporary Employees for Maximum Cost-Control," *Human Resource Management* 2, no. 1 (1963): 9.

14. Elmer Winter, "Your Work Force—1976 Style," n.d., 2, folder 7, "Speeches, 1971-1973," box 13, EWP.

15. Manpower, *Annual Report*, 1973, 9, Mergent.com.

16. Manpower, *Annual Report*, 1971, 7, Mergent.com.

17. Philip Vivian, "Manpower: Managing a Fixed Investment," *McKinsey Quarterly* (Spring 1977): 49.

18. Manpower, *Annual Report*, 1971, 7.

19. American Management Society, "Temporary Help Survey Results," AMS professional managements bulletins (January 1971), 6. This 15,000-firm survey with 3,489 respondents was done in 1970 jointly by the Administrative Management Society and the Institute of Temporary Services.

20. Winter, "Managing Temporary Employees," 8.

21. Winter, "Your Work Force—1976 Style," 1.

22. Manpower, *Annual Report*, 1974, 18.

23. "Annette Hopkins," folder "Correspondence 1974-75," carton 15, item 945, 9to5.

24. Local 925, "Why Unionize and How to Do It," n.d., folder "1978 Convention," item 131, 9to5.

25. Lucinda Smith, "Temporary Workers Ask Better Benefits," *Boston Globe*, October 14, 1974, 53.

26. "The Future of 9to5," September 8, 1973, 1, folder "The Future of 9to5," carton 1, 9to5.

27. "Organization for Women Office Workers," folder "1978 convention," item 131, 9to5.

28. "The Future of 9to5."

29. Names of those who wrote in to 9to5 have been changed. I selected names at random from an online name generator. Some attempt has been made to maintain the evident ethnicity of the names. I kept the real names of those who were part of 9to5 or publicly testified.

30. "A 9 to 5 Report on Temporary Office Work," folder "Drafts of a 9to5 Report on Temp Office Work," carton 15, 9to5.

31. "I'm Here Today," 1.
32. "Temporary Survey" (c. 1974), n.p., folder 951, 9to5.
33. Smith, "Temporary Workers Ask Better Benefits," 53.
34. "Temporary Workers' Testimony," 4, folder "Testimony in Support of Senate Bill 303," carton 15, 9to5.
35. "Olsten Sheet," folder "Temp Report Sheet," ibid., 9to5; "Grid Form," folder "Surveys: Agencies' Responses," ibid., 9to5. The information is somewhat inconsistent. What is clear, and is the larger point, is that temps experienced a world with few benefits and no information.
36. "Temp Report Sheet," folder "Temp Report Sheet," ibid., 9to5.
37. "Manpower Sheet," folder "Temp Report Sheet," ibid., 9to5.
38. "A 9 to 5 Report on Temporary Office Work."
39. "Temporary Survey."
40. Ibid.
41. "Rose Senatore," 4, folder "Testimony in Support of Senate Bill 303," carton 15, 9to5.
42. Smith, "Temporary Workers Ask Better Benefits," 53.
43. "Olsten Bonuses," folder "Temps—Our Leaflets, Reports, etc., 1974-75," carton 15, 9to5.
44. Interview #46, folder "Interviews #45-47," box 2, Jean Tepperman Papers, Schlesinger Library, Harvard University, Cambridge, MA.
45. American Management Society, "Temporary Help Survey Results," 3.
46. "Patty Chase Testimony" (c. 1975), 3, folder "Testimony in Support of Senate Bill 303," carton 15, 9to5.
47. Ibid.
48. "Temporary Survey."
49. "Dynamic Temporaries," folder "Survey Returns," box 2, 9to5.
50. American Management Society, "Temporary Help Survey Results," 2.
51. Ibid., 4. While only 1.8 percent reported using more than seven agencies, 12.3 percent reported using four to seven agencies.
52. American Management Society, "Temporary Help Survey Results," 5.
53. "Patty Chase Testimony," 5.
54. "Charlotte Cooper Testimony" (c. 1975), 2-3, folder "Testimony in Support of Senate Bill 303," carton 15, 9to5.
55. "Temp Report Sheet."
56. "Temporary Workers' Testimony."
57. "TAD-Power," folder "Survey Returns," box 2, 9to5.
58. "The Future of 9 to 5."
59. The struggle of women trade unionists had a long and complex history. For the classic histories, see Alice Kessler-Harris, *Out to Work: A History of Wage-Earning Women in the United States* (New York: Oxford University Press, 2003) and Meredith Tax, *The Rising of the Women: Feminist Solidarity and Class Conflict, 1880-1917* (Champaign, IL: University of Illinois Press, 1980).
60. "The Future of 9 to 5," 2.
61. Ibid., 2-3.
62. Ibid., 3.

63. "Temporary Workers' Testimony," 5. This document is unsigned but it is the same voice and language that Janet Selcer used elsewhere, so I am attributing it to her.

64. "Mr. Chairman," 1, folder "Testimony in Support of Senate Bill 303," carton 15, 9to5.

65. "Tuesday, 2–11," 2, folder "Testimony in Support of Senate Bill 303," carton 15, 9to5.

66. "Comments, Questions, and Clarifications," 2, folder "Drafts of Legislation," carton 15, 9to5.

67. "Annette Hopkins," 2.

68. Interview with Chris Carlsson, founder of *Processsed World*, November 5, 2015.

69. Chris Carlsson [Lucius Cabins], "The Making of a Bad Attitude: An Abridged History of My Wage Slavery," *Processed World*, Autumn 1986, 5.

70. Ibid.

71. Untitled, *Processed World*, Winter 1985–86, 1.

72. Christopher Winks, "Manuscript Found in a Typewriter," *Processed World*, Spring 1981, 2.

73. Ibid.

74. Ibid., 4.

75. Debra Wittley, "Blue Shield and the Union: A Post-Mortem," *Processed World*, Summer 1983, 46.

76. Lucio Cabanas [Chris Carlsson], "Office Workers on Strike," *Processed World*, Spring 1981, 14.

77. Ibid.

78. Tom Athanasiou, "New Information Technology: For What?," *Processed World*, Spring, 1981, 16.

79. gidget digit, "Sabotage!: The Ultimate Video Game," *Processed World*, Spring 1982, 2.

80. Ibid.

81. Athanasiou, "New Information Technology," 16.

82. Ibid.

83. William Serrin, "Part-time Work New Labor Trend," *New York Times*, July 9, 1986.

84. Edwin McDowell, "Audrey Freedman Dies at 68; Specialized in Labor Issues," *New York Times*, April 16, 1998.

85. Anne Polivka and Thomas Nardone, "On the Definition of 'Contingent Work,'" *Monthly Labor Review* (December 1989): 9.

86. George L. Beiswinger, "Turning Temporary Workers into Permanent Solutions," *The Office*, August 1989, 55.

87. Carolyn Fryar, "Managing Fluctuating Workloads with Temps," *Management Solutions*, February 1988, 23.

88. "Office Automation and the Clerical Worker," 1, folder "Speeches 1975-1980" box 1, item 719, 9to5.

89. Ibid., 6.

90. Ibid., 7–9.

91. Ibid., 1.

92. Ibid., 4.
93. Ibid., 10.
94. Interview with Felix Kaufman, n.d., 1-41, tape 1, folder "Interviews & Bios J-Ke," 1-24, box 7, PWC.

Chapter Ten: **Restructuring the American Dream**

1. Here I am pushing back on the literature that sees economists as the primary intellectual agents behind the changes in American capitalism in this period. Clearly economists matter, especially the portfolio theorists and the omnipresent Milton Friedman. I don't think their ideas simply skipped from journals into corporations. Consultants were paid to remake firms. Their journals, unlike *Econometrica*, were read by the entire C-suite. Businesspeople, more than academics, made these changes happen. For outstanding histories (with different perspectives) of the economists' ideas, see Brian Domitrovic, *Econoclasts: The Rebels Who Sparked the Supply-Side Revolution and Restored American Prosperity* (Wilmington, DE: Isi Books, 2009); Nancy MacLean, *Democracy in Chains: The Deep History of the Radical Right's Secret Plan for America* (New York: Penguin, 2017); and Angus Burgin, *The Great Persuasion: Reinventing Free Markets Since the Depression* (Cambridge, MA: Harvard University Press, 2012).
2. Peter Drucker, *Managing in Turbulent Times* (New York: Harper & Row, 1980), 3.
3. As discussed earlier, the postwar feud between the UE and IUE made organizing electronics factories very challenging, especially when combined with the subcontracted workforce and the antiunion attitudes of employers—and many employees. On the UE strikes of the late 1960s, see Ramon C. Sevilla, "Employment Practices and Industrial Restructuring: A Case Study of the Semiconductor Industry in Silicon Valley, 1955-1991," (PhD diss., UCLA, 1992), 172.
4. P. T. Bolwijn and T. Kumpe, "Toward the Factory of the Future," *McKinsey Quarterly* (Spring 1986): 40.
5. "Apple Streamlines," *Apple Connection*, June 24, 1984, 1, folder 9, box 1, series 2, APL.
6. María Patricia Fernández-Kelly and Saskia Sassen, "A Collaborative Study of Hispanic Women in the Garment and Electronics Industries," executive summary presented to the Ford, Revson, and Tinker Foundations, 1991, distributed by the Center for Latin American and Caribbean Studies, New York University, 118.
7. The numbers varied a bit, depending on the source, but the rough percentages were the same. See Sevilla, "Employment Practices," 164.
8. David Pellow and Lisa Park, *The Silicon Valley of Dreams* (New York: NYU Press, 2002), 48-49.
9. Glenna Matthews, *Silicon Valley, Women, and the California Dream* (Palo Alto, CA: Stanford University Press, 2002), 109.
10. So many of the debates over Silicon Valley have centered on why it has been so hard to replicate elsewhere, like North Carolina or Boston. Electronics has only ever really taken off in California and Texas, the same places where a large post-braceros migrant population live. To my knowledge, this point has not been emphasized.

11. Quoted in Dennis Hayes, "Lonely Trails, Itinerant Cultures: Work's Diminishing Connections," *Processed World*, Spring 1987, 14.

12. Ibid.

13. Interview with Fred Herr, n.d., 31, 34142.doc, box 36, PWC.

14. Ibid., 32.

15. John A. Byrne, "Are All These Consultants Really Necessary?" *Forbes*, October 10, 1983, 136.

16. Alonzo McDonald, "State of the Firm: Speech Outlines #1," Shareholders Conference, Freeport, Grand Bahama Island, March 22-23, 1976, 1, 2, box 6, folder 3, State of the Firm, Speech Outline #1, by Alonzo L. McDonald for Shareholders Conference, Freeport, Grand Bahama Island, March 22, 1976, exhibits, MBM.

17. Ibid., 9.

18. Ibid., 11, 12.

19. Ibid., 5.

20. Ibid.

21. Ron Daniel, "Closing Remarks," Shareholders Conference, Monte Carlo, September 27, 1977, 1, 2, box 6, folder 14, Closing Remarks by Ron Daniel, Shareholders Conference, Monte Carlo, September 26-27, 1977, MBM.

22. Ibid., 3.

23. Robert E. Kelley, "Should You Have an Internal Consultant?" *Harvard Business Review*, November–December 1979, 111.

24. John Huey, Joyce E. Davis, and Jane Furth, "How McKinsey Does It," *Fortune* 128, no. 11, November 1, 1993, 56-81.

25. Jean Pierre Frankenhuis, "How to Get a Good Consultant," *Harvard Business Review*, November–December 1977, 134.

26. Ibid., 136.

27. Byrne, "Are All These Consultants Really Necessary?," 136.

28. Bruce Henderson, "A Consultant Speaks Up," *Boston Globe*, January 4, 1983, 48.

29. Courtney Beinhorn and William Dunk, "This Looks Like a Job for Superconsultant," *Across the Board* (March 1988), 46.

30. Huey, Davis, and Furth, "How McKinsey Does It."

31. Ibid.

32. Thomas Peters and Robert Waterman, *In Search of Excellence: Lessons from America's Best-Run Companies* (New York: Harper & Row, 1982), 311-13.

33. David Packard, *The HP Way* (New York: HarperCollins, 1995).

34. "Historical Commitment to Flexibility and Employment Security," n.d., 21, folder "Flex Force/Temps Pool," box "Series 5—Subject Files Personnel F-Personnel G," HP.

35. "Involuntary Terminations," *Personnel Lines*, September 17, 1986, 2, folder "Personnel Lines 1980-1991," box "Series 1—Publications Titles K-P," HP.

36. "Behind the Reorganization," *FYI*, October 5, 1984, 1, folder "FYI to HP Senior Management 1980-1993," box "Series 1—HP Publications Titles A-F," HP.

37. Robert Waterman, "Coping with Change at HP—An Outsider's Perspectives," January 25, 1984, 1, folder "Management Meeting 1984," box "Series 5—Subject Files Management Meeting 1978-1996," HP.

38. "An Outsider's Inside Look at HP," *FYI*, February 16, 1984, 1, folder "FYI to HP Senior Management 1980-1993," box "Series 1—HP Publications Titles A-F," HP.

39. Waterman, "Coping with Change at HP," 1.

40. Ibid.

41. "Behind the Reorganization," 1.

42. "Everyone into the Pool," *Feature Report*, 1981, 1, folder "Flex Force/Temps Pool," box "Series 5—Subject Files Personnel F-Personnel G," HP.

43. "Have Computer, Will Travel," *Bandley Shuffle*, February 1986, 10, folder 2, box 2, APL.

44. "Watch Use of Temps," *Personnel Lines*, March 18, 1982, 2, folder "Personnel Lines 1980-1991," box "Series 1—Publications Title K-P," HP.

45. "Historical Commitment to Flexibility and Employment Security," 21.

46. "Adding Flexibility to the Work Force," *FYI*, February 27, 1987, 5, folder "FYI to HP Senior Management 1980-1993," box "Series 1—HP Publications Titles A-F," HP.

47. Ibid.

48. "Historical Commitment to Flexibility and Employment Security," 21.

49. "Managing Headcount Is a Priority," *FYI*, February 1989, 4, folder "FYI to HP Senior Management 1980-1993," box "Series 1—HP Publications Titles A-F," HP.

50. "Special Issue Preferred Supplier Contracts for External Temporary Workers," *In Touch*, October 4, 1994, 1, folder "Flex Force/Temps Pool," box "Series 5—Subject Files Personnel F-Personnel G," HP.

51. Ibid.

52. Kenichi Ohmae, *The Mind of the Strategist* (New York: McGraw-Hill, 1982), 219.

53. Ibid., 206-7.

54. Ibid.

55. Ibid., 224.

56. Ibid., 225.

57. "Ford's Fastest Whiz Kid," *Time*, November 21, 1960, 100.

58. Kenichi Ohmae, "Japan: From Stereotypes to Specifics," *McKinsey Quarterly* (Spring 1982): 19.

59. Ibid.

60. "Views Different on Value of Toyota-GM Venture," *New York Times*, February 16, 1983.

61. Ibid.

62. Daniel, "Closing Remarks," 6.

63. Ibid., 5.

64. Ibid., 15.

65. "Apple 1984 Super Bowl Commercial Introducing Macintosh Computer," You-Tube, www.youtube.com/watch?v=axSnW-ygU5g, accessed November 27, 2017.

66. Apple, "Values and Culture," 1986, 11, folder 8, box 5, APL.

67. "Steve Jobs Presenting the First Mac in 1984," YouTube, www.youtube.com/watch?v=8bepzUM1x3w, accessed November 27, 2017.

68. "When We Invented . . . ," *Wall Street Journal*, February 10, 1981, 7, folder 11, box 4, APL.

69. Apple, "A Sense of Our History," 1986, 6, 7, folder 8, box 5, APL. The document was the orientation presentation for new employees in 1986, explaining the history of the company.

70. Thomas & Company, "Competitive Dynamics in the Microcomputer Industry: IBM, Apple Computer, and Hewlett-Packard," 25, folder 5, box 14, APL.

71. Apple, "A Sense of Our History," 7.

72. Ibid., 9.

73. Ibid., 10.

74. "Poma Ads: Apple Shareholders Meeting (1984) 5/6," YouTube, www.youtube.com/watch?v=fl2fbkSmvnk, accessed November 27, 2017.

75. Ibid.

76. Untitled, *Fifth: A Fremont Flash special*, December 1988, 2, folder 13, series 2, APL.

77. Marty Olmstead, "Apple Polisher," *Savvy*, May 1986, 26, folder 11, box 4, APL.

78. Ibid.

79. "News," *Apple Connection*, November 6, 1984, 1, folder 9, box 1, series 2, APL.

80. "Macintosh Factory Is Doubling Its Capacity," *Apple Connection*, August 6, 1984, 1, folder 9, box 1, series 2, APL.

81. Marty Olmstead, "Apple Polisher," 26.

82. Ibid., 27.

83. "Coleman: Financial Wiz, Fremont Vet," *Fremont Flash*, September 1988, 8, folder 13, box 1, series 2, APL.

84. "Congratulations, Chiat/Day. Seriously," *Wall Street Journal*, May 27, 1986, 30.

85. "Playboy Interview: Steven Jobs," *Playboy*, February 1985, 58, folder 11, box 4, APL.

86. Jean-Louis Gasse, "I Shall," *Fifth: A Fremont Flash special*, 5.

87. "Train the Trainers," *Fremont Flash*, August 1989, 4, folder 13, box 1, series 2, APL.

88. "SE Assemblers Provide Charts and Graphs," *Fremont Flash*, 8, June 1989, folder 13, series 2, APL.

89. Untitled, *Fifth: A Fremont Flash special*, 9.

90. "Sharing Skills with Singapore," *Fremont Flash*, 1, June 1989, folder 13, series 2, APL.

91. Anthony Chan to Lynn Bidwell, May 9, 1988, 1, folder 2, box 9, APL.

92. Christopher Schmitt, "Imported Asians Doing Seagate Production Work: INS to Determine if Visa Restrictions Are Being Violated," *San Jose Mercury News*, August 31, 1986.

93. Ibid.

94. Matthews, *Silicon Valley*, 137.

95. Sevilla, "Employment Practices," 466.

96. Ibid., 479.

97. Karen Southwick, "High-Tech Industry Relies on Temporary Workforce," *San Jose Mercury News*, December 7, 1984, 18E.

98. Ibid.

99. Sevilla, "Employment Practices," 472–73.

100. Southwick, "High-Tech Industry Relies on Temporary Workforce," 18E.

101. Sevilla, "Employment Practices," 474.

102. Karen Southwick, "Temps Vital to High-Tech Firms," *San Jose Mercury News*, December 7, 1984, 19E.
103. Interview with Dennis Hayes, *Processed World* writer, November 27, 2015.
104. James Quinn, "High-Tech Firms Find Edge in Use of Illegal Aliens," *Los Angeles Times*, April 28, 1985, A10.
105. Interview with Dennis Hayes, November 27, 2015.
106. Dennis Hayes, "Lonely Trails, Itinerant Cultures: Work's Diminishing Connections," *Processed World*, Spring 1987, 15.
107. Fernández-Kelly and Sassen, "A Collaborative Study," 28.
108. Ibid., 62–63.
109. Ibid., 74.
110. Ibid., 65.
111. Ibid., 75.
112. Ibid.
113. Ibid., 74.
114. Interview with Dennis Hayes, November 27, 2015.
115. Hayes, "Lonely Trails," 16.
116. Joseph LaDou, "Occupational Health in the Semiconductor Industry," in Ted Smith, David A. Sonnenfeld, and David N. Pellow, *Challenging the Chip: Labor Rights and Environmental Justice in the Global Electronics Industry* (Philadelphia: Temple University Press, 2006).
117. "Search for Superfund Sites Where You Live," Environmental Protection Agency, www.epa.gov/superfund/search-superfund-sites-where-you-live. Calculation by author.
118. Leslie Byster and Ted Smith, "From Grassroots to Global," in Ted Smith, David A. Sonnenfeld, and David N. Pellow, *Challenging the Chip: Labor Rights and Environmental Justice in the Global Electronics Industry* (Philadelphia: Temple University Press, 2006),111.
119. Fernández-Kelly and Sassen, "A Collaborative Study," 67.
120. Ibid., 78.
121. Thomas Petzinger, Jr., "Vital Resources: Illegal Immigrants Are Backbone of Economy in States of Southwest," *Wall Street Journal*, May 7, 1985.
122. Fernández-Kelly and Sassen, "A Collaborative Study," 78.
123. Interview with Dennis Hayes, November 27, 2015.
124. Fernández-Kelly and Sassen, "A Collaborative Study," 71.
125. Ibid., 68.
126. Clara Germani, "U.S. Tackles High-Tech Firms' Illegal Aliens," *Christian Science Monitor*, April 24, 1984.
127. Ibid.
128. Laurie Becklund, "Regional INS Chief Nurtures His Image," *Los Angeles Times*, December 8, 1985.
129. Germani, "U.S. Tackles High-Tech Firms' Illegal Aliens."
130. Petzinger, "Vital Resources."
131. *Velasquez v. Senko*, U.S. Court of Appeals, Ninth Circuit, April 6, 1987, 643 F. Supp. 1172 (N.D. Cal. 1986), https://law.justia.com/cases/federal/district-courts/FSupp/643/1172/1908711.

132. David Schrieberg, "Ruling Would Let INS Resume Workplace Raids," *San Jose Mercury News*, September 12 1986, 1A.

133. Becklund, "Regional INS Chief Nurtures His Image."

134. "S.F. Declares a Sanctuary: Police Need Not Report Illegal Salvadorans, Guatemalans," *San Jose Mercury News*, December 25, 1985, 8B.

135. Schrieberg, "Ruling Would Let INS Resume Workplace Raids."

136. Germani, "U.S. Tackles High-Tech Firms' Illegal Aliens."

137. Ibid.

138. Jennifer Foote, "Aliens Held in Old-Age Homes, Jails," *San Jose Mercury News*, June 9, 1985.

139. "Illegal Aliens Make Massive Contribution to U.S. Firms," *Santa Cruz Sentinel*, May 9, 1985, 6.

140. David M. Heer, *Undocumented Mexicans in the United States* (Arnold and Caroline Rose Monograph Series of the American Sociological Association) (New York: Cambridge University Press, 1990), 78.

141. Petzinger, "Vital Resources."

142. Historians have excluded the slippage from bracero to undocumented from historical narratives because of political concerns. Historian Stephen Pitti prefers the use of "ethnic Mexican" over the more politicized and ahistorical "Chicano" or "*mexicano*." The term leaves nationality undecided (unlike Mexican American) and emphasizes the shared cultural life, even across lines of citizenship. Official histories, as historian Mireya Loza writes, like those offered by "NMAH [National Museum of American History], the Bracero Justice Movement, and policy makers thus have engaged in the solidification of a 'bracero' identity that purposely divorces itself from that of the undocumented laborer. But acknowledging that the flow of Mexican temporary workers was intricately tied to that of undocumented workers, or how easy it was to move in and out of these categories, would have made creating a cohesive narrative about bracero history difficult" (Loza, 173). Inclusion of legal braceros, she points out, is an important step toward a broader narrative of the U.S. Nonetheless, excluding the undocumented people who did the labor that made our economy possible seems to me a gross gap in the historical narrative, however inconvenient it is for an uncomplicated story, as Loza agrees. I also agree with Pitti that the shared cultural background is important, but just as important are the very real differences in legal and economic power among those who are native-born, legal migrants, and undocumented migrants. Mireya Loza, *Defiant Braceros: How Migrant Workers Fought for Racial, Sexual, and Political Freedom* (Chapel Hill: University of North Carolina Press, 2016); Stephen Pitti, *The Devil in Silicon Valley* (Princeton, NJ: Princeton University Press, 2003).

143. Petzinger, "Vital Resources."

144. Heer, *Undocumented Mexicans in the United States*, 150.

145. Ibid., 147.

146. Ibid., 148.

147. Ibid., 151.

148. Kitty Calavita, *California's Employer Sanctions: The Case of the Disappearing Law* (Research Report No. 39, Center for US-Mexican Studies, June 1982), 3–4.

149. Ibid.

150. Ibid., 41.

151. Ibid., 34.

152. "Making Sure the New Immigration Law Works," *Apple Bulletin*, May 20, 1987, 1, folder 8, box 1, series 2, APL.

153. Magnus Lofstrom, Laura Hill, and Joseph Hayes, "Wage and Mobility Effects of Legalization: Evidence from the New Immigrant Survey," *Journal of Regional Science* (February 2013): 171–97, doi:10.1111/jors.12005.

154. Lori Rodriguez, "Houston Employers Finding Few Problems with Immigration Bill," *Houston Chronicle*, January 21, 1987, in folder "Immigration," box 20 "Central Files I-L," AGC.

155. T. J. Wray, "Employer Responsibilities Under the Immigration Reform and Control Act of 1986," 1, April 23, 1987, ibid., AGC.

156. "Everything—and More—That You Ever Wanted to Know About the New Immigration Reform Law," May 21, 1987, 7, ibid., AGC.

157. David Schrieberg, "Beleaguered INS Chief Trading San Jose Job for Quieter Post," *San Jose Mercury News*, March 26, 1987.

158. Petzinger, "Vital Resources."

159. Becklund, "Regional INS Chief Nurtures His Image."

160. John Huey, Joyce E. Davis, and Jane Furth, "How McKinsey Does It," *Fortune* 128, no. 11, November 1, 1993, 56–81.

161. Thomas Peters, *Thriving on Chaos: Handbook for a Management Revolution* (1987; repr., New York: HarperPerennial, 1991).

162. Ibid., 3.

163. Ibid., 45.

164. Ibid., 30.

Chapter Eleven: **Permatemp**

1. *Consultants News*, July 1996, 15.

2. Sociologist Eileen Applebaum pointed at the time to the lack of investment in "high performance work systems" as the alternative to contingent work: "Firms appear to be responding to competitive pressures by adopting cost-cutting strategies that improve the bottom line in the short run, but do not lead to the continuous improvements in quality and efficiency that are required to remain competitive in world markets." U.S. Senate, Hearings Before the Subcommittee on Labor of the Senate Committee on Labor and Human Resources, "Toward a Disposable Work Force: The Increasing Use of 'Contingent' Labor," 103rd Congress, 1st Session, June 15, 1993, 32, 35.

3. Karen E. Debats, "Temporary Services Flourish," *Personnel Journal* 62, October 1983, 780.

4. Erica Groshen and Simon Potter, "Has Structural Change Contributed to a Jobless Recovery," Federal Reserve Bank of New York, *Current Issues in Economics and Finance* 9, no. 8, August 2003, 1.

5. Audrey Freedman, "How the 1980's Have Changed Industrial Relations," *Monthly Labor Review*, May 1988, 38.

6. *Consultants News*, July 1999, 6.

7. *Consultants News*, April 1997, 7.
8. *Consultants News*, October 1998, 7.
9. Ibid., 1.
10. *Consultants News*, April 1997, 11.
11. *Consultants News*, October 1998, 6.
12. Sallie Gaines, "Computing Stars at Arthur Andersen," *Chicago Tribune*, March 19, 1989.
13. "Arthur Andersen to Stay as One," *Chicago Tribune*, November 29, 1988.
14. Berton Lee, "Arthur Andersen Weighs Restructuring to Make Consulting Practice Separate," *Wall Street Journal*, September 26, 1988, 5.
15. Arsenio Oloroso, Jr., "Andersen Consulting HQ Move," *Crain's Chicago Business*, August 21, 1995, 18, 4.
16. "Arthur Andersen to Stay as One."
17. *Consultants News*, May 1998, 5.
18. *Consultants News*, July 1997, 11.
19. This shift, though not as large, was similar to how GE shifted into finance. See Louis Hyman, *Borrow: The American Way of Debt* (New York: Vintage, 2012).
20. *Consultants News*, July 1997, 6.
21. *Consultants News*, September 1997, 1.
22. John Huey, Joyce E. Davis, and Jane Furth, "How McKinsey Does It," *Fortune* 128, no. 11, November 1, 1993, 56–81.
23. "Associate Opinions Taken . . . ," 5, box 8, folder 15 Associate Opinions Taken from Confidential ITP Questionnaire Survey of 60 Associates, Attachment B, September, 1990, Marvin Bower, MBM.
24. "The Strategic Approach . . . ," 2, box 7, folder 9 The Strategic Approach to Consulting Staff Development, by Marvin Bower, paper based on remarks at shareholders conference, Washington, D.C., April 18, 1985, MBM.
25. Ibid., 7.
26. Ibid., 4.
27. Ibid., 7.
28. Ibid., 18.
29. *Consultants News*, May 1998, 7.
30. *Consultants News*, April 1997, 1.
31. "The Strategic Approach," 16.
32. "New McKinsey Boss," 1, *Frankfurter Allegemeine Zeitung*, March 7, 1995, box 8, folder 53 New McKinsey Boss Against Success-Based Fees, Translation from *Frankfurter . . .* , MBM.
33. Ibid.
34. "May Letter—Sculley/Spindler" May 20, 1991, 1, folder 12, box 4, APL.
35. "Playboy Interview: Steven Jobs," *Playboy*, February 1985, 52, folder 11, box 4, APL.
36. "Letter from John Sculley and Michael Spindler," June 20, 1991, 1, folder 12, box 4, APL.
37. "Jim Forquer Announces New Strategy," 1, September 9, 1992, folder 6, box 9, APL.
38. Freedman, "How the 1980's Have Changed Industrial Relations," 37–38.

39. "NATS Submits Testimony to Labor Subcommittee on 'Contingent Work-force,'" *Contemporary Times*, Fall 1993, 37.

40. "Annual Update," *Contemporary Times*, Spring 1994, 11; U.S. Senate, Subcommittee on Labor, "Toward a Disposable Work Force," 1.

41. U.S. Senate, Subcommittee on Labor, "Toward a Disposable Work Force," June 15, 1993, 22.

42. "Annual Update," 11.

43. U.S. Senate, Subcommittee on Labor, "Toward a Disposable Work Force," June 15, 1993, 28.

44. Ibid., 5.

45. Anne E. Polivka, "A Profile of Contingent Workers," *Monthly Labor Review* 119, no. 10 (October 1996): 10.

46. Steven Hipple, "Contingent Work: Results from the Second Survey," *Monthly Labor Review* (November 1998): 34.

47. Anne E. Polivka, "Contingent and Alternative Work Arrangements, Defined," *Monthly Labor Review* 119, no. 10 (October 1996): 3–9.

48. For a criticism of the narrow definition, see Susan N. Houseman, "A Report on Temporary Help, On-Call, Direct-Hire Temporary, Leased, Contract Company, and Independent Contractor Employment in the United States," U.S. Department of Labor, *Futurework*, August 1999, www.dol.gov/dol/aboutdol/history/herman/reports/futurework/conference/staffing/2.1_workers.htm.

49. Marisa DiNatale, "Characteristics of and Preference for Alternative Work Arrangements, 1999," *Monthly Labor Review* 124, no. 3 (March 2001): 39.

50. Jeff Kelly, Introduction to *Best of Temp Slave!* (Madison, WI: Garrett County Press, 1997), vii–ix.

51. Mark Maynard, "The Untold Story of Zines: Jeff 'Keffo' Kelly on TempSlave!," *Mark Maynard Blog*, markmaynard.com/2014/03/the-untold-history-of-zines-jeff-keffo-kelly-on-tempslave.

52. Jack Kear, "Paid in Full," *Best of Temp Slave!*, 17.

53. Jeff Kelly, "I Get a Real Temp Job," *Best of Temp Slave!*, 39.

54. Ibid., 41.

55. Ibid.

56. Jeff Kelly, "Life Denied," *Best of Temp Slave!*, 158.

57. To think about slackers is to think, inevitably, about Gen X. Much of what is being said today about millennials was being said about Xers in the 1990s. Andersen Consulting cautioned boomer managers about the generational conflict that arose from misunderstandings between the age groups. While boomers wanted to be part of the conglomerate, Xers wanted to be free agents. Xers wanted to make a mark while boomers sought to fit the mold. The desire for autonomy was naturalized as a generational quality, reduced to culture, rather than to the changing economy in which work happened. Xers had a competency in technology while boomers excelled in business acumen. These distinctions were, and are, silly. The cultural experiences of a generation are not monolithic. What was monolithic was the structural change in the workplace. *Consultants News*, June 1999, 9.

58. "Profile of the Temporary Workforce," *Contemporary Times*, Spring 1994, 33.

59. The surveys of temps never address this survivorship bias, which would wildly alter the results of the surveys.

60. "Profile of the Temporary Workforce," 33.

61. Ibid., 35.

62. DiNatale, "Characteristics of and Preference for Alternative Work Arrangements, 1999," 48. Only 4 percent of temps reported that childcare (0.5 percent) or "family or personal obligations" (3.4 percent) were the reason they took a temporary job.

63. Donna Rothstein, "Entry in and Consequences of Nonstandard Work Arrangements," *Monthly Labor Review* 119, no. 10 (October 1996): 76.

64. Elizabeth Dietz, "A Look at Temporary Help Wage Rates," *Compensation and Working Conditions* (September 1996), 46.

65. DiNatale, "Characteristics of and Preference for Alternative Work Arrangements, 1999," 40.

66. "NATS Submits Testimony to Labor Subcommittee on 'Contingent Workforce,'" 37.

67. "Weighing the Future," 5 *Star News*, July 21, 1993, 1, folder 3, box 3, series 2, APL.

68. "Dear Apple Employees," July 6, 1993, 1, folder 18, box 8, APL.

69. "Editor's Note," 5 *Star News*, July 21, 1993, 2, folder 3, box 3, series 2, APL.

70. "The Changed Nature of Workers and Work," 5 *Star News*, July 21, 1993, 3, folder 3, box 3, series 2, APL

71. "Vox Populi," 5 *Star News*, July 21, 1993, 5, folder 3, box 3, series 2, APL.

72. "A Message from Mike Markkula," February 4, 1996, 1, folder 12, box 4, APL.

73. Michael Spindler, "Q1 Performance and Restructuring," 1, January 17, 1996, folder 19, box 8, APL.

74. Gil Amelio, "Letter to Employees from Gil Amelio," February 4, 1997, 1, folder 20, box 8, APL.

75. Ibid., 2.

76. James M. Degnan, "A Consultant Can Help to Boost Productivity," *The Office*, November 11, 1987, 148.

77. Terrence J. Arter, "Contract the Independent Computer Consultant," *Journal of Systems Management* (January 1988): 36.

78. U.S. Senate, Subcommittee on Labor, "Toward a Disposable Work Force," June 15, 1993, 8.

79. Ibid., 16.

80. Ibid., 1.

81. Ibid., 8.

82. Ibid., 10.

83. Ibid., 81.

84. Ibid., 82.

85. Arter, "Contract the Independent Computer Consultant," 36.

86. Hewlett-Packard, "Professional Services Requestor Reference Manual," March 1, 1994, folder "Flex Force/Temps Pool," box "Series 5—Subject Files Personnel F-Personnel G," HP.

87. "Do You Qualify for Relief Under Section 530?," Office of the Treasury, IRS.gov, revised January 2017, accessed December 3, 2017, www.irs.gov/pub/irs-pdf /p1976.pdf; William Hays Weissman, *Section 530: Its History and Application in Light of the Federal Definition of the Employer-Employee Relationship for Federal Tax Purposes*, National Association of Tax Reporting and Professional Management, February 28, 2009, www.irs.gov/pub/irs-utl/irpac-br_530_relief_-_appendix_natrm_paper_09032009.pdf, accessed December 1, 2017.

88. Weissman, *Section 530: Its History and Application*, 6.

89. "Do You Qualify for Relief Under Section 530?"

90. "NATS Submits Testimony to Labor Subcommittee on 'Contingent Workforce,'" 40.

91. George L. Beiswinger, "Turning Temporary Workers into Permanent Solutions," *The Office*, August 1989, 56.

92. Ibid.

93. "The Not So Great Mystery of Flexible Employment," *Contemporary Times*, Spring 1994, 17.

94. Ibid., 20. The article covers a series of speeches on the economy of the 1990s, centered on William Styring III, a speaker from the Indiana Policy Review Foundation, a conservative think tank.

95. "The Not So Great Mystery of Flexible Employment," 21.

96. U.S. Senate, Subcommittee on Labor, "Toward a Disposable Work Force," June 15, 1993, 19.

97. Ibid., 16.

98. "Temps Staff Chemical Lockbox Operation," ABA *Banking Journal*, April 1990, 90.

99. Ibid., 93.

100. *Consulting News*, January 1996, 6.

101. "Trends: Outsourcing with a Vengeance," *Training*, November 1989, 11.

102. "Profile of the Temporary Workforce 1997," *Contemporary Times*, Spring 1998, 53.

103. Ibid.

104. Ibid., 54.

105. Beiswinger, "Turning Temporary Workers," 56.

106. Kristi Heim and Margaret Steen, "Firm Settles with Temps; Microsoft Will Pay $97 Million to End Suit," *San Jose Mercury News*, December 13, 2000, 1C.

107. *Donna Vizcaino, et al., v. Microsoft Corporation*, No. C93-178d, United States District Court for the Western District of Washington, Seattle Division, 1993 U.S. Dist. LEXIS 21068.

108. John Young, "Remarks," 1, folder "Management Meeting 1992," box "Series 5—Subject Files Management Meeting 1978-1996," HP.

109. David Packard, "Perspective on HP," January 17, 1989, 1, folder "Management Meeting 1989," HP.

110. Ibid., 15.

111. "Management Council Meeting," *FYI*, December 17, 1991, 3, folder "FYI to HP Senior Management 1980-1993," box "Series 1—HP Publications Titles A-F," HP.

112. *Hewlett-Packard Guidelines for Managing a Temporary Workforce*, (June 1995), folder "Temporary Employment," box "Series 5—Subject Files Personnel, "Resource Guide . . . ," HP.

113. Ibid., 10.

114. "Staffing Alternatives [1996]," 6, folder "Flex Force/Temps Pool," box "Series 5—Subject Files Personnel F-Personnel G," HP.

115. Terri L. Darrow, "Temporary Expertise Develops into a Permanent Solution," *Management Review*, November 1989.

116. "Manpower Proves Staying Power," *Milwaukee Sentinel*, April 1, 1996, folder 7, box 11, EWP.

117. *Consultants News*, October 1997, 1.

118. "Andersen Consulting May Be Moving Toward a Breakup with Parent Firm," *Wall Street Journal*, December 17, 1997.

119. Melody Petersen, "How the Andersens Turned into the Bickersons," *New York Times*, March 15, 1998.

120. "Andersen Consulting May Be Moving."

121. *Consultants News*, December 1998, 2.

122. Ibid.

123. Floyd Norris, "Accounting Firm to Pay a Big Fine," *New York Times*, June 20, 2001; Ken Brown, "Questioning the Books," *Wall Street Journal*, March 12, 2002.

124. Brown, "Questioning the Books."

125. *Consultants News*, February 2000, 1.

126. *Consultants News*, July 2000, 1.

127. *Consultants News*, December 2000, 1.

128. Ibid., 9.

129. For a recent take, see Gavin Benke, *Risk and Ruin: Enron and the Culture of American Capitalism* (Philadelphia: University of Pennsylvania Press, 2018).

130. Malcolm Gladwell, "The Talent Myth," *New Yorker*, July 22, 2002, 33.

131. Ed Michaels, Helen Handfield-Jones, and Beth Axelrod, *The War for Talent* (Boston: Harvard Business School Press, 2001).

132. Ibid., 28.

133. Interview with Fred Herr, n.d., 35, 34142.doc, 1, box 36, PWC.

134. Interview with Vincent O'Reilly, n.d., 1–9, 3151-1.doc, box 36, PWC.

135. Ibid., 1–13.

136. Ibid.

137. "KPMG Consulting Signs Deal to Buy Andersen Operations," *Wall Street Journal*, May 9, 2002.

138. *Consultants News*, October 2000, 1.

139. *Consultants News*, December 1996, 1.

140. Microsoft, *Annual Report*, 2000.

141. "Temporary Help Update for 1997," *Contemporary Times*, Spring 1998, 34, 38.

142. "Profile of the Temporary Workforce 1997," *Contemporary Times*, Spring 1998, 46.

143. Ibid., 44.

144. DiNatale, "Characteristics of and Preference for Alternative Work Arrangements, 1999," 28.

145. "Workforce Reduction FAQs," August 23, 2001, 1, folder "Personnel Expense Reduction Measures, July–Dec 2001," box "Series 5–Subject Files Personnel–Expense Reduction Measures 2001-," HP.

Chapter Twelve: **Flexible Labor in the Digital Age**

1. Interview by author with Craig Newmark, founder of Craigslist, Palo Alto, CA, February 12, 2016.
2. Interview by author with Stephane Kasriel, CEO of Upwork, Mountain View, CA, December 4, 1015.
3. Ibid.
4. Interview with Nikhil Shanbhag, general counsel of Instacart, Palo Alto, CA, January 28, 2016.
5. "Etsy Common Stock," www.sec.gov/Archives/edgar/data/1370637/000119312 515132943/d806992d424b41.pdf, accessed December 1, 2017.
6. Etsy, Seller Census 2017, 8, http://extfiles.etsy.com/advocacy/Etsy_US_2017_ SellerCensus.pdf.
7. Ibid., 2.
8. Diana Farrell and Fiona Greig, "Paychecks, Paydays, and the Online Platform Economy Big Data on Income Volatility," JPMorgan Chase and Co. Institute, February 2016, 3, www.jpmorganchase.com/corporate/institute/document/jpmc -institute-volatility-2-report.pdf.
9. Most of that variation in income (86 percent) came from "variation in pay within distinct jobs." Ibid., 15.
10. Jonathon Hall and Alan Krueger, "An Analysis of the Labor Market for Uber's Driver-Partners in the United States," January 22, 2015, 10, 11, https://s3.amazon aws.com/uber-static/comms/PDF/Uber_Driver-Partners_Hall_Krueger _2015.pdf.
11. Farrell and Greig, "Paychecks, Paydays, and the Online Platform Economy," 25–26.
12. Etsy, Seller Census 2017, 9.
13. Ibid., 4.
14. After this experience, I found out about the 2008 film *Sleep Dealer*, which lays out this very scenario.
15. "ILO Global Estimates on Migrant Workers," International Labor Organization, www.ilo.org/wcmsp5/groups/public/—dgreports/—dcomm/documents/publication /wcms_436343.pdf, accessed November 27, 2017.
16. "The Declaration of Interdependence," B Corp Declaration, www.bcorporation .net/what-are-b-corps/the-b-corp-declaration, accessed December 1, 2017.
17. Ibid.
18. "Etsy CEO Chad Dickerson Is Out—Along with 8 Percent of Its Workforce," *Fast Company*, May 2, 2017, www.fastcompany.com/4036454/etsy-ceo-chad -dickerson-is-out-along-with-8-of-its-workforce.
19. Faiz Siddiqui, "#DeleteUber Will Have Lasting Fallout for Ride-Hailing App, Study Says," *Washington Post*, May 5, 2016, www.washingtonpost.com/news /dr-gridlock/wp/2017/05/16/deleteuber-will-have-lasting-fallout-for-ride -hailing-app-study-says/?utm_term=.1f3bcef407e2.

20. Recently, though, there has been pushback on the environmental costs of this technology. Unlike paper money, which once printed has no environmental cost, every blockchain transaction requires vast computational power. Currently, in 2017, bitcoin uses 27.3 terawatt-hours per year, about the same power consumption as 2.5 million U.S. households. That number is growing. See https://digiconomist.net/bitcoin-energy-consumption.

21. Frances Coppola, "Ethereum's Latest Hard Fork Shows It Has a Very Long Way to Go," *Forbes*, November 26, 2016, www.forbes.com.

Chapter Thirteen: The Second Industrious Revolution

1. Seth D. Harris and Alan B. Krueger, "A Proposal for Modernizing Labor Laws for Twenty-first-Century Work: The 'Independent Worker,'" Hamilton Project, December 2015, www.hamiltonproject.org.

2. "Aggregate Reserves of Depository Institutions and the Monetary Base—H.3," Board of Governors of the Federal Reserve System, www.federalreserve.gov /releases/h3/current, accessed May 30, 2017.

3. As this book went to press, Congress passed the Tax Cuts and Jobs Act of 2017, which reduced the mortgage cap. Needless to say, the act did not create a minimum safety net, though it did offer low taxes to S-corporation businesses. Some contractors and small businesses might be able to take advantage of these lower taxes to hire more workers or simply to buy benefits, but it appears that service-oriented firms are largely excluded from these deductions.

4. See Joseph R. Blasi, Richard B. Freeman, and Douglas L. Kruse, *The Citizen's Share: Putting Ownership Back into Democracy* (New Haven, CT: Yale University Press, 2013).

INDEX